Prepared by Grace, for Grace

Prepared by Grace, for Grace

The Puritans on God's Ordinary Way of Leading Sinners to Christ

Joel R. Beeke
and
Paul M. Smalley

Reformation Heritage Books
Grand Rapids, Michigan

Prepared by Grace, for Grace
© 2013 by Joel R. Beeke and Paul M. Smalley

Reformation Heritage Books
2965 Leonard St. NE
Grand Rapids, MI 49525
616-977-0889 / Fax 616-285-3246
orders@heritagebooks.org
www.heritagebooks.org

Printed in the United States of America
13 14 15 16 17 18/10 9 8 7 6 5 4 3 2 1

Library of Congress Cataloging-in-Publication Data

Beeke, Joel R., 1952-
  Prepared by grace, for grace : the puritans on god's ordinary way of leading sinners to Christ / Joel R. Beeke and Paul M. Smalley.
     pages cm
  Includes bibliographical references and index.
  ISBN 978-1-60178-234-2 (pbk. : alk. paper) 1. Salvation—Puritans. 2. Grace (Theology) 3. Puritans—Doctrines. I. Smalley, Paul M. II. Title.
  BX9323.B439 2013
  234—dc23
                                    2013006563

For additional Reformed literature request a free book list from Reformation Heritage Books at the above regular or e-mail address.

To

Derek Thomas

my faithful friend and fellow-laborer in Christ

Thanks so much for all you are and have done
for me, our seminary, and book ministry.

—JRB

* * *

To

Dawn

my godly wife and faithful *ezer kenegdi*

Though you were not part of my preparation for conversion,
you have been exactly the helper I need to prepare for glory.

—PS

Contents

Foreword

Prepared By Grace, For Grace is a welcome addition to the mounting literature on the subject of "preparatory grace" in the writings of the Puritan theologians of the late sixteenth and seventeenth centuries. It makes a very distinctive contribution to an ongoing and complex discussion, and will be eagerly read by students of seventeenth-century theological literature, whether literary scholars, historians, or theologians. Academics in all three of these disciplines have had an interest in, and made contributions to, our knowledge and understanding of the teaching of post-Reformation thinkers on the process and psychology of conversion.

The general *tendenz* of the scholarship of the twentieth century was critical to varying degrees of the way in which Puritan writers understood the morphology of conversion. This was so for a variety of reasons. On occasion any emphasis on "preparation" for conversion was seen to be inimical to the pristine theology of the Genevan Reformation whose heirs the Puritans were seen to be. As is well known, Calvin was "subdued by a sudden conversion (*subita conversione*)."[1] What room therefore for "preparation" for salvation in his theology?

Or again, especially in theology influenced by Karl Barth, the idea that anything could "prepare" for grace was seen to be a contradiction in terms. Furthermore, theologians who distrusted the federal orthodoxy of the Puritans also viewed it as a mother who gave birth to preparationism, and thus turned people back into themselves instead of pointing them towards Christ. Famously, John McLeod Campbell (1800–1872) had reworked the very nature of the atonement against a background of encountering individuals who did not feel themselves to be "prepared" to receive grace. Any

---

1. John Calvin, author's preface to *Commentary on the Book of Psalms*, trans. James Anderson (Calvin Translation Society; repr., Grand Rapids: Eerdmans, 1948), 1:xl.

investigation of the morphology of conversion was thus seen to be either Christ-diverting, or stimulating a subjectivity that stood in the way of the free offer of Christ and the joyful acceptance of Him.

Something rather obvious, however, has been missing in almost all of these discussions. Characteristically they have been carried on by scholars whose world is that of books and journals, lecture rooms and research libraries. But the writings they have placed under the microscope have been those of pastors and preachers. These are two different universes of discourse. On occasion it seems clear that historians have not been sufficiently sensitive to theology to be able to grasp the nuances of what is being said. Calvin, for example, almost certainly meant he underwent an *unexpected* conversion, not a conversion without precursors.[2] In addition, most academic scholars—although they also live in a fallen environment—are not normally operating in a context in which they regularly spend time with people expressing profound spiritual need, conviction of sin, a deep sense of guilt and shame, and are seeking pastoral counsel. It is all too easy, therefore, to misjudge the kinds of analyses of the morphology of human experience that are delineated in the Puritan literature. As scholars we would be slow to discuss and critique the morphology of subjective experience to be found in psychiatric literature. We would recognize that we needed experience with many patients to enable us with any confidence to pass judgment on any morphology of psychological experience. There would be at least one significant dimension lacking—experience with and observation of the reality discussed. Is it possible there is an analogous liability in the discussion of the morphology of individual spiritual conversion?

Dr. Joel Beeke brings to this study well-honed skills in both history and theology. In addition he has already demonstrated in his other writings a prodigious and enviable familiarity with both the primary texts of the Puritan writings and the growing corpus of secondary literature.[3]

---

2. He had so understood *subita* in his *Commentary on De Clementia*. See *Calvin's Commentary on Seneca's 'De Clementia,'* trans. and ed. F. L. Battles and A. M. Hugo (Leiden: Renaissance Society of America, 1969), 55–56.

3. As, for example, in his *The Quest for Full Assurance: The Legacy of Calvin and His Successors* (Edinburgh: Banner of Truth Trust, 1999) and in his trilogy, *Puritan Reformed Spirituality* (Darlington, U.K.: Evangelical Press, 2004), *Meet the Puritans* (Grand Rapids: Reformation Heritage Books, 2006) with Randall Pederson, and, *A Puritan Theology: Doctrine for Life* (Grand Rapids: Reformation Heritage Books, 2012) with Mark Jones.

But in addition to his academic expertise, Dr. Beeke also brings thirty-five years of continuous pastoral ministry to substantial congregations. During the course of these years he has been engaged in weekly preaching to and in the pastoral counseling of men, women, and young people whose stories have often been strikingly similar in morphology to those with whom Puritan pastors regularly engaged. Mr. Paul Smalley likewise served for over a decade in pastoral ministry before becoming Dr. Beeke's teaching assistant and graduating with a Th.M. in Puritan theology. This combination of authors almost inevitably creates a sensitivity to pastorally-rooted texts which may be absent in other works. For one thing, long experience in closely observing the ways of God with a wide variety of individuals inevitably creates a distinctive sensitivity to the divine morphology in conversion. Indeed, it may mean that when the writings of fellow pastor-teachers are read, albeit from another generation, there is an immediate sense that the spiritual analysis given is instantly recognizable. This in turn creates a capacity to make discriminating judgments—which the reader will discover the Puritan writers also made in relationship to each other (as, for example, in Thomas Goodwin's criticisms of Thomas Hooker).

Prepared By Grace, For Grace merits a special welcome because its authors bring this rare pastoral perspective to the table. But this is not to say that pastoral experience trumps careful research. For they have read widely on this theme and ransacked the secondary literature. Their study, which ranges beyond the English and New England Puritans to Continental divines and at least one noted Scot, is immensely valuable as a whole, and also in its discrete parts. Readers will appreciate the cameo expositions of the thought of the various Puritan authors whose works are placed under the microscope. They will also want to know what are the conclusions of Dr. Beeke and Mr. Smalley—but those should be disclosed by the authors of the book, not the writer of a foreword!

Students and scholars who think and write on the theme of "preparation" may well wish (as Calvin did with the term "free will") that the expression be laid aside because it is subject to so many interpretations and so much difference in use. The difficulty lies, of course, in coining a different term whose definition is more immediately understood and agreed upon. Until then, we must content ourselves with the vocabulary that has served now for hundreds of years. For now, *Prepared By Grace, For Grace* is an important monograph. It will surely remain a standard work in the field for years to come and, hopefully, encourage the scholarly and pastoral balance which Dr. Beeke and Mr. Smalley seek to exhibit. It merits careful reading and, unless I misjudge its worth, should stimulate further study on the topic of preparation in general and on the theologians discussed here in particular.

—Sinclair B. Ferguson
First Presbyterian Church
Columbia, S.C.

I Would I Were Converted

When Adam was deceived,
I was of life bereaved;
Of late (too) I perceived,
I was in sin conceived.

I have in sin abounded,
My heart therewith is wounded,
With fears I am surrounded,
My spirit is confounded.

I would I were converted
Would sin and I were parted,
For folly I have smarted;
God make me honest-hearted!

Lord: thou wast crucified
For sinners, bled and died,
I have for mercy cried,
Let me not be denied.

—John Bunyan[1]

---

1. John Bunyan, *A Book for Boys and Girls* (1686; facsimile repr., London: Elliot Stock, 1889), 2–3, 5, 9 [incorrect pagination, actually p. 6].

INTRODUCTION

The Question of Preparation

For thus saith the LORD to the men of Judah and Jerusalem, Break up your fallow ground, and sow not among thorns.

—Jeremiah 4:3

This book is based on the conviction that a righteous and holy God saves sinners "by grace through faith" (Eph. 2:8). The human race fell into sin and misery when Adam despised God's glory and disobeyed His commandment, but God has provided a way of salvation through the death and resurrection of His Son. The gospel is the good news that God saves sinners who trust in Christ alone. This gospel of grace was the heartbeat of Puritanism. Perry Miller said, "The fundamental problem of life for English Puritans was not social: it was salvation of the soul, out of which would flow a purification of the church and a regeneration of the state."[1]

This book addresses the question of how God ordinarily brings sinners to the point of trusting in Christ alone for salvation. Specifically, is conversion an event or a process? If a process, how does the work of conversion begin? There may be exceptional cases, but in general, is there a pattern to conversion? This subject has massive implications for how we preach the gospel. Should we portray God as nothing but love, and try to woo people to this loving God who can ease their pain and fill the emptiness of their lives? Or should we also tell people that emptiness and pain are symptoms of sin, and God hates sin with a burning, righteous fury? Does God ordinarily begin the work of conversion by first convincing sinners of their guilt and His coming judgment?

---

1. Perry Miller, *The New England Mind: From Colony to Province* (Cambridge: Harvard University Press, 1953), 54.

How we answer that last question determines the role of God's law in our evangelism. If we minimize the need for conviction of sin in conversion, the law may be regarded as a distraction or hindrance to unbelievers, keeping them from Christ. But if conviction of sin is part of God's normal way of leading a sinner to salvation, then we must preach the law with the gospel.

Many Puritans of England and New England answered these questions with the doctrine known as *preparation*. People must be prepared to believe in Christ before they exercise such faith. Such preparation of the heart may be viewed as a part of the process that leads to conversion. Owen Watkins observes that, "The normal pattern of a Puritan conversion followed the sequence: peace, disturbance, and then peace again.... The casting down and raising up, the wounding and making whole, referred to the two landmarks already mentioned—conviction of sin and coming to Christ."[2] Complacency in sin, conviction of sin, and conversion to Christ constituted the Puritan process of personal salvation.

Most Puritans believed that God uses the law to prepare the way for the gospel in men's souls, much as John the Baptist's preaching of divine wrath and repentance prepared the way for the coming of the Lord Jesus. This doctrine of preparation for grace shaped their evangelistic preaching, their doctrine of assurance, and their personal piety. Because such preparation for salvation is the work of the Holy Spirit using the truths of God's Word, we have chosen to describe the Puritan doctrine as "preparation by grace, for grace."

Preparation for What?

The word *preparation* was used by the Puritans in many contexts. Charles Cohen writes, "Preparation has several definitions in Puritan theological discourse. While signifying the preliminaries to faith, the subject discussed here, it also refers to the activity of the Saints as they renew themselves for God's work or ready themselves to meet Christ in glory."[3] The Puritans urged people to prepare for many things: prepare to hear the preaching of the Word, prepare for conversion, prepare to partake of

2. Owen C. Watkins, *The Puritan Experience* (London: Routledge and Kegan Paul, 1972), 37.

3. Charles L. Cohen, *God's Caress: The Psychology of Puritan Religious Experience* (Oxford: Oxford University Press, 1986), 78n9.

the Lord's Supper, prepare to face trials, and prepare for the Lord's coming in glory. Lumping all these meanings together under the banner of preparation can only create confusion.

We misunderstand the Puritans if we fail to ask, in any given context, what kind of preparation is intended? For example, in critiquing Edward Taylor's (c. 1642–1729) notion of preparation for grace, David Parker uses a quotation from Taylor to support his argument: "our preparation consisting in the graces of the Spirit, oh we by preparing should stir up those shining spangles of the divine image upon our souls" so that they are "pleasing to God."[4] Does this statement describe the preparation of the unconverted for saving faith? If so, Taylor has significantly departed from Reformed theology by ascribing the ability to please God to an unconverted, unbelieving sinner. It is far more likely that Taylor spoke not of preparation for conversion but instead, the preparation of those already converted to use the means of grace, such as the Lord's Supper, in a profitable manner.

Certainly that is the case when Parker quotes Taylor as saying, "The wedding garment is that whereby a person is evangelically prepared for fellowship with God in all gospel ordinances."[5] Parker seizes on the phrase *evangelically prepared* as illustrative of Taylor's doctrine of preparation for conversion, while plainly Taylor was speaking of preparation for using the means of grace, such as the Lord's Supper. Rather than preparation *for* conversion, the preparation *was* conversion itself, symbolized by putting on the wedding garment (Matt. 22:11–14), which gave a person the right to join in the sacramental feast.

Mark Dever thus warns, "Ambiguity is particularly dangerous in this question because one can lose sight of the point of the preparation under discussion.... Carelessness at this point has led some to take any statement of call for human action...as proof of 'preparationism.'"[6] Therefore let us be clear that in this book we are not talking about Puritan preparation for good works, trials, Christ's return, taking the Lord's Supper, hearing the sermon, or other such matters. We are specifically speaking of *preparation for saving faith in Christ.*

4. David L. Parker, "Edward Taylor's Preparationism: A New Perspective on the Taylor-Stoddard Controversy," *Early American Literature* 11, no. 3 (Winter 1976/1977): 263.

5. Parker, "Edward Taylor's Preparationism," 271.

6. Mark E. Dever, *Richard Sibbes: Puritanism and Calvinism in Late Elizabethan and Early Stuart England* (Macon, Ga.: Mercer University Press, 2000), 126.

To focus our study on preparation for faith, we must bypass other topics that the Puritans cherished. The danger of this book is that it may give the impression that the Puritans were obsessed with instilling preparatory guilt and fear. On the contrary, they generously wrote about the doctrines of God, Christ's redemptive work, regeneration by the Holy Spirit, saving faith, repentance, assurance of salvation, the Christian life, and heaven.[7] But to dig deeply into the subject of preparation for grace, we must set aside these other matters while not forgetting that the Puritans had a full-orbed theology and a God-centered approach to all of life.

We may then address other definitional questions, such as: Does this preparation for grace consist of outward actions, such as going to church, or inward attitudes, such as grieving over our sins and longing for Jesus Christ to save us? We will focus on inward preparation of the heart, while recognizing the practical exhortations of the Puritans to be obedient to God in outward conduct. Reformed Christians have generally acknowledged that unregenerate people could perform such outward acts as attending church, hearing the Word, and praying to God, and exhorted them to do so. But this book has to do with preparing the heart for saving grace.

Furthermore, we should address the issue raised by Dever: Is there a distinction between preparation and preparation*ism*? The latter is generally used as a negative term for a doctrine of preparation that contradicts the principle of salvation by grace alone. We will avoid using the label *preparationism* (and the related noun *preparationist*) with respect to the Puritans, since, as we will see, they consistently opposed any notion of preparation based upon the exercise of human free will or any supposed merit in the actions of sinful men. Prejudice and preconceptions about preparationism have often hindered people from making objective judgments about the Puritan doctrine of preparation for grace.

Some might distinguish between *God's* preparation of sinners by conviction, and *man's* preparation of himself. But this distinction is not helpful because as Reformed, experimental Christians, the Puritans believed that all of man's works are done under the sovereignty of God. Therefore

---

7. For an overview of Puritan teachings on most major topics of systematic theology, see Joel R. Beeke and Mark Jones, *A Puritan Theology: Doctrine for Life* (Grand Rapids: Reformation Heritage Books, 2012).

reality cannot be divided into two separate compartments between God's sovereignty and man's responsibility, as this distinction attempts to do.

Further, as experimental Christians, the Puritans believed that God's saving plan unfolds in human life both in experiences and duties. If God is working upon people through the preaching of the Word, do not people have an obligation to respond rightly? Should not preachers press this obligation upon them? Most Christians would say yes to these questions. The inseparable connection between God's work and man's works makes it unwise to force them into opposing categories.

Finally, we must discuss how to distinguish preparation from repentance, given that both involve sorrow over sin, humiliation before God, and changes in one's conduct to some degree. We will include in preparation all those forms of repentance that precede the sinner's trusting in Christ alone for salvation. Sometimes this distinction is referred to as the difference between legal repentance and evangelical repentance. We realize this distinction leaves open the question of the timing of the actual birth or onset of justifying faith. As we will see, the Puritans also wrestled with that question.

Preparation: Evangelical or Legalistic, Reformed or Arminian?

The teachings of the Puritans on preparation have evoked very different reactions. Some support the use of the law in evangelism as a helpful or even necessary tool to awaken sinners to their need of Christ. They see no contradiction between preaching the requirements and curse of the law to the lost and proclaiming the promise of salvation and call to faith that is essential to the gospel of grace. They invoke the law not as an alternative way to be justified before God, but in order to convince sinners that they can only be justified through Christ's work, not their own.

Others condemn such preparation as a sub-Christian legalism that falls back into the salvation-by-works mentality that Paul so strongly opposed in his Epistle to the Galatians. They believe evangelism should speak of nothing but free grace. Preaching God's law to fallen sinners only breeds morbidity, they say. Some even believe that frightening people with the curse of the law causes them psychological harm and contradicts God's unconditional love.

Others agree that preaching should use the law to convict sinners, but they also think that the Puritans went to an unhealthy extreme, inclining their hearers to endless introspection that undermines faith and assurance. Even those who affirm the law in principle may feel so uncomfortable with it in practice that they rarely preach of God's law and His wrath against sin so as to stir the fear of damnation in anyone's heart.

Controversy has also risen regarding the Puritans' concept of preparation for grace and the Reformed doctrine of sovereign grace. Arminian theology teaches that God helps the lost sinner up to a point, then allows him to decide whether or not he will believe in Christ. Thus the human will is the decisive factor for determining who goes to heaven and who goes to hell. That is possible, the Arminian says, because fallen men still retain some ability to turn towards God. By contrast, Reformed theology teaches that mankind is so lost that no one would choose to trust in Christ unless God first changed the sinner's heart, causing him to believe. God's will is the decisive factor in determining who will be saved, for man is dead in sin. This point of view was articulated well by the apostle John in his gospel (John 1:12, 13 *et passim*), but obscured in the teaching of the church for many centuries prior to the sixteenth-century Reformation, when it was once more clearly and powerfully preached by Martin Luther (1483–1546), Ulrich Zwingli (1484–1531), Martin Bucer (1491–1551), Heinrich Bullinger (1504–1575), and, most famously, John Calvin (1509–1564).

Some people argue that when the Puritans developed their theology of conversion, especially the doctrine of preparation, they diluted the pure Reformed teachings they inherited from Calvin. We are told that though they considered themselves Reformed, the Puritans actually paved the way for Arminianism in England. This "Calvin versus the Puritans" argument has massive negative implications for Christians and churches that embrace the Westminster Confession of Faith, for it asserts that Westminster theology is not true to the Protestant Reformation.

Others argue that Puritan theology is the natural development of Calvin's teachings and may be found in seed form in Calvin's writings. More specifically, they say the doctrine of preparation for saving faith fits well in the Reformed system of beliefs, for it is one step in God's sovereign work toward saving sinners through Christ.

It should be plain by now that preparation is a controversial subject. Nonetheless, it is an important subject, for it addresses some of the most essential matters of Christian faith and experience, such as how the gospel is to be preached, and how sinners are converted.

We authors believe that the doctrine of preparation generally received among the Puritans is biblical, evangelical, and Reformed (though we will point out cases where some individual Puritans have carried certain aspects of this doctrine beyond biblical boundaries). Neglecting to preach law and judgment to lost sinners is one reason (though not the only one) why many churches are unhealthy today. Too many of their members are self-righteous, self-satisfied Christians in name only, whose spiritual pride has never been broken by the Spirit of Christ working through the Word of God. They have never come to see their true plight as sinners abiding under God's wrath, who merit nothing but condemnation and punishment, with no one to turn to for help other than Jesus Christ. A shallow view of sin must inevitably produce a shallow kind of faith. Feeling little need for grace, they want very little from God or from Christ apart from what they think they are entitled to.

On the other hand, we recognize that it is possible to abuse the doctrine of preparation. The Puritans knew that when confronted with the demands of the law, one can sink into despair of salvation, or be driven to cling all the more to legalism and self-righteousness, instead of fleeing to Christ for salvation. Preachers can dwell too long on the evils of sin without offering the sweet promises of the gospel. Steps to conversion can become roadblocks to trusting in Christ if they are viewed as conditions to be met in order to be worthy of receiving Him. Though we affirm the fundamentals of the Puritan doctrine of preparation, we do not always agree with the details of each Puritan's way of working out the implications of this doctrine.

We mean no disrespect to those who view these teachings as unbiblical, unhealthy, and/or contradictory to Reformed theology. Many of the scholars cited in this book have made significant contributions to the study of the Puritans. Even while we critique them, in some respects we stand upon their shoulders. When we argue that they have misunderstood the Puritans in various matters, we acknowledge that we also are liable to mistakes as fallen human beings. May God raise up students and scholars who will correct our own errors.

Our goal is to let Calvin and the Puritans speak for themselves. Please forgive us if the following pages are crowded with quotes and footnotes. We want you to hear these voices speaking from the past, rather than us telling you only what we think they said. We have conformed spelling and capitalization to modern standard usage to make the quotes more readable. As Cohen says, "Seventeenth-century orthography is wonderful to behold, a salve for everyone who did not win his fourth grade spelling bee."[8] But we have not substituted new words in place of old, or rearranged sentences.

We want you to taste some of the spiritual sweetness in Puritan writings. If that whets your appetite for further research, let our footnotes offer you some places to start. There is always more study to be done![9]

---

8. Cohen, *God's Caress*, xi

9. A large collection of Puritan writings and many rare books are available at the Puritan Research Center, housed at Puritan Reformed Theological Seminary, Grand Rapids, Michigan.

CHAPTER ONE

Preparation and Modern Scholarship

Prepare ye the way of the LORD, make straight in the desert a high-way for our God. Every valley shall be exalted, and every mountain and hill shall be made low: and the crooked shall be made straight, and the rough places plain.

—Isaiah 40:3b–4

The Puritans believed that the Holy Spirit labors for the conversion of sinners. Specifically, since salvation is by grace through faith, the Spirit labors to work faith in the heart of the sinner. Without this work of the Spirit, no one can acknowledge or confess that Jesus is Lord (1 Cor. 12:3). Sadly, in addition to the utter inability of the sinner to exercise saving faith, during his years in the natural state many obstacles have piled up, such as habits of sin and settled attitudes of self-righteousness, which have so hardened his conscience that the sinner cannot even acknowledge his need for Christ. The omnipotent Spirit could sweep aside such obstacles and bring the sinner immediately to faith, but that is not the Spirit's usual or ordinary way, for He created the mind and conscience of man and generally prefers to work through those faculties. So the Spirit begins by removing obstacles to the gospel call in the mind and conscience. The gospel requires only faith in Christ, but ordinarily it is necessary to remove such obstacles to prepare the way for faith. So the Spirit works to prepare the lost sinner's soul for grace. This is the essence of the Puritan doctrine of preparation.

The Puritans sought to apply the doctrines of sovereign grace to human experience, in order to understand God's way of bringing sinners to Christ. Edmund Morgan says that before New England was settled, the Puritans already had created "a morphology of conversion, in which each stage could be distinguished from the next, so that a man could check his eternal condition by a set of temporal and recognizable signs."[1] In the sciences, morphology refers to the study of the shape and structure of words and objects, whether a galaxy, rock formation, or body of an animal. Applied to the Puritan doctrine of salvation, it refers to the idea that God's eternal predestination of a sinner to eternal life unfolds in personal experience according to a discernible pattern of events and experiences. Since we are saved by faith in Christ, this pattern revolves around faith. Morgan says, the Puritans "broke down the operation of faith into a succession of recognizable stages,"[2] The initial stage or stages serve as a preparation for faith.

To speak of "the Puritan morphology of conversion" is something of an overstatement, for it suggests a fixed, universal pattern of salvation. In reality the Puritans' teaching on conversion included various patterns, which they often presented while commending the mystery and variety of God's ways. But in general the Puritans' view was that conviction of sin and active seeking of God's mercy usually preceded conscious resting and relying upon Christ. This doctrine of preparation has prompted much scholarly discussion since the middle of the twentieth century. Modern scholars have charged the Puritan doctrine of preparation with being implicitly legalistic and Arminian, and denying salvation by grace alone.

Perry Miller on Preparation

Perry Miller (1905–1963), a professor at Harvard University, was an influential historian of the Puritans. He helped shift scholarship away from analyzing the Puritans from political, economic, and psychological perspectives to understanding them in terms of their theology. Miller argues that the doctrine of preparation was part of the Puritans' covenantal solution to the problem of absolute divine sovereignty. It gave human effort a place in the predestined world.

Since regeneration was an act of God in no way based upon human merit or effort, Miller said, the New England Puritans turned to the doctrine of

---

1. Edmund S. Morgan, *Visible Saints: The History of a Puritan Idea* ([New York]: New York University Press, 1963), 66.
2. Morgan, *Visible Saints*, 68.

preparation held by their predecessors to call their society back to morality and to refute antinomianism.[3] According to Miller, the Puritans could not say that all people were called to salvation without contradicting their view of predestination. Miller apparently misread the Reformed doctrine of predestination as fatalism, allowing for no explanation for conversion but an unanticipated lightning bolt from heaven. He grossly misunderstood Calvin's doctrine of conversion as "a forcible seizure, a rape of the surprised will."[4] Richard Goode says Miller's starkly contrastive view of predestination versus preparation was later propagated by such scholars as Alfred Habegger, David Parker, and George Selement.[5]

In the preparation doctrine of early covenant theologians such as William Perkins (1558–1602), Miller said the New England Puritans found a basis to demand moral action that was neither saving nor meritorious. Miller said, "This much a corrupt man might do, for it was really no motion of his soul; it was not lifting of himself up by his own bootstraps, but simply an attitude of expectancy."[6] Miller wrote, "Preparation was not a supernatural work. All men could achieve it."[7] Yet the expectation was that God normally saved those who prepared themselves.[8] Miller made the doctrine of preparation sound remarkably like the medieval nominalist idea that God will give grace to those who do what is in them (*facere quod in se est*), i.e., what is in their natural power to do.[9]

Miller's statements misrepresented Puritan preparation. The Puritan doctrine of preparation did not offer men something they could accomplish on their own. Instead, the Puritans taught that God prepared sinners for the gospel by His Spirit working in their hearts through the Word. Later, Miller quoted Thomas Hooker (1586–1647), saying that the beginnings of man's turning to God require more than the natural will power of man. But Miller went on to say, "Yet at this point God is still acting from the outside, as when He moves any object in nature, not from

---

3. Perry Miller, "'Preparation for Salvation' in New England," *Journal of the History of Ideas* 4, no. 3 (June 1943): 257–60, 278.

4. Miller, *The New England Mind: From Colony to Province*, 56.

5. Richard C. Goode, "'The Only and Principal End'; Propagating the Gospel in Early Puritan New England" (PhD Dissertation, Vanderbuilt University, 1995), 223–25.

6. Miller, "'Preparation for Salvation' in New England," 261.

7. Miller, "'Preparation for Salvation' in New England," 263.

8. Miller, "'Preparation for Salvation' in New England," 262.

9. See Heiko A. Oberman, *The Harvest of Medieval Theology: Gabriel Biel and Late Medieval Nominalism* (Cambridge: Harvard University Press, 1963), 53, 128ff.

within as He does after He has filled the heart with His Spirit."[10] Though Hooker distinguished between God's works before and after justification, he did not describe divine preparation for faith as merely an act of providence "as when he moves any object in nature," but as an operation of the Spirit accompanying the Word. Hooker wrote, "The Lord by his Spirit prepares the soul."[11] Preparation is a work of the supernatural God upon the soul, even though supernatural grace is not infused within the soul to become part of our inherent motivational structure.

Miller also accused the so-called preparationists of being nominally Calvinists in their doctrinal declarations while undermining absolute divine sovereignty in their practical applications by calling all men, even the unconverted, to do all they could to embrace the means of grace.[12] Miller said they shifted the focus from the majestic and sovereign God to the religious efforts of men.[13] Hooker and Thomas Shepard (1605–1649) were said to have planted the seeds of later English Arminianism, and to have dethroned the Lord.[14] Miller spared no words in emphasizing the dire effects of the Puritan doctrine of preparation on the God-centered worldview of the Reformers.

To maintain his position, Miller discarded as irrelevant every Puritan affirmation of divine sovereignty and human inability. He discounted these affirmations as hollow attempts to cling to orthodoxy without any real significance in the deepest convictions of Puritanism. This is an unfair reading of the Puritans, who passionately defended the doctrines of divine election and human depravity. From their perspective, the doctrine of preparation was an application of the larger biblical themes of God's sovereign grace and man's innate opposition to holiness.

Norman Pettit on Preparation
Norman Pettit was professor of English at Boston University. His book, *The Heart Prepared,* offers a remarkable assessment of the views of the

10. Miller, "'Preparation for Salvation' in New England," 265. Miller cited Hooker, *The Unbeleevers Preparing for Christ* (London, 1638), 32. But neither this page nor those immediately before and after it support his statement.
11. Thomas Hooker, *The Sovles Preparation for Christ* (The Netherlands: n.p., 1638), 219.
12. Miller, "'Preparation for Salvation' in New England," 277–78.
13. Miller, "'Preparation for Salvation' in New England," 284.
14. Miller, "'Preparation for Salvation' in New England," 286.

Reformers and some of the Puritans on preparation for faith. His scholarship is impressive and his research into primary sources helpful, but his thesis is marred by assumptions derived from scholarly sources such as Miller but foreign to the Puritans themselves. Pettit says: "In the orthodox Reformed theology of the sixteenth century no allowance had been made for the biblical demand to prepare the heart for righteousness. In strict predestinarian dogma the sinner was taken by storm—his heart wrenched from depravity to grace."[15] Dever writes, "Pettit seems to have assumed that an adherence to a theology of predestination would also necessitate a belief in both an immediate conversion, and in a conversion that was, by its violence, inconsistent with natural human faculties."[16] Thus Pettit pits the Calvinistic idea of divine sovereignty against the Puritan doctrine of preparation.

According to Pettit, Puritan preparation was the struggle to find liberty from "the shadow and tyranny of the doctrine of divine coercion" taught by earlier Reformed theologians.[17] Strangely, this pursuit of liberty ultimately degenerated, we are told, into "moralism and sentimentalism."[18] But to its credit, preparation was a rediscovery via covenant theology of "the great Prophetic exhortations to return to God" found in the Scriptures.[19] Pettit makes the curious statement that,

> Both the gradual workings of the Holy Spirit and the extreme emphasis on covenant ideals were fundamentally opposed to the basic tenets of Reformed theology. Both contradicted the dogmatic stand that anything done on man's part diminishes God's sovereignty. Yet the ultimate convictions behind Reformed dogmatics remained at the core of Puritan thought.[20]

Pettit thus places the Puritans at the heart of an impossible tension between divine sovereignty and human responsibility, apparently attributing divine sovereignty to the Reformed confessions and human responsibility to the Scriptures.

---

15. Norman Pettit, *The Heart Prepared: Grace and Conversion in Puritan Spiritual Life* (New Haven: Yale University Press, 1966), vii.
16. Dever, *Richard Sibbes*, 126–27.
17. Pettit, *The Heart Prepared*, 217.
18. Pettit, *The Heart Prepared*, 217.
19. Pettit, *The Heart Prepared*, 218.
20. Pettit, *The Heart Prepared*, 218.

Yet it appears that Pettit is entangled in contradictions. How can Puritanism be "fundamentally opposed to the basic tenets of Reformed theology," yet hold at its "core" the "ultimate convictions behind Reformed dogmatics"? How can predestination be a basic tenet but not an ultimate conviction of the Reformed viewpoint? Furthermore, how did the pursuit of liberty from divine coercion degenerate into moralism, which is legalism? How did turning back to the Bible with its robustly God-centered perspective produce mere sentimentalism? Rather than resolving those questions, Pettit's conclusions further muddy the waters that surround the Puritan doctrine of preparation.

At the heart of Pettit's confusion is his belief that Reformed dogma teaches that "anything done on man's part diminishes God's sovereignty."[21] Certainly the Reformation doctrine of justification by faith alone excludes all merit in human works. But the Reformed doctrine of divine sovereignty also includes God's use of human means in conversion and sanctification. God does not treat men like stocks of wood and blocks of stone but deals with them according to their created nature as beings of mind, feelings, and will.

Samuel Willard (1640–1707), New England Puritan pastor, wrote a massive exposition of the Westminster Shorter Catechism. Seymour Van Dyken called Willard "one of the most important preachers among the second generation of New England Puritans, one who summarized the theological thought of seventeenth century American Puritanism."[22] Willard said, "There is no cooperation of the man with the Spirit in the producing of the habit of faith in him…. It is a regeneration, and none ever helped to beget himself."[23] By the "habit" of faith he meant the inward disposition to trust Christ, which logically precedes our actual trusting in Him. So regeneration is an act of sovereign grace alone. Willard also argued against the idea that sovereign grace saved men by "violent compulsion," writing,

> It is named, *effectual calling*. *Calling* because it is a voice of God speaking to the soul of a sinner, inviting and alluring of him to come over to the Lord Jesus Christ…. The Spirit of God, in the work of application, treats with men as reasonable creatures, and causes

---

21. Pettit, *The Heart Prepared*, 218.

22. Seymour Van Dyken, *Samuel Willard, 1640–1707: Preacher of Orthodoxy in an Era of Change* (Grand Rapids: Eerdmans, 1972), 7.

23. Samuel Willard, *A Compleat Body of Divinity* (1726; facsimile repr., New York: Johnson Reprint Corp., 1969), 434.

by counsel; not carrying them by violent compulsion, but winning them by arguments, by which they are "made willing in the day of his power" (Ps. 110:3).... *Effectual*, because it always gains the sinner to accept of, and close in with it.[24]

 Regeneration is monergistic—by grace alone—but it does not bypass the preaching and hearing of the Word. Sidney Rooy says of the theology of Richard Sibbes (1577–1635), "God uses means, he saves through means, he gives grace through means. Men are damned who despise the means."[25] Predestination does not lull men into passivity as they wait for lightning to strike their souls. God works out His predestination through providence, the means of grace, the work of the Spirit, and the responses of the soul. God rules over all of life, so it should not surprise us that He prepares His elect prior to their conversion.

Pettit believes that any attempt to believe in both divine sovereignty and human responsibility is "bound to be self-contradictory," a contradiction that left the Puritans trapped between the Bible and the Reformed creeds.[26] But the historian must understand the doctrinal positions of men within the context of their larger theological perspectives. William Stoever comments,

> The Reformed doctrine of divine sovereignty was not regarded in the orthodox period as excluding human activity from regeneration. That a person was predestined to a certain end, and saved by grace alone, did not affect his nature as a rational, willing agent, nor did it mean that he could "do nothing" morally significant in daily life, but only that he was impotent to effect his own salvation. Denial of such efficacy to individuals, however, was not regarded as inconsistent with the assertion that human activity, in the context of the ordained means for dispensing grace, is instrumental in the application of redemption.[27]

Though Pettit's account of preparation is revealing, it distorts preparation because it forces it to lie upon a Procrustean bed of assumptions

24. Willard, *A Compleat Body of Divinity*, 432, emphasis original.

25. Sidney H. Rooy, *The Theology of Missions in the Puritan Tradition: A Study of Representative Puritans: Richard Sibbes, Richard Baxter, John Eliot, Cotton Mather, and Jonathan Edwards* (Delft, Netherlands: W. D. Meinema, 1965), 36.

26. Pettit, *The Heart Prepared*, 219.

27. William K. B. Stoever, *'A Faire and Easie Way to Heaven': Covenant Theology and Antinomianism in Early Massachusetts* (Middleton, Conn.: Wesleyan University Press, 1978), 195.

that most Puritan theologians did not hold. Puritans such as Perkins and Hooker developed their doctrine of preparation believing there were ways in which the sovereign God ordinarily worked out His eternal decree in human lives. Pettit's presuppositions hinder him from seeing the fundamental unity between Calvin and the Puritans, which we will show in more detail later in this book.

R. T. Kendall on Preparation

American-born Robert T. Kendall (b. 1935) spent much of his life serving as a pastor in England and writing on both an academic and a popular level. Kendall published his doctoral thesis for Oxford University as *Calvin and English Calvinism,* a major reassessment of Puritanism in relation to the Genevan Reformer. His book focuses upon the doctrine of saving faith especially in its connections to Christ's atonement, preparation for faith, and assurance of salvation.

Kendall's basic thesis is that Puritanism degenerated from pure Calvinism into an emphasis upon works as opposed to grace. He lays much of the blame on Theodore Beza (1519–1605), Calvin's successor at Geneva. Beza's doctrine, Kendall says, has a qualitative difference from Calvin's: he was "the architect of a system fundamentally different from Calvin's."[28] With some help from other theologians, Beza allegedly hijacked the Reformed movement. Kendall's work was preceded by similar assertions by Basil Hall.[29] It is a startling claim, given that Reformed theologians have studied Calvin for centuries and never noticed this supposed radical departure from his views, either in Beza or among the Puritans.

Certainly as part of the international Reformed movement the Puritans did not consider themselves dependent on Calvin as the authority or inspiration of their teachings. They relied on the Bible for both, and identified themselves by the Reformed confessions. It is wrong to view Reformed Christianity as literal Calvinism, that is, as if Calvin invented it. Carl Trueman writes, "So-called Calvinists were not those who looked to Calvin as the major theological authority but rather those who looked to the tradition of Reformed confessions. This thus makes room for

28. R. T. Kendall, *Calvin and English Calvinism to 1649* (Carlisle, U.K.: Paternoster Press, 1997), 38.

29. Basil Hall, "The Calvin Legend," and "Calvin against the Calvinists," in *John Calvin,* ed. G. E. Duffield (Grand Rapids: Eerdmans, 1966), 1–37.

Calvin as an important source for the tradition without making him the sole dominating theological force, a point that reflects both his status in his own day…and in the years following his death."[30]

The Reformed churches believed they stood in fundamental unity with one another as orthodox Christians, as opposed to Arminians, Roman Catholics, and Socinians. That is why Kendall's contention is revolutionary in asserting that Beza's influence mediated through William Perkins led the English Reformed churches into a system that contradicted the fundamentals of Calvin's theology.

The Calvin-versus-the-Calvinists thesis has been sufficiently refuted in other books.[31] The differences between the Reformers and Reformed Scholasticism (of which Puritanism was a part) have been shown to be largely differences of method, not message.[32] In addition, Beza did not attempt secretly to reinvent Reformed theology. David Steinmetz writes, "Theologically, Beza was less original than Calvin, whose teaching he attempted faithfully to expound. Beza was not in marked disagreement with Calvin over any theological issue."[33] Covenant theology does not betray Calvin but is a systematic outworking of themes already present in Calvin.[34]

Conclusion

Puritan preparation is the doctrine that God prepares sinners for faith by overcoming obstacles in their minds and consciences to the claims of

---

30. Carl R. Trueman, "Calvin and Calvinism," in *The Cambridge Companion to John Calvin,* ed. Donald K. McKim (Cambridge: Cambridge University Press, 2004), 226.

31. Paul Helm, *Calvin and the Calvinists* (Edinburgh: Banner of Truth, 1982); Richard A. Muller, *Christ and the Decree: Christology and Predestination in Reformed Theology from Calvin to Perkins* (Durham, N.C.: Labyrinth Press, 1986); *Post-Reformation Reformed Dogmatics: The Rise and Development of Reformed Orthodoxy, c. 1520 to c. 1725,* 2nd ed., 4 vols. (Grand Rapids: Baker, 2003); *After Calvin: Studies in the Development of a Theological Tradition* (Oxford: Oxford University Press, 2003); Joel. R. Beeke, *The Quest for Full Assurance: The Legacy of Calvin and His Successors* (Edinburgh: Banner of Truth, 1999). For a brief overview of the issues, see Richard A. Muller, "Was Calvin a Calvinist?" http://www.calvin.edu/meeter/lectures/Richard%20Muller%20-%20Was%20Calvin%20a%20Calvinist.pdf (accessed July 21, 2011).

32. See Willem J. Van Asselt, et al., *Introduction to Reformed Scholasticism,* trans. Albert Gootjes (Grand Rapids: Reformation Heritage Books, 2011).

33. David C. Steinmetz, *Reformers in the Wings: From Geiler Von Kayserberg to Theodore Beza* (Oxford: Oxford University Press, 2001), 117.

34. Peter A. Lillback, *The Binding of God: Calvin's Role in the Development of Covenant Theology* (Grand Rapids: Baker Academic, 2001).

the gospel. This teaching has prompted much criticism from twentieth-century historians.

Perry Miller says Puritan preparation is a covenantal distortion of Calvin's doctrine of pure divine sovereignty. Norman Pettit, while dealing more carefully with the primary sources, similarly assumes that in calling men to act prior to their conversion, the Puritans were denying the Calvinistic doctrine of salvation by seizure. R. T. Kendall places this view of preparation in the larger context of the Calvin-versus-the-Calvinists thesis. However, later scholars say the portrayal of the Puritans by such men is skewed by false assumptions and misreading of the evidence.

So far we have dealt with these matters in general terms. As we go on to consider the teachings of specific Puritans on preparation, we will interact in more detail with the work of these scholars. The burden of this book is to depict the Puritan doctrine of preparation as they presented it themselves. First, however, we must consider the Puritan view in the context of such theologians as Augustine and Calvin.

CHAPTER TWO

Precedents to Puritan Preparation: Augustine to John Calvin

Man, blinded and drunk with self-love, must be compelled to know and to confess his own feebleness and impurity.

—John Calvin[1]

Aurelius Augustinus (354–430) was a successful orator and teacher of rhetoric in the late Roman Empire. Though his mother, Monica, was a devout Christian, Augustine was more interested in the philosophies of the Greco-Roman world than in Christianity. He and his female companion of thirteen years had a son, and for a time Augustine seemed content to live for sex and academic success. However, after listening to the preaching of Ambrose, bishop of Milan, Augustine found himself torn between wanting to believe in Christ and holding onto his lusts. He found that he was unable to master himself.

One day in a garden, he was so overwhelmed with grief over his sins that he began weeping. He opened a Bible and read Romans 13:13–14, "Let us walk honestly, as in the day; not in rioting and drunkenness, not in chambering and wantonness, not in strife and envying. But put ye on the Lord Jesus Christ, and make not provision for the flesh, to fulfil the lusts thereof." The light of faith flooded into his heart as Augustine's restless soul found rest in Christ. He was baptized and later became a bishop in the church and one of the preeminent teachers in Christian history. In hindsight, he understood that God had been drawing Augustine to

---

1. John Calvin, *Institutes of the Christian Religion*, ed. John T. McNeill, trans. Ford Lewis Battles (Philadelphia: Westminster Press, 1960), 2.7.6.

Himself. He prayed, "I call Thee into my soul, which by the desire which Thou inspirest in it Thou preparest for Thy reception."[2]

When the Puritans wrote about preparation for conversion, they did not come to this understanding on their own. Their view of conversion was shaped by hundreds of years of teaching. In particular, they stood in a tradition shaped by Augustine and the Reformation. In this chapter we will take a brief look at the Augustinian tradition as part of the historical background for the doctrine of preparation. Then we will examine the teachings of John Calvin.

Preparation as the Augustinian Language of Grace

The term *preparation* has roots in the patristic and medieval discussions of divine grace. Long before the Puritans, Augustine had analyzed grace as a progressive series of steps corresponding to the stages of the journey of the elect from unbelief to glory. Philip Schaff explained,

> Grace, finally, works progressively or by degrees. It removes all the consequences of the fall; but it removes them in an order agreeable to the finite, gradually unfolding nature of the believer.... Augustine gives different names to grace in these different steps of its development. In overcoming the resisting will, and imparting a living knowledge of sin and longing for redemption, grace is *gratia praeveniens* or *praeparans* [prevenient or preparing grace]. In creating faith and the free will to do good, and uniting the soul to Christ, it is *gratia operans* [operating or working grace]. Joining with the emancipated will to combat the remains of evil, and bringing forth good works as fruits of faith, it is *gratia cooperans* [cooperating grace]. Finally, in enabling the believer to persevere in faith to the end, and leading him at length, though not in this life, to the perfect state, in which he can no longer sin nor die, it is *gratia perficiens* [perfecting grace].[3]

Augustine wrote, "And who was it that had begun to give him his love, however small, but He who prepares the will, and perfects by His co-operation what He initiates by His operation? Forasmuch as in

---

2. Augustine, *Confessions*, 13.1, in *A Select Library of the Nicene and Post-Nicene Fathers of the Christian Church*, ed. Philip Schaff (repr., Grand Rapids: Eerdmans, 1991), 1:190.

3. Philip Schaff, *History of the Christian Church*, 3rd ed. (New York: Charles Scribner's Sons, 1891), 3:849.

beginning He works in us that we may have the will, and in perfecting works with us when we have the will" (Phil. 1:6).[4]

Augustine rebuked those who claimed to have prepared themselves and thus merited the grace of freedom, for salvation comes not of man's will but of God's (Phil. 2:13; Rom. 9:16). He affirmed that sinners must believe, hope, love, and, indeed, voluntarily pursue eternal life. But he also affirmed that God generates man's willing response, saying: "The preparation of the heart is from the Lord" (Prov. 16:1). He wrote, "The whole work belongs to God, who both makes the will of man righteous, and thus prepares it for assistance, and assists it when it is prepared.... It goes before the unwilling to make him willing; it follows the willing to make his will effectual."[5]

Augustine also recognized that the law, though unable to save sinners, had a part in leading men to saving grace. Yet he opposed any idea of receiving grace by preceding merit. He wrote, "Must then the unrighteous man, in order that he may be justified—that is, become a righteous man—lawfully use the law, to lead him, as by the schoolmaster's hand [Gal. 3:24], to that grace by which alone he can fulfill what the law commands? Now it is freely that he is justified thereby—that is, on account of no antecedent merits of his own works." How does the law function as a schoolmaster without granting merit to the sinner? Augustine said one must "lawfully use the law, when he applies it to alarm the unrighteous, so that...they may in faith flee for refuge to the grace that justifies."[6]

We have already spoken of Augustine's account of his own conversion. This became a model for others. Augustine's way to faith in Christ was filled with struggles, both moral and intellectual, and set a precedent for a lengthy and difficult conversion process, but nonetheless one that unfolded by grace alone. John Owen (1616–1683) used Augustine's experience as a paradigm for "the manner of conversion," thus demonstrating that the Puritans were influenced by Augustine.[7] Owen wrote, "I must say, that, in my judgment, there is none among the ancient or modern

---

4. Augustine, *On Grace and Free Will*, ch. 33, in *Nicene and Post-Nicene Fathers*, 5:458.

5. Augustine, *The Enchiridion on Faith, Hope, and Love* (Washington, D.C.: Regnery, 1996), 39–40 [ch. 32].

6. Augustine, *On the Spirit and the Letter*, ch. 16, in *Nicene and Post-Nicene Fathers*, 5:89–90. See also *On Christian Doctrine*, 2.7.10.

7. *Pneumatologia, or, A Discourse Concerning the Holy Spirit*, in *The Works of John Owen* (1850–1853; repr., Edinburgh: Banner of Truth, 1965), 3:337–66.

divines unto this day, who, either in the declarations of their own experiences, or their directions unto others, have equaled, much less outgone [excelled] him, in an accurate search and observation of all the secret actings of the Spirit of God on the minds and souls of men, both towards and in their recovery or conversion."[8]

We are not saying that Augustine's idea of preparatory grace was identical to that of the Puritans. Much theological reflection took place during the successive twelve centuries after Augustine. But we do say that the language of preparation is deeply rooted in the Augustinian tradition of sovereign grace. To speak of preparation for conversion does not deny salvation by grace but strikes notes that resonate with the mighty chords of grace that the church has played throughout history.

The medieval theologian Thomas Aquinas (1225–1274) also said that man cannot prepare himself to receive grace except by the grace of God preparing him.[9] God's preparatory grace may come at the same moment as the infusion of habitual grace, or it may precede habitual grace and lead to it step by step. Either way it is God's grace acting upon the soul.[10]

Richard Muller says Reformed scholars likewise differentiated between several acts of divine grace. These include the following:

1) *Gratia praeveniens*, or prevenient grace, which precedes repentance.

2) *Gratia praeparans*, or preparing grace, which communicates a sense of one's inability and a desire to come to Christ. This is preparation for conversion by the law.

3) *Gratia operans*, or operating grace, which regenerates the soul and creates faith.

4) *Gratia cooperans*, or cooperating grace, which continues to support the renewed soul during the process of sanctification.

5) *Gratia conservans*, or preserving grace, which enables believers to persevere.[11]

---

8. Owen, *Pneumatologia*, 3:349.

9. Thomas Aquinas, *Summa Theologica*, 2.1, Q. 109, art. 6.

10. Aquinas, *Summa Theologica*, 2.1, Q. 112, art. 2. See also Pettit, *The Heart Prepared*, 25–26, and Bernard of Clairvaux, *On the Love of God*, chs. 8–9.

11. Richard A. Muller, *Dictionary of Latin and Greek Theological Terms Drawn Principally from Protestant Scholastic Theology* (Grand Rapids: Baker, 1985), 129–30.

In taking the term *preparation* and deducing from it a Pelagian or legalistic theology, one fails to recognize the church's language of grace. By contrast, Augustine's view of prevenient grace bears some resemblance to the centuries-later Puritan doctrine of preparation, which says that God's grace operates in successive steps or phases, the first of which is "overcoming the resisting will, and imparting a living knowledge of sin and longing for redemption," as Schaff wrote.[12]

Before moving on from the Augustinian tradition, we would be remiss if we did not mention Martin Luther, the Augustinian monk who became a reformer. Though the Puritans did not read as much from Lutheran theologians as from Reformed writers, they certainly loved to read and quote Luther himself.[13] Richard Sibbes quoted Luther more often in his sermons than any other theologian besides Augustine.[14] Luther went through a prolonged and intense experience of guilt and fear before coming to Christ in assured faith. He disowned any concept of merit through penitential works, or of sinners effecting their own conversion. Yet he saw legal guilt and fear as God's means to awaken sinners and spur them to seek salvation. Sinners did not prepare themselves for faith, but, as Marilyn Harran observes, "God, through the Law, His alien work, brings man to despair and humility and to a recognition of his need, and through the Gospel, His appropriate work, He gives man faith and the knowledge of His forgiveness."[15]

In those respects, the Reformed and Puritan traditions are in continuity with Luther.[16] That suggests the doctrine of preparation is not rooted in the theology of Perkins or Beza but in the earliest leaders of the Reformation, and those who came prior to them. It would be fascinating to examine the similarities of Puritan preparation with Luther's view of the law and conversion, but that is beyond the scope of this book. Let us now turn to the French Reformer who is at the center of the academic debate about preparation.

---

12. Schaff, *History of the Christian Church*, 3:849.

13. For example, the English translation of Luther's commentary on Galatians was printed in England in 1575, 1577, 1588, 1602, 1615, and 1644, and his preface to Romans in 1590 and 1632.

14. Stephen P. Beck, "The Doctrine of *Gratia Praeparans* in the Soteriology of Richard Sibbes" (PhD Dissertation, Westminster Theological Seminary, 1994), 38.

15. Marilyn J. Harran, *Luther on Conversion: The Early Years* (Ithaca, N.Y.: Cornell University Press, 1983), 186.

16. Beck, "*Gratia Praeparans* in the Soteriology of Richard Sibbes," 44–46, 52–54.

John Calvin: Reformed Preparation

We have seen that the idea of *preparation* for faith does not represent a radical departure from Augustinian tradition. However, the Reformation of the sixteenth century did bring about significant shifts in theology, especially the renunciation of some conclusions of medieval scholasticism. John Calvin (1509–1564), though not the founder of the Reformed movement, nevertheless was a prominent pastor and theologian in the early years of the Reformed church. The specifics of his conversion from Roman Catholicism to Reformation Christianity are not known. But at some point in his early twenties, Calvin was changed from a man devoted to academic studies and to the papacy to a man who trusted in Christ alone as his righteousness. He then lived devoted to the motto, "Lord, I offer my heart to Thee, promptly and sincerely." His great book, *The Institutes of the Christian Religion,* has long been regarded as a classic statement of the Reformed faith. And Calvin's commentaries on Scripture, sermons, treatises, and personal letters constitute a massive body of Reformed, experiential theology.

In regard to Calvin's view of preparation for faith, some scholars have drawn a line between preparation and unadulterated Calvinism. Kendall insists that Puritan preparation was absolutely foreign, indeed contradictory, to Calvin's theology. He said Calvin's theology "rules out any preparation for faith on man's part…. There is nothing in Calvin's doctrine that suggests, even in the process of regeneration, that man must be prepared at all—including by the work of the Law prior to faith." While the law might stir men to seek salvation, Kendall said Calvin views it as "but an accidental effect."[17] Was Puritanism a relapse into pre-Reformation doctrine of preparation? What did John Calvin truly believe about preparation, faith, and conversion?

Certainly Calvin taught that men are saved by grace alone. God saves sinners through Christ; sinners do not save themselves. But this is not a violent act of compulsion on God's part. Commenting on Christ's statement in John 6:44 that "No man can come to me, except the Father which hath sent me draw him," Calvin wrote, "True indeed, as to the kind of 'drawing,' it is not violent, so as to compel men by external force; but still

---

17. Kendall, *Calvin and English Calvinism,* 26.

it is a powerful impulse of the Holy Spirit, which makes men willing who formerly were unwilling and reluctant."[18]

Calvin's Rejection of Meritorious Preparation by Free Will
In harmony with Augustine's view of sin and grace, Calvin said that fallen man cannot produce even "puny" impulses toward God (Gen. 6:5; 8:21). He exclaimed, "Away then with all that 'preparation' which many babble about!"[19] According to an editorial footnote from John McNeill, Calvin was specifically referring here to John Fisher (c. 1459–1535), Johann Cochlaeus (1479–1552), and Alphonsus de Castro (1495–1558), who were all Roman Catholic theologians. Calvin went on to say that Christ's teaching in John 6 about the drawing of the Father does "utterly overturn the whole power of free will, of which the Papists dream. For if it be only when the Father has 'drawn' us that we begin to 'come to Christ,' there is not in us any commencement of faith, or any preparation for it."[20] Calvin also rejected the idea that God's grace works upon man's will "in such a way that, having been prepared, it then has its own part in the action."[21] God does not create a state of human ability so that sinners are converted by any power but grace alone, he said.

At first glance, Calvin seems to have forcefully rejected all forms of preparation for conversion. But a closer look reveals that Calvin was rejecting the concept of preparation that sprang from the nominalist school of medieval theologians, such as William of Ockham (c. 1288– c. 1348). Aquinas had taught that God infused grace into a sinner apart from any merit or effort of men; men then exercised the divine gift of love to merit eternal life. The Reformers opposed this notion of justification by merit with the doctrine of justification by faith alone. But medieval nominalists went beyond Aquinas, teaching that God will give the infusion of grace as a fitting reward (congruent merit) to the person who does the best he can with his natural abilities. Steven Ozment summarizes the nominalist view of salvation in four steps: "1) moral effort: doing the best one can on the basis of natural moral ability, 2) infusion of grace as

---

18. John Calvin, *Commentary on the Gospel according to John*, trans. William Pringle (repr., Grand Rapids: Baker, 1996), 1:257 [on John 6:44].

19. Calvin, *Institutes*, 2.2.27.

20. Calvin, *Commentary on the Gospel according to John*, 258–59 [on John 6:45].

21. Calvin, *Institutes*, 2.3.7.

an appropriate reward, 3) moral cooperation: doing the best one can with the aid of grace, and 4) reward of eternal life as a just due."[22]

Calvin and the other Reformers forcefully opposed the nominalist view of preparation by stressing the total inability of fallen man to move towards God, and teaching that salvation is by grace alone.[23] However, this opposition did not exclude the idea that God may sovereignly lead sinners through a process of preparation that culminates in conversion by grace alone. We must be careful not to take Calvin's condemnation of preparation as taught by some Roman Catholic theologians and apply it to Reformed notions of preparation unless guilty of the same errors. Nor should we assume that the mere use of the word *preparation* means the same thing to Roman Catholics as to the Reformed.

Calvin himself spoke about God preparing men to trust in Christ. One example of God preparing a sinner for Christ is, according to Calvin, the desire that moved Zacchaeus to climb a tree to see Christ (Luke 19:1–10). Calvin wrote, "Now, though faith was not yet formed in Zacchaeus, yet this was a sort of preparation for it; for it was not without a heavenly inspiration that he desired so earnestly to get a sight of Christ…. In this manner, before revealing himself to men, the Lord frequently communicates to them a secret desire, by which they are led to Him."[24]

Knowing God with Mind and Heart

To understand Calvin's view of preparation, we must consider his view of knowing God. Calvin opened his *Institutes* with the statement that "true and sound wisdom, consists of two parts: the knowledge of God

---

22. Steven Ozment, *The Age of Reform, 1250–1550: An Intellectual and Religious History of Late Medieval and Reformation Europe* (New Haven: Yale University Press, 1980), 234. We are indebted for this reference to Philip A. Craig, "The Bond of Grace and Duty in the Soteriology of John Owen: The Doctrine of Preparation for Grace and Glory as a Bulwark against Seventeenth-Century Anglo-American Antinomianism" (PhD Dissertation, Trinity International University, 2005), 6.

23. Calvin also made strong arguments against Roman Catholic preparationism in his treatise against Albert Pighius (c. 1490–1542), *The Bondage and Liberation of the Will* (Grand Rapids: Baker, 1996), 26, 49, 69, 108, 110, 131–32, 135, 153, 173–74, 176, 187–88. Cited in Craig, "The Bond of Grace and Duty," 18–19.

24. John Calvin, *Commentary on a Harmony of the Evangelists*, trans. William Pringle (repr., Grand Rapids: Baker, 1996), 2:433–34 [Luke 19:1–10]. Cf. Victor A. Shepherd, *The Nature and Function of Faith in the Theology of John Calvin*, NABPR Dissertation Series, Number 2 (Macon, Ga.: Mercer University Press, 1983), 110.

and of ourselves."[25] Kendall says Calvin's emphasis on knowledge marks a clear boundary between him and the Puritans. Calvin supposedly says that faith consists merely of the knowledge and passive reception of God's promise, "a passive persuasion in the mind."[26] Thus the Puritans departed from Calvin in their emphasis upon the will and faith's activity in desiring and embracing God.

But Calvin did not drive a wedge between the mind and the will in his view of saving faith. He said, "Indeed, we shall not say that, properly speaking, God is known where there is no religion or piety," where "I call piety that reverence joined with love for God which the knowledge of his benefits induces."[27] Calvin spoke of a "twofold knowledge of God," which is, first, "to feel" the sovereign goodness of the Creator and God of providence, and second, "to embrace the grace of reconciliation offered to us in Christ."[28] Faith "is more of the heart than of the brain, and more of the disposition than of the understanding," Calvin said, for "faith embraces Christ as offered to us by the Father."[29] Thus the saving knowledge of God involves the persuasion of the mind but also the heart's embrace of Christ.

Like the Puritans after him, Calvin said the fulcrum of conversion was the will. He said of Philippians 1:6, "There is no doubt that through 'the beginning of a good work' he denotes the very origin of conversion itself, which is in the will. God begins his good work in us therefore, by arousing love and desire and zeal for righteousness in our hearts; or, to speak more correctly, by bending, forming, and directing, our hearts to righteousness." Continuing to use "heart" and "will" interchangeably, Calvin wrote about the promise of the gift of a new heart (Ezek. 36:26–27), explaining that means "the will…is changed from an evil to a good will."[30]

In the matter of saving faith, Calvin said, "no mere opinion or even persuasion" will suffice.[31] He did emphasize faith as knowledge, in part because he believed that faith must rest on the clear teaching of God's

---

25. Calvin, *Institutes*, 1.1.1.
26. Kendall, *Calvin and English Calvinism*, 3, 19.
27. Calvin, *Institutes*, 1.2.1.
28. Calvin, *Institutes*, 1.2.1.
29. Calvin, *Institutes*, 3.2.8.
30. Calvin, *Institutes*, 2.3.6.
31. Calvin, *Institutes*, 3.2.1.

Word, not a blind submission to the church's authority which leaves people in "the grossest ignorance."[32] But Calvin's concept of knowledge included both head knowledge as well as heart knowledge. He wrote, "Now we shall possess a right definition of faith if we call it a firm and certain knowledge of God's benevolence toward us, founded upon the truth of the freely given promise in Christ, both revealed to our minds and sealed upon our hearts through the Holy Spirit."[33] He said, "For the Word of God is not received by faith if it flits about in the top of the brain, but when it takes root in the depth of the heart."[34] "Can faith be separated from love?...we do not attain salvation by a frigid and bare knowledge of God."[35]

Preparatory Knowledge of Sin
Saving faith thus involves knowledge that engages both the head and heart. But true knowledge of God and of self involves a painful and humbling awareness of one's sins in the light of God's holiness. Calvin said, "It is certain that man never achieves a clear knowledge of himself unless he has first looked upon God's face, and then descends from contemplating him to scrutinize himself. For we always seem to ourselves righteous and upright and wise and holy—this pride is innate in all of us—unless by clear proofs we stand convinced of our own unrighteousness, foulness, folly, and impurity."[36]

Graham Harrison writes, "According to Calvin, it is part of the plight of man that although his spiritual state is desperate in the extreme, he is unaware of that fact. There exists, therefore, an urgent necessity for him to be brought to a right state of self awareness, an apprehension of his real condition before God, if he is to go on and benefit from the work of the Mediator."[37] Calvin said, "Now it is impossible that men become rightly converted to God unless they are condemned in themselves and they have conceded both the terror and the agony of

---

32. Calvin, *Institutes*, 3.2.2.

33. Calvin, *Institutes*, 3.2.7.

34. Calvin, *Institutes*, 3.2.36; cf. 1.5.9.

35. John Calvin, *Commentaries on the Catholic Epistles*, trans. John Owen (repr., Grand Rapids: Baker, 1996), 310 [on James 2:14].

36. Calvin, *Institutes*, 1.1.2. See *Institutes*, 2.1.1–3.

37. Graham Harrison, "'Becoming a Christian'—In the Teaching of John Calvin," in *Becoming a Christian* (London: The Westminster Conference, 1972), 25.

the malediction which is prepared for them unless they are restored to grace with God."[38]

To see ourselves in the light of God's holiness requires an act of God upon the soul. Calvin said, "Besides the wickedness that is in us, there is also such a great hardness and willfulness that God has to wake us, as it were by force, that we may have some sense of our vices that we may hate them. It is true that this is done chiefly when God calls us and pulls us out of the confusion we were in. But yet every Christian must continue in it all the time of his life."[39] This awakening thus lays the foundation for the entire Christian course of life-time repentance.

Calvin said the law is one means God uses to awaken us. Though Calvin emphasized the use of the law in guiding believers in following Christ, he also taught the use of the law in driving unbelievers to Christ for salvation. He said,

> Therefore the law summoneth all the world before God, not one except[ed]: it condemneth all the children of Adam, and showeth that they are worthy to be cast away of God, and that they have nothing else to look for, nor any other hope but to be swallowed up in hellfire. This is first of all, why the law of God is given us. Now seeing God thundereth against us, we must needs run to that mercy which is offered unto us in our Lord Jesus Christ…being humbled we should seek our salvation in our Lord Jesus Christ, seeing that in us there is nothing but mere damnation.[40]

Calvin spoke of three uses of the moral law. David Jones describes those as "preparative, preservative, and restorative." He explains, "The first use of the law is to prepare sinners to seek salvation in Christ, and particularly justification, through faith alone."[41] Though Calvin emphasized the uses of the law as a restraint on society and as a rule of living

---

38. John Calvin, *The Deity of Christ and Other Sermons*, trans. Leroy Nixon (Audubon, N.J.: Old Paths Publications, 1997), 54.

39. John Calvin, *Sermons on the Epistle to the Ephesians* (Edinburgh: Banner of Truth, 1987), 531.

40. John Calvin, *Sermons on Timothy and Titus* (1579; facsimile repr., Edinburgh: Banner of Truth, 1983), 50–51.

41. David C. Jones, "The Law and the Spirit of Christ," in *A Theological Guide to Calvin's Institutes*, ed. David W. Hall and Peter A. Lillback (Phillipsburg, Pa.: P & R Publishing, 2008), 302.

for the believer, he did not neglect the use of conviction and condemnation to drive sinners to Christ.

In that respect, the law assists the natural conscience of sinners, which Calvin described as "a certain mean between God and man, because it does not allow man to suppress within himself what he knows, but pursues him to the point of convicting him."[42] Though a person's conscience may slumber or give way to hypocrisy, when awakened it torments sinners and strips away all their excuses. The preaching of God's Word becomes the vehicle through which the divine glory of Judgment Day shines on the conscience, searches the soul, and strikes the sinner with dread.[43]

We therefore disagree with William Chalker when he asserts that Calvin could not conceive of any "preparation for faith," or when he asserts that a pre-conversion awareness of one's sins and need for salvation is "foreign to Calvin," or when he says, "Calvin discredited all other self-knowledge prior to faith."[44] Certainly Calvin viewed self-knowledge as a work of God as well as a work prior to and preparatory for saving faith in Christ. Thus the seeds of Puritan preparation can be found in John Calvin's theology.

Preparation, Faith, and Repentance

To understand how preparation by the law relates to faith and repentance, Calvin said we must know our depravity, but our pride hinders us until God awakens us in part by the law. Calvin said repentance does not come from a bare preaching of the law but is induced by the gospel of grace and reconciliation.[45] Evangelical repentance comes through faith in Christ.[46] But Calvin also saw the command to "prepare ye the way of the Lord" as meaning "that we may take out of the way those sins which obstruct the kingdom of Christ, and thus may give access to his grace."[47] A conviction of sin, even a moral reformation, generally precedes saving faith and evangelical repentance.

---

42. Calvin, *Institutes*, 3.19.15.

43. David L. Foxgrover, "John Calvin's Understanding of Conscience" (PhD Dissertation, Claremont Graduate School, 1978), 143–45, 369–80.

44. William H. Chalker, "Calvin and Some Seventeenth Century English Calvinists" (PhD Dissertation, Duke University, 1961), 50–51, 115, 126.

45. Calvin, *Commentary on a Harmony of the Evangelists*, 1:179 [on Matt. 3:2]; *Institutes*, 3.3.2.

46. Calvin, *Institutes*, 3.3.1.

47. Calvin, *Commentary on a Harmony of the Evangelists*, 1:182 [on Matt. 3:3].

So it is wrong to read Calvin's location of repentance as a consequence of faith as if he thereby denied any preparatory work of the law.
His view is more complex. Shepherd says, "It would appear that Calvin
speaks of repentance as preceding faith when by 'repentance' he means
regret, remorse, fear of the coming judgment, disgust at sin; and conse-
quent to faith when by 'repentance' he means that newness of life which
Jesus Christ is."[48]

Consider what Calvin wrote with regard to persons not yet regenerate: "Because they are too full of their own virtue or of the assurance of
their own righteousness, they are not fit to receive Christ's grace unless
they first be emptied. Therefore, through the recognition of their own
misery, the law brings them down to humility in order thus to prepare
them to seek what previously they did not realize they lacked."[49] The law
is the mirror that confronts us with our sins and condemnation before
God, humbles our pride, and drives us to receive Christ as our righteousness and God's grace.[50]

Preparatory conviction must be distinguished from saving repentance. Calvin said many people are confused about the order of faith
and evangelical repentance "by the fact that many are overwhelmed by
qualms of conscience or compelled to obedience before they are imbued
with the knowledge of grace."[51] This initial fear, however, does not properly belong to the true obedience which can only be found where the
Spirit reigns through union with Christ. Instead it pertains to "how
variously Christ draws us to himself, or prepares us for the pursuit of
godliness."[52] This striking use of preparatory language in Calvin anticipates what later appeared in Puritan writings.

Calvin surveyed distinctions made by others with respect to repentance, such as the distinction between mortification and vivification. He
spoke highly of their view of mortification:

> Mortification they explain as sorrow of soul and dread conceived
> from the recognition of sin and the awareness of divine judgment.
> For when anyone has been brought into a true knowledge of sin, he
> then begins truly to hate and abhor sin; then he is heartily displeased

---

48. Shepherd, *The Nature and Function of Faith*, 37.
49. Calvin, *Institutes*, 2.7.11. See also Shepherd, *The Nature and Function of Faith*, 139–43.
50. Guenther H. Haas, "Calvin's Ethics," in *The Cambridge Companion to John Calvin*, 100.
51. Calvin, *Institutes*, 3.3.2.
52. Calvin, *Institutes*, 3.3.2.

with himself, he confesses himself miserable and lost and wishes
to be another man. Furthermore, when he is touched by any sense
of the judgment of God (for the one straightway follows the other)
he then lies stricken and overthrown; humbled and cast down he
trembles; he becomes discouraged and despairs.[53]

Vivification is finding consolation and life by faith in Christ. Calvin
accepted this description of repentance but clarified it, saying that vivification need not be the end of all fears yet involves "the desire to live in a
holy and devoted manner, a desire arising from rebirth."[54]

Similarly, Calvin commends the distinction made by others between
"repentance of the law" and "repentance of the gospel," noting that the
former can sometimes be "nothing but a sort of entryway of hell" such
that sinners already in this life begin to feel God's wrath.[55] Calvin said
"all these things are true," but he preferred to offer his own definition of
repentance as, "the true turning of our life to God, a turning that arises
from a pure and earnest fear of him; and it consists of the mortification of
our flesh and of the old man, and in the vivification of the Spirit."[56]

Of particular interest to us in regard to preparation is Calvin's concept that repentance arises from the fear of God. He said, "Before the
mind of the sinner inclines to repentance, it must be aroused by thinking
upon divine judgment."[57] Fixing the mind upon Judgment Day "will not
permit the miserable man to rest nor to breathe freely even for a moment
without stirring him continually to reflect upon another mode of life
whereby he may be able to stand firm in that judgment."[58]

Calvin wrote, "Inasmuch as conversion begins with dread and hatred
of sin, the apostle makes 'the sorrow...according to God' the cause of
repentance [2 Cor. 7:10].... There is, besides, an obstinancy that must be
beaten down as if with hammers. Therefore, the depravity of our nature
compels God to use severity in threatening us. For it would be vain for
him gently to allure those who are asleep."[59]

---

53. Calvin, *Institutes*, 3.3.3.
54. Calvin, *Institutes*, 3.3.3.
55. Calvin, *Institutes*, 3.3.4.
56. Calvin, *Institutes*, 3.3.5.
57. Calvin, *Institutes*, 3.3.7.
58. Calvin, *Institutes*, 3.3.7.
59. Calvin, *Institutes*, 3.3.7.

We note several themes in Calvin's writing that recur in the Puritans: the necessity of sorrow and fear to awaken proud, hard hearts; the emotional nature of such contrition; distinguishing the fear of judgment from evangelical obedience; linking gracious obedience to faith in Christ; and the character of the fear of God in the reprobate, for whom such fear is not a road to life but only an anticipation of their future in hell.

These themes refute the sharp contrast that Pettit draws between Calvin and Bullinger, attributing to Calvin a predestinarian view of conversion by "coercion," and to Bullinger a covenantal view of conversion by "repentance and acknowledgment." Pettit writes, "For Calvin there is no divine offer to which the heart must respond, but only God's omnipotence, through [which] the heart, though invited to prepare, is compelled toward grace."[60] By contrast, we have observed in Calvin's writings his view that God does not merely coerce men's hearts but addresses them in a personal manner to awaken them to their need and terrible danger so that when He regenerates them to behold the spiritual beauty of Christ, they embrace Christ as their Savior from sin as a reasonable choice of their wills.

Calvin openly taught in his sermons on Deuteronomy that God, as the first part of a "double grace" in conversion, "prepareth our hearts to come unto him to receive his doctrine."[61] He compared the heart to a rough piece of stone that must be made smooth before God writes His laws upon it. Even when men come to church, they may come with hearts roughened by lusts and are "not disposed to receive God's word."[62] Since some scholars deny the compatibility of the Puritan doctrine of preparation with the Calvinistic doctrine of divine sovereignty, we quote Calvin here at length:

> True it is, that we cannot do this of our own self-moving, but he
> must direct us thereto by his Holy Spirit. Notwithstanding, it is to be
> noted, that God bestoweth two distinct graces upon us. The one is in
> preventing us, to the intent we should be ready and forward to yield
> him obedience: and the other is in enlightening us, and in giving
> us a present affection to serve him as soon as we know his will....
> Before men are brought to the faith...they have some good prepara-
> tive aforehand.... They have not faith, but an entrance unto faith....
> Now cometh this inmoving, of men, or of their own nature? No, it is

---

60. Pettit, *The Heart Prepared*, 44.

61. John Calvin, *Sermons on Deuteronomy* (1583; facsimile repr., Edinburgh: Banner of Truth, 1987), 423.

62. Calvin, *Sermons on Deuteronomy*, 422.

God's working in their hearts, who maketh that preparation there by
the grace of his Holy Spirit.... God hath taught him aforehand, and
prepared him to the doing thereof. Ye see then that that is one grace
which God bestoweth: and yet nevertheless, God showeth us that it
is our duty to do it, though we cannot do it of our own ability.[63]

Calvin thus clearly affirmed that God's preparatory grace clears the way
for faith, and the duty of the unconverted to pursue this preparation,
even though only God can make it possible.

Calvin said, "Christ...reveals himself to none but poor and afflicted
sinners, who groan, toil, are heavy-laden, hunger, thirst, and pine away
with sorrow and misery."[64] However, Calvin did not view this miserable
condition as an end; rather, he said one must press forward through it to
Christ. He wrote,

> Therefore, I think he has profited greatly who has learned to be very
> much displeased with himself, not so as to stick fast in this mire
> and progress no farther, but rather to hasten to God and yearn for
> him in order that, having been engrafted into the life and death of
> Christ, he may give attention to continual repentance. Truly, they
> who are held by a real loathing of sin cannot do otherwise. For no
> one ever hates sin unless he has previously been seized with a love
> of righteousness.[65]

Calvin's words here suggest what would later develop into Thomas Hooker's theology of conviction and implanting into Christ, as well as John
Bunyan's Slough of Despond. They also prompt a question that puzzled
the Puritans long after Calvin's death: at what point does preparatory
grief over sin become true love for God? In many ways Calvin's writings
on these matters anticipated the later work of the Puritans.

Conclusion

The language of preparation is the language of grace. The Puritan doctrine of preparation did not communicate legalism to its hearers in the
church; rather, it resonated with the church's discussions of grace over the
centuries. To be sure, the Protestant Reformation required clarification

---

63. Calvin, *Sermons on Deuteronomy*, 422.
64. Calvin, *Institutes*, 3.3.20.
65. Calvin, *Institutes*, 3.3.20.

of what was included in this preparation. All forms of meritorious self-
improvement as steps to salvation were rejected by Calvin. But Calvin
also recognized that God's grace precedes faith, not only in the moment
of creating faith itself but in the mysterious influences that lead to faith
over time. Faith is not bare knowledge or passive persuasion but the
embrace of Christ by the heart, resulting in personal knowledge of God.
The heart must therefore be prepared by the law awakening the sinner
to his need of Christ. The law beats on the stony heart as a hammer to
smooth its surface before God writes His Word upon it. Though some
men called this repentance, Calvin preferred to think of it as preparation
for faith, which in turn leads to true repentance.

This leads us to the conclusion that Calvin himself taught that the
ordinary way of conversion included preparation for faith, both as a grace
from God and a duty incumbent on man. Therefore, attempts to drive a
wedge between Calvin and the Puritans at this point is only an attempt
to split apart what is fundamentally one. Paul Helm writes, "Thus Calvin,
together with the Puritans, insisted that one important function of the
moral law is to convict men of sin, but also taught that it requires the grace
of God in the gospel to bring such men to repentance and saving faith."[66]
To further demonstrate this unity between Calvin and the Puritans, let us
now consider the teachings of the Puritans on preparation for faith.

---

66. Helm, *Calvin and the Calvinists,* 69.

CHAPTER THREE

The Early English Puritans:
William Perkins, Richard Sibbes,
and John Preston

First, the law prepares us by humbling us: then comes the gospel, and
it stirs up faith.

—William Perkins[1]

John Winthrop (1588–1649) was a founding father of Massachusetts Bay
Colony. He thought he had been converted at age eighteen through the
preaching of Ezekiel Culverwell, for he subsequently became a godly
man, gave spiritual counsel to others, and considered entering the pastoral ministry. But then he read some of the old Puritan writers, who
convinced him that he had gone no further in spirituality than a reprobate man. That, he said, "was a dart in my liver."

Winthrop worked harder to live a righteous life. He shunned recre-
ations and worldly employments, thinking they might distract him from
God. When he was age thirty, Winthrop experienced a remarkable time
of humiliation during which God showed him his emptiness. After that,
Winthrop wrote, "The good Spirit of the Lord breathed upon my soul,
and said I should live." Though he experienced some trials and temptations after that, Winthrop had an abiding sense of peace with God.[2] His
experience illustrates the typical Puritan motif of passing through preparatory humiliation prior to attaining assurance of salvation.

Observation of the effect of the law in assisting the gospel in conversion predates the Puritan movement. It also predates the Reformation.
Thomas Bilney (c. 1495–1531) said that during his conversion experience
(c. 1516) he read 1 Timothy 1:15: "Christ Jesus came into the world to save

---

1. William Perkins, *A Commentary on Galatians*, ed. Gerald T. Sheppard (1617; facsimile repr., New York: Pilgrim Press, 1989), 200.
2. Morgan, *Visible Saints*, 71–72.

sinners; of whom I am chief." He wrote, "This one sentence, through God's instruction and inward working, which I did not then perceive, did so exhilarate my heart, being before wounded with the guilt of my sins, and being almost in despair, that immediately I felt a marvelous comfort and quietness." Bilney was later instrumental in the conversion of Hugh Latimer (c. 1490–1555). He went to Latimer to confess his sins but did so in such a way that Latimer recognized his own sins and inability to save himself.[3]

As the Reformation proceeded in England, Erasmus's Greek New Testament and the teachings of Luther and Calvin changed people's view of conversion. They became increasingly convinced that the law was useful not just for regulating society and directing the life of believers but also in awakening unbelievers to their sin and weakness. John Bradford (1510–1555) wrote, "For how can it be, that such as find no terror of conscience, and see not their just damnation in the law of God, which commandeth things impossible to man's nature and power; how can it be, I say, that such should find sweetness in the gospel of Christ?"[4] The bitter must go before the sweet.

This preparatory work of the law is not a matter of attaining merit or achieving self-salvation. The Thirty-Nine Articles of the Church of England (1563, 1571) had made it clear that fallen man has no power or merit to prepare himself for salvation:

> The condition of man after the fall of Adam is such, that he cannot turn or prepare himself by his own natural strength and good works, to faith and calling upon God: wherefore we have no power to do good works pleasant and acceptable to God, without the grace of God by Christ preventing us, that we may have a good will, and working in us, when we have that good will.[5]

Works done prior to conversion were not instrumental in salvation, "as they spring not of faith in Jesus Christ; neither do they make men

---

3. F. W. B. Bulluck, *Evangelical Conversion in Great Britain, 1516–1695* (St. Leonards on Sea, Eng.: Budd & Gillatt, 1966), 1–10.

4. *The Writings of John Bradford*, [Volume 1] (Cambridge: The Parker Society, 1848), 5. On Bradford's view of personal salvation as sorrow for sin, faith, and new life, see Lynn B. Tipson, Jr., "The Development of a Puritan Understanding of Conversion" (PhD Dissertation, Yale University, 1972), 141–42.

5. "The Thirty-Nine Articles of the Church of England," article 10, in Philip Schaff, *The Creeds of Christendom* (repr., Grand Rapids: Baker, 1998), 3:493–94.

meet to receive grace, or (as the school-authors say) deserve the grace of congruity."[6]

These statements set the Church of England against teachings of the Roman Catholic Church. The Counter-Reformation Council of Trent had pronounced an anathema in 1547 upon anyone who denied that human free will cooperated with God's grace to prepare a sinner for justification. The council had also anathematized anyone who said that all of man's acts prior to justification were sinful and hateful before God, or that man's will does not cooperate with God's grace prior to faith to prepare the sinner for justification.[7]

The Thirty-Nine Articles excluded meritorious preparation, preparation by human strength, and preparation through virtue or works pleasing to God prior to conversion. But they did not exclude preparation that reveals our own guilt, weakness, and sin. Thus the Heidelberg Catechism (1563), which many English Protestants loved, confessed both conversion by the sovereign grace of the Holy Spirit (Q. 21, 65) and the necessity of knowing our sin and misery through the law (Q. 2–11).[8] Indeed the catechism's three-fold structure of misery, deliverance, and thankfulness helped to instill in Reformed believers an intuitive sense that conviction of sin precedes assurance of salvation.

This combination of salvation by grace alone and preparation by the humbling of a sinner was passed on from the Reformers to the Puritans. The early Puritan Richard Greenham (c. 1542–1594) affirmed divine predestination and exhorted men to bring themselves to God to be humbled by His laws.[9] In his *Short Form of Catechising,* Greenham asked, "What is required for our right and sound entrance to our salvation?" He then answered,

1. To know and to be persuaded of the greatness of our sin and the misery due to the same,

6. "Thirty-Nine Articles," article 13, in Schaff, ed. *The Creeds of Christendom,* 3:495.

7. "The Canons and Decrees of the Council of Trent, Sixth Session, held January 13, 1547, Decree on Justification," canons 4–5, 7–9, in Schaff, *The Creeds of Christendom,* 2:111–12.

8. *The Summe of Christian Religion,* the English translation of Ursinus's lectures on the Heidelberg Catechism, was printed in England in 1587, 1589, 1591, 1595, 1601, 1611, 1617, 1633, and 1645. See also William Ames, *The Substance of Christian Religion: Or, a Plain and Easie Draught of the Christian Catechisme* (London: by T. Mabb for Thomas Davies, 1659). On preparation in the catechism and Ursinus, see chapter 13.

9. Pettit, *The Heart Prepared,* 50.

2. To know and be persuaded how we may be delivered from them, and

3. To know and be persuaded what thanks we owe to God for our deliverance.[10]

The foundation of Greenham's belief was clearly the Heidelberg Catechism, which says that we must preach the law and the gospel, for "the law is to prepare, the gospel is to follow after."[11]

Richard Rogers (1551–1618), author of *Seven Treatises* (1592), similarly explained conversion as: first, "the clear knowledge of man's misery"; second, "his redemption and deliverance"; and third, "how both these ought to work upon men's hearts, and what fruit they will bring forth by the operation of the Holy Ghost."[12] The effect of knowing one's misery, he said, "will wound and humble their hearts, when they shall see thereby, that they are but dead and damned people." A person with this knowledge perceives himself "not only a loathsome creature in God's sight, through the leprosy of sin, but withal a most cursed and damned person."[13]

People attain this knowledge, according to Rogers, by the internal power of being "secretly drawn, he cannot tell how, by the unspeakable work of the Spirit of God" and by the external means of "the doctrine of the law preached."[14] Most people are no more moved by the law than birds are frightened by a familiar scarecrow, but some hear God's "thundering voice, by his law arraigning men for their sins: which is no less fearful to them than the roaring of a lion."[15] Rogers said conversion then proceeds through the stages of considering oneself and one's state, humiliation before God, confession of sin and hungering after divine mercy with a soft heart of sorrow, prizing and pursuing Christ above all things, and applying Christ to oneself by faith.[16]

---

10. Paul E. G. Cook, "Becoming a Christian—In the Teaching of Richard Rogers and Richard Greenham," in *Becoming a Christian*, 60.

11. Cook, "Becoming a Christian—In the Teaching of Richard Rogers and Richard Greenham," 61.

12. Richard Rogers, *Seven Treatises* (London: by Felix Kyngston, for Thomas Man and Robert Dexter, 1603), 2.

13. Rogers, *Seven Treatises*, 2.

14. Rogers, *Seven Treatises*, 10.

15. Rogers, *Seven Treatises*, 11.

16. Rogers, *Seven Treatises*, 13–28. Cf. Pettit, *The Heart Prepared*, 51–53.

Pettit says Rogers got his views from experience, not orthodox dogma: "For Rogers the facts of regeneration along experiential lines take precedence over prescribed theological dogma.... Rogers let experience itself determine the process of conversion."[17] However, Rogers constantly referred, not to human experiences, but to the Holy Scriptures.[18] There is also no evidence that Rogers was resisting or departing from Reformed dogma.

This understanding of preparation was not confined to England. Robert Rollock (1555–1598), a Scottish theologian and first principal of Edinburgh University, wrote, "Our effectual calling is effected, first by the Law, then by the Gospel."[19] The law pronounces a curse on all law-breakers, convincing sinners in their consciences that they are accursed. As a result, "we are amazed and affected with the feeling of our misery." Though this feeling is "the first degree of our salvation," Rollock qualified this by saying it "belongs not so much to the calling itself, as to our preparation to that effectual calling which is properly effected by the doctrine of the Gospel."[20]

Arthur Hildersam (1563–1632), a Puritan theologian, further detailed the steps leading to true conversion, not, Pettit says, "so much to impose a rigid pattern as to establish guideposts along the way." In quoting Hildersam, Pettit says, "Ordinarily the Lord useth by the Spirit of bondage and legal terrors to prepare men to their conversion."[21] *Ordinarily* is a key word in this statement, for the Puritans believed that God had the freedom to convert people in whatever manner He chose. Hildersam wrote, "They that would win souls to God, must plainly and particularly discover to men their sins," yet not always sharply and bitterly, but in whatever manner is "most likely to prevail and do them good."[22]

Someone might object to this, saying that people already know they are sinners, but Hildersam said their knowledge is like a sleeping

---

17. Pettit, *The Heart Prepared*, 54.

18. A quick scan of this section shows 92 Scripture references in 19 pages, about 5 per page (Rogers, *Seven Treatises*, 9–28). This does not count unmarked allusions to Scriptures or biblical themes.

19. *Select Works of Robert Rollock* (repr., Grand Rapids: Reformation Heritage Books, 2008), 1:194.

20. Rollock, *Select Works*, 1:194–95.

21. Pettit, *The Heart Prepared*, 58.

22. Arthur Hildersam, *CVIII Lectures upon the Fourth of John*, 3rd ed. (London: by Moses Bell for Edward Brewster, 1647), 59.

watchdog that inspires no fear. Their conscience must yet be awakened, for "till men have the true knowledge and sense of sin, they can never know Christ to the comfort and salvation of their souls."[23]

When God convicts people of sin, they must respond by humbling themselves and grieving over their sins—not just because of the punishment their sin deserves but because of their inherent wrongness towards God. This humiliation culminates in repentance. Hildersam did not clearly locate these stages of conversion with respect to unregenerate deadness and regenerate life—or somewhere in between.[24]

To further explore early English Puritan views on preparation, let us now examine the work of three influential men: William Perkins, Richard Sibbes, and John Preston.

William Perkins: Steps of Salvation

William Perkins (1558–1602) was a towering influence in the English Reformed movement and similar movements in the European Continent and New England. Converted after a wild life of alcohol abuse, Perkins became a member of the spiritual brotherhood of Puritans at Cambridge. He had the unusual ability both to minister to criminals on death row and to write profound theological treatises. He was especially concerned with how God's predestination of chosen sinners to eternal life worked itself out in everyday life.

Perkins asserted both the absolute predestination of men to salvation or damnation, and the utter deadness and inability of sinners to do anything of spiritual value until God regenerates them. He rebuked as "semi-Pelagian papists" those who "ascribe God's predestination partly to mercy and partly to man's foreseen preparations."[25] No preparations by the unconverted can merit or cause conversion,[26] he said. Given that Perkins taught a kind of legal preparation prior to evangelical faith, he clearly put Roman Catholic preparation in a different class than his own.

Perkins did not say that dead sinners were unable to do anything at all or to be prepared for conversion in any sense. He said the natural and

---

23. Hildersam, *The Fourth of John*, 60–61.
24. Pettit, *The Heart Prepared*, 59–61.
25. Quoted in Pettit, *The Heart Prepared*, 62.
26. Yong Jae Timothy Song, *Theology and Piety in the Reformed Federal Thought of William Perkins and John Preston* (Lewiston, N.Y.: Edwin Mellen Press, 1998), 132–35.

corrupt will could still move people to intellectual study, civic virtue, morality, and outward religious actions such as listening to the Scriptures and discussing them. After all, humanity still possessed a conscience by which they could apply God's law to themselves and experience guilt.[27]

While denying the Roman Catholic concept of preparation, Perkins proposed preparation of another kind. He wrote:

> *Q. But how mayest thou be made partaker of Christ and his benefits?*
>
> A. A man of a contrite and humble spirit, by faith alone apprehending and applying Christ with all his merits unto himself, is justified before God and sanctified....
>
> *Q. How doth God bring men truly to believe in Christ?*
>
> A. First, he prepareth their hearts, that they might be capable of faith, and then he worketh faith in them.
>
> *Q. How doth God prepare men's hearts?*
>
> A. By bruising them, as if one would break a hard stone to powder; and this is done by humbling them (Ezek. 11:19; Hos. 6:1–2).
>
> *Q. How doth God humble a man?*
>
> A. By working in him a sight of his sins, and a sorrow for them."[28]

Perkins said that just as the body of an infant develops in stages within a mother's womb, so the Holy Spirit works faith in the soul "not suddenly, but by certain steps and degrees."[29] He begins by enlightening the mind, first "with a further knowledge of the law than nature can afford," and, second, "to understand and consider seriously" Christ and His grace. Then the Holy Ghost inflames the will to "hunger after Christ" and to pray for reconciliation with God. This weak faith then grows and develops into the sealing of the heart with "a lively and plentiful assurance."[30]

Perkins said that in saving a man, God ordinarily follows a series of ten steps in two stages, the first stage being preparatory. In the first stage, (1) God gives a sinner the outward means of grace, especially preaching,

27. Tipson, "The Development of a Puritan Understanding of Conversion," 209, 214.

28. *The Work of William Perkins*, ed. Ian Breward (Appleford: Sutton Courtenay Press, 1970), 147, 156.

29. William Perkins, *Exposition of the Creede*, in *A Golden Chaine* (London: Iohn Legat, 1600), 192.

30. Perkins, *Exposition of the Creede*, 192–93.

plus some inward or outward affliction to subdue his stubbornness. (2) God makes him attentive to the law to see what is good and what is evil. (3) God causes him to (see and know his own peculiar and proper sins, whereby he offends God." (4) God "smites the heart with a legal fear...makes the sinner fear punishment and hell, and despair of salvation, in regard of anything in himself." These four steps are the works of preparation prior to grace; the actions which follow are effects of grace.[31] One may experience the first four stages and yet not be born again.

In the stage of preparation the law is a "schoolmaster unto Christ" (Gal. 3:24). Perkins elsewhere explained, "The law, especially the moral law, urgeth and compelleth men to go to Christ. For it shows us our sins, and that without remedy: it shows us the damnation that is due unto us: and by this means, it makes us despair of salvation in respect of ourselves: and thus it enforceth us to seek for help out of ourselves in Christ. The law is then our schoolmaster not by the plain teaching, but by stripes and correction."[32] Perkins summarizes this stage in the explicit language of preparation: "In this verse, Paul sets down the manner and way of our salvation, which is on this manner; first, the law prepares us by humbling us: then comes the gospel, and it stirs up faith."[33]

Preparation for conversion by the law involves three agents: God, the minister, and the sinners. Ministers must so preach the law that men will be made willing to hear the gospel.[34] God works through the law with restraining (but not renewing) grace. The sinner must listen, read, think, and pray.[35]

The second stage of saving grace includes these next six steps: (5) God stirs the person's mind seriously to consider the gospel.[36] (6) God kindles in the heart sparks of faith consisting of a persistent desire to

---

31. William Perkins, *The Whole Treatise of the Cases of Conscience* (Cambridge: Iohn Legat, 1609), 15.

32. Perkins, *A Commentary on Galatians*, 200.

33. Perkins, *A Commentary on Galatians*, 200.

34. Tipson, "The Development of a Puritan Understanding of Conversion," 237–42.

35. Song, *Theology and Piety in the Reformed Federal Thought of William Perkins and John Preston*, 138–39.

36. Elsewhere Perkins said that a serious consideration of the gospel belongs to the first actions of the Holy Spirit, and hunger for Christ is the most basic act of saving faith, thus putting #5 with #1–4 above. See William Perkins, *An Exposition of the Symbole or Creede of the Apostles*, in *The Workes of that Famovs and VVorthy Minister of Christ in the Vniuersitie of Cambridge, Mr. William Perkins* (London: Iohn Legatt, 1612), 1:125.

trust Christ. This is the beginning of justifying faith. (7) God sustains this faith to combat doubt, despair, and distrust. (8) God quiets the conscience so that the soul rests on the promise of salvation. (9) God stimulates the heart to "evangelical sorrow for sin, because it is sin, and because God is offended." This is evangelical repentance. (10) God gives grace to the saved sinner to labor to obey God's commandments.[37] Perkins elsewhere presented the same ideas in a somewhat different scheme, showing the flexibility of his analysis.[38]

Perkins placed sorrow for sin in the steps preceding faith, but he placed evangelical repentance after faith. In this ordering he echoed the teachings of Calvin. Like Calvin, Perkins noted that the reprobate person may experience sorrow for sin, but evangelical repentance comes only to the elect in their spiritual rebirth.

At the same time, Perkins taught that *in human experience* godly sorrow often precedes an awareness of faith. He said, "Humiliation is indeed a fruit of faith; yet I put it in place before faith, because in practice it is first. Faith lieth hid in the heart, and the first effect whereby it appears, is the abasing and humbling of ourselves."[39] This humiliation consists of grief and shame over sin, confessing sin to God and our worthiness of damnation, and praying to God for mercy. Although the sinner may not yet perceive his own faith in Christ, the promises of Scripture to the broken-hearted (Isa. 57:15; Ps. 51:17; Prov. 28:13; 1 John 1:9) reveal that he has already "entered into the state of salvation."[40] So the order of sorrow/saving faith/repentance in objective reality may actually manifest itself as sorrow/repentance/saving faith in subjective experience.

Richard Sibbes: Sweet Mercy and Bruised Reeds

Richard Sibbes (1577–1635) was a kindhearted Puritan known for the sweetness of his writings. He was converted through the ministry of Paul Baynes, Perkins's successor at Cambridge. He trained many preachers and cultivated a remarkable network of friendships with ministers and political figures. His classic book on repentance, *The Bruised Reed*,

---

37. Perkins, *Cases of Conscience*, 15. See Pettit, *The Heart Prepared*, 63–64; Beeke, *The Quest for Full Assurance*, 88–92.

38. Perkins, *A Golden Chain*, 117–21 [ch. 36].

39. Perkins, *Cases of Conscience*, 16.

40. Perkins, *Cases of Conscience*, 16.

was so popular that it went through six editions between 1630 and 1638.[41] In that work Sibbes said that God's people are all "bruised reeds" prior to conversion (cf. Isa. 42:3), except for those saved in childhood, "yet in different degrees, as God seeth meet; and as difference is in regard of temper, parts, manner of life."[42]

This bruising, which Christ described as being "poor in spirit" (Matt. 5:3), refers to a sense of heinousness of our sins against God, mingled with desire for Christ and a "spark of hope."[43] Affliction itself does not bring sinners to sorrow for sin, rather, they are "brought to see their sin… when conscience is under the guilt of sin."[44] Sibbes wrote, "Our hearts (like malefactors) until they be beaten from all shifts, never cry for the mercy of the Judge. Again, this bruising maketh us set a high price upon Christ, the gospel is the gospel indeed then, then the fig-leaves of morality will do us no good."[45] Thus a sound and lasting conversion to Christ requires "the lash of the law."[46]

Pettit says that of all the "preparationists," Sibbes was "by far the most extreme in terms of the abilities he assigned to natural man."[47] Similarly, Bruce Elliott says, "Sibbes has gone beyond anything that Calvin or Perkins would have come out and stated." He says this is a sign of "seismic shifts" with massive implications for "the theoretical foundations of the Puritan movement."[48]

Yet Sibbes himself said, "This bruising is required before conversion, so that the Spirit may make way for itself into the heart, by leveling all proud high thoughts."[49] Thus preparation is not our hearts opening themselves by our own power to let the Spirit enter, but rather, the Spirit opening our hearts by His power so that He may come in. Sibbes viewed bruising as both "a state into which God bringeth us" and "a duty to

41. Dever, *Richard Sibbes*, 228.
42. Richard Sibbes, *The Brvised Reede and Smoaking Flax*, 3rd ed. (London: by M. F. for R. Dawlman, 1631), 10.
43. Sibbes, *The Brvised Reede and Smoaking Flax*, 11–12.
44. Sibbes, *The Brvised Reede and Smoaking Flax*, 30.
45. Sibbes, *The Brvised Reede and Smoaking Flax*, 14.
46. Sibbes, *The Brvised Reede and Smoaking Flax*, 15.
47. Pettit, *The Heart Prepared*, 73.
48. Bruce S. Elliott, "The Wrights of Salvation: Craft and Conversion among 17th Century English Puritans" (PhD Dissertation, University of California, Berkeley, 2001), 156–57.
49. Sibbes, *The Brvised Reede and Smoaking Flax*, 13.

be performed by us." Sibbes said, "when he humbles us, let us humble ourselves."[50] He wrote,

> We must lay siege to the hardness of our own hearts, and aggravate sin all we can: we must look on Christ, who was bruised for us, look on him whom we have pierced with our sins. But all directions will not prevail, unless God by his Spirit convinceth us deeply, setting our sins before us, and driving us to a stand. Then we will make out for mercy. Conviction will breed contrition, and this humiliation.[51]

Though painful, bruising is a labor of love, like the lancing and cutting of a surgeon intent on healing, Sibbes said.[52] Christ bruises but does not destroy the elect sinner: "Christ his course is first to wound, then to heal."[53] This view is far removed from legalism or Pelagianism; it says that sovereign grace must stir the hearts of sinners to sense their need of salvation and act accordingly.[54] In a manner that anticipates Jonathan Edwards more than a century later, Sibbes urged those not yet in a state of grace to "seek" and "strive" after salvation.[55]

Sibbes's clearest teaching on preparation for saving faith may be in his sermon, "Lydia's Conversion."[56] The conversion of Lydia, briefly noted in Acts 16:13–14, was the subject of a number of Puritan sermons.[57] Noting that Lydia worshiped God *prior to* her conversion, Sibbes made the following points about the work of preparation:

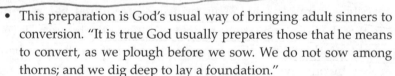

- This preparation is God's usual way of bringing adult sinners to conversion. "It is true God usually prepares those that he means to convert, as we plough before we sow. We do not sow among thorns; and we dig deep to lay a foundation."

50. Sibbes, *The Brvised Reede and Smoaking Flax,* 33.

51. Sibbes, *The Brvised Reede and Smoaking Flax,* 34–35.

52. Sibbes, *The Brvised Reede and Smoaking Flax,* 19.

53. Sibbes, *The Brvised Reede and Smoaking Flax,* 27.

54. Paul R. Schaefer, Jr., *The Spiritual Brotherhood: Cambridge Puritans and the Nature of Christian Piety* (Grand Rapids: Reformation Heritage Books, 2011), 205–17.

55. Beck, "*Gratia Praeparans* in the Soteriology of Richard Sibbes," 180–84.

56. Dever, *Richard Sibbes,* 126. Beck, "*Gratia Praeparans* in the Soteriology of Richard Sibbes," 162.

57. For different Puritan perspectives on Lydia, see Charles L. Cohen, "Two Biblical Models of Conversion: An Example of Puritan Hermeneutics," *Church History* 58, no. 2 (June 1989): 186–91.

- This preparation is necessary. "There is such a distance between the nature and corruption of man and grace, that there must be a great deal of preparation, many degrees to rise by before a man comes to that condition he should be in."

- This preparation is divine grace before salvation to prepare for more divine grace unto salvation. "All preparations are from God. We cannot prepare ourselves, or deserve future things by our preparations; for the preparations themselves are of God."

- This preparation has no merit or power to effect conversion. "We grant no force of a meritorious cause in preparations to produce such an effect as conversion is. No. Only preparation is to remove the hindrances, and to fit the soul for conversion."

- This preparation does not make a soul good enough to be saved; rather, preparation makes Christ precious enough to move the soul to pursue Him as its treasure. Preparation is sufficient when "the soul is so far cast down as it sets a high price on Christ, and on grace, above all things in the world."

- This preparation first breaks the "natural rudeness and fierceness" of a man (Job 11:12) and "civilizeth people," and, second, casts them down by "a work of the law.[58]

Though Sibbes did not say so here, one can infer that the concept of preparation civilizing people contributed to Puritan views on child-rearing and mission work among people such as the Native Americans.

Sibbes was known as "the sweet dropper." One man said after his death, "Heaven was in him before he was in heaven." Yet Sibbes also taught that God prepares the soul for faith in Christ by bruising us in regard to our sins. The doctrine of preparation did not arise out of cruel or emotionless spirits; it was taught by loving men who delighted in the saving work of Christ.

John Preston: Plowing for the Gospel Seed

John Preston (1587–1628), like many other Puritans, studied at Cambridge University. He was converted under the preaching of John Cotton. His

---

58. "Lydia's Conversion," in *The Complete Works of Richard Sibbes,* ed. Alexander B. Grosart (Edinburgh: James Nichol, 1863), 6:522–23.

teaching and preaching in turn greatly influenced other Puritans such as Thomas Goodwin and Thomas Shepard. Like Perkins, Preston believed that the covenant was the outward means by which God executed His eternal decree of predestination.[59] He said preparation is the immanent, temporal means by which God makes way for faith in those whom He eternally, transcendently, has elected. Preparation does not lead to faith as a meritorious cause, but only as a logical precedent.[60] 🔏

Preston stated his doctrine of preparation in a work titled *Paul's Conversion*, based on Acts 9:6.[61] He wrote, "Whoever will receive Christ, and be ingrafted into him, and receive the gospel as he ought to do he must first be humbled."[62] By humbled he meant the trembling fear and astonishment that comes when "he who is a sinner sees into the holiness and purity of God, and the vileness of his own nature." It is the double knowledge that Calvin had commended.[63] Far from meriting salvation, this humiliation prepares for faith by showing the sinner his need for Christ.

Preston said there were two kinds of sorrow over sin: "preparative sorrow" and "godly sorrow" (cf. 2 Cor. 7:9–11). Preparative sorrow is grief over sin only because sin brings punishment. It is the "work of the flesh" that was evident in Judas, Cain, and Ahab. Its tendency is to make people run away from Christ. By contrast, godly sorrow brings the soul to repentance and obedience. It grieves not just over the consequences of sin but over sin itself as a betrayal of God. It is "a work of the sanctifying Spirit." Its tendency is to make people run *to* Christ. The man with godly sorrow "hath an eye given him whereby he sees into the riches of God's love unto him, and then reflects upon himself," and is ashamed, Preston said.[64]

Preparation does not limit the free offer of the gospel, for it is not about the warrant to trust in Christ. Preparation instead addresses the motivation for trusting in Christ. Like Sibbes, Preston wrote about preparation, saying, "It is a necessary condition, because no man will receive Christ till then: till he be cast down, Christ will not be prized, grace will not be

---

59. Song, *Theology and Piety in the Reformed Federal Thought of William Perkins and John Preston,* 157–58.

60. Song, *Theology and Piety in the Reformed Federal Thought of William Perkins and John Preston,* 203–205.

61. "Pavls Conversion. Or, The Right VVay to be Saved" in *Remaines of that Reverend and Learned Divine, John Preston* (London: For Andrew Crooke, 1634), 179.

62. Preston, "Pavls Conversion," in *Remaines,* 182.

63. Preston, "Pavls Conversion," in *Remaines,* 180.

64. Preston, "Pavls Conversion," in *Remaines,* 193–97.

esteemed…. He that is not broken hearted and wounded with sin, will not seek to the Physician to be healed" (cf. Matt. 9:12; 13:44–46).[65] He said, "We preach Christ generally unto all, that whosoever will, may receive Christ; but men will not receive him, till they be humbled, they think they stand in no need of Christ."[66] Christ will receive all who come to Him, but Christ will not be sweet to them until sin is first bitter in them.

Preston said the Scripture speaks of preparation in piercing ("pricking") and breaking the heart (Acts 2:37; Isa. 61:1), poverty of spirit and mourning (Matt. 5:3; Isa. 61:2; Rev. 3:17), melting the heart with shame (2 Chron. 34:27; Jer. 31:19), and trembling at the Word (Isa. 66:2).[67] Thus godly preachers who "generally labour to humble men in preaching of the law, and then after persuade them by the promises to come to Christ" were following in the footsteps of the Lord's dealings with Adam (Gen. 3:8), the prophets with Israel, John the Baptist with the people (Matt. 3:7), Christ with the Samaritan woman (John 4:16–18), Peter at Pentecost (Acts 2:37), Paul with Felix (Acts 24:24–25) and in his Epistle to the Romans (chap. 1–3).[68] Preparation makes preachers as well as people responsible for the "humiliation of spirit." Preston said some of the means for this preparation were as follows:

1) Get a right mental view of sin as God's enemy, our greatest evil in separating us from God and his holiness, the cause of all bitter effects, and the cost it required to be healed: Christ crucified.[69]

2) Labor "to make your hearts fit to be humble" by gaining an inward sense of holiness by the Spirit so that sin becomes a burden and by considering the inescapable and awful judgment of God.[70]

3) Apply to yourself how much you owe God for all His mercies to you and how little you have given Him by way of thankful obedience, especially in your great sins.[71]

4) Look upon your past sins as if they were all present with you, and upon God's future judgment as if it were presently coming upon you.[72]

65. Preston, "Pavls Conversion," in *Remaines*, 182–83.
66. Preston, "Pavls Conversion," in *Remaines*, 187.
67. Preston, "Pavls Conversion," in *Remaines*, 182–84.
68. Preston, "Pavls Conversion," in *Remaines*, 184–86.
69. Preston, "Pavls Conversion," in *Remaines*, 207–210.
70. Preston, "Pavls Conversion," in *Remaines*, 210–13.
71. Preston, "Pavls Conversion," in *Remaines*, 213–16.
72. Preston, "Pavls Conversion," in *Remaines*, 216–18.

5) Remove your excuses for sin that shelter your conscience, such as, trusting in outward religious duties, pretending to have a good heart despite sinful actions, and saying that it's just your nature to do a particular sin.[73]

6) Pray earnestly for the work of the Holy Spirit, "for this makes the law effectual." Preston said, "The law and the letter of the law will not work grace in you no more than the flesh will, except the Spirit go with it: it is the Spirit that always enlighteneth the mind and works a change in the whole man." Make use of Christ's promise that God will give His Spirit to those who ask Him (Luke 11:13).[74]

7) Strive to gain knowledge of the Word, for it is the instrument of the Spirit. Know the Bible, receive it as God's Word, and apply it to your conscience.[75]

The packed soil, rocky soil, and thorny soil of Christ's parable beckoned the Puritans to plow deep into men's souls with the law of God.[76] If they did not, the seed sown might make a superficial change but would lack the roots and persevering fruits of salvation. Preston wrote,

A man may be said to receive Christ by a common light of knowledge, and hereupon do many things for Christ; but yet he will not take Christ for his King as well as a Saviour, except he be humbled, he will not take Christ so, as to be ruled by his laws, and to live under his commands, he will not take him with losses and crosses, disgrace and reproach...but when a man is thoroughly humbled, then he will part with all things for Christ, nothing shall be so dear and precious unto him, as Christ will be.[77]

The Puritans did not value humiliation for its own sake but believed that "the least measure of humiliation necessary is that which makes a man believe in Christ."[78]

73. Preston, "Pavls Conversion," in *Remaines*, 218–226.
74. Preston, "Pavls Conversion," in *Remaines*, 226–28.
75. Preston, "Pavls Conversion," in *Remaines*, 228–32.
76. Preston, "Pavls Conversion," in *Remaines*, 189–90.
77. Preston, "Pavls Conversion," in *Remaines*, 193.
78. Preston, "Pavls Conversion," in *Remaines*, 200.

Conclusion

The English Reformation produced a church that confessed that no one could prepare himself for God's grace by his own power. Salvation is totally of the Lord (Jonah 2:9). At the same time, men as early as Bradford confessed that God prepared men by His law. The English stood with Calvin in simultaneously denying merit by the law and affirming conviction by the law. This is application of the law without legalism as well as legal impulses that create a sense of need for justification but which do not earn justification in any way.

Elizabethan Puritans such as Richard Greenham, Richard Rogers, and Arthur Hildersam embraced the Reformed doctrine of predestination and the experiential emphasis of the Heidelberg Catechism. They then labored to express the way predestination works itself out in personal experience. The preeminent teacher among them was William Perkins, who explained the process of conversion in ten steps, identifying the first four or five steps as preparatory for faith. Perkins also realized that these steps might not be easily discerned in human experience and that repentance might sometimes become evident prior to faith even though spiritually it flows from it. Faith may evidence itself as desire prior to assurance.

These early Puritans found much evidence in Scripture for the doctrine of preparation, *biblically* developing it, whether on the basis of Isaiah's metaphor of the bruised reed or Luke's account of Lydia, the pierced hearts at Pentecost or the broken man on the road to Damascus. They also considered this doctrine of preparation *theologically*, fitting it together with the doctrines of unconditional election, the utter destitution of any saving merit in man, and the free offer of the gospel. And they considered it *practically*, as Preston did when he gave instructions to the unconverted about how to humble themselves before God, or when Sibbes comforted tender consciences with images of Christ's sweet mercy to the bruised reed.

However, we have observed that the Puritans never found it necessary to deny God's sovereignty in salvation. On the contrary, the early Puritans consistently viewed preparation as part of the practical outworking of predestination. Preparation had its place on the chart of God's eternal, Christ-centered plan, whether it was softening the heart of the elect prior to saving faith or temporarily illuminating the heart of the reprobate before it was finally hardened by the deceitfulness of sin.[79]

Our overview of early Puritanism also has not revealed a harsh, vindictive spirit in regard to the doctrine of preparation, as if preachers delighted in whipping men with the law. Rather, they demonstrated an intense longing for sinners to wake up and flee the house of sin before it burned down around them. The call to preparation was rooted in an evangelistic longing for the salvation of sinners.

---

79. One topic which we did not treat here but deserves further exploration is the relationship between early Puritan preparationism and the covenant, which Perkins saw as the means by which God implemented His decree.

CHAPTER FOUR

William Ames and
Preparation for Conversion

Dryness of wood tends to fire.
—William Ames[1]

One of Perkins's most prominent students was William Ames (1576–1633).[2] Educated at Cambridge, Ames experienced conversion under the preaching of Perkins after realizing that a person can be outwardly moral and religious but still not know God. He believed that "theology is the doctrine or teaching of living to God," according to His will, for His glory, and by His grace. After several years of fruitful teaching and preaching at Cambridge, Ames was suspended for his Puritan beliefs and for his criticism of dissolute living and gambling at the school. He attempted to minister in London, but the bishop of London banned him from preaching.

Knowing he would face further persecution in England, Ames went to the Netherlands, where he served as the pastor of congregations of English exiles. He also spent much time defending the doctrines of God's sovereignty in salvation as opposed to Arminianism which was on the rise in the Netherlands. Ames's reputation as the "Augustine of Holland" led to the call to serve as the main theological adviser to the presiding officer of the Synod of Dort, where Reformed theologians formulated the Canons of Dort as their response to the five doctrinal points contested by the Remonstrants.

1. William Ames, "The Preparation of a Sinner for Conversion," trans. Steven Dilday, thesis 6 (see the appendix to this book), in *Disceptatio Scholastica de circulo pontificio* (1644).
2. See Keith L. Sprunger, "The Learned Doctor Ames" (PhD Dissertation, University of Illinois, 1963).

Ames taught for eleven years at Franeker University, where he became embroiled in controversy with his colleague, Johannes Maccovius (1588–1644).[3] When Maccovius was charged with false teaching and examined by the Synod of Dort in 1619, Ames had defended him. The synod acquitted Maccovius with an admonition to avoid overly subtle scholastic language. However, after Ames joined the faculty of Franeker University in 1622, his relationship with Maccovius deteriorated. In 1626 Ames and some colleagues tried to have Maccovius removed from the faculty primarily because of his purportedly ungodly lifestyle.[4]

Later Ames moved to Rotterdam to serve as a pastor. Shortly thereafter, the river flooded his house, and Ames contracted pneumonia and died at age 57. If he had lived he most likely would have immigrated to New England, whose leaders he admired.

Though Ames never got to the New World, his writings did, circulating as well throughout Europe and Great Britain. His *Medulla Theologiae* (1627), or *Marrow of Theology,* was highly regarded by Thomas Hooker, Increase Mather, and Thomas Goodwin. It became the standard textbook for theology in New England for more than a hundred years. His companion volume which expanded his system of ethics was *Conscience with the Power and Cases Thereof* (1630 Latin; 1639 English). This book was reprinted nearly twenty times in less than thirty years. Ames's theology of living to God profoundly shaped the Dutch Further Reformation, which stretched from Willem Teellinck (1579–1629) to Theodorus van der Groe (1705–1784). Van Vliet says that if "Perkins was the father of English Puritanism, and Teellinck the father of the Dutch Second [Further] Reformation, then surely Ames was the connecting link, introducing to the continent an informed, system-based theology and an experiential theology."[5]

Whatever Ames said about preparation for faith in his *Marrow* and *Conscience* echoed throughout the Reformed world for a century, especially in New England. So let us now consider the doctrine of preparation Ames worked out in those two treatises.

3. Jan van Vliet, "William Ames: Marrow of the Theology and Piety of the Reformed Tradition" (PhD Dissertation, Westminster Theological Seminary, 2002), 275.

4. Van Vliet, "William Ames," 277–78; Michael D. Bell, *"Propter Potestatum, Scientiam, ac Beneplacitum Dei:* The Doctrine of the Object of Predestination in the Theology of Johannes Maccovius" (ThD Dissertation, Westminster Theological Seminary, 1986), 24–25.

5. Van Vliet, "William Ames," 297.

The Marrow of Ames's Teachings on Preparation

Ames said in *Marrow of Theology* that God planned redemption in eternity, accomplished redemption in history, and applies redemption in the personal experience of the believer. These three dimensions of salvation are centered in Jesus Christ.[6] The application of redemption has two parts: "union with Christ and partaking of the benefits that flow from this union."[7] God creates this saving union with Christ by calling people to Christ. This calling consists of two parts: "the offer of Christ and the receiving of him." The offer consists of the presentation of Christ in the gospel as the only and sufficient Savior. The offer has an outward component in preaching, and an inward component in spiritual enlightenment with respect to the promises. Preaching and enlightenment may result in salvation, or they may not.[8] Thus these are not effectual graces specific to the elect.

Men and women are joined to Christ when they receive Him. It is here that Ames locates regeneration, conversion, and a new creation. In receiving Christ, men are passive and active in different respects. They are passive in that "a spiritual principle of grace is generated in the will of man," and they are born again by God's power. Even the enlightenment of man's mind cannot produce this effect; it requires a divine act upon his will. Men are active in that, having been given grace, they now come to Christ in faith "freely but also surely, unavoidably, and unchangeably." With this faith comes repentance.[9]

In the midst of the offer of Christ, but prior to the reception of Christ, comes preparation. Ames wrote, "But so that men may be prepared to receive the promises, the application of the law usually precedes, in order to uncover sin and lead to *anapologia*, a sense of guilt, and humiliation in the sinner (Rom. 7:7)."[10] The Greek word *anapologia* means "without excuse" or "without a defense" (compare *anapologētos* in Rom. 1:20).[11] Benjamin Boerkel says this is "recognition of one's defenselessness before

---

6. William Ames, *The Marrow of Theology*, trans. and ed. John D. Eusden (1968; repr., Grand Rapids: Baker, 1997), 1.18; 1.24; 1.25.27–29.

7. Ames, *The Marrow of Theology*, 1.26.1.

8. Ames, *The Marrow of Theology*, 1.26.3, 4, 7, 8, 10, 11, 14, 15.

9. Ames, *The Marrow of Theology*, 1.26.17–29.

10. Ames, *The Marrow of Theology*, 1.26.12.

11. William Ames, *Conscience with the Power and Cases Thereof* (n.p., 1639), 2.4.2.

the tribunal of God."[12] Ames may be alluding here to the work of the law described in Romans 3:19–20, "Now we know that what things soever the law saith, it saith to them who are under the law: that every mouth may be stopped, and all the world may become guilty before God. Therefore by the deeds of the law there shall no flesh be justified in his sight: for by the law is the knowledge of sin." Boerkel says Ames was also following Calvin's statement of the first use of the law: "But, in order that our guilt may arouse us to seek pardon, it behooves us, briefly, to know how by our instruction in the moral law we are rendered more inexcusable."[13]

In preparation, Ames said, the convicting power of the law, through the Spirit's enlightenment, "is sometimes and in a certain way granted to those who are not elected (Heb. 6:4; 10:29; Matt. 13:20ff)."[14] Thus it is a supernatural work of grace but is not an infusion of supernatural grace. It is the usual work of the Spirit upon men who are as yet dead in sin. The Spirit's work produces a kind of repentance in preparation, but it is not saving repentance. Ames explained,

> Repentance, so far as it comprises the care, anxiety, and terror connected with the law, precedes faith in order of nature, as a preparing and disposing cause, and is even found in the unregenerate; but insofar as it turns man away effectively and genuinely from sin, by which God is offended, it follows faith and depends upon it as an effect upon its cause and so belongs to those who have faith.[15]

Therefore we disagree with Pettit's assessment that in Ames's view of the unconverted sinner, "He seizes upon the Law, the Law does not seize him."[16] While Ames exhorts sinners to prepare themselves, he views this act as the means by which the Holy Spirit takes hold of sleepy sinners and with knowledge and fear motivates them to seek salvation. Here again Pettit's false dichotomy between divine action and human action pulls apart what was held together in the minds of the Puritans.

Ames expanded this concept of preparation in his book on *Conscience.* He titled one chapter, "How a sinner ought to prepare himself

---

12. Benjamin J. Boerkel, "Uniqueness within the Calvinist Tradition—William Ames (1576–1633): Primogenitor of the *Theologia Pietatis* in English-Dutch Puritanism" (ThM Thesis, Calvin Theological Seminary, 1990), 119.

13. Boerkel, "Uniqueness within the Calvinist Tradition," 119–20; Calvin, *Institutes,* 2.7.3.

14. Ames, *The Marrow of Theology,* 1.26.14–15.

15. Ames, *The Marrow of Theology,* 1.26.31.

16. Pettit, *The Heart Prepared,* 83.

to conversion,"[17] which is notable given that he believed sinners are passive in the first act of regeneration. He distinguished between things that pulled a man out of a state of sin, and things that put a man into the state of grace. The goal of the former is "to shake a man out of that carnal security, in which he slept before, and to work in him a carefulness of his salvation above all things else."[18]Ames said this includes these four steps:

1) You take a serious look into the law of God and into your life (James 1:23–25).

2) You are convicted by conscience that you are shut up in sin and without excuse (Rom. 1:20; 2:20; 7:7; 11:32).

3) You despair of salvation by your strength or by any other means (Rom. 7:9, 11, 13).

4) You are humbled in grief, fear, and confession of sin. This humiliation includes confession of particular sins (Rom. 7:7; Acts 2:23, 37). It is often preceded by some painful circumstances (2 Chron. 33:12). Though people feel various degrees of humiliation, "all those that are truly converted are also truly humbled."[19]

Similarly, Ames taught that there were four steps of putting a man into grace: (5) recognition from the gospel that forgiveness is possible; (6) the earnest desire or hunger to be saved; (7) union with Christ by faith worked in effectual calling; (8) and true repentance from sin towards God.[20]

In comparing the steps of Perkins and Ames, we note the following:

- Ames omitted or assumed Perkins's first step of the means of grace and affliction.

- Ames's first step corresponds to Perkins's second step of attention to the law.

- Ames's second step matches Perkins's third step of conviction of one's sins.

- Ames's third and fourth steps correspond to Perkins's fourth step of fear and despair.

---

17. Ames, *Conscience,* 2.4.
18. Ames, *Conscience,* 2.4.
19. Ames, *Conscience,* 2.4.1–7.
20. Ames, *Conscience,* 2.4.7.

- Ames's fifth step lines up with Perkins's fifth step of attention to the gospel.

- Ames's sixth step matches Perkins's sixth step of desire for salvation.

- Ames did not mention here Perkins's seventh step of combat with doubt.

- Ames's seventh step corresponds to Perkins's eighth step that faith rests on Christ.

- Ames's eighth step matches Perkins's ninth step of repentance.

- Ames did not here mention Perkins's tenth step of obedience.

Steps that Ames did not mention here are developed elsewhere in his writing, though not necessarily in this order. For example, though Ames did not include Perkin's step of combat with doubt, he did recognize that a person of weak faith could lack assurance yet be made steadfastly to sorrow over sin, to desire Christ, and to choose Him and His Word as his chief good.[21]

Regarding the means of grace, Ames did not see a contradiction between divine predestination and human activity because God accomplishes His electing will through means.[22] He distinguished between natural means and supernatural grace, saying the Holy Spirit applies Christ and His redemption to sinners through means, though "no external means properly have the power to communicate grace to us in any real sense."[23] Therefore "external means naturally concur and operate in the preparation of man to receive grace, yet in themselves they do not properly confer grace. It is the Spirit that works together with them (1 Cor. 3:7)."[24]

So while affirming divine sovereignty, Ames also exhorted men to use the means given to them to seek the grace of effectual calling: first, to settle their minds to consider the Word of God worth more than all riches; second, to be serious and diligent about their salvation; third, to use the means by which God gives saving grace; fourth, to bring themselves to the point of being willing to sell everything to gain this pearl.[25]

21. Ames, *Conscience*, 2.6.13–22.
22. Ames, *The Marrow of Theology*, 1.25.14–16, 23.
23. Ames, *The Marrow of Theology*, 1.33.1–3.
24. Ames, *The Marrow of Theology*, 1.33.3.
25. Ames, *Conscience*, 2.5.11–15.

That summarizes Ames's teaching on preparation for conversion in his famous books *The Marrow of Theology* and *Conscience*. However, in another, less-well-known work, Ames gives even more attention to this topic.

Ames's Disputation on Preparation

We are referring here to Ames's disquisition titled *Praeparatione peccatoris ad conversionem* ("The Preparation of the Sinner for Conversion"), published in 1633 along with his treatise *Disceptatio Scholastica de circulo pontificio*. Written with the same precision as the *Marrow*, Ames's disputation offers a focused version of his teaching on preparation. As we will see in our consideration of John Norton and Giles Firmin, this disputation was often cited as an influential work in later debates about preparation.[26] Cotton Mather owned a copy in which he made notes.[27] In this chapter we will use the English translation of the disputation, which is included in the appendix to this book.

This scholastic disputation on preparation consists of twelve positive theses. The first seven theses offer clear distinctions regarding the meaning of the preparation that Ames defended. The next five theses present proofs for this preparation, largely from Scripture. They are followed by answers to seven objections, two questions, and one corollary.

Distinctions and Definitions of Preparation

From the outset Ames rejected any concept of meritorious preparation for justification as an error of "the Papists," that is, Roman Catholicism. He implied that this error involved Pelagianism or semi-Pelagianism by stating that they imagine that such preparations come "either only from free will, or partly also of grace."[28] The Puritans were well aware of the medieval theological debates on grace, sin, nature, and merit and purposely developed their views according to Augustinian and Reformation beliefs.

On the other hand, Ames argued that Reformed opposition to the Roman Catholic view of preparation does not "remove all preparatory affections and motions...by which in a human sinner God provides for Himself a way unto his congruous conversion."[29] To do so would be like

---

26. See chapters 9 and 10.
27. Julius H. Tuttle, *The Libraries of the Mathers* (Worcester, Mass.: Davis Press, 1910), 48.
28. Ames, "The Preparation of a Sinner for Conversion," thesis 1.
29. Ames, "The Preparation of a Sinner for Conversion," thesis 2.

rejecting all good works since we cannot earn merit with God by our works. Ames said rather that God forms "certain dispositions" when doing the work of "converting and regenerating every sinner after the use of means."[30] Ames's reference to "means" allied him with the Reformed tradition that God, who needs no assistance to accomplish His will, nonetheless ordinarily works His will through created means.

In his first thesis, Ames carefully distinguished the Reformed view of preparation from the Roman Catholic view. The English Reformed writers were highly critical of the Roman Catholic view of preparation, saying that it undermined the doctrine of justification by faith by introducing meritorious works prior to conversion. The Roman Catholics also opposed the doctrine of regeneration by grace alone by teaching the cooperation of the unregenerate will. This criticism was also true for Arminianism, which English Reformed believers tended to associate with Roman Catholicism.[31]

While rejecting the Roman Catholic view, Ames strongly advocated a Reformed understanding of preparation. If we fail to distinguish between these two different views of preparation, we will mistakenly read attacks on Roman Catholic "preparationism" as if they were attacks on the Reformed view of preparation. Whenever we read a writer arguing against preparation, we must immediately ask whether his target was the Roman Catholic or the Reformed view. Otherwise we will misread anti-Papist polemics as a controversy among the Reformed, an error that has often led to confusion about preparation.

In the next two theses, Ames positioned himself more precisely in reference to other theologians. Contrary to the early Reformer Martin Bucer, Ames did not allow for natural gifts that incline certain men towards grace, not even in the elect. He wrote, "We embrace only those preparations which depend upon and proceed from vocation by the word."[32] Ames wrote of preparatory grace as an external, divine work of God's Spirit upon men through the ministry of preaching, not as an internal impulse originating from within fallen men. Ames aligned himself with the British representatives at the Synod of Dort who believed that the

---

30. Ames, "The Preparation of a Sinner for Conversion," thesis 3.

31. English Arminians such as Archbishop Laud not only objected to the Calvinist doctrine of predestination, but also pleaded for sacramental grace and a sacerdotal understanding of the presbyter's office.

32. Ames, "The Preparation of a Sinner for Conversion," thesis 4.

Holy Spirit works through the Word to produce "certain internal" effects and "certain external works" leading to conversion. He also identified with Perkins's doctrine of "four preparatory works preceding grace." Ames clarified this by saying that preparatory works precede "habitual grace," implying that he considered preparation also to be of grace, but a different kind of grace than that which creates new spiritual habits or dispositions of the heart.[33]

Ames offered an analogy to explain the difference between preparatory "dispositions" and the habitual grace born of regeneration. Preparatory works are not like the heat that a fire produces in wood before it catches on fire, he said, for they do not share the same nature as regenerate graces nor do they have the power to produce those graces. Rather, preparation is like drying the wood before putting it in the fire, which makes it more receptive to the flame. Preparation makes a person more receptive to the Word, Ames said, by removing or reducing obstacles to conversion and producing qualities useful for conversion. It diminishes ignorance, unrestrained delight in sin, and audacity in sinning, then through illumination, increases shame and horror over sin, as well as desires for salvation.[34]

Ames presented a sharply focused image of preparation, which we might call Reformed preparation, with the following seven theses:

- It does not merit further grace from God.

- It is not the natural impulse of any lost sinner.

- It is not the first stirrings of the graces of faith or love.

- It is not a mechanism by which sinners produce their own conversion.

- It is, instead, a work of God's Spirit through the Word.

- It produces the effect of internal guilt and fear and external works.

- It renders the soul more receptive to the free gift of regenerating grace.

---

33. Ames, "The Preparation of a Sinner for Conversion," thesis 5. For the views of the British delegates at Dort, see "Via Media: The Way of Peace in the Five Busy Articles, Commonly Known by the Name of Arminius," in *The Works of the Right Reverend Joseph Hall* (Oxford: Oxford University Press, 1863), 9:493–94.

34. Ames, "The Preparation of a Sinner for Conversion," thesis 7.

Proofs of Reformed Preparation

The next five theses of Ames (8–12) argued for the doctrine of preparation. Almost all of his proofs came from Scripture, but he began with tradition and reason. He wrote, "The evidence of this truth is so great, that he who resists the same, by one rash opinion, would appear to expunge the whole first part of the Catechism, with a large part of the second; and also to abrogate the entire ministry of the word in order to the conversion of sinners."[35] Ames, who was in the Netherlands, used this potent argument to say that much of the Heidelberg Catechism's three-fold structure of misery, deliverance, and gratitude stood upon a work of the law in the sinner's heart prior to conversion. Ames clearly felt that he had Reformed opinion on his side, which was reaffirmed when the Synod of Dort officially adopted the Heidelberg Catechism as a standard for the Dutch church. Ames also argued that without a doctrine of preparation, preachers would be crippled in their ability to exhort lost sinners to believe the truths of God's Word and to practice those truths.

Ames was convinced that many Scriptures taught preparation ("this doctrine is found everywhere"), but he offered a few "illustrious texts" together with commentary from John Calvin. In Mark 12:34, Christ said to a scribe, "Thou art not far from the kingdom of God." Ames quoted Calvin, who said, "We are taught that many, while they, as men confused, are yet held by error, yet approach unto the way with closed eyes, and in this manner are prepared, so that in the fullness of time they might run in the race of the Lord."[36] Against those who say this text referred to people who drew closer to the church by a profession of faith, Ames said the entire Jewish nation was the visible church when Christ called people by faith and repentance to the reign of God within them.[37] From this text Ames argued that some unconverted people were closer to the kingdom than others. This was also the view of Calvin.

The second text that Ames cited was Acts 2:37, which includes the phrase "they were pricked in heart." He cited Calvin's commentary on the phrase: "Sorrow over sin is the beginning of repentance, the entrance into

---

35. Ames, "The Preparation of a Sinner for Conversion," thesis 8.

36. Ames, "The Preparation of a Sinner for Conversion," thesis 9. See Calvin, *Commentary on a Harmony of the Evangelists*, 3:65.

37. Ames, "The Preparation of a Sinner for Conversion," thesis 10.

piety."[38] Within its context in Acts 2, this comment refers to people who were not yet publicly identified with Christ but were broken down by Peter's preaching of Christ in the power of the Holy Spirit. This Scripture became a *locus classicus*, a prime example of Puritan preparation. Ames anticipated the argument that the "initial fear" and "desire of salvation" in this verse are actually part of regeneration by the Holy Spirit. He said that the fear of judgment can only be considered a part of regeneration in that it leads to it, and that the term *regeneration* is often used in a broad sense "for the entire series of helps, by which we are moved unto it."[39] Ames thus acknowledged that preparation was a work of the Holy Spirit, and that the language of regeneration, like conversion, may be viewed in a narrow or broad sense.

Ames's third proof text was cited in his answer to the objection that the law produces servile fear, which makes people turn away from God. Ames quoted Romans 8:15, which speaks of "the spirit of servitude unto fear," to show that the Holy Spirit produces this kind of fear (he also cited Acts 2). He argued that the Holy Spirit would never drive people away from God. Furthermore, God can use even evil things for good. Servile fear is a mixture of a right view of God as the awesome Judge and the "deformity" that our sinful nature adds to the term. The Spirit produces only the former type of fear, which becomes incorporated into filial (childlike) fear of God after regeneration. To support his position, Ames cited Calvin's commentaries and the *Institutes* as well as the writings of French Reformed author Daniel Chamier (1565–1621).[40]

The proofs that Ames used to support his Reformed view of preparation show that he believed he was standing upon firm biblical ground. Rather than perceiving the doctrine of preparation as a Puritan or scholastic aberration, Ames said preparation had been the doctrine of Reformed theologians from the days of the Reformation down to his own time.

Objections against the Reformed View
Ames's next seven theses (13–19) refuted objections to his doctrine of preparation. Whereas the previous proofs focused on biblical texts, these objections took a more theological direction.

---

38. Ames, "The Preparation of a Sinner for Conversion," thesis 9. See John Calvin, *Commentary on the Acts of the Apostles*, trans. Christopher Fetherstone, ed. Henry Beveridge (repr., Grand Rapids: Baker, 1996), 1:115.

39. Ames, "The Preparation of a Sinner for Conversion," thesis 11.

40. Ames, "The Preparation of a Sinner for Conversion," thesis 12.

Objection #1: *Unregenerate men are not able to do good, and so are like beasts.*

In response, Ames argued that even if people could not prepare themselves, God could prepare them. Furthermore, people can do something; they can hear the preaching of the Word. Even sinful deeds can set up circumstances or "a material disposition" to do good. Thus selling Joseph into slavery set up a situation in which Joseph could do much good.[41]

Objection #2: *Unregenerate people have an appetite only for things of the flesh.*

Ames responded with the observation that those with no taste for good can learn that they have no taste for it, indeed, might even sip it before developing a taste for it.[42]

Objection #3: *Sin reigns in unregenerate men.*

The kingdom of sin in people does not mean that God does not rule over them with His power, nor that God could not prepare them before setting them free from sin. Indeed, the reign of sin does not exclude "material dispositions to the grace of regeneration."[43]

In his response to Objection #2 and #3, Ames argued that just as people who have the Holy Spirit have some inclinations to evil and unbelief, so also people of the flesh have some dispositions to spiritual life. This is a curious argument, since Ames has already said that preparation excludes even the heat of the fire of grace from the wood of the unconverted soul. Preparation only dries the wood before it is fired. The unconverted do not possess the first elements of holiness. What then does he mean by "material dispositions" to life? Remember that he has already spoken of an illuminated understanding and fear of the holy Judge. These form psychological dispositions in the mind and heart in which godliness could dwell, but they themselves are not godliness. Ames further clarifies the nature of these preparatory dispositions in the next objections.

Objection #4: *Unregenerate people are dead in sins.*[44]

This objection reflects the opposition of Maccovius, Ames's colleague at Franeker, who in his *Theologia Polemica* (Ch. 16, Q. 1) said there can be no internal preparations for regeneration in a person who is still dead in

---

41. Ames, "The Preparation of a Sinner for Conversion," thesis 13, objection 1.
42. Ames, "The Preparation of a Sinner for Conversion," thesis 14, objection 2.
43. Ames, "The Preparation of a Sinner for Conversion," thesis 15, objection 3.
44. Ames, "The Preparation of a Sinner for Conversion," thesis 16, objection 4.

sin; therefore, any work of God that lifts man out of natural blindness is not preparation but regeneration.[45]

In response, Ames said, "The consequence is null, concerning a material disposition. For, just as in Adam's fashioned body, in itself there was a disposition to life afterwards to be instilled; and in the bones, in Ezekiel 37, gathered, conjoined, clothed with flesh and skin, after they had the spirit infused, there was a greater disposition to life, than while they remained dry and divided; so also it happens in certain men destitute of spiritual life."[46] Thus a "material disposition" towards spiritual life is analogous to the relation of the body to the soul: it provides a structure in which the soul can function in a human way. Similarly, the dead faculties of a sinner's soul can be arranged to provide a disposition which, while still dead, could house life if God breathed into it.

Objection #5: *Preparation creates a middle state between the regenerate and the unregenerate.*

Ames's response is that material dispositions do not change the state of a person. The gathering and assembly of bones in Ezekiel's vision does not put them in a state between life and death; they are still dead.[47]

Objection #6: *If a disposition to regeneration precedes regeneration, then an unregenerate person is not merely passive but active.*

Ames responds by affirming that this is true. The orthodox do not teach that the unregenerate are passive in every way but only passive with respect to the first act of regenerating grace. They recognize that conversion involves human activity, from the fearful cries of the convicted sinner to the operation of the regenerated will in trusting Christ. But human activity is not the cause of regeneration, not even partly by cooperating with God's regenerating grace.[48]

In this response, Ames seemed to be drawing upon the multiform view of grace in the Augustinian tradition (which we examined earlier).[49] In the *preparatory grace of conviction*, a sinner can cooperate to a degree by

---

45. Hugo Visscher, "William Ames: His Life and Works," in *William Ames*, trans. Douglas Horton (Cambridge: Harvard Divinity School Library, 1965), 93–94, 98n59.

46. Ames, "The Preparation of a Sinner for Conversion," thesis 16, objection 4.

47. Ames, "The Preparation of a Sinner for Conversion," thesis 17, objection 5.

48. Ames, "The Preparation of a Sinner for Conversion," thesis 18, objection 6. Ames again cited Perkins.

49. See chapter 2.

thinking about God and His Word, praying, and physically attending the means of grace. In the *regenerating grace of conversion*, the sinner does not cooperate but is the passive object of a faith-giving God. *Sanctifying grace* precedes each motion of our faith and obedience and cooperates with it. *Regenerating grace* is a cause of sanctifying grace, much as a seed is the cause of the tree. But preparatory grace does not cause regenerating grace anymore than plowing soil causes a seed to be planted. The foundation of Puritan preparation is this complex Reformed view of God's grace.

Ames's view of the unregenerate person's "material dispositions" to life also reflects the complexity of the Reformed view of fallen people. We will consider this in further detail in Ames's closing corollary.

Objection #7: *Preparation implies that those who appear better than others will be regenerated.*

Ames responds by saying that the proposition is nonsense. Many hypocrites appear to be better than sinners, much like the Pharisees and false apostles put on a show of holiness (Luke 18; 2 Cor. 11). Also, the "material dispositions" of preparation do not have "a certain/definite connection with regeneration." God is able to take people of "inferior quality" and prepare them, sometimes "by one sermon."[50] With this last objection Ames once more rejected the Roman Catholic idea that preparation grants unconverted people some kind of merit, even a congruent merit. He also said that preparation does not necessitate a long process but can take place suddenly.

Conclusions from Reformed Preparation
In the remainder of his disputation on preparation, Ames addressed two questions and posed a corollary. They set forth some implications of the view that he defined and defended.

The first question is whether men can hear the Word "savingly" prior to regeneration. Karl Reuter says that Maccovius had "expressly denied" that there was any saving hearing of the Word prior to regeneration.[51] Ames offered a distinction here, saying that if "savingly" means that "the very action presupposes the state of salvation, and in formal order, and in a certain/definite connection, cleaves to salvation," then no sinner can

---

50. Ames, "The Preparation of a Sinner for Conversion," thesis 19, objection 7.
51. Karl Reuter, "William Ames: The Leading Theologian in the Awakening of Reformed Pietism," in *William Ames*, trans. Horton, 257.

hear the Word "savingly" prior to regeneration. Thus preparation is not part of the golden chain of the inseparable links of God's saving acts: foreknowledge, predestination, calling, justification, and increasing conformity to Christ unto glory (Rom. 8:29–30). Grasping any one of those links meant holding the entire chain and thus being assured of salvation. But preparation does not belong to the "things that accompany salvation" (Heb. 6:9), Ames said.[52]

But, if "savingly" means "that what is done confers anything to the salvation afterwards to be communicated," then, yes, people can hear the Word "savingly" prior to regeneration. By this Ames meant that although attentive listening to preaching without faith cannot save a sinner, it can lead to his later salvation by faith. He cited the example of Timothy, whose instruction in the Word of God when he was a child later resulted in his salvation (2 Tim. 3:15). He also quoted Augustine's account of how God prepared him for conversion with the "harsh eye-salve of salutary griefs" (*Confessions*, 7.8; 8.8). This citation reminds us once more how the Bishop of Hippo influenced later Reformed views of the process leading to conversion. To those who object that the Word cannot be heard savingly except in the good soil of an opened heart, Ames responded that the first effect of the Word is to make the soil good.[53]

The second question pertains to how the faculties of the soul relate to regenerating grace, namely, whether it is right to say that "the will necessarily follows the judgment of the intellect." Therefore saving grace does not operate directly on the will but is only infused by means of the mind. Reuter says this question reflects the position of Maccovius,[54] which Ames rejected as "very ignorantly spoken." Ames said the intellect presents objects to the will but does not change the quality of the will itself. Regenerating grace is "supernaturally infused," which by definition means it is produced in the will by an immediate creative act of God. God infuses spiritual love into the will. This love is not a property of the intellect, so the intellect cannot be a means to produce it.[55]

Ames's distinction between the role of the intellect and that of the will is a key feature of Puritan preparation. This distinction allowed the Puritans

---

52. Ames, "The Preparation of a Sinner for Conversion," question 1.

53. Ames, "The Preparation of a Sinner for Conversion," question 1.

54. Reuter, "William Ames," in *William Ames,* trans. Horton, 258.

55. Ames, "The Preparation of a Sinner for Conversion," question 2.

to argue that God prepares the sinner by operating upon the mind, but the mind's understanding, even with the affections it stirs, cannot transform the will. The will remains corrupt and dead until God creates within it the new principle of divine love. Thus preparation has a significant function in the soul, but it is not a saving power. The person's salvation remains wrapped up in the regeneration of the will. Ames also suggested there is a vital relationship between saving faith and love, for the turning point of regeneration is the infusion of love into the will. Jonathon Beeke observes that though Ames said saving faith involves the understanding, its proper place is in the will, so "the definition of faith must revolve or hinge upon the presence or absence of a restored will."[56] Calvin also identified the will as the place in which God begins conversion.

Ames concluded with the brief corollary that it is crude to say that unregenerate man has no more power or disposition than a stone.[57] His polemical target appears to be the predestinarian current within Lutheranism championed by Matthias Flacius Illyricus (1520–1575).[58] The Lutheran churches were wracked by controversy over this matter in the decades following Luther's death. The Canons of Dort (Head 3/4, Art. 16) also addressed the matter, saying, "This grace of regeneration does not treat men as senseless stocks and blocks, nor takes away their will and its properties, neither does violence thereto."[59] Ames's closing comment in his thesis highlights a key point in the doctrine of preparation: the complexity of the Reformed view of fallen human nature. Though sinners are dead in sin and hostile to God, they are not inanimate objects. They still have souls, and those souls include active minds, consciences, affections, and wills.

Franciscus Gomarus (1563–1641) was a theologian and Bible scholar at Leiden University, who became famous for his debates with Arminius over predestination. Gomarus presided over a disputation on free will, asserting that unregenerate sinners are dead in sin and have no power to do anything but sin. They cannot even cooperate with God's grace

---

56. Jonathon Beeke, "The Watchman William Ames: The Nature of Justifying Faith in Ames's Soteriology in Light of his Emphasis on the Divine and Human Wills" (MA Thesis, Westminster Seminary West, 2006), 53–54.

57. Ames, "The Preparation of a Sinner for Conversion," corollary.

58. Schaff, *The Creeds of Christendom*, 1:269–271.

59. Joel R. Beeke, ed., *Doctrinal Standards, Liturgy, and Church Order* (Grand Rapids: Reformation Heritage Books, 2003), 109.

in their first conversion to God. But Gomarus also asserted that sinners have an intellect, will, and desires that enable them to do some external good, to practice morality, and to understand many things about God from the Bible—though "not out of a godly devotion and godly inclination towards God."[60] Puritan preparation was a thoughtful attempt to do justice both to man's total inability to love God apart from spiritual renewal and his remaining dignity, responsibility, and ability as a person created in God's image. That twofold emphasis is what gave Puritanism its tremendous evangelistic appeal.

Conclusion

William Ames organized Reformed and Puritan theology into a scholastic system notable for its pithy declarations and biblical arguments. He repeated the same essential steps of salvation that were evident in the thought of his teacher, William Perkins. Yet he also developed this concept to a degree of theological sophistication that is not evident in the work of Perkins, Sibbes, or Preston. By making use of the complex Reformed doctrines of grace and human inability, Ames defined preparation in an orthodox manner by making careful distinctions.

Ames also clarified the difference between Roman Catholic preparation and Reformed preparation, rejecting the former but asserting the latter as biblical and consistent with salvation by grace alone. Calvin and Perkins similarly attacked meritorious or free-will preparation while affirming that God prepares sinners by His Word before giving them faith. This crucial distinction must be kept in mind whenever we read discussions of preparation by Reformed authors. Failing to take this distinction into account has led some scholars to misread Reformed attacks on "the Papists" as an intramural controversy among the Reformed about preparation.

John Eusden does not believe that Ames's preparation for faith makes him "an Arminian-within-the-gates, or a quasi-Remonstrant"; rather, he says Ames remained faithful to Reformed orthodoxy but was also sensitive to the human side of religious life which the Arminians

---

60. Franciscus Gomarus, "Theological Disputation on Free Choice," in *Reformed Thought on Freedom: The Concept of Free Choice in Early Modern Theology*, eds. Willem J. van Asselt, J. Martin Bac, and Roelf T. te Velde (Grand Rapids: Baker Academic, 2010), 131–33.

emphasized.[61] Eusden says this led Ames to view the orthodoxy of his opponent Maccovius as "artificial" due to its neglect of "experience" and "the inescapable nature of the religious life."[62] Ames was simultaneously orthodox in his Reformed view of salvation, and sensitive to the human experience of the process of conversion.

Ames's description of preparation seems to overflow into regeneration at times. For example, his call for men to *seek* effectual calling by esteeming the Word of God above all riches strangely echoes his teaching that "a vehement longing after the Word of God" is a *sign* of effectual calling.[63] One wonders what the difference is between the duty of seeking salvation by being willing to sacrifice all for the pearl of great price, and the sign that you already have salvation because your will is steadily inclined towards God and enjoying Him as "the chief good."[64] Perhaps Ames would make further distinctions here, but on a practical level readers might be confused about whether a spiritual quality precedes conversion or flows from it. That is the perennial danger of preparation.

Nonetheless, Ames's treatment of preparation set a standard that other theologians would refer to for generations. His metaphors of drying wood, assembling Adam's body, or joining together the bones in Ezekiel's vision reappear in the writings on preparation by later authors such as David Dickson, John Norton, John Owen, and Peter van Mastricht.[65] The translation of this disputation in the appendix to this book provides modern scholars with a treasure box of insights into the doctrinal framework for preparation. This translation also demonstrates that the Puritans did not naïvely embrace a practical preparation that contradicted their doctrinal positions. They carefully analyzed preparation, using the tools of scholasticism and Renaissance humanism to make this doctrine a coherent part of their biblical, theological, experiential, and practical system.

---

61. Eusden, introduction to Ames, *The Marrow of Theology,* 7.
62. Eusden, introduction to Ames, *The Marrow of Theology,* 50.
63. Ames, *Conscience,* 2.5.9.
64. Ames, *Conscience,* 2.5.7.
65. David Dickson, *Therapeutica Sacra* (Edinburgh: Evan Tyler, 1664), 18; John Norton, *The Orthodox Evangelist, or A Treatise Wherein many Great Evangelical Truths... Are briefly Discussed* (London: by John Macock for Henry Cripps and Lodowick Lloyd, 1654), 177, 257, 259; Owen, *Pneumatologia,* 3:229; Peter van Mastricht, *On Regeneration* (New Haven: Thomas and Samuel Green, [1769]), 30.

CHAPTER FIVE

Preparation in Early New England (1): Thomas Hooker

The heart of a man is the highway wherein Christ comes. Now there are mountains of pride and untoward stoutness of heart, and many windings and turnings.

—Thomas Hooker[1]

Early in the seventeenth century, a student at Emmanuel College, Cambridge, was seized with terror about God's wrath against his sin. Simeon Ash, another student who had to work serving other students to pay his bills, spent many nights with this fear-struck young man trying to comfort him by pointing him to the Savior. Eventually the young man experienced peace with God. He said, "The promise of the gospel was the boat which was to carry a perishing sinner over into the Lord Jesus Christ."

Several years later, the converted student counseled a deeply distressed woman who was also convinced she was hopelessly damned. His counsel bore fruit as she, too, found peace with God. The student was Thomas Hooker (1586–1647), who went on to become a widely heralded preacher of conversion and physician of souls, as well as a defender of Congregationalism. He worked as a pastor in England, then immigrated to Massachusetts. Later he helped to found Connecticut.

Perhaps no Puritan is as famous on the subject of preparation as Hooker. Pettit writes, "Hooker, it is safe to say, wrote more on preparation than any other pastor in New England."[2] The titles of some of Hooker's books indicate this emphasis, such as *The Soul's Preparation for Christ, Being a Treatise of Contrition. Wherein is discovered How God breaks the*

---

1. [Thomas Hooker], *The Sovles Humiliation* (London: by T. Cotes for Andrew Crooke and Philip Nevill, 1640), 4.

2. Pettit, *The Heart Prepared*, 101.

Heart, and wounds the Soul, in the conversion of a Sinner to Himself. However, R. T. Kendall went too far in saying that "the whole of Hooker's soteriological preaching may be summed up in one word: *preparation*."[3] In Books 1–8 of *The Application of Redemption,* Hooker devoted many pages to developing a Christ-centered, trinitarian theology of saving grace, including a defense of particular redemption.[4] John Ball says that this extensive treatment was Hooker's definitive statement of his beliefs. He writes, "Early therefore in the volume, Hooker's orthodoxy as to the main points in Calvinistic theology is clearly reaffirmed."[5] Hooker also wrote treatises on trusting in Christ and our union with Him,[6] including 142 pages on "spiritual love and joy" in Christ.[7]

Hooker certainly spent much time preaching about conversion. Cotton Mather said of Hooker, "The very spirit of his ministry lay in the points of the most practical religion, and the grand concerns of a sinner's preparation for, implantation in, and salvation by, the glorious Lord Jesus Christ."[8] Robert Horn says Hooker preached like a Hebrew prophet, explaining:

> The Old Testament prophets called on the circumcised to acknowledge their sins and then turn to the promise of a new heart; the preacher, in Hooker's view, was to urge people in the same way. This is why his teaching is so experimental and practical. He believed in the great biblical and Reformation truths of divine sovereignty and election and of human responsibility and inability, but his sights were on how divine truth affected and broke the heart. He wanted his hearers not only to see the truth but to feel its power and weight.[9]

3. Kendall, *Calvin and English Calvinism,* 128.

4. Thomas Hooker, *The Application of Redemption, By the effectual Work of the Word, and Spirit of Christ, for the bringing home of lost Sinners to God, The First Eight Books* (1657; facsimile repr., New York: Arno Press, 1972). Hooker devoted pages 11–23 and 72–81 of this work to establish the particular or limited extent of the atonement.

5. John H. Ball, III, *Chronicling the Soul's Windings: Thomas Hooker and His Morphology of Conversion* (Lanham, Md.: University Press of America, 1992), 212–13, 215.

6. Thomas Hooker, *The Soules Vocation or Effectval Calling to Christ* (London: by John Haviland for Andrew Crooke, 1638); *The Soules Implantation into the Natural Olive* (London: by R. Young, 1640); *The Soules Exaltation* (London: by Iohn Haviland for Andrew Crooke, 1638); *The Soules Possession of Christ* (London: by M. F. for Francis Eglesfield, 1638).

7. Hooker, *The Soules Implantation into the Natural Olive,* 179–320.

8. Cotton Mather, *Magnalia Christi Americana: Or, the Ecclesiastical History of New-England* (London: for Thomas Parkhurst, 1702), 2:65.

9. Robert Horn, "Thomas Hooker—The Soul's Preparation for Christ," *The Puritan Experiment in the New World* (London: Westminster Conference, 1976), 21.

From the outset of his ministry in England, Hooker had to deal with nominal Christianity in the churches. Some bishops even sneered at the idea of an experiential knowledge of Christ. In response, Hooker preached like a lion to expose superficial faith and to call people to true faith. He said, "If you desire any evidence to your souls or testimony to your hearts that God hath wrought grace in you, then show it in your lives.... Be holy in buying, selling, travelling, trading...."[10] Ironically, Hooker's passionate preaching to the lost is what has provoked the most fiery criticism from modern historians.

Hooker and Modern Criticisms

Iain H. Murray writes, "Hooker, a modern school of critics unite to say, was a legalist who directed men more to duties and to their own abilities than to Christ."[11] Perry Miller charges Hooker with subtly betraying Reformed theology. He writes, "In many passages describing the extent to which an unregenerate man may go in the work of preparation, some of these writers passed beyond any limits that could be reconciled with Calvinism. In New England clearly the most extreme was Thomas Hooker, who with great eloquence magnified the possibilities of a man's producing in himself a receptive frame of mind."[12]

Kendall says Hooker's doctrine of preparation so vastly expands common grace that man "initiates the process of preparation" which ultimately leads to grace.[13] Kendall writes, "All his pleadings about an 'effectual' calling of God are rendered meaningless by his appeal—indeed, his urgent and impassioned counsel—directly to man's will."[14] Kendall seems to assume that Calvinism logically results in preaching without much application, or at least preaching without passion. But Hooker wrote in the midst of his exhortations, "The Lord by his Spirit prepares the soul."[15] He

---

10. Iain H. Murray, "Thomas Hooker and the Doctrine of Conversion," *Banner of Truth*, no. 196 (Jan 1980): 26. This series of articles is available at http://www.puritansermons.com/pdf/murray4.pdf (accessed June 13, 2011).

11. Iain H. Murray, "Thomas Hooker and the Doctrine of Conversion," *Banner of Truth*, no. 197 (Feb 1980): 12.

12. Perry Miller, *Errand into the Wilderness* (Cambridge: Harvard University Press, 1956), 87n154.

13. Kendall, *Calvin and English Calvinism*, 132.

14. Kendall, *Calvin and English Calvinism*, 138.

15. Thomas Hooker, *The Sovles Preparation for Christ* (The Netherlands: n.p., 1638), 219.

viewed preparation as a work of divine grace, and biblical exhortations as the most ordinary means by which the Lord worked.

John Fulcher says Miller's thesis should be qualified or even revised by recognizing that Hooker described preparation as a work of the Spirit in the unconverted, especially in his later writings.[16] E. Brooks Holifield says, "Neither Hooker nor the other ministers ever meant to suggest that sinners could prepare their own hearts."[17] John Ball says, "Kendall is correct in regard to Hooker's voluntaristic emphasis. Yet he fails to see that, for Hooker, sovereign grace is maintained from the very first stirrings of preparation."[18] By voluntarism Ball means Hooker's emphasis on the will over the intellect as the primary ruler within the soul, which is therefore the center of saving religion.[19] Jones noted a similar voluntarism in John Cotton's work.[20] Regardless, Hooker's appeals did not contradict divine sovereignty over the human will. They sprang from recognizing that God works through the means of preaching to prepare the hearts of sinners and to breathe spiritual life into them.

Another criticism is that the doctrine of preparation hinders the sinner from coming to Christ. Interestingly, this criticism came from Charles Haddon Spurgeon, who said that "some preachers in the Puritanic times" such as Rogers but "especially the American, Thomas Hooker," encouraged sinners to think, "I possess such-and-such a degree of sensibility on account of sin, therefore I have a right to trust in Christ."[21] Spurgeon argued against this, asserting the command of God that men believe in His Son (1 John 3:23). J. I. Packer, in response, says, "Spurgeon's theological judgment is surely sound; but equally surely he has put the wrong people in the dock. One wonders whether he has read the authors to whom he refers (after all, he was only twenty-nine at the time); certainly, he misrepresents their teaching. To state the facts correctly, we

---

16. John R. Fulcher, "Puritan Piety in Early New England: A Study in Spiritual Regeneration from the Antinomian Controversy to the Cambridge Synod of 1648 in the Massachusetts Bay Colony" (PhD Dissertation, Princeton University, 1963), 203, 214.

17. E. Brooks Holifield, *Theology in America: Christian Thought from the Age of the Puritans to the Civil War* (New Haven: Yale University, 2003), 44.

18. Ball, *Chronicling the Soul's Windings*, 75.

19. Ball, *Chronicling the Soul's Windings*, 90–91.

20. Jones, "The Beginnings of American Theology," 34.

21. C. H. Spurgeon, *The Metropolitan Tabernacle Pulpit, Volume 9* (1863; repr. Pasadena, Tex.: Pilgrim Publications, 1979), 531.

must distinguish two questions: that of the *warrant of faith*, and that of the *way to faith.*"[22]

Preparation does not oppose the free offer of the gospel to all people. Hooker preached on Revelation 22:17, "Whosoever will, let him taste of the water of life freely," saying that God freely offers salvation to all people: "the freeness of the offer of his grace" and "the universality of this offer of grace.'"[23] He thus encouraged unbelievers, saying, "Why, it is a free mercy, and therefore why mayest not thou have it as well as another?" (Isa. 55:1).[24] He said, "If you will but come and take grace, this is all God looks for, all that the Lord expects and desires, you may have it for the taking."[25] All sinners have a warrant to trust in Christ.

However, it is precisely in the invitation to "whosoever will" that Hooker saw the need of preparatory conviction and humiliation. To receive this offer, he said, "man must will to receive Christ and grace." Corruption makes man oppose this grace of God.[26] Therefore, for the free offer of the gospel to become effective in saving sinners, God must "work a will in his servants to receive the Lord Jesus Christ."[27]

To support Hooker's views on preparation, Robert Horn wrote,

> Hooker in one place gives four reasons for the necessity of a preparatory work: (a) "Every man by nature doth entertain sin as his God, and seeks and loves that most of all"; (b) "There cannot be two gods in one heart.... You cannot have Christ, and yet be an underling to sin"; (c) "You must have your first god—pride and malice and the like—unthroned before the Lord Christ will set up his scepter"; and (d) "The soul will not part with his corruption and lust...unless he be wearied with them and find (their) gall and bitterness."[28]

Hooker's view of conversion did not hold people back from Christ, but it did hold them back from a false assurance of salvation. He warned people who lacked true contrition, "Do not thou think to fall upon the

---

22. J. I. Packer, *A Quest for Godliness: The Puritan Vision of the Christian Life* (Wheaton, Ill.: Crossway Books, 1990), 171–72, emphasis original.

23. T[homas] Hooker, *The Vnbeleevers Preparing for Christ* (London: by Tho. Cotes for Andrew Crooke, 1638), 2.

24. Hooker, *The Vnbeleevers Preparing for Christ*, 19.

25. Hooker, *The Vnbeleevers Preparing for Christ*, 20.

26. Hooker, *The Vnbeleevers Preparing for Christ*, 2.

27. Hooker, *The Vnbeleevers Preparing for Christ*, 3.

28. Horn, "Thomas Hooker—The Soul's Preparation for Christ," 21–22.

promise presently." Yet he quickly added, "Indeed you cannot fall upon it too soon upon good grounds; but it is impossible that ever a full soul or a haughty heart should believe."[29] In other words, by all means come to Christ immediately, but do not think that you are coming to Christ if your heart remains proud and self-satisfied.

Hooker's Doctrine of Contrition

Hooker taught that when God draws sinners to Christ, He does a "great work of preparation" upon them which consists of "contrition" and "humiliation" (Isa. 57:15).[30] These two preparations slide back the two great bolts that lock the door of the heart against Christ: contrition, which destroys the sinner's contentment in his present spiritual condition; and humiliation, which destroys the sinner's confidence in his self-sufficiency to solve his spiritual problem.[31] Let us look first at Hooker's view of contrition, to which he devoted several hundred pages in his *The Soul's Preparation* and *The Application of Redemption, the Ninth and Tenth Books*.

Contrition consists of the *sight* of sin and its punishment, a *sense* of sin inducing hatred against it, and *separation* of the heart from sin (Acts 2:37).[32] Hooker wrote, "All these are not wrought so much by any power that is in us, as by the almighty power of God working in us."[33]

Contrition prepares a person to be joined to Christ as the Savior from sin. Christ came to seek and to save the lost (Luke 19:10). Only those who know they are lost will be saved by Him. No one comes to Christ, that is, believes in Him, unless the Father draws him (John 6:44). In this drawing, God opens a person's eyes to the vileness of his sin. Thus Christ calls the weary and heavy-laden to come to him (Matt. 11:28). God promised that Christ would save broken-hearted mourners (Isa. 61:1–3).[34] Sargent Bush writes, "The essential argument of Hooker's sermons on contrition is that

---

29. Hooker, *The Sovles Preparation for Christ*, 174.

30. Thomas Hooker, *The Application of Redemption By the Effectual Work of the Word, and Spirit of Christ, for the bringing home of lost Sinners to God. The Ninth and Tenth Books* (London: Peter Cole, 1657), 2; *The Sovles Preparation for Christ*, 1–2; *The Soules Implantation*, 2.

31. Hooker, *The Soules Implantation*, 6–13.

32. Hooker, *The Sovles Preparation for Christ*, 2; *The Application of Redemption… The Ninth and Tenth Books*, 16.

33. Hooker, *The Sovles Preparation for Christ*, 2.

34. Hooker, *The Sovles Preparation for Christ*, 147–50.

the individual must be made aware of his dire spiritual condition before anything can be done to change it."[35]

Contrition begins with a sight or knowledge of sin (Ezek. 36:31; Jer. 31:19). This must not be a superficial glance but a clear and searching view into the depths of sin. In true contrition the passing pleasures and false peace of sin are stripped away so the sinner may see sin's venom, like that of a snake with a pretty skin but with a poisonous bite.[36] One must peer through "a little peep-hole into hell," witness the pains of the damned, and realize that sin is a greater evil than any pain. For sin robs us of the greatest good, "communion with God," sets itself against the Lord and provokes His justice, and "procures all plagues and punishments to the damned." Sin is nothing less than hatred against God and warring against the Lord of hosts.[37]

True contrition is not an abstract, theoretical view of sin but one that convicts us of our personal guilt. Our hearts must cease treating others' sins as worse than our own and say to ourselves, *"Thou* art the man" (2 Sam. 12:7).[38] Furthermore, in true contrition, we abandon all our excuses and yield our consciences to the conviction of God's wrath against us for our sin.[39] To come to this point, we must first pray that God causes us to see our hearts the way He sees them; second, "labor to acquaint ourselves thoroughly with God and his law" in the many sins it forbids and duties it requires; and third, cease to quarrel with God's Word and submit to its rebukes.[40]

A true view of sin leads to such piercing of the heart that it shivers to pieces (Acts 2:37).[41] This is the beginning of alienating the will from its sins. Hooker wrote, "Unless the Lord should thus wound and vex the soul, the heart that prized corruption as a god (as every natural man doth) would never be severed from it."[42] The Lord wounds the heart by amazing it with "some flashes of his wrath" against sin and "the hammer

---

35. Sargent Bush, Jr., *The Writings of Thomas Hooker: Spiritual Adventure in Two Worlds* (Madison: University of Wisconsin Press, 1980), 171.

36. Hooker, *The Sovles Preparation for Christ,* 11–13.

37. Hooker, *The Sovles Preparation for Christ,* 13–16.

38. Hooker, *The Sovles Preparation for Christ,* 21–23.

39. Hooker, *The Sovles Preparation for Christ,* 23–25.

40. Hooker, *The Sovles Preparation for Christ,* 32–35.

41. Hooker, *The Sovles Preparation for Christ,* 112.

42. Hooker, *The Sovles Preparation for Christ,* 113.

of God's law layeth a sudden blow upon the heart, and this discovers the vile nature of sin."[43]

The sinner who was once careless now, with smitten heart, returns to hear the preaching of the Word. His initial amazement becomes a convicted fear that he is in bondage to sin and death. As the Scriptures indicate, "the Spirit shows our bondage, and thence comes this fear" (Rom. 8:15; 2 Tim. 1:7; Deut. 28:66).[44] Though the sinner tries to distract himself with business and play, "the Lord pursueth the soul" and sets his conscience on fire with His wrath.[45] Preparatory contrition culminates in moving the soul away from its formerly cherished sins "with a secret dislike" and even "hatred" for them. This is not caused by active holiness within the soul (wrought by regeneration) but is the passive disgust pressed upon the soul by the Spirit's revelation of sin's evil effects.[46] Yet even though the sinner may hate sin because of the fire of punishment, he still loves sin for itself and is not yet converted.[47]

Calvin also compared God's work of convincing people of their sin to a hammer blow upon the mind.[48] Such images are rooted in Scripture, in texts such as Jeremiah 23:29: "Is not my word like as a fire? saith the LORD; and like a hammer that breaketh the rock in pieces?"

The Culmination of Contrition: Separation and Saving Sorrow

Contrition ultimately produces separation from sin. As we have seen, Hooker indicated that contrition separates the heart from sin by creating hatred against it with "saving sorrows."[49] He noted an analogy between Adam's fall and Christ's restoration. He said Adam fell first by an "aversion, or turning from God; then a conversion or turning of the soul to the creature" with inordinate desire. Christ, the second Adam, saves by reversing this process: "There must be an aversion and turning from the

---

43. Hooker, *The Sovles Preparation for Christ*, 117.
44. Hooker, *The Sovles Preparation for Christ*, 118–19.
45. Hooker, *The Sovles Preparation for Christ*, 121.
46. Hooker, *The Sovles Preparation for Christ*, 217–18.
47. Hooker, *The Sovles Preparation for Christ*, 125–26.
48. Calvin, *Institutes*, 3.3.7.
49. Hooker, *The Sovles Preparation for Christ*, 2, 144–45, 217–18; *The Application of Redemption... The Ninth and Tenth Books*, 16, 670, 700.

creature before there can be a conversion unto God."[50] Hooker referred to this as "saving preparation before the infusion of faith."[51]

This initial turning from idolatry, according to Hooker, is not due to the power of natural man, nor is it a "habit of grace" infused by the Holy Spirit, nor is it a human virtue pleasing to God. Rather it is the "irresistible power" of the "Spirit of contrition" working upon the soul prior to inhabiting that soul.[52] The soul is divorced from its idol but not yet remarried nor in love with the heavenly Husband. It is "an act of the Spirit of Christ, whereby it doth fling down those strongholds, dispossess the power of Satan, and quit the soul from those overpowering and prevailing claims which Satan and sin challengeth over it, as to exercise their tyranny and authority over it…. It's a cutting off of the branch that it grow not upon its old root, and receive not sap and influence therefrom."[53] Hooker wrote, "We cannot be under two covenants; in the first Adam, and the second; grow upon two stocks together."[54]

Hooker did not say whether this cutting off from sin precedes engrafting into Christ *in time*. Did he believe that the elect stood for a while in an intermediate state prior to conversion, where they were neither in Adam nor in Christ? Could covenant theologians conceive of man existing apart from some covenant with God? Or did they regard this cutting off as logically preceding but temporally coincident with regeneration? Hooker said that once the soul is fully prepared by Christ, the Lord enters into His temple immediately.[55] He wrote, "When this preparation is fully wrought, faith is certainly, and will undoubtedly be infused, and cannot be hindered, when (I say) it is complete."[56] John Gerstner and Jonathan Gerstner comment on this, saying, "Thus this state of preparation is probably a logical not a chronological one."[57] But Hooker portrayed the preparatory hatred of sin as a process of seeking and laboring to destroy sin that

---

50. Hooker, *The Application of Redemption… The Ninth and Tenth Books*, 673.

51. Hooker, *The Application of Redemption… The First Eight Books*, 150.

52. Hooker, *The Application of Redemption… The Ninth and Tenth Books*, 674–75.

53. Hooker, *The Application of Redemption… The First Eight Books*, 151.

54. Hooker, *The Application of Redemption… The Ninth and Tenth Books*, 679.

55. Hooker, *The Soules Preparation for Christ*, 143–44.

56. Hooker, *The Application of Redemption… The First Eight Books*, 152.

57. John Gerstner and Jonathan Gerstner, "Edwardsean Preparation for Salvation," *Westminster Theological Journal* 42, no. 1 (Fall 1979): 10.

unfolded over time, not something that happened at the moment of sav-ing conversion.[58] So there is ambiguity here that invites further research.

At issue is the timing of regeneration in the process of preparation and conversion. Hooker believed that "we cannot tell exactly when faith is born, whether after a man has fully apprehended Christ or when he first hungers for Him," as Miller wrote.[59] Just as the forming of a child's body in the womb is a fearful, wonderful, and mysterious process (Ps. 139:13–16), so the Spirit's forming of faith in the soul is a secret, as Christ Himself taught (John 3:8).[60] Hooker concurred with John Rogers, who said, "It is hard to say at what instant faith is wrought, whether not till a man apprehends Christ and the promise, or even in his earnest desires, hungering and thirsting; for even these are pronounced blessed."[61] Hooker wrote, "It is not only possible, but it is too ordinary" that the soul has become united to Christ but does not yet know it.[62] Like a man in a dark basement who cannot see the sun shining into the windows of his house, so humbled believers may not perceive that Christ is already shin-ing in their souls. Hooker wrote, "It is the Spirit of Christ that makes you willing to part with sin. Hath Christ been so long with you, and do you not know him?"[63]

God's saving work upon the soul includes both "saving contrition… before faith" and progressive sanctification unto glory after faith. The first is a "sorrow of preparation" by which the Spirit brings us to Christ; the latter involves the "sorrow of sanctification" produced by the Spirit's indwelling after we receive Christ. The sorrow of preparation is the seed of faith. As Hooker wrote, "In the hungerings and thirstings of the soul, there is as it were the spawn of faith, not yet brought to full perfection, the soul is coming towards God, but not yet come to him to rest so fully and wholly on him as hereafter it will."[64] The "spawn of faith" probably refers to faith in its undeveloped, "egg" form. The Puritans often used the embryonic metaphor in describing the new birth.

58. Hooker, *The Sovles Preparation for Christ,* 219–22.
59. Miller, "'Preparation for Salvation' in New England," 265.
60. Thomas Hooker, "To the Reader," in John Rogers, *The Doctrine of Faith* (London: for Nathanael Newbery and William Sheffard, 1627), [no pagination].
61. Rogers, *The Doctrine of Faith,* 175.
62. Hooker, *The Soules Ingrafting into Christ,* 133.
63. Hooker, *The Soules Ingrafting into Christ,* 138.
64. Hooker, "To the Reader," in Rogers, *The Doctrine of Faith.* See Hooker, *The Sovles Preparation for Christ,* 144.

At the point of conversion, the "sorrow in preparation" becomes "sorrow in sanctification." In preparation the soul grieves because of the Holy Spirit's piercings and woundings, yet it does not yet have an inward principle of grace to love God and hate sin as sin. In sanctification the soul's sorrow over sin flows out of the grace infused into it by God's Spirit. Hooker called both of these griefs "saving sorrows," even though preparative sorrow lacks spiritual holiness. Both preparation and sanctification are part of the golden chain of God's saving acts (Rom. 8:30).[65] Hooker said this process could be viewed as a clock that does not keep the right time. First the workman stops the clock and sets its wheels right. Then he puts the weights on the clock so it runs by its internal principles.[66] Likewise, after Christ dwells in the heart by the Holy Spirit, the prepared sinner becomes a regenerated sinner in union with the Lord.

In speaking of preparation as the "saving sorrow" that precedes faith, Hooker went beyond Calvin and the majority of the Puritans. His view of preparation began to merge into saving conversion. That brought him into dispute with other Puritans who also taught preparation for grace, but reserved all saving habits and acts for union with Christ. At the same time, the ambiguity Hooker built into his theology about when Christ actually enters the soul allows for the possibility of accepting the idea that "saving sorrow" precedes *conscious* faith, for Christ may live in the soul before the soul senses His presence or its faith in Him.

Hooker's Doctrine of Humiliation

Hooker explored humiliation, the second aspect of his doctrine of preparation, in his book *The Soul's Humiliation*. Perhaps if he had lived longer, he would have given us a more developed explanation of this doctrine in a supplement to his *Application of Redemption,* as he did with *The Soul's Preparation.*[67] Sadly, he died before the revision could be done, leaving us only with the notes that someone took from his sermons on *Humiliation.*

Hooker based his doctrine on an exposition of the parable of the prodigal son (Luke 15:14–18).[68] Just as conviction breaks the heart and makes sin wearisome by its bitter consequences, humiliation "pares

---

65. Hooker, *The Sovles Preparation for Christ,* 144–45.
66. Hooker, *The Sovles Preparation for Christ,* 146.
67. Ball, *Chronicling the Soul's Windings,* 87; Bush, *The Writings of Thomas Hooker,* 187.
68. Hooker, *The Sovles Humiliation,* 3.

away all self-sufficiency" and "confidence in a man's privileges, and all
his good performances, and all his duties, by which he is ready to shelter
himself."[69] Conviction moves sinners to use the means of grace in seeking
peace of conscience; humiliation shows sinners that their use of religious
means cannot save them, only Christ working through the means.[70] The
humiliated soul does not despair of God's mercy but despairs of all help
from self and so "submits himself wholly to God…and is content to be at
his disposing."[71]

Hooker identified three stages in humiliation:

1) The prodigal son, impoverished by his partying and famine, does
   not go home to his father but takes a job to earn a living. Likewise
   the sinner, awakened to his misery, tries to find help by his ability
   but not from Christ who alone can help him.

2) The prodigal's labors leave him desperately needy. After every
   help he can find fails to bring him peace, the sinner despairs of
   finding salvation in himself or any creature.

3) The lost son goes home to his father and submits to him as a servant because he is unworthy of being counted a son. The lost soul
   falls down before the throne of God, submits to His justice, and
   hopes for His mercy.[72]

Hooker interpreted the story of the prodigal son as stages of humiliation but left no place for contrition as a distinct work of God prior to
humiliation. That suggests he may not have viewed contrition and humiliation as sequential steps as much as dimensions of preparation that can
take place simultaneously. If so, his detailed analysis of preparation
may not have been intended as a structure of the conversion experience
through time.

The most controversial aspect of Hooker's doctrine of humiliation is
the last step, in which he asserts that the humbled sinner not only submits to justice but is content to be damned. John McNeill said of this
assertion, "The soul, he [Hooker] argued, must be so 'at God's disposing'
as to be content to be damned if God wills it—a doctrine advanced by

---

69. Hooker, *The Sovles Humiliation*, 5.
70. Ball, *Chronicling the Soul's Windings*, 131.
71. Hooker, *The Sovles Humiliation*, 7.
72. Hooker, *The Sovles Humiliation*, 8–9, 20–21, 79.

St. Francis de Sales and Fénelon."[73] Frances de Sales (1567–1622) and Francois Fénelon (1651–1715) were Roman Catholic theologians in France. Fénelon, of course, lived after Hooker, and could not have influenced him. De Sales's writings were translated and published in English as early as 1613.[74] However, de Sales's self-abandonment to damnation was supposedly an act of love to God, and no Reformed theologian would attribute the love of God to an unconverted man.[75] But the doctrinal convergence of Hooker and de Sales is intriguing. Jones said of Hooker's preparation, "Before the soul can join with Christ, it must have no wishes of its own. It must be in a state of total self-negation"—or, more accurately, self-renunciation.[76] This concept of total self-renunciation as a precursor to union with God suggests a link with medieval mysticism. The Puritans were influenced by medieval thinking and read widely outside of Reformed circles.[77] Hooker might have drawn upon a medieval stream of thought that also influenced de Sales and Fénelon. But it would be premature to infer such a connection without further research.

Regardless, Hooker's book *The Soul's Humiliation* asserts the doctrine of preparatory humiliation to the point of being content to be damned. Hooker wrote, "The heart truly abased, is content to bear the estate of

---

73. John T. McNeill, *The History and Character of Calvinism* (New York: Oxford University Press, 1954), 339.

74. Francis de Sales, *An Introduction to the Deuout Life,* trans. I[ohn] Y[akesley] (Douai: by G. Patt for Iohn Heigham, 1613).

75. Francis de Sales said, "Whatever may happen, O God, you who hold all things in your hand, whose ways are justice and truth, whatsoever you may have decreed concerning me in the eternal secret of your predestination and reprobation, you whose judgments are unfathomable, you who are a very Just Judge and Merciful Father, I will love you always, O Lord, at least in this life! At least in this life will I love you, if it is not given me to love you in eternity!... If my merits demand it, and I am to be one damned among the damned,...grant that I should not be among those who curse your name." E. J. Lajeunie, O.P., *Saint Francis de Sales: The Man, The Thinker, His Influence,* trans. Rory O'Sullivan, OSFS (Bangalore, India: S.F.S. Publications, 1986), 1:71, cited by Alexander T. Pocetto, "From Despair to Hope: One College Student's (Francis de Sales 1567–1622) Struggle with Truth, http://www4.desales.edu/~salesian/resources/articles/english/despair.hope2.html#_ftn-ref10 (accessed July 11, 2011).

76. Jones, "The Beginnings of American Theology," 127. Self-negation is not quite the same thing as self-abnegation, or renunciation. To be willing to be damned is, properly speaking, more of an act of radical self-renunciation than self-negation.

77. For example, on one page Firmin quoted "three Popish authors," Alvarez, Cornelius a Lapide, and Cardinal Cajetan (*The Real Christian,* 235). Ames said of the casuistry of "the Papists" that "in a great deal of earth and dirt of superstitions, they have some veins of silver" ("To the Reader," in *Conscience*).

damnation: because he hath brought this misery and damnation upon himself."[78] He also said this content was not a gross negligence "either of God's glory or his own good," which is not lawful nor preparatory, for "God will make him prize mercy, and care for it too before he have it" so that he "is ever improving all means."[79] It is rather a state of being "content to be at God's disposing" without "quarrelling with the Almighty."[80] The Judge has every right to condemn the sinner to hell and no sinner deserves mercy. Hooker admitted that the soul by nature desires its own preservation ("it is a rule that God hath stamped in the creature"), but the humbled sinner will fight against his tendency to quarrel with God's justice.[81]

In a rather unique way, this book calls men to submit to hell to get to heaven. To those tempted to murder themselves in despair, Hooker wrote, "Why will you not bear the wrath of the Lord? It is true indeed, your sins are great, and God's wrath is heavy, yet God will do you good by it; and therefore be quiet…. Lie low, and be content to be at God's disposing."[82] In its concluding pages, the book makes this appeal for humiliation, "Will you outbrave the Almighty to his face, and will you dare damnation? As you love yourselves take heed of it."[83] Thus Hooker simultaneously appealed to self-love and called sinners to submit to the prospect of eternal punishment for their sins.

As we will see, Hooker's view on contentment to be damned was continued in the theology of Thomas Shepard; nonetheless, the majority of Puritans found fault with it, especially Giles Firmin, whom we will consider in a later chapter.

Preparation and Fallen Man's Ability

Hooker plainly taught the Reformed doctrine of human inability. He said unsaved men are totally deprived of the ability to serve God. All men are flesh (John 3:6). Until they are born again, they will have no good thought nor do any good action (Rom. 7:18). They may be morally good but not spiritually good until God gives them saving grace. By nature they are

---

78. Hooker, *The Sovles Humiliation*, 112.
79. Hooker, *The Sovles Humiliation*, 113–14.
80. Hooker, *The Sovles Humiliation*, 114.
81. Hooker, *The Sovles Humiliation*, 115–17.
82. Hooker, *The Sovles Humiliation*, 141.
83. Hooker, *The Sovles Humiliation*, 222.

dead in trespasses and sins (Eph. 2:1), like a senseless, rotting corpse. God has already condemned them (John 3:18), and they are indeed ruled by the devil (John 6:70; 13:27; Eph. 2:2; Acts 26:18).[84]

Hooker pressed upon sinners to "get out of this natural corruption."[85] Modern critics view Hooker's view of preparation as a covert denial of human inability and salvation by grace alone. Indeed, Hooker himself referred to the "cavil of Bellarmin," the Roman Catholic apologist, that if a natural man does not have the power to receive God's grace, he cannot be exhorted.[86] Here we must again be careful not to judge the Puritans according to presuppositions that they did not hold, such as the belief that "obligation always implies ability," which, as Mark Dever says, is foreign to Augustinian thinking.[87] The Reformed divines saw no inconsistency in exhorting men to spiritual acts that they could not perform without divine grace. In the Reformed view, exhortation refers to duty, not ability, and such an exhortation might be the means by which God freely grants grace needed to heed it. Gospel preaching requires a preacher to press upon men the duties of faith, repentance, and new obedience.

Another element in Reformed theology is the Word's instrumentality in salvation. "Faith cometh by hearing, and hearing by the word of God," Paul said (Rom. 10:17). Accordingly, Reformed Christians believe that by the faithful preaching of the Word, God may communicate supernatural, life-giving grace to those dead in sin. Charles White says that as a result, the Puritans could teach the total inability of sinners to come to Christ of their own power in the doctrinal portion of a sermon, but exhort sinners to human action in the application of the sermon without being "closet Arminians."[88] Reformed Christians believed that God could use exhortations addressed to the spiritually dead to give them life.

Though these distinctions of ability, duty, and instrumentality clarify some aspects of Hooker's doctrine of preparation, they do not entirely solve the problem involved. Hooker told unconverted men they already had certain abilities. He called upon them "to begin speedily and persevere constantly in the means that God hath appointed," such as listening

---

84. Hooker, *The Sovles Humiliation*, 33–37.

85. Hooker, *The Vnbeleevers Preparing for Christ*, 119.

86. Hooker, *The Vnbeleevers Preparing for Christ*, 120.

87. Dever, *Richard Sibbes*, 127.

88. Charles E. White, "Were Hooker and Shepard Closet Arminians?" *Calvin Theological Journal* 20, no. 1 (April 1985): 42.

to sound preaching.[89] He summoned them even prior to conversion to use the means of grace while doing "three things which are in the power of natural men to perform," first, to know their misery and inability; second, to confess to God their stubbornness; and third, to be convicted that the Holy Spirit can change their hearts.[90]

Kendall says Hooker took "a huge step" beyond Perkins in affirming natural human ability, implicitly charging Hooker with leading the church away from Reformed doctrine, even further from Calvin than Perkins allegedly went.[91] But Calvin acknowledged that the darkness of the fallen human mind does not extinguish its moral awareness. Calvin quoted pagan authors to show that the heathen sometimes sense that they are stubbornly rushing into actions which they know are wrong.[92]

Calvin even said, "Their understanding extends so far that evasion becomes impossible for them, and they, convicted by the witness of their own consciences, begin even now to tremble before God's judgment seat."[93] In this context Calvin spoke of men's gropings in the dark, apart from the biblical revelation of God's law. How much more then can the natural mind, when pressed under the spiritual preaching of the law, see something of its depravity?[94] Calvin wrote, "For man, blinded and drunk with self-love, must be compelled to know and to confess his own feebleness and impurity" by the moral law.[95] Hooker did not leap beyond Reformed theology in his exhortations but was firmly planted in it. Yet he did emphasize preparation more strongly than Calvin and most other Puritans would have done.

Preparation and the Grace of Christ

We cannot say that Hooker proposed a formula in which a prolonged period of profound conviction of sin was necessary for every conversion. He said that sometimes God works "punctually," meaning all at once, or at one point in time; but also asserted that God "is bound to no time, and

---

89. Hooker, *The Vnbeleevers Preparing for Christ*, 119.
90. Hooker, *The Vnbeleevers Preparing for Christ*, 121–22.
91. Kendall, *Calvin and Calvinism*, 132.
92. Calvin, *Institutes*, 2.2.23.
93. Calvin, *Institutes*, 2.2.24.
94. Calvin, *Institutes*, 2.7.3.
95. Calvin, *Institutes*, 2.7.6.

therefore we must not limit the Holy One of Israel."[96] He wrote, "All this may be done at one sermon, in one doctrine, or in one part of a use."[97]

Furthermore, "all are not alike wounded for sin." Hooker explained, "Two men are pricked, the one with a pin, and other with a spear: two men are cut, the one with a pen-knife, the other with a sword: so the Lord deals kindly and gently with one soul, and roughly with another."[98] He gently melted Lydia's heart, but the jailer, who was "an outrageous rebellious wretch," had to be shaken to the point of near suicide. Every person's heart is locked up by sin, but some require less force than others to open.[99] The Lord gives to each person what is needed to drive that person to seek mercy. When God works preparation quietly, it may be that "the work is secret, and the soul apprehends it not."[100] Therefore it is not necessary to discern this work of preparation prior to coming to Christ, but rather to glorify God when we are converted for overcoming our hearts' enthrallment to sin and drawing us to His Son.

The goal of preparation is to bring sinners to Christ. Hooker said, "That soul which was cured by any other means save only by Christ, was never truly wounded for sin.... But if the soul were truly wounded for sin, then nothing can cure him but a Savior to pardon him, and grace to purge him."[101] Godly sorrow drives a person to God for mercy; carnal sorrow drives the person away from God in despair.[102]

Godly sorrow for sin is thus good for the soul. The soul feels the weight of sin as its greatest evil, for men were created for God and to find happiness only in Him. Godly sorrow wearies the soul of its sin and fits the soul for the Lord Christ to come in. It makes the heart "set a high price upon Christ and grace."[103] A man under godly sorrow is not yet "in Christ" but only "prepared for Christ." This sorrow is not "sanctifying sorrow." Here Hooker diverged from most Puritans in teaching a true, godly sorrow in the unregenerate. However, "undoubtedly that soul which hath this work upon it, shall have faith poured into it." Though the person is

---

96. Hooker, *The Sovles Preparation for Christ*, 128.
97. Hooker, *The Sovles Preparation for Christ*, 129.
98. Hooker, *The Sovles Preparation for Christ*, 155.
99. Hooker, *The Sovles Preparation for Christ*, 157.
100. Hooker, *The Sovles Preparation for Christ*, 159.
101. Hooker, *The Sovles Preparation for Christ*, 133.
102. Hooker, *The Sovles Preparation for Christ*, 134–36.
103. Hooker, *The Sovles Preparation for Christ*, 137–42.

not yet settled on Christ, he will be saved. Hooker wrote, "When the heart is fitted and prepared, the Lord Christ comes immediately into it."[104] This view fits with Hooker's overall theology that Christ Himself prepares the soul by contrition, therefore no one need fear that a true sorrow over sin will abort before coming to birth. On the other hand, it raises the question about how an unconverted man, not yet united to Christ, can have the godly sorrow that will assuredly bring him to salvation. Again we face the question of whether there is an intermediate state of preparation, between being altogether dead in sin and coming to conversion.

Behind the process of preparation looms an invisible war between Christ and sin. The "over swaying authority of carnal reason" resists conviction, Hooker said. In this, Christ wages a merciful war: "The Lord Christ forceth the understanding to bear that almighty stroke of his Spirit, whereby he destroys the sovereign power of carnal reason, and fits it to receive the prevailing impression of his spiritual light, which searcheth the secrets of sin in the soul."[105]

Hooker used the image of a holy war against the citadel of sin in the human soul.[106] He said the mind of fallen man has become "the stronghold of Satan." Therefore, "the Lord Christ, he first forceth this fort, demolisheth and casteth down the frame of it" (2 Cor. 10:4). Hooker wrote, "Jesus, the head of the second covenant," who made satisfaction for the first Adam's sin, comes with the truth in his hand, and "the Lord Jesus forceth the understanding to submit" (Acts 26:18). Then, "There is room made for the ready entertainment of light, of the guidance of the Spirit of Christ, as the head of the covenant, who begins to set up his throne, where Satan had his hold."[107]

It is ironic that, whereas Miller and others contrast a gradual conversion theology with a sovereignly coercive conversion theology, here in Hooker, the man regarded as the prince of preparationists, we find some of the strongest language of coercion.[108] So there is no direct correlation between viewing the conversion process as a forceful seizure and

---

104. Hooker, *The Sovles Preparation for Christ*, 143–44.
105. Hooker, *The Application of Redemption… The Ninth and Tenth Books*, 47–48.
106. Hooker, *The Application of Redemption… The Ninth and Tenth Books*, 98–99.
107. Hooker, *The Application of Redemption… The Ninth and Tenth Books*, 49–50.
108. James W. Jones III, "The Beginnings of American Theology: John Cotton, Thomas Hooker, Thomas Shepard and Peter Bulkeley" (PhD Dissertation, Brown University, 1970), 124.

opposing any idea of preparation for conversion. Furthermore, Hooker's view of conversion as spiritual conquest also contradicts the insistence by some scholars that forceful conversion must be an event rather than a process, that is, sudden and not gradual. At the same time, Hooker's rhetoric of spiritual war should not mislead us into thinking that God violently drags sinners into the kingdom, kicking and screaming. Hooker said that sometimes conviction comes like a sword but at other times it is like a pinprick. Furthermore, in this context he is talking about God's conviction and humiliation of unregenerate God-haters. He said that in regeneration God changes the heart from the inside out with new desires so they are made willing in the day of His power. This wooing of the heart is not coercion but a drawing of sinners by the cords of love.

Hooker also used the image of a door upon which Christ knocks by His Word.[109] But the same Christ who knocks on the door also moves the sinner to unlock the door that Christ may come in. He wrote,

> Christ is said to stand at the door and knock, and if any man will open unto him, he will come in and sup with him (Revelation 3:20). Saving contrition is a shooting back the bolts of our base lusts, a severing and unlocking the heart from the sovereignty of one's noisesome corruptions, that stop the passage and hinder the coming of our Savior; this clear and convicting sight of our sins, is as it were the lifting up of the latch, or letting in of the key, the powerful dispensation of the truth and operation of his Spirit whereby the knot and combination between sin and the soul is broken and severed, and the way made that the authority of the truth may come at the heart and work kindly upon it for good.[110]

Therefore Christ works through the preacher's sermons and the sinner's meditations and seeking, for Christ alone has the key to unlock the sin-bound heart.

The centrality of Christ makes Hooker's doctrines of predestination and preparation sweet and evangelical, not legalistic and morose, as was also true of most of the Puritans. Bush observes this in Hooker, and says of the Puritans, "It is easy to forget that for them predestination was not a mechanical, impersonal, legalistic operation simply imposed on men by

---

109. Hooker, *The Application of Redemption… The Ninth and Tenth Books*, 101.
110. Hooker, *The Application of Redemption… The Ninth and Tenth Books*, 111–12.

a distant Power. Their Christology brings Jesus…front and center."[111] We may say the same of the Puritan doctrine of preparation. Preparation is Christ's loving pursuit of the hostile soul, casting down everything that exalts itself against the knowledge of God, so that ultimately, through the gift of faith, the sinner receives Him. Thus preparation is Christ-centered, not man-centered. We may draw a number of conclusions from this study of Thomas Hooker, but we will wait to do so until the end of the next chapter, in which we consider the teaching of another New England divine, Thomas Shepard.

---

111. Bush, *The Writings of Thomas Hooker*, 158.

CHAPTER SIX

Preparation in Early New England (2): Thomas Shepard and William Pemble

Those that are saved, are saved with much difficulty…. It is a wonderful hard thing to be saved. The gate is strait, and therefore, a man must sweat and strive to enter.

—Thomas Shepard[1]

John Stansby was a farmer and clothier in England who later immigrated to New England. He joined Thomas Shepard's church sometime before 1641. When confessing his faith before the congregation, Stansby said, "I know I came in the world a child of hell, and if ever any a child of hell, [it was] I." He vividly recalled the years he spent in sexual immorality and drunkenness. He not only sinned but enticed others to join him in sin. When he heard that unrepentant sinners such as adulterers and drunkards could not enter the kingdom of God (1 Cor. 6:9–10), he realized that he was truly lost. Though he did not want to give up his sins, he was greatly moved by the preaching of the Word and sometimes made resolutions to change. Yet his heart remained "rotten."

The Spirit often came to Stansby through the means of grace, offering him Christ's blood and mercy, but he loved his lusts too much. He says he saw "my hellish, devilish nature opposite to God and goodness," which separated him from God; but he also sensed the "mercy of the Lord breaking my heart." He began praying for the Lord to draw him to Christ. In the promises of God he gained "a sight of his beauty and glory and excellency, and hereupon I went with boldness to [the] throne of grace." Stansby discovered that Christ's death could break the power

---

1. Thomas Shepheard [Shepard], *The Sincere Convert, Discovering the Paucity of true Believers; and the great Difficultie of Saving Conversions* (London: by T. P. and M. S., 1643), 144.

of his sin as he began to live conscientiously in the fear of the Lord. Now, before the church, he confessed that he believed his nature had been changed because now, when sin rose in his heart he ran to the fountain of grace in Christ.[2]

In the last chapter, we reviewed the preparation doctrine of Thomas Hooker, one of the founding fathers of Puritan New England. In this chapter we will examine the teachings of his son-in-law, Thomas Shepard, a strong advocate of Hooker's position. We will then look at an English theologian whom Miller presented as a Calvinistic opponent of preparation. Then we will draw some conclusions about early New England views of preparation for conversion.

Thomas Shepard: Sound and Sincere Conversion

Thomas Shepard (1605–1649) was converted through the preaching of John Preston. He immigrated to New England in 1635. Four months later, he lost his wife to tuberculosis. Over the years, Shepard became known as an effective evangelist and a fervent supporter of missions to native Americans. He also helped establish Harvard College.

Shepard had listened to Thomas Hooker's preaching in the old world. He married one of Hooker's daughters after arriving in the new world. Shepard's books remained influential after his death. He was one of the authors most frequently quoted by Jonathan Edwards.

Shepard taught that although Christ did not come to save all men, He is offered to all who hear the gospel. Christ's priestly sacrifice and intercession save the elect; but as King, He commands every person to bow before Him and depend upon His grace.[3] Even if the sinner despises the means of grace, rejects grace, and plays the whore with God's rivals, the Lord still calls him to return to Him (Jer. 3:1).[4] Even if the sinner is not willing to receive Christ, Christ still offers Himself to the sinner (Matt. 23:37). Shepard asked, "Upon what conditions may Christ be had? Make an exchange of what thou art or hast with Christ" (Matt. 13:44).[5]

Shepard explained this process as a four-fold exchange:

2. Michael McGiffert, ed., *God's Plot: Puritan Spirituality in Thomas Shepard's Cambridge*, rev. ed. (Amherst: University of Massachusetts Press, 1994), 180–81.

3. Shepard, *The Sincere Convert*, 106–107.

4. Shepard, *The Sincere Convert*, 107 [pagination incorrect; actually page 109].

5. Shepard, *The Sincere Convert*, 111.

- Give Christ yourself and He will give you Himself.

- Give Christ your sins and He will take them on Himself.

- Give Christ your sweet pleasures and glory, and He will be your sweetness and glory.

- Give Christ the rags of your righteousness, and He will give you His righteousness.[6]

Despite the free offer of grace, sinners resist salvation with all their might. Shepard wrote, "Those that are saved, are saved with much difficulty.... It is a wonderful hard thing to be saved. The gate is strait [narrow], and therefore, a man must sweat and strive to enter; both the entrance is difficult, and the progress of salvation too."[7] Becoming a Christian and staying one to the end is hard. Shepard said we must pass through four strait gates to enter heaven: humiliation, faith, repentance, and overcoming the opposition of the devil, the world, and the flesh.[8]

Such is the "lamentable captivity of all men" that we must be redeemed by the price of Christ's blood to satisfy divine justice, and be indwelt by the power of Christ's Spirit to be rescued from Satan's prison.[9] Shepard accused the Socinians of denying salvation by price, and the Arminians, of denying salvation by power.[10]

Conviction, Compunction, Humiliation, and Faith
In the process of preparation, Shepard wrote, "God saveth none but first he humbleth them; now it is hard to pass through the gates and flames of hell, for a heart as stiff as a stake to bow, as hard as a stone to bleed." Humiliation is "not to mourn for one sin, but all sins, and not for a bit, but all a man's lifetime." It is not just to drop a tear at a sermon, but to have "a heart rent for sin, this is true humiliation, and this is hard."[11]

---

6. Shepard, *The Sincere Convert*, 112.
7. Shepard, *The Sincere Convert*, 144.
8. Shepard, *The Sincere Convert*, 146–48.
9. Thomas Shepard, *The Sound Beleever. Or, a Treatise of Evangelicall Conversion* (London: for R. Dawlman, 1645), 2.
10. Shepard, *The Sound Beleever*, 4.
11. Shepard, *The Sincere Convert*, 146. Cf. Richard Alan Humphrey, "The Concept of Conversion in the Theology of Thomas Shepard (1605–1649)" (PhD dissertation, Drew University, 1967), 185–206.

Shepard said the powerful work of Christ includes the following elements:

- Conviction to remedy ignorance of our misery,

- Compunction, or pain, to remedy our security and lack of a sense of our misery,

- Humiliation to remedy our self-confidence in our works, and

- Faith in Christ to remedy our presumptuous resting upon God's general mercy.[12]

Like Hooker before him, Shepard wrote that Christ is applied to us by faith, but "no man can or will come by faith to Christ to take away his sins, unless he first see, be convicted of, and loaded with them."[13] Shepard said, "The Lord Christ by his Spirit begins the actual deliverance of his elect" with "conviction of sin" (John 16:8–9).[14] In this, the Spirit makes use of the law, for "the main end of the law is to drive us to Christ."[15] "The Lord Jesus by his Spirit" does not reveal sin in a vague way but reveals a person's particular sins of nature, of each faculty, of each activity, and the coming wrath for them (Rom. 3:9–18; 4:15).[16] Shepard emphasized that Christ does this as part of His saving office. Though conviction is a "common mercy" and not a saving grace peculiar to the elect, nonetheless, "conviction is a work of the Spirit."[17] Therefore, Jones rightly says that Miller's thesis of expanded natural ability fails to indict Shepard, for Shepard "linked preparation wholly to the work of God's Spirit."[18]

Conviction of sin is not merely rational knowledge but "a clear, certain, and manifest light" that silences arguments with an intuitive vision of sin and death.[19] Sin becomes real by spiritually "beholding really the greatness of God [and then being] smitten by sin," Shepard said. "God comes in and appears immediately to the soul in his greatness and glory."[20] As a result conviction does not rest merely in the understanding

---

12. Shepard, *The Sound Beleever*, 4.
13. Shepard, *The Sound Beleever*, 4.
14. Shepard, *The Sound Beleever*, 6.
15. Shepard, *The Sound Beleever*, 8.
16. Shepard, *The Sound Beleever*, 9, 18.
17. Shepard, *The Sound Beleever*, 44.
18. Jones, "The Beginnings of American Theology," 250.
19. Shepard, *The Sound Beleever*, 23, 26.
20. Shepard, *The Sound Beleever*, 28.

but enters into the affections and will, producing "compunction" or piercing of the heart with a sense of sin (Acts 2:37).[21] Conviction lights a candle by which a man can see his sin; compunction burns his fingers and makes him dread the fire.[22] Compunction consists of fear, sorrow, and separation from sin.[23] It is not merely due to a natural fear arising from the conscience but to "supernatural arrows shot into the conscience by the arm of the Spirit."[24] It is not just something due to God's "moral" persuasion but is a true, physical action.[25] Thus, while conviction and compunction do not introduce supernatural graces such as faith or love *into* the soul, they are supernatural acts *upon* the soul. "This compunction or sense of misery is wrought by the Spirit of Christ, not the power of man to prepare himself for further grace."[26] Compunction goes beyond the anticipation of torment and anguish to actually feel the evil of separation from God, like lost sheep (Luke 19:10). Upon regeneration, this compunction will become the grief of wronging God.[27]

Effectual Preparation and Contentment to Be Damned
Like Hooker, Shepard said there was an intermediate act of grace given to the elect alone that precedes regeneration. In this act God cuts off a branch from the tree of Adam before grafting it into the tree of Christ.[28] He said that the divine work of bringing the elect into union with Christ consists of two parts, first, being cut off from the wild olive tree, the old Adam; and second, being engrafted into the good olive tree, the second Adam. "The first must go before the second; for where there is perfect resistance, there can be no perfect union. But take a man growing upon his old root of nature, there is nothing but perfect resistance (Rom. 8:7) and therefore that resistance must first be taken away, before the Lord draws the soul to Christ, and by faith implants it into Christ.[29]

Shepard did not regard this as a crucial point in the doctrine of preparation. He recognized that many holy and learned men thought "there

---

21. Shepard, *The Sound Beleever*, 45.
22. Shepard, *The Sound Beleever*, 57.
23. Shepard, *The Sound Beleever*, 65.
24. Shepard, *The Sound Beleever*, 69.
25. Shepard, *The Sound Beleever*, 88–89.
26. Shepard, *The Sound Beleever*, 98.
27. Shepard, *The Sound Beleever*, 91.
28. Shepard, *The Sound Beleever*, 99, 115.
29. Shepard, *The Sound Beleever*, 101.

is no such special work of the Spirit as separates the soul from sin before it comes unto Christ, but that this is done after the soul is in Christ by faith, viz. in sanctification, being first justified by faith."[30] Shepard said all believed that the Holy Spirit works in sinners a sense of the misery of sin. This effectively drives the elect to Christ but does not save the reprobate. Shepard went on to say there is in the elect a "farther stroke of severing the soul from sin, conjoined with the terrors and sorrows [before their closing with Christ], which is not evident in the reprobate."[31]

Shepard cited the Reformed scholastic doctrines of grace found in Paulus Ferrius's *Scholastici Orthodoxi Specimen* (1616) and William Pemble's *Vindiciae Gratiae* (1627) to demonstrate that his view was consistent with orthodox views of grace.[32] He defended his doctrine at some length, laying out the following *ordo salutis:* common preparatory sorrows, the special grace of cutting off the old man, grafting into Christ by faith (calling), justification, and sanctification.[33]

However, Shepard did not appear to be comfortable with Hooker's language of "saving" preparation. He wrote, "Trouble me no more therefore in asking… whether there is any saving work before union? I answer, No, for what is said is one necessary ingredient to the working up of our union, as cutting off the branch from the old stock, is necessary to the ingrafting it into the new; indeed, 'without faith it is impossible to please God' [Heb. 11:6]."[34]

Shepard propagated Hooker's doctrine of humiliation up to the point of contentment to be damned. He wrote, "Be not careless whether the Lord help or no, but be humble, not to quarrel in case he should not."[35] If it was arrogant for a beggar to quarrel with a man for not giving him great treasures of gold, then it is far more arrogant for a sinner to murmur at God for not giving him the unsearchable riches of Christ.[36] Shepard said some people may not yet have come to peace of conscience because "they never came to be quieted with God's will, in case they think they shall never partake of his love: but are above that, oppose and resist and

---

30. Shepard, *The Sound Beleever,* 97.
31. Shepard, *The Sound Beleever,* 98.
32. Shepard, *The Sound Beleever,* 98, 100, 105, 107.
33. Shepard, *The Sound Beleever,* 97–116.
34. Shepard, *The Sound Beleever,* 115.
35. Shepard, *The Sound Beleever,* 147.
36. Shepard, *The Sound Beleever,* 148–49.

quarrel with that, unhumbled under that; the Lord therefore intending to bestow his favor only upon humbled sinners, he will therefore hide his face until they lie low, and acknowledge themselves worthy of nothing but extremity of misery; unworthy of the least mercy."[37]

Preparatory Preaching to the Lost

Though Shepard regarded preparation as the sovereign work of God, that did not stop him from calling on the unconverted to act. Shepard wanted them to wake up. He said, "Awaken therefore all you secure creatures; feel your misery, that so you may get out of it."[38] "What? No sigh, no tears?" he exclaimed, "Canst thou carry all thy sins upon thy back, like Samson the gates of the city, and make a light matter of them?... Oh get thine heart to lament and mourn under thy miseries, who knows then but the Lord may pity thee."[39] He called upon the ministers of Christ to "co-work with Christ" by faithfully preaching sin and judgment to their congregants.[40]

An unconverted person can be affected with a sense of his misery, Shepard said, by first taking a good look at his own sin and God's wrath against it (to destroy false hope), then, second, to look at "the Lord's readiness and willingness to receive thee yet unto mercy" (to avoid hopelessness).[41] He said, "Bring thy soul to the light; desire the Lord in prayer.... Set the glass [mirror] of God's law before thee, look up in the ministry of the word unto the Lord, and say, Oh Lord search me."[42] Yet Shepard also warned people against finding peace by relying upon "humiliations, repenting, tears, sorrows, and confessions" by "making these things their God and their Christ."[43] If we refuse to come to Christ because we think we are not humble enough, we are showing pride in our humiliation—as if we could be worthy.[44] Humiliation is not an end to itself, Shepard said. It must drive us to Christ so that He saves us.

Therefore we should not prescribe how much conviction and grief a sinner needs, for God works variously in each one of His elect.[45] Shepard

---

37. Shepard, *The Sound Beleever*, 154.
38. Shepard, *The Sincere Convert*, 224.
39. Shepard, *The Sincere Convert*, 224.
40. Shepard, *The Sound Beleever*, 34.
41. Shepard, *The Sincere Convert*, 225.
42. Shepard, *The Sound Beleever*, 39.
43. Shepard, *The Sincere Convert*, 238–39.
44. Shepard, *The Sound Beleever*, 86.
45. Shepard, *The Sound Beleever*, 5, 32, 48–52, 79.

also acknowledged that God can work in an "unusual and extraordinary way" apart from humiliation. He said, "A man may be converted only by the gospel, and God may let in sweetness and joy without any sense of sin or misery, and in my experience I have found it so."[46] But these cautions may have been swallowed up by Shepard's thundering proclamation of soul-shaking convictions and fears as the usual manner of God's working. He believed that denying the doctrine of preparation undermined the gospel. He declared, "Mark those men that deny the use of the law to lead unto Christ, if they do not fall in time to oppose some main point of the gospel."[47]

Shepard's remark may have hinted at a division within English Reformed Christendom. Miller apparently thought so. To explore this question further, we must turn our attention now to an English theologian reputed for his defense of salvation by sovereign grace.

William Pemble: Grace and Preparation

William Pemble (c. 1591–1623) was a teacher of divinity at Magdalen Hall in Oxford. He has sometimes been called a "high Calvinist" or even "hyper-Calvinist," especially because of his teaching in *Vindiciae Gratiae* (1627) that justification precedes faith.[48] Nevertheless Pemble was highly respected by the Puritans for his scholarly defense of Reformation doctrine. Miller said that Pemble criticized Hooker for counting as preparation actions that could not be done by the unregenerate, though Pemble did not mention Hooker by name.[49] Miller said, "Hooker's line smelled to him of sophistical Arminianism"; these were not preparations but fruits of conversion, "and instead of elevating natural abilities, he was cheapening grace."[50] If that is true, it would confirm the thesis that the Puritan doctrine of preparation for grace undermined the Reformed doctrines of total inability and salvation by grace alone. In this section, we will examine Pemble's teachings, particularly in response to Hooker, and by implication, to Shepard.

---

46. Shepard, *The Sound Beleever*, 48.

47. Shepard, *The Sound Beleever*, 96.

48. William Pemble, *Vindiciae Gratiae*, in *The Workes of the Late Learned Minister of God's Holy Word, Mr William Pemble*, 4th ed. (Oxford: by Henry Hall for John Adams, 1659), 24.

49. Miller, "'Preparation for Salvation' in New England," 266.

50. Miller, *The New England Mind: From Colony to Province*, 57.

Pemble admitted that conversion is shrouded in such profound mystery that the saved must say, "Only one thing we know, that we were blind, but now we see" (cf. John 9:25).[51] Yet Pemble was also certain that conversion and the implanting of holiness and faith is entirely of God's grace without the least contribution from fallen human nature.[52] The converted person must confess "that it is impossible there should be in and of himself such preparations and forward dispositions to work his own conversion."[53] Pemble also opposed the Arminian teaching that God promised to bestow grace on those who are better prepared for the gospel by their proper use of the "natural light" of reason, since the wise of this world often reject the gospel as foolishness. Pemble considered this Arminian idea another form of the Roman Catholic doctrine of "preparatory merits of congruity, preceding the gift of grace."[54]

At first it seems that Pemble opposed all ideas of preparation, but a further look reveals that he made a strong distinction between preparation and conversion, saying the former cannot produce the latter. He said, "Civility is a hopeful preparation, but no working cause of sanctity."[55] No degree of preparation in natural man has the power to produce the spiritual holiness of conversion. Yet Pemble did say that someone who has the preparation of a Christian education so that "the violence of corruption is somewhat broken in him…is not far from the kingdom of God…according to the usual course of God's working" (cf. Mark 12:34).[56]

Hooker would have heartily agreed with this approach. Though there is a marked contrast between the emphases of Hooker's works on preparation and Pemble's treatise on *sola gratia*, they both believed in both the reality of preparation for conversion and the inability of the prepared to save themselves.

Pemble also opposed the Arminian notion that "the affections may be *excitati*, stirred up and quickened with true love of goodness and hatred of evil, before such time as a man be converted."[57] The key phrase here is

---

51. Pemble, *Vindiciae Gratiae*, 26.
52. Pemble, *Vindiciae Gratiae*, 27–29.
53. Pemble, *Vindiciae Gratiae*, 29. On this page Pemble did state that *after* the first divine act of conversion man has an "actual concurrence with the Spirit of God" to move himself to perform spiritual duties, being now inwardly moved by the Spirit.
54. Pemble, *Vindiciae Gratiae*, 56.
55. Pemble, *Vindiciae Gratiae*, 30.
56. Pemble, *Vindiciae Gratiae*, 30.
57. Pemble, *Vindiciae Gratiae*, 75.

true love, for Pemble believed that biblical truths could stir the affections of an unconverted man but not with true holiness prior to regeneration. Note the distinction Pemble made in the following statement:

> The Arminians give a very large allowance of grace to an unregener-
> ate man, and they tell us, that besides a knowledge of sin, a sorrow
> for it in regard of punishment, a fear of God's wrath, and desire to
> be free from it (all which we confess may be in a man unregenerate),
> besides these, there are, say they, in such a one, a deploring of his
> spiritual death in sin, and utter impotency to do any good, a grief for
> the offending of the divine Majesty, a desire of grace and the Spirit of
> regeneration to be given him, a hungering and thirsting after righ-
> teousness and life; in brief, an unregenerate man may offer to God
> the sacrifice of a contrite and broken heart.[58]

It is striking that even this committed Calvinist could acknowledge that the unregenerate may experience knowledge of sin, sorrow over its consequences, and long for salvation. Pemble's point was to question not whether such preparation precedes conversion, but only whether such preparation may include true spiritual contrition and hunger after righteousness. In other words, the dispute was not about the reality of preparation but its spiritual content.

Pemble wrote, "We deny not, but that there are ordinarily many preparations whereby God brings a man to grace, and that the Word works many effects both upon the hearts and lives of men even whilst they are as yet destitute of true grace."[59] He included in "the antecedent preparations to bring men unto conversion" both outward actions, such as attending church and meditation on Scripture; and inward acts, such as knowing God's revealed will; sensing sin in the conscience; fear, hor-ror, and grief over God's punishment; desiring liberty; and a small hope and even joy in the possibility of salvation because of the general prom-ises of the gospel.[60]

Pemble said such works of preparation are "good and necessary."[61] The unconverted sinner's inability to perform spiritual duties with the right love of God must not stop him from doing what he can. Pemble

---

58. Pemble, *Vindiciae Gratiae*, 76.
59. Pemble, *Vindiciae Gratiae*, 78.
60. Pemble, *Vindiciae Gratiae*, 81.
61. Pemble, *Vindiciae Gratiae*, 81.

wrote, "Ministers then are to urge upon all men indifferently the necessity of all Christian endeavors tending to their conversion; and hearers are not to balk God's commands upon pretences of their own sinful abilities: God must be obeyed as far as we can go."[62]

However, he refuted the Arminian contention that men may grieve about displeasing God while they are still His enemies, or love God without being born of God. Determining the exact nature of a person's desires was difficult. A desire for salvation could be motivated by mere self-love, and not love for God. William Perkins had said, however, that the desire to come to Christ was an early sign of true justifying faith.[63] Pemble said the most skillful divines taught "that he who truly desires grace, hath true grace." He was perhaps alluding to Perkins.[64] As we saw earlier, Hooker agreed with Rogers that spiritual hunger and thirst could be indications of regeneration.[65]

It does not seem likely that Miller was right in saying that Pemble had Hooker in his sights when he wrote *Vindiciae Gratiae*, because, first, Pemble identified his adversaries in this matter as Arminius and Arminians. He was not critiquing Reformed ministers whom he thought were undermining their theological heritage but those who were outside the Reformed camp.

Second, the historical order of books by these authors raises questions. Pemble's book was published in 1627, two years prior to Hooker's first book, *The Poor Doubting Christian*, and five years before *The Soul's Preparation for Christ*. It is possible that Pemble was acquainted with Hooker's preaching, for the latter had a significant ministry in England before departing for the Netherlands, then to the New World. But Hooker's ministry through books had not yet begun.

Third, Thomas Shepard, Thomas Hooker's son-in-law, cited the *Vindiciae Gratiae* of the "blessed and learned Pemble" to support an aspect of Shepard's own doctrine of preparation.[66] So obviously Shepard, a university-educated scholar, did not regard Pemble as an opponent of preparation. Rather, he believed Pemble's theology supported this doctrine.

---

62. Pemble, *Vindiciae Gratiae*, 82.
63. Perkins, *Cases of Conscience*, 15.
64. Pemble, *Vindiciae Gratiae*, 77.
65. Rogers, *The Doctrine of Faith*, 175. See Hooker's preface in "To the Reader."
66. Shepard, *The Sound Beleever*, 105.

Fourth, Pemble believed in the preparation of the unconverted man through teachings and terrors. He commended the preaching of preparation in terms that Hooker would have applauded. In the end, this supposed critic of preparation proves to be one of its advocates and a staunch champion of sovereign grace. Pemble's case therefore militates against the thesis that preparation was a significant departure from Calvin's doctrine of predestination.

Concluding Observations on Early New England Preparation

As a founding father of New England, Thomas Hooker had enormous influence on succeeding generations. He was also well respected in England. True to the Reformed heritage rooted in Calvin and others, Hooker taught preparation as one part in the big picture of God's sovereign grace to sinners. Though he frequently exhorted the lost to seek salvation by meditating deeply on their sins (more than most Puritans did), he also taught them that any step that took them closer to the kingdom resulted from Christ knocking at the door of their hearts. Preparation was due not to natural man seeking God but to God's Spirit pursuing fallen man.

Miller presented William Pemble as *prima facie* evidence that faithful Calvinists opposed Hooker's doctrine of preparation, but we have found that Pemble himself advocated a kind of Reformed preparation. Rather than critiquing Hooker, Pemble attacked Roman Catholic and Arminian concepts of preparation. Thus the theory that Pemble, a Reformed teacher at Oxford, had launched a missile of protest across the Atlantic Ocean at perceived semi-Arminians in New England proves to be a fiction of historiography.

Hooker said that the Spirit prepares sinners for salvation by working contrition and humiliation in them. He said that this contrition consisted of a sight of sin, a sense of sin, and a separation from sin. While insisting that separation from sin does not include true sanctification of the soul, Hooker did at least speculate that cutting the soul off from sin precedes its implanting in Christ. That left his readers with questions regarding a possible intermediate state between spiritual death and life. Yet Hooker also acknowledged that we cannot easily discern when faith is born in the soul. So his innovative view of unregenerate sinners being cut off from sin was somewhat balanced by the practical mystery that sinners may be born again earlier in the process than they realize.

Humiliation begins with man's efforts to save himself, then moves into despairing of the possibility of self-salvation, then finally brings the sinner to quiet submission before God. Hooker's only novelty was to posit that at this point sinners had to become content to be damned by God. This idea was rejected by the majority of Puritans, particularly those who thought it reflected Roman Catholic mysticism.

Still, the charge that Hooker was a closet Arminian is not well grounded. He operated within the Reformed system of thought, in which duty does not imply ability, and the means of grace, such as preaching the Word, are instruments that God uses to give spiritual life to dead sinners even as the preacher calls them to believe. Furthermore, Hooker said that unconverted sinners had the same moral sensibilities that Calvin said existed in the pagan world. Nor was Hooker a legalist. Though the law was at the forefront of his doctrine of preparation, it functioned as a tool in the hand of Christ to beat the bushes and drive sinners out of hiding so they might hide themselves in Christ's grace. Christ prepares His people in a process that varies as to time and intensity. Hooker did not say that to be converted everyone must pass through a prescribed experience for a set length of time.

Similarly, Thomas Shepard taught that Christ not only purchased redemption but applies it to His elect by powerful works upon their souls. This involves imparting the spiritual sight of sin and judgment in the light of God's glory, instilling heart-felt grief and fear, and effecting separation from sin in one's affections. Although the law plays a significant role in this process, its purpose is not to reinforce our natural legalism but, rather, to bring us to contrition and humiliation through the grace of Jesus Christ. Christ seeks the lost to save them. In preparation, a sinner does not work himself up to the door of heaven, rather, the Savior clears and plows the field of a man's heart so that He may plant the living seed of faith in it.

Goode says that these Puritans, like other orthodox Reformed theologians, believed that God's sovereign grace and man's responsibility happily coexisted. In preparation for faith, the Puritans saw divine and human activity intertwining by (1) rejecting any concept of merit in preparatory works, (2) asserting God's initiative in every aspect of the process, and (3) explaining the divine purpose in preparation, namely, that by striving after salvation men would learn how impotent they are to actually reach up to God.[67] Therefore preparation for conversion prepared men to be saved by grace alone, not by their own works.

Puritan preparation in general did not move towards Arminianism but was a practical refutation of it. Goode explains, "Because the Puritans designed preparation to teach a lesson about self-justification, the language of the preparationists had the look and feel of Arminianism. Preparationists were telling prospective Christians, 'So, you think that you can get right with God? Go ahead! See how many rungs of the ladder you can climb.' All the while preparationists knew that the only thing a candidate could really do was to yearn to climb the ladder. No unjustified sinner could even achieve the first rung…. Once individuals understood how bereft of merit they were, they would cry out to God for grace."[68]

The ladder metaphor is helpful as long as we see that it refers to more than just using the means of grace or thinking about God and sin, which the unconverted can do. The ladder thus refers to steps of trusting, hoping in, and loving God. Pressing on men their duty to ascend this ladder is intended only to frustrate them with the powerlessness of their paralysis. Thus, when the Lord Jesus was asked, "What must I do to inherit eternal life?" He directed the inquirer to the demands of God's law for perfect love. He said, "This do, and thou shalt live" (Luke 10:25–28). Christ was not a legalist. He wisely employed a strategy to expose the wickedness and inability of his inquirer to choose God. Goode concludes by saying, "Preparationism was a means to advance Calvinistic orthodoxy, not a means to attack it."[69] Preparation teaches sinners by experience that Arminianism is false, for sinners cannot turn from sin to Christ unless God raises them from the dead.

The formulations of preparation by Hooker and Shepard are not above criticism, however. Packer offers this assessment of these early New England theologians:

- "First, they gave the impression (despite parenthetical disclaimers) that God's work of humbling men for sin invariably followed the same course, in every detail of the process, and if you had not experienced it all you must be a stranger to true grace."

---

67. Goode, "Propagating the Gospel in Early Puritan New England," 235, 239.
68. Goode, "Propagating the Gospel in Early Puritan New England," 242–43.
69. Goode, "Propagating the Gospel in Early Puritan New England," 243.

- "Second, Hooker and Shepard went beyond Scripture in teaching that the sign of true humiliation for sin was that the sinner, acknowledging his guilt, should be content to be damned for the glory of God."

- "Third, by concentrating attention on this preliminary work of grace, and harping on the need for it to be done thoroughly, these writers effectively discouraged seeking souls from going straight to Christ in their despair."[70]

As we continue this study, we will see that the Puritans also criticized one another, resulting in a more balanced expression of the doctrine of preparation. In addition to the objections raised by Packer, the Puritans questioned the possibility of "saving sorrow" prior to faith, asking such questions as, Is there some way of cutting the elect away from the old man prior to regeneration? Winship says that this view, though advocated by Hooker and Shepard and the very popular early Puritan preacher John Rogers, was not the view of most Puritans. He says, "Puritans on both sides of the Atlantic, if they even raised the issue of preparation's having a middle stage between faith and unregenerate nature, generally rejected that argument."[71] In this they may have been influenced by Ames, who said that preparation does not posit a "middle state" between spiritual life and death.[72] In any case, this would not result in a debate over the validity of preparation itself, for the orthodox divines agreed that the Spirit must work a supernatural sense of misery in the elect sinner to drive him to Christ.[73] Rather, the Puritans debated the precise nature of the operations of the Spirit in preparation.

The rigorous preaching of preparation in New England tended to be balanced by the pastors' gracious care of anxious sinners. In practice, Hooker and Shepard did not demand deep, protracted experiences of conversion. Many people came to salvation under Hooker's preaching. Cotton Mather said of Hooker's ministry in England, "Hereby there was a great reformation wrought, not only in the town, but in the adjacent

---

70. Packer, *Quest for Godliness*, 172.
71. Winship, *Making Heretics*, 70, 269n18.
72. Ames, "The Preparation of a Sinner for Conversion," thesis 17, objection 5.
73. Shepard, *The Sound Beleever*, 98.

country, from all parts whereof they came to hear the wisdom of the Lord Jesus Christ, in his gospel."[74]

Pettit says Hooker required candidates for church membership to give an account of their conversion only if they were willing to do so. He says that in actual practice, Hooker said that "if a man could give 'a reason of his hope towards God,' this casts the cause, with judicious charity, to hope and believe there is something of God and grace in the soul."[75]

As for Shepard, we have a rather full record of many conversion accounts ("relations") of members whom he and his church received into full communion.[76] Those accounts, for the most part, show that sinners were brought to a moderate degree of conviction of sin that resulted in a longing for Christ and a desire to live for His glory. The accounts demonstrate there were many ups and downs in people's quest for conversion and assurance. But the converts whom Shepard's church accepted as members were not required to demonstrate a hell-on-earth depth of humiliation nor a minutely prescribed pattern of experiences. Rodger Payne writes, "The relations exhibit only a general adherence to the detailed morphologies of conversion worked out by the theologians. None of the existing relations attempted to communicate an experience that fully demonstrated a systematic morphology."[77] Therefore we doubt that Shepard "enforced strict admissions" (in Pettit's words), at least with respect to strict adherence to a morphology of conversion, or a specified level of intensity of experience.[78]

Patricia Caldwell relates the conversion narrative of a maid who was converted during this time: "Her narrative, though brief, is thickly woven with Bible quotations ranging from Psalms to St. John and calling especially on the Old Testament prophets (not only Isaiah and Jeremiah but also Hosea and Zephaniah), giving the reader an impression not so much of being marched through a morphology as of being led through

---

74. Mather, *Magnalia Christi Americana*, 3:59.

75. Pettit, *The Heart Prepared*, 100.

76. McGiffert, ed., *God's Plot*, 149–225. See also George Selement and Bruce C. Woolley, eds., *Thomas Shepard's Confessions* (Boston: The Colonial Society of Massachusetts, 1981).

77. Rodger M. Payne, "'When the Times of Refreshing Shall Come': Interpreting American Protestant Narratives of Conversion, 1630–1830" (PhD Dissertation, University of Virginia, 1989), 134.

78. Pettit, *The Heart Prepared*, 101.

the Bible."[79] Caldwell notes that the narratives of Shepard's membership interviews quoted the Bible 544 times, an average of 11 per person, drawing upon 52 of the 66 biblical books.[80] That does not suggest superficial conformity to a prescribed pattern of experiences but rather a heart's reliance on the Scriptures to the degree that Scripture provided the language of personal experience of conversion as "seen through a biblical lens."[81]

The theology of preparation made quite an impression on New England Puritans. Many who sought church membership did not testify of their own experiences along precise lines, and some were anxious about not doing so, but these people were still welcomed into the church, showing that the Puritan understanding of preparation and conversion was more flexible than their doctrine might suggest. Similarly, Cotton said that the New England churches accepted as members those with "the least measure of breathing and panting after Christ, in their sensible feeling of a lost estate."[82] The order and structure of preparatory teaching was intended for pedagogical clarity, not experiential rigidity.

---

79. Patricia Caldwell, *The Puritan Conversion Narrative* (Cambridge: Cambridge University Press, 1983), 168–69.

80. Caldwell, *The Puritan Conversion Narrative*, 171.

81. Caldwell, *The Puritan Conversion Narrative*, 177.

82. John Cotton, *The Way of the Churches of Christ in New England* (London: 1645), 58; quoted by Baird Tipson, "Invisible Saints: The 'Judgment of Charity' in the Early New England Churches," *Church History* 44, no. 4 (Dec. 1975): 468.

CHAPTER SEVEN

Preparation and the Antinomian Controversy: John Cotton

It is the usual manner of God to give a covenant of grace by leading men first into a covenant of works.

—John Cotton[1]

Puritans who advocated preparation also spoke of the dangers of going too far with the doctrine. Richard Sibbes warned preachers, "It is dangerous (I confess) in some cases with some spirits, to press too much, and too long this bruising; because they may die under the wound and burden, before they be raised up again. Therefore it is good in mixed assemblies to mingle comforts, that every soul may have its due portion."[2] Preston wrote, "A man cannot have too much faith, or repentance, or love," but he can experience an unhealthy degree of humiliation (2 Cor. 2:7).[3]

However, some scholars have argued there was some controversy among the Puritans over the legitimacy of preparation, not just its degree. The Antinomian Controversy that threatened to split New England has been depicted as a battle between covenantal preparationists and the Calvinistic purist John Cotton. Therefore, let us now discuss one of the most controversial figures of early New England, John Cotton.

John Cotton (1584–1652) once secretly rejoiced at the death of William Perkins because Perkins's preaching had laid siege to his heart. But Cotton was later converted through the ministry of Sibbes. After serving for twenty-one years as the pastor of St. Botolph's Church in Boston,

---

1. John Cotton, *The New Covenant, Or, A Treatise, unfolding the order and manner of the giving and receiving of the Covenant of Grace to the Elect* (London: by M. S. for Francis Eglesfield and John Allen, 1654), 21.

2. Sibbes, *The Brvised Reede and Smoaking Flax*, 37.

3. Preston, "Pavls Conversion," in *Remaines*, 191.

England, efforts to prosecute him for nonconformity compelled him to move to Boston in New England in 1633. Controversy awaited him there.

The Antinomian Controversy (1636–1638) has attracted an enormous amount of scholarly attention.[4] Antinomianism refers to the idea that a Christian is released by Christ from the necessity of obeying God's law as a rule of conduct. It so emphasizes the union of Christians with Christ and His Spirit that it effectively negates human effort and obedience. At the center of the storm in the 1600s was Anne Hutchinson (1591–1643), who, according to Miller, rejected preparation for conversion entirely as a "covenant of works." She also insisted that works cannot function as evidence of justification.[5] Hutchinson appealed to Cotton as one of the few preachers of free grace in New England. Let us take a closer look at Cotton's doctrine as we continue to test Miller's interpretation of preparation.

Cotton is one of the most enigmatic figures in Puritan New England. Even his own contemporaries had difficulty understanding where he stood on certain issues. He was a powerful and influential preacher and a preeminent defender of Puritanism, yet antinomian mystics claimed Cotton's teachings as their own. It should not surprise us, then, that he has prompted conflicting interpretations among modern scholars. While we do not claim to answer all the questions surrounding Cotton, we do believe that a careful reading of his writings reveals that he was neither antinomian nor anti-preparation. At the same time, we acknowledge that Cotton made statements that are difficult to understand. A careful examination of these statements in their context can help clarify his meaning.

---

4. See *The Antinomian Controversy, 1636–1638: A Documentary History*, ed. David D. Hall (Durham: Duke University Press, 1990); Emery Battis, *Saints and Sectaries: Anne Hutchinson and the Antinomian Controversy in the Massachusetts Bay Colony* (Chapel Hill: University of North Carolina Press, 1962); Theodore D. Bozeman, *The Precisianist Strain: Disciplinary Religion and Antinomian Backlash in Puritanism to 1638* (Chapel Hill: University of North Carolina Press, 2004); Donald R. Come, "John Cotton: Guide of the Chosen People" (PhD Dissertation, Princeton University, 1948); Philip F. Gura, *A Glimpse of Sion's Glory: Puritan Radicalism in New England, 1620–1660* (Middletown: Wesleyan University Press, 1984); Janice Knight, *Orthodoxies in Massachusetts: Rereading American Puritanism* (Cambridge: Harvard University Press, 1994); Amanda Porterfield, *Female Piety in Puritan New England: The Emergence of Religious Humanism* (Oxford: Oxford University Press, 1992), 95–106; Selma R. Williams, *Divine Rebel: The Life of Anne Marbury Hutchinson* (New York: Holt, Rinehart, and Winston, 1981); Michael P. Winship, *Making Heretics: Militant Protestantism and Free Grace in Massachusetts, 1636–1641* (Princeton: Princeton University Press, 2002).

5. Miller, "'Preparation for Salvation' in New England," 268–69.

John Cotton and the Use of the Law

He who has the Son has life (1 John 5:12), Cotton said, and part of having the Son is worshiping Him as our God by obeying all the commandments of God.[6] To have the Son is to be united with Him by His Spirit dwelling in us. This Spirit works in us to conform us to the Son in His graces, and to liberate us from the reigning power of sin.[7] Theodore Bozemen says that while Cotton was a minister in England, he considered holy obedience a sign that a person was justified by faith.[8] However, later in New England, Cotton qualified sanctification as a sign of true conversion. He wrote, "I would not wish Christians to build the signs of their adoption upon any sanctification, but such as floweth from faith in Christ Jesus."[9] In other words, works that do not proceed from faith are sin; such works could not therefore be any part of our sanctification. Nevertheless, Cotton wrote, "Christ hath as it were revived Moses; but as the law given by Christ is not a covenant of works, but a commandment of well-doing; and he having given it, we take ourselves to be bound to be subject unto it."[10]

Cotton also urged ministers to preach the demands of the law to unbelievers. He said, "There is a generation of preachers that would now have no law preached, but now only to draw men on to Christ, by the love of Christ. It is true, this we should labor to do, but how must we do it? Do you think God will marry us to Christ, before our first husband be dead? Unless the sinful hearts of men be pricked, unless the proud, wanton, and stubborn heart be pierced and wounded to the death?"[11] Cotton thus applied the law to men both before and after conversion. He said ministers should preach against particular sins, showing how these sins are offenses against God's greatness and goodness, to pierce the hearts of sinners.[12]

Janice Knight contrasts the stern views of most New England ministers regarding sin with those of Cotton, arguing that Cotton "consistently

6. John Cotton, *Christ the Fountaine of Life* (1651; facsimile repr., New York: Arno Press, 1972), 1, 6, 12.

7. Cotton, *Christ the Fountaine of Life*, 58–60, 67.

8. Bozeman, *The Precisianist Strain*, 218–21.

9. Sargent Bush, Jr., ed., *The Correspondence of John Cotton* (Chapel Hill: University of North Carolina Press, 2001), 232.

10. Cotton, *The New Covenant*, 117.

11. John Cotton, *The Way of Life, Or, Gods VVay and Course, in Bringing the Soule into, and keeping it in, and carrying it on, in the ways of life and peace* (London: by M. F. for L. Fawne and S. Gellibrand, 1641), 134.

12. Cotton, *The Way of Life*, 162.

modified" the common depiction of the sinner as a "vile creature" or "a filthy rag" and instead portrayed the unconverted person as an errant child or hopeful bride waiting for Christ.[13] This contrast is misleading, however, for Cotton compared sin to mire, dirt, vomit, scum, a dead carcass, a menstrual cloth, and dung—all biblical metaphors (Isa. 57:20; 2 Peter 2:22; Ezek. 24:6; Jer. 16:18; Isa. 64:6; Ps. 83:10).[14] Given the evil of sin but man's general blindness to it, Cotton wrote, "Hence we see a necessity laid on ministers to preach the law; or else how shall people see their sins?"[15] Cotton's writings reveal that he had a strong view of the law as both the moral guide of believers and the mirror that shows unbelievers their moral filth.

John Cotton, the Lone New England Calvinist?

Miller says Cotton opposed New England's doctrine of preparation. He wrote, "The majority of New England divines followed Hooker, but there was one ominous exception, John Cotton."[16] Miller portrayed Cotton as a faithful Calvinist who said that only divine grace could bridge the vast gulf between the state of lost mankind and the state of the regenerate. Cotton said a blind man cannot prepare himself to see, so the first motions of our souls towards Christ indicate a spiritual union that already exists between Him and us. Because of this, Miller said Cotton was "the better Calvinist" than Hooker.[17] A careful examination of the sources does not support Miller's thesis at any point, however.

Here is the "blind man" statement that Miller quoted, as it appeared in its immediate context:

> Use 1. To reprove the Papists of their merit *ex congruo*; they say when men are converted, they are prepared for it, by some good fore-going works, some merit of congruity, for which God shows them mercy: but what preparation is there in a blind man to see, or in an ignorant man to understand? Here are men as much unprepared for mercy, as

13. Knight, *Orthodoxies in Massachusetts*, 20–21.
14. John Cotton, *An Exposition of First John* (Evansville, Ind.: Sovereign Grace Publishers, 1962), 60.
15. Cotton, *Exposition of First John*, 55.
16. Miller, "'Preparation for Salvation' in New England," 266.
17. Miller, "'Preparation for Salvation' in New England," 267.

ever you knew any, scorned Christ, made themselves merry to pour
contempt upon the apostles' gifts, yet came to have pricked hearts.[18]

Let us observe that, first, Cotton was not attacking the Puritan doctrine of preparation but the Papist doctrine of merit. The word *preparation*
here does not refer to Hooker's view but to the preparationism of Roman
Catholicism. We do not agree with Michael Winship's statement that,
"When pushed and angry enough, Cotton could work himself into considering Hooker and Shepard's doctrine as not only wrong but papist."[19]
Perhaps Winship misunderstood Cotton's statement that, "To take a
man's sanctification, for an evident cause or ground of his justification, is
flat Popery."[20] Cotton is not criticizing his fellow Puritans here for using
the fruits of sanctification as evidence for justification, for the Puritans all
believed that sanctification was not a "cause" of justification. Thus prior to
and after this statement, Cotton wrote, "It is granted of all hands.... Thus
far we consent."[21] Cotton's rejection of Roman Catholic preparationism
was not an indictment of Hooker and Shepard's views on preparation;
rather, for the most part, it was a position he shared with them.

Second, the doctrine that Cotton reproved was that God gave saving
grace to men who first did good works. Late medieval scholastic theology
had taught that prior to regeneration, a man in a purely natural condition
could do works of "congruent merit" (*meritum de congruo*). This type of
merit was not by itself sufficient for salvation, but it did make the recipi-
ent worthy of grace by doing the best they could in their natural ability.[22]
Hooker refuted this idea, saying that in fact God prepared men for salvation by showing them they could do nothing meritorious.

Third, Cotton argued that unregenerate man could not do works of congruent merit because under the work of the Spirit, they went from being
scorners to having "pricked hearts." In other words, they did not go from
performing good works to trusting Christ, but went from being proud, hard-
hearted sinners to being pierced, broken-hearted sinners. That is precisely
what Hooker taught about preparation. Cotton did not oppose Reformed
preparation but used it as a weapon against Roman Catholic preparation.

---

18. Cotton, *The Way of Life,* 182.
19. Winship, *Making Heretics,* 71.
20. Hall, ed., *The Antinomian Controversy,* 177. Winship references but does not quote
this text in his footnote with respect to this point (*Making Heretics,* 270n26).
21. Hall, ed., *The Antinomian Controversy,* 177–78.
22. Muller, *Dictionary of Latin and Greek Theological Terms,* 191–92.

A few pages earlier in the same treatise, Cotton answers the question, "What preparation is there in a blind man to see?" by urging the following duties: "First, hearken to the word of God (Prov. 2:1) and your souls shall live (Isa. 55:2–3).... Second, apply the word unto your hearts.... Third, cry after wisdom (Prov. 2:3), that is, pray heartily to God, mourn before him.... The blind man cried after our Savior (Mark 10:51), and though the people rebuked him, yet he cried till he received sight.... Fourth, seek after knowledge as for hidden treasure (Prov. 2:4)."[23]

Cotton's conclusion was that the blind man cannot prepare himself by good works, but should cry out to the Savior to heal his blindness. That sounds very much like Reformed preparation. Therefore we must disagree with Pettit, who wrote, "Unlike Calvin, Cotton carried his doctrine to such an extreme that he was unable even to accept the divine exhortations to preparation as 'useful.'"[24]

Miller also offered other evidence of Cotton's alleged opposition to preparatory grace. Seven years after the trial of Ann Hutchinson, Francis Cornwell published an account of Cotton's response to other New England divines. This account was quite popular; it was printed in three editions in four years (1644–1647), and no doubt strongly influenced people's opinion of Cotton.[25] It contained strong statements against "saving preparatives" and also limited the role of sanctification as evidence of justification.[26] This document is what Miller cites as evidence that Cotton was appealing to Calvin against preparationists with the cry, "Let Calvin answer for me!"[27] But in its context this appeal to Calvin clearly did not pertain to preparation for salvation, but the use of the fruits of sanctification as evidence for justification.[28] Furthermore, as Miller acknowledges, Cotton said that Cornwell's publication did not accurately represent his statements.[29] To ascertain Cotton's own views, we should look at the writings that were indisputably his.

23. Cotton, *The Way of Life*, 184–85.
24. Pettit, *The Heart Prepared*, 139.
25. Miller, "'Preparation for Salvation' in New England," 269.
26. *Gospel Conversion... Opened by John Cotton, at a Conference in New-England... Now published for the generall good by Francis Cornwell* (London: by J. Dawson, 1646), 5, 9, 15–28.
27. Miller, "'Preparation for Salvation' in New England," 268.
28. *Gospel Conversion*, 22.
29. Miller, "'Preparation for Salvation' in New England," 272.

John Cotton and the Covenant of Grace

Bozeman views English Reformed covenantal thought as an ellipse, a geometric space defined by two centers, which are faith and works, or gospel and law.[30] This view of the covenant is balanced. By 1636, however, Bozeman says Cotton's teaching had taken "a sharper turn" towards "semi-antinomian" ideas by spiraling away from the center of moral obedience and towards union with God by faith.[31] Bozeman refers to this as "a severe but silent shift in [Cotton's] theological center that ran counter both to the major trend of his English doctrine and to central Reformed tenets."[32] He says Cotton became more hesitant and critical of the use of conditions and qualifications in the covenant of grace, but at the same time he never ceased to affirm the conditional promises of the covenant to people who possess the spiritual qualifications.[33] But does this warrant saying that Cotton departed from the main line of Reformed doctrine? Perhaps it would be better to say that Cotton remained orthodox in his Reformed views but developed an emphasis that antinomians exploited contrary to his intentions. Bozeman does acknowledge, however, that Cotton stopped "well short of the positions taken by Eaton" and other antinomians.[34]

One document that Bozeman cites as evidence for a shift in Cotton's views in 1636 is *The New Covenant* (though it was not published until late 1654).[35] This document does strongly emphasize union with Christ as the heart of the covenant of grace. But what does it say about the law? Surely the use of the law was at the heart of antinomian debates. And, as we will see, Cotton affirmed a significant place for the law, even prior to faith.

Cotton understood that the essence of the covenant of grace was God giving Himself to His elect: "I will be their God" (Gen. 17:8).[36] The first gift God offers in the covenant of grace is Himself as Father, Son, and Holy Spirit. Christ is the foundation of all "saving qualifications," that is, qualifications that show one belongs to the covenant.[37] Bozeman help-

30. Bozeman, *The Precisianist Strain*, 18, 27.

31. Bozeman, *The Precisianist Strain*, 242.

32. Bozeman, *The Precisianist Strain*, 244–45.

33. Bozeman, *The Precisianist Strain*, 254–55.

34. Bozeman, *The Precisianist Strain*, 254.

35. Bozeman, *The Precisianist Strain*, 242n17. See Larzer Ziff, *The Career of John Cotton: Puritanism and the American Experience* (Princeton: Princeton University Press, 1962), 265.

36. Cotton, *The New Covenant*, 4, 8.

37. Cotton, *The New Covenant*, 52.

fully explains here, "Reflecting scholastic Latin usages, 'qualification' and 'quality' in this context signified any divinely worked attribute in the self's nature and behavior, and 'disposition' was an approximate synonym for 'habit,' or an infused virtuous inclination."[38] So Christ alone, dwelling in the heart of the saint, can produce the character and conduct revealing that a person belongs to the covenant of grace and possesses salvation.

Cotton did not believe that preparations prior to possessing Christ count as saving qualifications. He wrote, "Here were indeed preparations for Christ, but these were not saving, they were still children of wrath."[39] However, Cotton nuanced his statement by saying: "Indeed there is a saving preparation before consolation in Christ, and the manifestation of our gracious union with him; but for our first union with him; there are no steps unto the altar (Ex. 20:26)."[40]

In this way Cotton allowed for some ambiguity in the process of conversion. On the one hand, he carefully guarded against any view of preparation involving the exercise of gracious habits (faith, hope, and love) prior to possessing Christ. We need Christ even to trust in Christ. Thus Cotton carefully avoided the Arminianism that Pemble attacked. He did not say there was any pre-conversion preparation that is saving. On the other hand, he said that a person may have Christ before he knows it with conscious assurance of faith. Though he does not know it, such a person is in "union with Christ" by a yet undiscerned faith, which allows for a state of "saving preparation." That view corresponds to Perkins's teaching that the beginning of justifying faith is a desire for Christ.[41]

Some of these statements could be construed as a denial of preparation since God's first gift to the elect is Himself. The conclusion would then follow that there can be no preparation prior to union with Christ. But in its context, Cotton says that God is the first gift *of the covenant of grace*.[42] Therefore his teaching here on the covenant leaves open the question of whether God works in a person in a preparatory manner prior to bringing him into the covenant of grace. To see what Cotton taught about preparation for the covenant of grace, one must consider what he said about the law and the covenant of works.

---

38. Bozeman, *The Precisianist Strain*, 255n38.
39. Cotton, *The New Covenant*, 53–54.
40. Cotton, *The New Covenant*, 54.
41. Perkins, *Cases of Conscience*, 15.
42. Cotton, *The New Covenant*, 52.

Cotton anticipated the objection, "If God give himself before any blessing...to what use then serveth the law of God?"[43] He said the law has many uses for both the regenerate and unregenerate. Those united with Christ under the covenant of grace are still bound to keep the law, not as "a covenant of works but a commandment of well-doing" given by Christ with His enabling Spirit to His people.[44] With respect to people whom God has elected but has not yet regenerated, Cotton said the law "is of use unto them; to aggravate their sin, and to multiply it unto them as it were, that is to say, to aggravate the apprehension of the heinousness of sin upon their conscience, and to set home the burden of sin unto their souls, thereby to drive them to feel their great need of the Lord Jesus Christ, whom otherwise they should forever have despised" (Gal. 3:19).[45] Cotton wrote, "It is the usual manner of God to give a covenant of grace by leading men first into a covenant of works."[46] The law retains a principal place in life both prior to conversion (as a covenant of works driving men to Christ) and after conversion (in the covenant of grace driven by Christ). Therefore James Jones errs in saying that Cotton rejected any idea of preparation by the law for faith and could not conceive of God working on a man apart from union with Christ.[47]

Cotton's teaching "there are no steps unto the altar"[48] does not deny the process of conviction as God's normal way of bringing men to conversion. Nor does it encourage passivity. Instead it was Cotton's way of asserting that the difference between conviction and conversion is the difference between death and life, and there are no stirrings of true spiritual life prior to union with Christ. He may have aimed these words at the teaching of Hooker and Shepard that there is a preparatory step of cutting the elect away from sin before union with Christ as a kind of middle step between death and regeneration. Cotton denied this.

Citing Galatians 3:24, he went on to affirm, "As a school-master driveth his scholar [student] through fear unto this or that duty...so the law of God driveth the soul through fear unto Jesus Christ.... For being once made sensible of his own inability to redeem himself, and unworthiness

43. Cotton, *The New Covenant*, 106–107.
44. Cotton, *The New Covenant*, 115–19.
45. Cotton, *The New Covenant*, 108.
46. Cotton, *The New Covenant*, 21.
47. Jones, "The Beginnings of American Theology," 30, 52, 211, 213.
48. Cotton, *The New Covenant*, 54.

to be redeemed from the wrath of God; now is the soul fitted to hear the voice of the gospel, now is the news of Christ beautiful and glad tidings: and of this use is the law unto the elect of God, *before they come under the covenant of the grace of God.*"[49] These words so ably express the Puritan doctrine of preparation that Hooker could have written them himself.

In *The New Covenant*, Cotton offered a Reformed perspective on the law's role both before and after saving faith, but he also made potentially confusing statements about union with God. Bozeman wrote, "Because Cotton's antinomian tendency was peculiarly ambivalent, limited in range and contained by larger loyalties both social and theological, Cotton offers a far more elusive and intriguing problem in interpretation."[50] Cotton indeed is a challenge to interpret, and was so to his contemporaries, but that does not warrant the accusation that he took a sharp turn into semi-antinomian ideas. Bozeman admitted that Cotton's theological message included "a generous level of pietist and disciplinary content,"[51] and so rather than calling Cotton a semi-antinomian, or Hooker a semi-legalist, we suggest they were both orthodox Reformed theologians, but with different emphases. Each of their theologies had tendencies that they limited within the larger context of Reformed theology, that could be abused by critics who were prone to ignore or throw off the system of the doctrines of grace. The Christian faith contains many tensions and paradoxes because it is the rational revelation of an incomprehensible God. The constant challenge in Christian theology is to preach the whole counsel of God, while not emphasizing one point of doctrine in a way that denies another.

So far we have considered Cotton's criticism of Roman Catholic preparationism and his view of the covenant of grace. Now let us turn our attention to his teachings on contrition.

John Cotton on Sorrow for Sin

Cotton certainly believed that coming to Christ involved humility and brokenness over one's sins. Cotton wrote to Shepard in early 1636, "I conceive the soul closeth with Christ, by feeling himself a poor desolate soul,

---

49. Cotton, *The New Covenant*, 109–110, emphasis added.
50. Bozeman, *The Precisianist Strain*, 241.
51. Bozeman, *The Precisianist Strain*, 243.

lost for want of Christ, sensible of his own insufficiency to reach him, and unworthiness to receive him, yet seeking and longing for him in every ordinance, and spiritual duty, though finding itself unable to begin, or continue seeking or waiting, farther than Christ shall help, and work with him."[52] Donald Come regards this statement as an example of how Cotton ministered in the same tradition as Perkins and Sibbes.[53]

In *The Way of Life* Cotton said, "The very first work of living and saving grace gives a deadly stroke to the life of sinful nature."[54] This first grace wrought in a sinner is "the taking away of the stony heart and gift of a new heart" (Ezek. 36:26).[55] This grace is also identified with piercing the heart with sorrow and grief (Acts 2:37), resulting in the will coming to hate sin and oneself for sin (Ezek. 36:32).[56] This is sharing in Christ's death so that we might share in His resurrection.[57]

Cotton here appeared to have taken Hooker's preparation doctrine and subsumed it under saving grace, thereby denying preparation prior to regeneration and union with Christ. One can understand why Miller wrote, "He was persuaded that between the natural and the regenerate man lay a gulf so immense that only divine grace could bridge it. If a man performs a single action appropriate to the elect, he has then and there become one of them. There can be no half-way conversion.... Therefore what Hooker and Shepard called preparation was for Cotton simply the impact of grace, and the prepared were already saints."[58]

However, Miller's statement does not take account of the broader scope of Cotton's theology. Later in *The Way of Life*, Cotton made the following qualification: "A man may be pricked in the eye to weep for sin, in the tongue to cry out for sin, in the foot begin to amend his way, and yet not have his heart pricked, nor have any living or saving grace; a man may be fearful of sin, grow more careful of good duties, be more fruitful in good ways, and be not pricked in heart, but only in conscience or understanding."[59] Cotton thus allowed for the awakening of conscience,

---

52. Bush, ed., *The Correspondence of John Cotton*, 231.
53. Come, "John Cotton: Guide of the Chosen People," 271.
54. Cotton, *The Way of Life*, 125.
55. Cotton, *The Way of Life*, 126.
56. Cotton, *The Way of Life*, 125, 127–28.
57. Cotton, *The Way of Life*, 129.
58. Miller, "'Preparation for Salvation' in New England," 267.
59. Cotton, *The Way of Life*, 131.

conviction of sin, fear of judgment, and efforts at moral reformation prior to regeneration. Therefore we should not take Cotton's statements as rejecting Puritan preparation, but only as restricting true godly sorrow to the regenerate.

At the same time, we note some differences between Cotton and his colleagues. Cotton understood the pricking of the heart in Acts 2:37 as regenerate sorrow, whereas Hooker viewed it as the grief of unregenerate men. Cotton confined the piercing of the heart (i.e. the will) to saving contrition, whereas Hooker spoke of it in regard to preparatory contrition. Such a difference could easily have led to debate between Cotton and other New England divines. Cotton might have had this difference in mind when he wrote, "There is a difference between a pricked heart, and a pricked conscience. Generally Christians confound these two, and shuffle them up together, as if they were both one, but indeed they much differ; and without a discerning whereof, many a poor soul may be swallowed up, either by despair on the one hand, or presumption on the other."[60]

The pierced heart loves and respects biblical preaching, whereas the pierced conscience finds it a burden. The pierced heart turns away from this world, whereas the pierced conscience tries to bury itself in business and worldly pleasures. When God pierces the heart, He humbles a person to receive teaching, whereas when God only pricks the conscience, the person remains argumentative and stubborn.[61] The pricked heart grieves over sin for its own sake while the pricked conscience only grieves over punishment.[62]

Cotton may have had disputes with his American colleagues, but they did not argue about the sovereignty of divine grace or fidelity to the Reformed heritage. Rather they may have disputed the precise qualities that distinguish contrition before and after conversion. That was a debate about the nature of preparatory grace, not its reality.

John Cotton's Preparation

Pettit viewed Cotton as an extreme, polar opposite to upholders of the covenantal tradition. He wrote that according to Cotton, "Man cannot

---

60. Cotton, *The Way of Life*, 140.
61. Cotton, *The Way of Life*, 141–49.
62. Cotton, *The Way of Life*, 152.

turn to God, as did Abraham, but must be seized. Man cannot willingly acknowledge God until he is wrenched, turned about, forced to believe in a new relationship which until that moment has played no part in his life."[63] We have already noted that Pettit's analysis was driven by a faulty assumption that sovereign grace demands that conversion be imposed on the human soul. Contrary to this assumption, White has documented many cases in which Cotton exhorted unbelievers to give themselves up to Christ, to seek after Christ, to come home to God, to take pains to diligently use all good means of grace, and never to rest until they know they are united with Christ.[64]

Cotton's Reformed theology did not lead him to reject a process of preparation leading up to union with Christ. We have already seen that Cotton urged unbelievers to seek knowledge, apply the Word to themselves, and pray for divine illumination. Cotton also explicitly affirmed preparation for conversion.[65] In *The New Covenant,* he taught that the Lord took Abraham and his seed to be His covenant people by "a double act, as 1) of preparation, not on Abraham's part or on his seed's part, but on their own part as the Lord prepared them. 2) The Lord did invest him with the blessings of this covenant."[66] In the latter work of blessing, God "doth give himself unto us, and taketh possession of us by his blessed Spirit."[67] Preparation thus consists of "a double work of his Spirit" upon the elect of God:

- First, "a spirit of bondage" severs them from worldly entanglements and delights. God draws sinners away from all sinful lusts and false hopes of mercy. In this bondage God impresses the conscience with "the weight and danger of their sins."

- Second, "a spirit of burning" consumes the hypocrisy of sinners and the apparent beauty of their good works. As a result they find no comfort in their good deeds. People may go so far and not enter into adoption, but "hereby also the Lord useth to prepare his people."[68]

---

63. Pettit, *The Heart Prepared*, 138.
64. White, "Were Hooker and Shepard Closet Arminians?" 36–39.
65. Iain H. Murray, *Antinomianism: New England's First Controversy* (Edinburgh: Banner of Truth, 1978), 40–45.
66. Cotton, *The New Covenant*, 19–20.
67. Cotton, *The New Covenant*, 24.
68. Cotton, *The New Covenant*, 21–23. Cotton develops this two-fold work of the Spirit at length on pp. 174–84.

Those two stages of preparation correspond with Hooker's contrition and humiliation. Surprisingly, even in the midst of the Antinomian Controversy, Cotton affirmed the same fundamental doctrine of preparation as Hooker did.

It is therefore puzzling when Pettit says that Thomas Hooker was "preaching an entirely different doctrine of conversion" than Cotton.[69] Cotton did not collapse conviction of sin into union with Christ. He said that after the soul is "thus prepared," the Spirit of God takes up residence in it as His temple, infusing faith to receive the Lord Jesus Christ.[70] Wayne Christy says of Cotton's theology, "Preliminary to this acceptance by God, there must be preparation by God's Spirit."[71] Holifield says that the New England divines, including Cotton, agreed that God's usual way of conversion is to use the law to prepare the heart for faith in Christ.[72] Cohen says, "Cotton's use of the word *prepare,* his mention of the Spirit of Bondage, and the description of the Spirit's humiliating work clearly show his essential agreement with other Puritans that the soul passes through preparatory states that antecede calling."[73]

John Cotton's Consistency regarding Preparation

We have cited a number of texts that Cotton used to teach preparation for conversion. Some critics have questioned the sincerity of Cotton's statements on preparation. Miller suggested that Cotton folded under pressure from New England leaders and cloaked his views in diplomatic language so he could survive politically.[74] He wrote, "Cotton bent before the storm and saved his standing in the commonwealth at the expense

---

69. Pettit, *The Heart Prepared,* 133.

70. Cotton, *The New Covenant,* 25–26.

71. Wayne H. Christy, "John Cotton: Covenant Theologian" (MA Thesis, Duke University, 1942), 83. Christy wrongly pits Cotton against Calvin, saying that Cotton was dissatisfied with "a conception of a distant sovereign God arbitrarily imposing salvation by election," and seeking "a more kindly attitude" and "a more intimate relationship with God" (p. 73). On the contrary, at the heart of Calvin's theology was personal union with Christ. See Paul Wells, "Calvin and Union with Christ: The Heart of Christian Doctrine," in *Calvin: Theologian and Reformer,* ed. Joel R. Beeke and Garry J. Williams (Grand Rapids: Reformation Heritage Books, 2010), 65–88.

72. Holifield, *Theology in America,* 43.

73. Cohen, *God's Caress,* 84n25.

74. Miller, "'Preparation for Salvation' in New England," 272–75.

of his consistency."[75] Thus, he said that what Cotton wrote after the Antinomian Controversy reflects less his own view on preparation and more
a posture adopted for the sake of peace.

That accusation is difficult to verify or deny, given that we have few
of Cotton's writings published prior to the controversy with Hutchinson,
which began in 1636. Some of his later publications were based upon
sermons preached earlier, however. The only work by Cotton that was
published in this early period was *God's Promise to His Plantation* (1630),
but it discusses God's providence, not conversion.[76] Cotton wrote a preface to Hildersam's treatise on John 4 (first published in 1629), which, as
we saw earlier, supported preparation. But one author may commend
another author's book without endorsing everything in it.[77]

However, we do have access to some of Cotton's letters written prior
to the controversy. On May 31, 1626, Cotton wrote to James Ussher:

> I dare not preach the gospel indifferently unto all, before the law;
> nor the worth of Christ, before the need of Christ. Children's bread
> is not meet for whelps [young dogs]; and full souls will despise
> honeycombs. I see John Baptist was sent to humble, before Christ
> came to heal; and Christ himself preached repentance, before faith
> in the promises (Mark 1:15). Neither do I remember in the gospel any
> promise of grace, pardoning sin, nor any commandment to believe
> sin pardoned, but to the broken, the bruised, the poor, the weary, the
> thirsty, or the like. Faith in the promises, before the heart be changed
> from stoniness to brokenness, I fear is no better than the temporary
> faith, which is found in the stony soil (Luke 8:13).[78]

Cotton wrote this letter prior to moving to New England and well before
controversy erupted over antinomianism. He was forty-one-years old,
with about fifteen years of pastoral ministry under his belt. So it is reasonable to view this statement on the need for preparation as Cotton's
sincere theological position developed through years of reflection and

75. Miller, "'Preparation for Salvation' in New England," 271.

76. John Cotton, "God's Providence to His Plantation," in *Sermons that Shaped America: Reformed Preaching from 1630–2001,* ed. William S. Barker and Samuel T. Logan, Jr.
(Phillipsburg, N.J.: P & R Publishing, 2003), 5–17.

77. See I[ohn] C[otton], "To the Godly Reader," in Hildersam, *The Fourth of John,* [no
pagination]. Benjamin Brook said that Cotton's preface first appeared in the second edition of this book (1632), but Bush dates Cotton's preface to 1628 (*The Correspondence of John
Cotton,* 124–25).

78. Bush, ed., *The Correspondence of John Cotton,* 111–12.

preaching. He did not change his position later, nor did he cloak his true views in diplomatic language. John Cotton firmly believed that God ordinarily prepares the soul for faith by breaking the heart over sin.

Like other Puritans, Cotton did not preach the gospel to sinners irrespective of contrition and humiliation. That does not mean he refused to freely offer Christ to all people through the gospel or failed to call them all to repent and believe in Christ. It does mean, however, that he told people that the gospel promises of salvation are effectual in the poor in spirit.

Although Cotton's theological writings can be confusing, his affirmation of preparation after the Antinomian Controversy remained consistent with his stance prior to the controversy. Therefore we believe he should be fully acquitted of Miller's charge.

John Cotton, Preparation, and the Antinomian Controversy

After a careful examination of Cotton's writings and letters, we have seen that Cotton's teachings on God's regenerating grace do not contradict the idea of preparation for conversion. To the contrary, the documents prove that Cotton taught the divine preparation of unbelievers before union with Christ, and exhorted unbelievers to prepare themselves.

What then do we make of the Antinomian Controversy in New England? Pettit says that of the eighty-two errors condemned by the Massachusetts synod in 1637, the majority "either directly or indirectly denied the concept of preparation."[79] He offers the examples of two such errors. If it is true that the synod condemned forty or more errors related to preparation, it would strongly suggests that Cotton was against preparation, or at least was perceived to be so. But an examination of the list of errors does not bear this out. Of the eighty-two errors, only four can be reasonably seen as errors regarding preparation prior to saving conversion. When these errors are read in context with their confutations, we see that preparation was not singled out but was included under the broader consideration of conditions or the use of means in the covenant of grace, whether before or after conversion.

The first relevant error was this: "There can be no true closing with Christ in a promise that hath a qualification or condition expressed."[80]

---

79. Pettit, *The Heart Prepared*, 149.
80. *A Short Story of the Rise, Reign, and Ruine of the Antinomians* (1644), in *Antinomianism in the Colony of Massachusetts Bay, 1636–1638*, ed. Charles F. Adams (Boston: The Prince Society, 1894), 107 [error 38].

The confutation cites Scriptural invitations to the weary (Matt. 11:28) and thirsty (Isa. 55:1–2; John 7:37; Rev. 22:17), which support rather than refute preparation for salvation. What is more, the terms *qualification* and *condition* are used again of another error regarding whether faith should be preached "as the condition of the covenant of grace."[81] So this error does not specifically involve preparation. Rather it questions whether it is proper to speak of faith as a condition to the covenant of grace or qualification to a right to claim to be within the covenant.

The second relevant error cited by the synod was saying that, "The Spirit acts most in the saints when they endeavor least."[82] We note that the reference to "the saints" is to persons who profess conversion, or "visible saints." The confutation of this error does mention "the special seasons of God's preventing grace," including preparation for faith. The confutation broadens the scope of the original statement of error because, as it states, the debate was about "the use of lawful means." It was not about saving grace versus preparation for grace.

The third relevant error is that, "A man may not be exhorted to any duty, because he hath no power to do it."[83] The texts used to support the confutation of this error are Philippians 2:12–13, Ephesians 5:14, and 1 Corinthians 15:58.

The fourth error is that "Frequency or length of holy duties or trouble of conscience for neglect thereof are all signs of one under a covenant of works."[84] The confutation refers to the duties of "the faithful in Christ Jesus," and also cites 1 Corinthians 15:58, which says, "Therefore, my beloved brethren, be ye stedfast, unmoveable, always abounding in the work of the Lord, forasmuch as ye know that your labour is not in vain in the Lord." Since this last Scripture clearly pertains to believers and the confutation speaks of "the faithful," it does not seem likely that these third and fourth errors referred to preparation for conversion. Rather, they seem to pertain to antinomianism, which presses the doctrine of human inability so far that it undercuts all human responsibility. Reformed theology teaches both the inability and responsibility of man. Loss of ability through sin does not annul the duty man owes to his Maker.

---

81. *A Short Story*, 123 [error 81].
82. *A Short Story*, 109 [error 43].
83. *A Short Story*, 114 [error 59].
84. *A Short Story*, 118 [error 70].

Clearly, there was controversy in New England. There were also concerns about identifying the inner life of the believer with Christ and His Spirit, which were listed in fourteen errors.[85] There were questions regarding the role of sanctification in assurance, which were exhibited in twenty-one errors.[86] There were also errors about the law as a rule of life for believers,[87] the necessity of imitating Christ,[88] faith as a condition of the covenant of grace or means of union with Christ,[89] special revelations,[90] the use of Scripture and preaching,[91] leaving one's church,[92] and accusations that pious Christians were still under a covenant of works.[93]

John Winthrop believed the Antinomian Controversy centered on two fundamental issues: the indwelling of the Holy Spirit in believers, and the role of the fruits of sanctification as evidence of justification.[94] Together these two matters account for at least forty percent of the errors rebuked by the New England synod. But preparation is mentioned in, at most, five percent of the errors cited, and even in those errors, preparation is not the central issue. It does not seem that the controversy was about the doctrine of preparation *per se*.

After reviewing Miller's thesis that preparation is "crypto-Arminianism" and therefore is the "fundamental issue" in the Antinomian Controversy, William Stoever says preparation for conversion is "relatively inconspicuous" in the primary sources of that controversy.[95] Instead, communications between Cotton and his colleagues revolve

---

85. Christ in us: *A Short Story*, 95–100, 104, 106, 111–12 [errors 1–3, 6–8, 11, 14, 15, 18, 26, 35, 51, 52].

86. Sanctification in assurance: John Winthrop, *The History of New England from 1630 to 1649*, ed. James Savage (Boston: Little, Brown, and Co., 1853), 1:250; *A Short Story*, 98, 103, 100, 103–105, 110–11, 113–14, 116–17, 119–21, 123 [errors 10, 16, 25, 29–31, 44, 45, 47, 50, 58, 60, 65, 67, 69, 72, 73, 75–77, 81].

87. Law as a rule of life: *A Short Story*, 96, 105 [errors 4, 5, 33].

88. Imitating Christ: *A Short Story*, 96 [error 6].

89. Faith as a condition or means: *A Short Story*, 96, 106, 110, 123 [errors 27, 28, 37, 48, 81].

90. Special revelation: *A Short Story*, 103, 108, 118 [errors 24, 40, 71].

91. Usefulness of Scripture and preaching: *A Short Story*, 107, 112, 114 [errors 39, 53, 54, 61].

92. Leaving one's church: *A Short Story*, 122 [errors 79, 80].

93. Covenant of works: *A Short Story*, 98, 99, 101, 118–19 [errors 9, 12, 13, 20, 70, 74].

94. David D. Hall, ed., introduction to *The Antinomian Controversy, 1636–1638: A Documentary History*, 2nd ed. (Durham: Duke University Press, 1990), 11.

95. Stoever, *A Faire and Easie Way to Heaven*, 193.

around faith, justification, and sanctification with respect to their order and evidence.[96] It does not make sense, either, to say that preparation was a doctrine not yet formally developed and so was a hidden issue in the controversy, for, as Stoever says, "in stressing 'legal' preparation to receive Christ, they were elaborating a commonplace of Reformed divinity."[97] Already in 1633, as we have seen, William Ames was presenting a scholastic disputation on preparation.

Stoever says the debate was not about Arminianism but about God's use of means in salvation as opposed to His immediate work upon the soul apart from human ministry. He writes:

> In spite of the rhetoric about "legalism" and "going on in a covenant of works," the Antinomian Controversy at the theological level was not basically about meriting grace (in a Roman Catholic sense), or about human cooperation with grace (in an Arminian sense), or about unregenerate ability to "prepare" for "effectual calling" (in the sense of some modern interpreters). Rather, it concerned a broader and more fundamental issue; namely, the proper relationship between created nature and divine activity in the process of regeneration itself.... The elders [New England ministers]...believe that God in accomplishing salvation uses "means" which belong to the created order, and respects the inherent capacities of human beings. The dissenters, in contrast, maintained that God acts directly upon men, overruling natural capacities, and transforms men apart from, and in spite of, any activity of theirs.[98]

Stoever concludes by saying, "The suggestion that the elders were departing from normative Reformed doctrine, judged by the formal divinity of the period, is simply incorrect."[99]

Conclusion

No part of Miller's thesis that Cotton was a better Calvinist in taking a stand against preparationists is supported by the evidence. While Cotton was an ardent defender of sovereign grace and salvation through Christ alone, he

---

96. Stoever, *A Faire and Easie Way to Heaven*, 194.

97. Stoever, *A Faire and Easie Way to Heaven*, 193.

98. William K. B. Stoever, "Nature, Grace, and John Cotton: The Theological Dimension in the New England Antinomian Controversy," *Church History* 44, no. 1 (March 1975): 22.

99. Stoever, "Nature, Grace, and John Cotton," 32.

also taught preparatory grace. On the basis of a survey of the teachings of Perkins, Hooker, and Cotton, Cohen writes, "A review of three representative preachers shows that Puritans agreed on the essential framework of preparatory experience while contesting subordinate issues."[100]

Cotton did attack preparation, but it was Roman Catholic preparation. In this regard he stood in line with Calvin, Perkins, and Ames. While Cotton emphasized that God's first gift in the covenant of grace is Himself, he also taught that God brings people under a conscious bondage to the covenant of works before bringing them into the covenant of grace. Cotton was neither antinomian nor anti-preparation, for he placed the law of God both before and after conversion. Though Cotton's statements are at times confusing, his position on preparation was consistent before and after the Antinomian Controversy.

Furthermore, it is incorrect to say the controversy was based on the issue of preparation. The debate appears rather to have centered upon the relation of God's grace to human activity. This issue is related to preparation but is not the same, for the issue of grace and nature has implications not just for preparation but for sanctification after regeneration. The issue of sanctification and good works as evidence of regeneration was the primary focus of the controversy.

Winship summarizes the historiography of the issue of preparation by saying, "Perry Miller in 1943 pointed out that preparation was a critical flash point in the free grace [or antinomian] controversy.... Historians accepted Miller's argument until William K. B. Stoever demonstrated, easily enough, that Cotton was a preparationist and that the other ministers and their debates revolved around other topics."[101]

What then shall we make of Cotton's appeal to Calvin? Holifield says Cotton disturbed Calvin's "fragile equilibrium...between nature and grace."[102] He so emphasized union with Christ that human effort and obedience were diminished in significance. Bozeman says Cotton may have played into the antinomians' hands by strongly emphasizing that our graces are nothing without Christ, which is standard Reformed doctrine, but he may have exalted it to the point of neglecting the importance of

100. Cohen, *God's Caress,* 79.
101. Winship, *Making Heretics,* 69.
102. Holifield, *Theology in America,* 47.

human effort and agency in obedience.[103] This would not be the only time that orthodox preaching against legalism was abused by antinomians.

But as for preparation, Cotton stood within the mainstream of Puritan teaching. He denied that "preparation to union with Christ" can have any "moral merit of congruity," or "logical consequence of a safe estate," or "power, of efficiency to beget faith."[104] Nevertheless he affirmed the usefulness of external preparations like hearing and reading the Word, meditation, avoiding gross sins, and spending time often with godly people, and internal preparations such as conviction, grief, and humiliation.[105] In fact, Cotton wrote,

> Such preparatory dispositions are not proportionable to regeneration or union, as any degree of heat in wood begot by fire, is fit to be blown up to a flame. They have not the force of the least disposition, having either any necessary or certain connection with faith to be introduced: but are rather material dispositions, which make the subject more capable of faith, as *siccitas ligni ad ignem* [dry wood for fire]; more capable partly, 1. By removing (in part) impediments, as knowledge of the truth removeth ignorance; sorrow for sin, and fear, removeth delight in sin, and carnal security. 2. By conferring something, whereof there is use in regeneration, as illumination, shame and sorrow, and fear for sin.[106]

Without naming William Ames, Cotton here offered his paraphrase of theses 6 and 7 of Ames's *Praeparatione peccatoris ad conversionem*, which we examined in chapter 4 and include as an appendix in this book.[107] Remarkably, the man whom many supposed to be the great anti-preparationist quoted Ames's defense of preparatory grace! Again we see the unity of the Reformed and Puritan tradition on preparation by grace, for grace.

---

103. Bozeman, *The Precisianist Strain,* 223–25.

104. John Cotton, *A Brief Exposition with Practical Observations upon the whole Book of Canticles* (London: by T. R. and E. M. for Ralph Smith, 1655), 57.

105. Cotton, *Canticles,* 58.

106. Cotton, *Canticles,* 57–58. We are grateful to Murray, *Antinomianism,* 45, for this reference.

107. Not only do the same words and concepts appear in the same order, but the exact phrase *siccitas ligni ad ignem* appears at the end of thesis 6. See Ames, "De Preparatione peccatoris ad conversionem," in *Disceptatio Scholastica de Circulo pontificio* (1644), 31.

CHAPTER EIGHT

Preparation at the Apex of Puritanism: Westminster, Jeremiah Burroughs, and William Guthrie

He doth not say, thou art a wretched, wicked creature, and depart from me thou cursed, as he will say to sinners hereafter...but thou dost hear this voice this day from Christ, "Come to me all you that are weary." Christ is near to you; the Lord is near to the broken heart.
— Jeremiah Burroughs[1]

The Puritan doctrines of preparation and conversion were enshrined in pulpit messages and in personal narratives. The Puritan movement, born in the mid-sixteenth century, matured in the middle of the seventeenth century. Having survived the persecution of Archbishop William Laud (1573–1645), the Puritans gradually became more influential in the 1640s and 1650s. The Westminster Assembly produced three doctrinal standards that continue to inform the beliefs of Presbyterians around the world: the Westminster Confession of Faith (1647), the Westminster Larger Catechism (1647), and the Westminster Shorter Catechism (1648).[2] At this time Puritan practical and devotional literature also flourished.

The Puritan views and practice of preparation were evident in the precise formulations of the Westminster Assembly. They also appeared in the practical Puritan writings of the mid-seventeenth century. In this chapter we will examine how preparation was expressed in the Westminster Standards and by two writers of this period, Jeremiah Burroughs and William Guthrie.

---

1. Jeremiah Burroughs, *Four Books on the Eleventh of Matthew* (London: Peter Cole, 1659), 1:29.

2. *Westminster Confession of Faith* (Glasgow: Free Presbyterian Publications, 2003). Henceforth these doctrinal standards will be referred to as WCF, WLC, and WSC with appropriate chapter, paragraph, or question numbers.

The Westminster Standards: Sovereign Grace and Preparation

No chapter, section, or question and answer in the Westminster Standards is specifically devoted to preparation for saving faith. Furthermore, the several references to "preparing" in the standards most often speak not of preparing for faith but of preparing for a Christian duty such as hearing the Word or receiving the Lord's Supper.

Like the Thirty-Nine Articles, the Westminster Standards deny that man is "able, by his own strength, to convert himself, or to prepare himself thereunto" (WCF 9.3).[3] Man's will is so enslaved to sin that he is "dead in sin, and wholly defiled in all the faculties and parts of soul and body" (WCF 6.2).[4] There simply is nothing in human nature by which men may reach up to God. God must first reach down to men. Conversion is by grace alone.

Even the "common operations of the Spirit" cannot enable dead sinners to come to Christ, for conversion requires an "effectual calling" from God (WCF 10.4, 1).[5] In this heart-transforming call, man "is altogether passive...until being quickened and renewed by the Holy Spirit, he is thereby enabled to answer this call, and to embrace the grace offered and conveyed in it" (WCF 10.2).[6] "Works done by unregenerate men, although...they may be things which God commands" do not proceed from faith, are not done according the the Word, and are not done for the glory of God. These works "are therefore sinful, and cannot please God, or make a man meet to receive grace from God" (WCF 16.7).[7]

One might think the Westminster divines had abandoned the preparation doctrine of their forefathers. Pettit thought so, and says that the Confession of Faith "contains several statements contrary to the New Englanders' views on preparation."[8] However, the real purpose of this language in the confession was to reject the synergistic theology of Roman Catholicism, in which men prepared themselves for saving grace by works of congruent merit. If we assume that preparation is inherently synergistic and anti-Calvinistic, it would follow that the Westminster

---

3. Citing John 6:44, 65; Eph. 2:2–5; 1 Cor. 2:14; Titus 3:3–5.

4. Citing Gen. 2:17; Eph. 2:1; Titus 1:15; Gen. 6:5; Jer. 17:9; Rom. 3:10–18.

5. Regarding common operations of the Spirit, citing Matt. 7:22; 13:20–21; Heb. 6:4. Regarding effectual calling, citing Rom. 8:30; 11:7; Eph. 1:10–11.

6. Citing 1 Cor. 2:14; Rom. 8:7; Eph. 2:5; John 6:37; Ezek. 36:27; John 5:25.

7. Citing Hag. 2:14; Titus 1:15; Amos 5:21; Hos. 1:4; Rom. 9:16; Titus 3:5.

8. Pettit, *The Heart Prepared*, 164.

Assembly in tune with its theology of grace must also have rejected all ideas of preparation and exhortations to human activity prior to conversion. However, the Westminster divines did not reject Reformed preparation, nor did they encourage the unconverted to be fatalistically passive. If the confession denied New England preparation, how could the New England synod give its assent to the confession in the Cambridge Platform (1648), saying that it is "very holy, orthodox, and judicious in all matters of faith"?[9]

The Westminster Standards call men to action in being saved. To escape God's wrath, sinners were urged to make "the diligent use of the outward means whereby Christ communicates to us the benefits of his mediation" (WLC Q. 153),[10] especially the preaching of the Word, sacraments, and prayer (WLC Q. 154).[11] Those means cannot save a person unless they are accompanied by faith and repentance. Unconverted people defile all good works, even in using the means of grace, but "their neglect of them is more sinful, and displeasing unto God" (WCF 16.7).[12] Thus unconverted people must use the means and cry for mercy, for their passivity and inactivity is only "more sinful," not more honoring to God's sovereignty.

The Word of God becomes effective in saving sinners by the "Spirit of God" who makes "the preaching of the word" a powerful means of "enlightening, convincing, and humbling sinners; of driving them out of themselves, and drawing them unto Christ," then sanctifying and strengthening them in Christ (WLC Q. 155; cf. WSC Q. 89).[13]

The Westminster Standards indicate that the gospel and the law have key roles in saving men. It declares that all men, both unregenerate and regenerate, find the law useful as a means "to inform them...of their duty,

---

9. Williston Walker, *The Creeds and Platforms of Congregationalism* (Philadelphia: Pilgrim's Press, 1969), 195. Pettit observes that the New Englanders had "some debate" over chapter ten, paragraph one on effectual calling before voting to embrace the confession (*The Heart Prepared*, 164). However, it is in chapter *nine* that the remarks against preparationism appear, and there is no mention of debate on that point. See our subsequent discussion with regard to Westminster's doctrine of vocation in chapter ten.

10. Citing Prov. 2:1–5; 8:33–36.

11. Citing Matt. 28:19–20; Acts 2:42, 46–47.

12. Citing Ps. 14:4; 36:3; Job 21:14–15; Matt. 25:41–45; 23:23.

13. On enlightenment, citing Neh. 8:8; Acts 26:18; Ps. 19:8; on conviction and humiliation, citing 1 Cor. 14:24–25; 2 Chron. 34:18–19, 26–28; on driving them to Christ, citing Acts 2:37, 41; 8:27–39.

binding them to walk accordingly; to convince them of their disability to keep it, and of the sinful pollution of their nature, hearts, and lives: to humble them in the sense of their sin and misery, and thereby help them to acquire a more clear sight of the need they have of Christ, and of the perfection of his obedience" (WLC Q. 95).[14] The moral law's special use for unregenerate men is, "to awaken their consciences to flee from wrath to come, and to drive them to Christ" (WLC Q. 96).[15] Indeed, one proof that the Scriptures are the Word of God is "their light and power to convince and convert sinners" (WLC Q. 4).[16]

The Westminster Assembly regarded Spirit-worked conviction of sin as the foundation of both faith and repentance. The Larger Catechism offers the following definition of "justifying faith" (WLC Q. 72):

> Justifying faith is a saving grace, wrought in the heart of a sinner by the Spirit and word of God, whereby he, being convinced of his sin and misery, and of the disability in himself and all other creatures to recover him out of his lost condition, not only assenteth to the truth of the promise of the gospel, but receiveth and resteth upon Christ and his righteousness, therein held forth, for pardon of sin, and for the accepting and accounting of his person righteous in the sight of God for salvation.[17]

One might ask what the relation of conviction of sin is to justifying faith. Is conviction of sin, according to the Westminster divines, a part of faith? Note that the Larger Catechism's answer just quoted used passive verbs for some parts of faith and active verbs for others. The active verbs "receiveth and resteth" communicate the activity of faith. So the Shorter Catechism simply said that faith in Christ is that grace "whereby we receive and rest upon him alone for salvation, as he is offered to us in the gospel" (WSC Q. 86).[18] It did not mention conviction in its definition of faith. When the Larger Catechism did include conviction, it used the passive verb "being convinced" prior to the active verbs of faith.

---

14. On conviction by the law, citing Ps. 19:11–12; Rom. 3:20; 7:7; on humiliation by the law, citing Rom. 3:9, 23; on the law's display of our need of Christ, citing Gal. 3:21–22; on the law's demonstration of Christ's righteousness, citing Rom. 10:4.

15. On awakening, citing 1 Tim. 1:9–10; on driving men to Christ, citing Gal. 3:24.

16. Citing Acts 18:28; Heb. 4:12; James 1:18; Ps. 19:7–9; Rom. 15:4; Acts 20:32.

17. The portion of this definition regarding conviction of our sin and inability cites Acts 2:37; 16:30; John 16:8–9; Rom. 5:6; Eph. 2:1; Acts 4:12.

18. Citing John 1:12; Isa. 26:3–4; Phil. 3:9; Gal. 2:16.

Therefore the grammar and syntax of the Larger Catechism probably indicate that conviction is the work of God upon sinners which prepares them for faith.

Similarly the Larger Catechism defined "repentance unto life" as a Spirit-wrought grace in which a sinner turns from sin to God in his affections and will, "out of the sight and sense, not only of the danger, but also of the filthiness and odiousness of his sins" (WLC Q. 76; cf. WCF 15.2; WSC Q. 87).[19] Since repentance comes out of this sight and sense of sin, the catechism implies that conviction logically precedes repentance.

Thomas Vincent (1634–1678), in his work on the Shorter Catechism published in 1674, wrote that the one thing "requisite unto turning from sin in repentance" is "a true sight of sin."[20] He said that "without this sense of sin, sinners will not forsake sin, nor apply themselves unto the Lord Jesus for pardon and healing (Matt. 9:12–13)."[21] Though Vincent's work on the catechism appeared a generation after the Westminster Assembly, it was highly commended by older theologians such as John Owen (1616–1683), Joseph Caryl (1602–1673), and Thomas Case (c. 1598–1682). The latter two were Westminster divines.[22]

Conviction of sin is the first work that the Shorter Catechism mentions under effectual calling: "Effectual calling is the work of God's Spirit, whereby, convincing us of our sin and misery, enlightening our minds in the knowledge of Christ, and renewing our wills, he doth persuade and enable us to embrace Jesus Christ, freely offered to us in the gospel" (WSC Q. 31).[23] Conviction is not merely the work of a natural, fallen conscience but the work of God's Spirit. So far from being a hindrance to evangelism or to faith in Christ, conviction of sin, according to the Shorter Catechism, is a necessary part of the Spirit's work in effectual calling, as He persuades and enables the sinner to believe on the Lord Jesus Christ.

Vincent said that effectual calling consists of two parts: the work of the Holy Spirit upon our minds, and the work of the Holy Spirit upon our

---

19. On the sight of the danger of sin, citing Ezek. 18:28, 30, 32; Luke 15:17–18; Hos. 2:6–7; on the sight of the filth of sin, citing Ezek. 36:31; Isa. 30:22.

20. Thomas Vincent, *Explicatory Catechism, or, An Explanation of the Assembly's Shorter Catechism* (New Haven: Walter, Austin, and Co., 1810), 225 [on WSC Q. 87].

21. Vincent, *Explicatory Catechism*, 226 [on WSC Q. 87].

22. "Epistle to the Reader," in Vincent, *Explicatory Catechism*, 3–4.

23. Citing 2 Tim. 1:9; 2 Thess. 2:13–14; Acts 2:37; 26:18; Ezek. 36:26–27; John 6:44–45; Phil. 2:13.

wills. The work of the Spirit on our minds convinces us of sin by the law and enlightens us about Christ by the gospel.[24] Vincent wrote,

> The Spirit worketh in our mind a conviction of our sin and misery, when he giveth us a clear sight and full persuasion of the guilt of our sins, and a feeling apprehension of the dreadful wrath of God, and the endless miseries of hell, which we have deserved for sin, and every hour are exposed unto; which doth wound our hearts and consciences, and filleth us with perplexing care what to do to be saved (John 16:8; Acts 2:37).[25]

In the Shorter Catechism, conviction of sin is listed under the work of effectual calling. Does that mean the framers believed that the Spirit works conviction of sin only in the elect? Certainly the Assembly said, "All the elect, and they only, are effectually called" (WLC Q. 68),[26] but that does not mean the divines regarded conviction was limited to the elect. The Larger Catechism states: "although others may be, and often are, outwardly called by the ministry of the word, and have some common operations of the Spirit," under which, because of their own wickedness, they never come to Christ (WLC Q. 68; cf. WCF 10.4).[27] In accord with broader Puritan teachings, it is best to view conviction of sin as one of the "common operations of the Spirit" that precedes faith in effectual calling but does not necessarily lead to faith. The use of the law in convincing sinners of their pollution is "common to all men" (WLC Q. 94; cf. Q. 95). Similarly Rollock, who once called conviction of sin the first step of effectual calling, wrote later that conviction of sin is not so much part of effectual calling as is preparation for it.[28]

This interpretation of effectual calling in the standards was confirmed by the Confession of Faith (WCF 10.1) and the Larger Catechism (WLC Q. 67), which made no reference to conviction of sin in their definitions of effectual calling. The Shorter Catechism defines effectual calling in a broad sense to include the preparatory work of the Spirit, common to all men, in producing conviction of sin, whereas the Confession and Larger Catechism define it more narrowly as a work of "God's free and

---

24. Vincent, _Explicatory Catechism_, 86–87 [on WSC Q. 31].
25. Vincent, _Explicatory Catechism_, 87 [on WSC Q. 31].
26. Citing Acts 13:48.
27. Citing Matt. 22:14; 7:22; 13:20–21; Heb. 6:4–6.
28. Rollock, _Select Works_, 1:194–95.

special grace" (WCF 10.2) accomplished only in the elect. This explains why the Cambridge Synod in New England had some debate over the Confession's definition of effectual calling but was able to resolve it by recognizing that this effectual calling may be broadly or narrowly defined.[29] As we have seen, this was not a controversy between Westminster and the New England teachers of preparation but an expression of the diversity of views within the Westminster Assembly.

Thomas Watson (c. 1620–1686), in his exposition of the Shorter Catechism, published posthumously in 1692, said conviction is the "antecedent" of effectual calling: "Before this effectual call, an humbling work passeth upon the soul: a man is convinced of sin, he sees he is a sinner and nothing but a sinner; the fallow ground of his heart is broken up (Jer. 4:3).... Conviction is the first step in conversion."[30]

Thus the Westminster Standards express the two-fold approach to preparation embraced by most Puritans. First, they emphatically denied that natural man is capable of any meritorious preparation for conversion. This was the view of Reformed writers such as Calvin, Perkins, Pemble, and Cotton in opposition to Roman Catholicism. Second, the Westminster standards taught that the Spirit does a preparatory work through the law to convict sinners so that the soil of their souls is ready for faith and repentance, though this plowed soil will not produce faith and repentance until God plants this supernatural seed in them. We have footnoted the copious Scripture references for these quotations from the Westminster Standards to show that this doctrine was firmly rooted in the Bible, both in the Old and New Testaments.

Having explored the Westminster Confession and Catechisms, we turn next to the practical divinity of two men who preached and wrote in the 1640s and 1650s on this same subject.

Jeremiah Burroughs: Christ's Invitation to the Burdened

Jeremiah Burroughs (c. 1600–1646) was an advocate for the minority view of moderate Independency within the largely Presbyterian Westminster Assembly. He was a stellar preacher and promoter of peace among

---

29. Walker, *The Creeds and Platforms of Congregationalism*, 195.

30. Thomas Watson, *A Body of Practical Divinity in a Series of Sermons on the Shorter Catechism* (London: A. Fullarton, 1845), 150 [on WSC Q. 31].

various factions of Puritanism. He served as a pastor in England until increasing persecution in the 1630s forced him to move to the Netherlands. After Puritan power was reestablished, Burroughs returned to London to preach. A fall from his horse ended his life. Richard Baxter (1615–1691) said that if all the Episcopalians had been like James Ussher, all the Presbyterians like Stephen Marshall, and all the Independents like Jeremiah Burroughs, the divisions in the church would have been quickly healed.

After preaching a series of sermons particularly focused on the subject of divine reconciliation with sinners, Burroughs preached a series of sermons on Christ's saying recorded in Matthew 11:28–30, "Come unto me, all ye that labour and are heavy laden, and I will give you rest. Take my yoke upon you, and learn of me; for I am meek and lowly in heart: and ye shall find rest unto your souls. For my yoke is easy, and my burden is light." Burroughs said this was "a most gracious invitation of Jesus Christ to poor sinners to come in unto him…a heart-melting invitation… which hath been the comfort of many a wounded conscience, of many a troubled sinner."[31]

Burroughs observed from this text that when Christ calls to Himself all who labor and are heavy laden, He means especially people laboring under the burden of conviction of sin. He said these people were prompted by conscience, or the inward sense of obligation to God and condemnation for sin. He spoke of the burden of the law, guilt for sin, the corruption of sin, and affliction. Let us focus on the burden of the guilt of sin.

God lays upon people a sense of the burden of sin. Burroughs wrote, "God comes to make [the heart] to be sensible of the evil of sin."[32] The guilt of sin is so heavy that it dragged even angels down to hell and made Christ Himself sweat drops of blood. Burroughs then referred his readers to his treatise on the evil of sin,[33] in which he said that sin is a worse evil than the greatest of afflictions. Sin wrongs God, who is the sum of all good. Every sin at its root desires to destroy God, if that were possible. Sin wrongs man more than affliction does, for godly men may be impoverished and persecuted yet remain noble and worthy, but sin makes a man worthless. Sin destroys everything good. It is the evil in all evils;

---

31. Burroughs, *Four Books*, 1:1–2.
32. Burroughs, *Four Books*, 1:12.
33. Burroughs, *Four Books*, 1:14.

the very image of the devil. Sin, though committed by finite creatures, contains a kind of infinity of evil within itself.[34]

Burroughs wrote about the burden of sin so that people might know how that burden elicits Christ's invitation to come to Him. The words "heavy laden" imply that the truths about God and sin no longer "lay floating" or "hovering" in the mind but "now the Lord causes them to sink down within the heart" so that the sinner feels their crushing weight.[35] The comforts and pleasures that were supposed to accompany sin have come to nothing. The sinner sees himself as a "loathsome creature."[36] Sin and temptation make him tremble lest one more ounce added to his burden should "press the soul down to eternal misery." The greatest weight upon the sinner is realizing that he has been the enemy of "an infinite, blessed, holy God, that is so infinitely worthy of all honor from me."[37] This burden is so great that the sinner knows no angel or man can lift it from him; it is so great that he would rather bear any other burden instead of the burden of sin. Though "the heavy hand of God is upon him," the sinner acknowledges that God is righteous: "let him have glory whatsoever becomes of me, for the truth is, I have brought this burden upon myself."[38]

Burroughs knew that some people suffered from psychological burdens quite apart from a conviction of sin. Those who were not experientially Reformed tended to dismiss conviction of sin as mere "melancholy," which today might be called a mental illness or depression. He responded by pinpointing six differences between melancholy and conviction of conscience: (1) Melancholy can appear with great ignorance, but conviction comes with a new revelation of God and sin. (2) Melancholy generally comes gradually through bodily changes, but conviction can appear in a flash by something made known from the Word. (3) Melancholy brings confusion, but conviction gives clear insight about why one is in distress. (4) Melancholy makes outward afflictions difficult to bear, but conviction makes trials seem light compared to God's wrath. (5) Melancholy causes dullness and sluggishness, but conviction stirs people to thought, prayer,

---

34. Jeremiah Burroughs, *The Evil of Evils, or the Exceeding Sinfulness of Sin* (London: Peter Cole, 1654), *passim*. This book was revised and reprinted as Jeremiah Burroughs, *The Evil of Evils, or the Exceeding Sinfulness of Sin*, ed. Don Kistler (Grand Rapids: Soli Deo Gloria, 2008).
35. Burroughs, *Four Books*, 1:16.
36. Burroughs, *Four Books*, 1:17.
37. Burroughs, *Four Books*, 1:18.
38. Burroughs, *Four Books*, 1:19–20.

and action. (6) Melancholy can be cured sometimes with medicine and outward comforts, but conviction needs healing through the blood of Christ applied by the Spirit through the gospel.[39]

The burden of sin, though "almost intolerable," does not leave men in despair. Burroughs wrote, "But now those that are burdened with sin in such a manner as the Lord doth use to prepare the heart for his Son by; they feel the weight of it, but so feel that weight as they labor, that is, their hearts are yet active and stirring and working," listening to God's Word, praying for God's mercy, waiting on God's will, and ready to do His command. This is the kind of burdened sinner whom Christ especially invites to come to Him and find rest.[40]

At this point the sinner may feel that the burden of sin is as vast as a mountain that blocks access to Christ, which only a few, elite athletes can climb. He may not be sure that he has adequately experienced his burden of sin. One of the dangers of Puritan preparation is that it lays such stress on conviction of sin that it can discourage some people from coming to Christ. Burroughs, who sensed this danger, hastened to say that being burdened over sin is "not any condition of the covenant of grace...there is no other condition but believing in Christ."[41] He also warned against trying to find assurance of salvation in one's feeling of conviction, for faith must rest upon Christ alone. Being troubled for our sins does not save us, for only Christ's sufferings for sin on the cross can do that. Therefore the depth or weight of our burden over sins does not matter so long as it moves us to come to Christ.[42]

In Burroughs we see how the doctrines of creation and redemption intersect in the Puritan doctrine of conversion. God normally lays the burden of sin on the soul He intends to save because "Jesus Christ doth work upon the heart in a rational way, as a rational creature, although he doth work above reason, and conveys supernatural grace that is beyond reason."[43] God created man with a mind and a heart, and sin did not destroy those faculties. If a man trusts in Christ, he will do so in a rational and emotional manner, or he ceases to be a man. Therefore God ordinarily prepares sinners for faith by giving them an understanding

---

39. Burroughs, *The Evil of Evils*, ed. Kistler, 248–56.
40. Burroughs, *Four Books*, 1:20.
41. Burroughs, *Four Books*, 1:21.
42. Burroughs, *Four Books*, 1:21–22.
43. Burroughs, *Four Books*, 1:22.

and sense of their need for Christ. Yet redemption is a supernatural work of grace alone, both in its accomplishment by Christ and in its application through Christ's Spirit. The gap between conviction of sin and the exercise of faith remains an infinite distance because it is a qualitative change from death to life. Burroughs and other Puritans labored to hold creation and redemption together by viewing conversion through the processes of both preparation and regeneration.

From this doctrine of Christ's invitation to the burdened, Burroughs drew the following exhortations to sinners:

- Grieve over sin: "There is no other burden that we are to bring upon ourselves, but rather to seek to avoid them; but as for the burden of sin, we are to burden our hearts with that, and to labor to lay our sins to our hearts, and to press them there, and to charge them upon our own spirits with all the aggravations we can, and to join with the work of God's Spirit, when the Spirit of God comes to lay sin upon the soul."

- Do not despair, for Christ still calls you to come: "So I say to all burdened sinners; be of good comfort troubled soul, Christ calls thee; he saith come to me all ye that are weary, and heavy laden; he doth not say, thou that art so much laden."

- Remember that salvation is near: "He doth not say, thou art a wretched, wicked creature, and depart from me thou cursed, as he will say to sinners hereafter…but thou dost hear this voice this day from Christ, 'Come to me all you that are weary.'"

- Take your burden to God in prayer: "Go thy way, O soul, and get into the presence of God, and tell God of thy burdens that thou feelest, make thy moan unto him…and it is very probably, that thy soul shall be heard, and according to this invitation here."[44]

Nonetheless, the primary application of Matthew 11:28 that Burroughs pressed upon his hearers is to come to Christ. He wrote, "Is there any poor soul that is ready to perish under the weight of sin that goes under the load of it; Christ calls to that soul to come to him."[45] To come to Christ is to believe in Him, for, "It implies a beholding, a looking unto Jesus Christ, as being the all-sufficient Savior, to save our souls from all

---

44. Burroughs, *Four Books,* 1:26–30.
45. Burroughs, *Four Books,* 1:26.

the evils that are upon us, and to supply unto us all good we stand in need of."[46] Rest your heart in nothing until it rests in Him; stir up all your spirit to seek after Him. Roll all your burdens "upon the infinite, rich, free grace of God in Jesus Christ." Indeed, commit your souls to Christ for salvation and all good now and forever.[47]

Christ requires nothing of the burdened sinner to find rest but to come to Him (Isa. 55:1; Matt. 11:28; Rev. 22:17).[48] Burroughs thus wrote, "No man or woman that God is working upon to come to Christ, need trouble themselves about the degree of humiliation, or the time of humiliation…. If you would know what degree of humiliation is sufficient, only so much as can bring you to Christ."[49]

William Guthrie: Preparation and the Free Offer

Scottish preacher William Guthrie (1620–1665), though little known today, was a great preacher in his time. Guthrie studied under and experienced conversion through Samuel Rutherford, one of Scotland's commissioners to the Westminster Assembly. Guthrie saw hundreds of profane and careless people in his parish at Fenwick transformed into godly believers. John Owen read Guthrie's *The Christian's Great Interest* (1658), and said (with typical humility) that this little book contained more divinity than all of Owen's writings combined.

Guthrie wrote "of a preparatory work of the law, of which the Lord doth generally make use, to prepare his own way in men's souls."[50] However, he said, "the Lord doth not always take that way with men."[51] Some God calls from the womb or in early childhood, some "in a sovereign gospel-way…by some few words of love" without any apparent work of the law, and some at the brink of death.[52] Guthrie described these cases with such clarity that his readers could discern whether or not this was their experience.

46. Burroughs, *Four Books,* 1:116–17.
47. Burroughs, *Four Books,* 1:118–22.
48. Burroughs, *Four Books,* 1:130.
49. Burroughs, *Four Books,* 1:132.
50. William Guthrie, *The Christian's Great Interest* (Glasgow: for William Collins, 1833), 78.
51. Guthrie, *The Christian's Great Interest,* 78.
52. Guthrie, *The Christian's Great Interest,* 79–80, 82.

When God works in a preparatory, legal way, as He does with many, He "does not keep one way or measure in it," Guthrie said.[53] Sometimes God's work is "more violently and suddenly dispatched," and sometimes He "carries on this work more calmly, softly, and easily" over a period of time.[54] Guthrie described the steps of this process, noting that the Lord lays siege to the sinner, drives him out of his deceitful resting places, and makes salvation most precious and necessary to him. Reprobation, death, and the unpardonable sin may haunt a sinner with fears, but God upholds him with the possibility of salvation.[55]

Guthrie said the sinner must know that "he was born a rebel and out-law unto God," that he had committed many actual, particular sins, and that God's wrath "is standing in force against those very sins of which he is guilty."[56] He must know that he has no ability to make peace with this God who is at war against sin and sinners, and that he is "void of all the saving graces of the Spirit": true love, fear, godly sorrow, and faith.[57] He must know these things in a way that seriously affects his heart, so he counts salvation more important than anything. Indeed, it breaks his heart and makes him loath himself and long for speedy relief.[58]

The Lord stirs the desire for salvation, which sometimes provokes men to do many good works, only to fall under fresh revelations of their sin. Generally men in this condition want to be alone to think about their sins as well as God's mercy and patience. The sinner who is so con-victed then begins to pray, to confess his sins to God, and to grasp hold of God's promises.[59]

In this process, the sinner comes to know God's way of salvation through the satisfaction of divine justice by Christ's righteousness. He knows that God is willing to make peace with all who come to Him through Jesus Christ, invites all to come, and will most assuredly receive all who do come.[60] Embedded in Guthrie's view of preparation is the free offer of the gospel; indeed, he believed that one aspect of such preparation

---

53. Guthrie, *The Christian's Great Interest*, 79; cf. p. 99.
54. Guthrie, *The Christian's Great Interest*, 85, 86.
55. Guthrie, *The Christian's Great Interest*, 86–89.
56. Guthrie, *The Christian's Great Interest*, 178.
57. Guthrie, *The Christian's Great Interest*, 179–80.
58. Guthrie, *The Christian's Great Interest*, 180–81.
59. Guthrie, *The Christian's Great Interest*, 90–95.
60. Guthrie, *The Christian's Great Interest*, 181–83.

was convincing sinners of that free offer. In one sermon, Guthrie said, "Wherever he comes in the word of his gospel, he excludes none but those who exclude themselves. And so the promises are held out to all.... God offers the promises freely to all that will take them."[61]

In another sermon Guthrie declared that God gives "an invitation to all persons in all places,"[62] which is, "Ho, every one that thirsteth, come ye to the waters, and he that hath no money; come ye, buy, and eat" (Isa. 55:1a). In that invitation Guthrie found preparation, for one who comes must travel a certain road. God's road is the authoritative demonstration of the Spirit and the Word to show a man his sins and guilt and liability to God's curse, as well as to make him "willing to embrace the free offers of Jesus Christ."[63] The one who buys must first see his need of what is offered. And the one who eats must have hunger for the food.[64] Thus the free offer of the gospel and preparation go together: the free offer reveals God's willingness to save, and preparation makes men willing to heed the offer, and be saved.

Conclusion

Although the Westminster Standards did not include an express statement on preparation for conversion, the concept of conviction of sin appears in its treatment of effectual calling, saving faith, and repentance unto life. By consulting the three major Standards and comparing them to one another, we have seen that the Westminster divines upheld the general Puritan consensus that rejected Roman Catholic preparation but accepted Reformed preparation. That was confirmed by the seventeenth-century expositions of the Westminster Shorter Catechism written by Vincent and Watson. The confessional standards of British Presbyterianism declare that conviction of sin, though a common work of the Spirit, is an important prelude to God's effectual calling of His elect. They also warned that though the unconverted cannot please God in using the means of grace, neglecting the use of those means is far more displeasing to Him.

---

61. William Guthrie, sermon upon Isaiah 44:3, in *A Collection of Lectures and Sermons... mostly in the time of the Late Persecution*, ed. J[ohn] H[owie] (Glasgow: J. Bryce, 1779), 25.

62. Guthrie, sermons upon Isaiah 55:1–2, in *A Collection of Lectures and Sermons*, 98.

63. Guthrie, sermons upon Isaiah 55:1–2, in *A Collection of Lectures and Sermons*, 112.

64. Guthrie, sermons upon Isaiah 55:1–2, in *A Collection of Lectures and Sermons*, 113–14.

However, the Standards are silent about the details of preparation, presenting no "morphology of conversion" and no analysis of conviction and humiliation in its component parts. Nor do they address controversies about Reformed preparation regarding saving qualifications, or being cut off from Adam before engrafting into Christ, or contentment to be damned. Rather, a simple outline of the conversion process was laid down in the Shorter Catechism's description of effectual calling: conviction of our sin and misery, enlightenment regarding Christ, and renewal of the will resulting in the willing embrace of Jesus Christ as the gospel freely offers Him to us. Thus the Westminster Assembly affirmed the reality of preparation for faith but did not elevate any particular view of it to creedal status. Nor did the Assembly consider preparation to be a doctrine worthy of its own chapter, as it did of justification and adoption. They chose rather to subsume preparation under other doctrines such as effectual calling and repentance unto life.

The preaching of Burroughs and Guthrie also demonstrated that preparation remained at the heart of Puritan care of souls in the mid-seventeenth century. Puritan pastors guided sinners on the journey from spiritual indifference and complacency in sin, through conviction and humiliation for sin, to solid conversion. Their sermons exhibited great tenderness for broken-hearted sinners and a piercing portrayal of the evil of sin. They expected a period of struggle before peace but cautioned that God moves men with great variety in their experiences. Their sermons highlighted Scripture texts that were favorites in Puritan evangelism: Isaiah 55:1, Matthew 11:28, and Revelation 22:17. They thus wedded preparation with the free offer of the gospel, in which the free offer prevented preparation from becoming a condition for salvation, and preparation prevented the free offer from becoming easy believism.

CHAPTER NINE

Preparation under a Scholastic Lens:
John Norton

Preparatory work is said to be so; either by way of mere order, asserted by the Orthodox, according to the Scriptures: or by way of causation, merit, and congruity; asserted by the Papists, and Arminians; contrary to the Scriptures.

—John Norton[1]

John Norton (1606–1663), a New England Congregationalist minister, was a friend of John Cotton and wrote a short biography of Cotton after his death. Cotton handpicked Norton to succeed him as minister of First Church at Boston. Cotton also wrote the Epistle to the Reader in Norton's *The Orthodox Evangelist*. In it, Cotton praised Norton's book for its scholastic brevity and rational disputation, and especially for Norton's "holy dexterity" in searching out the mysteries of grace and free-will.[2]

That is ironic, given Miller's depiction of Cotton as a Calvinistic opponent of preparation, for Norton's book devotes more than thirty pages—a tenth of the book—to preparation.[3] The irony increases when we realize

---

1. John Norton, *The Orthodox Evangelist, or A Treatise Wherein many Great Evangelical Truths… Are briefly Discussed* (London: by John Macock for Henry Cripps and Lodowick Lloyd, 1654), 130.

2. John Cotton, "To the Judicious Christian Reader," in Norton, *The Orthodox Evangelist,* [no pagination]. Pettit writes that in this preface Cotton said that Calvin and others like him had been "slighted" in New England (*The Heart Prepared,* 178). But in fact Cotton did not use the word "slighted" nor did he specify New England in this remark. Instead he said that the medieval "schoolmen…of late years have crept (for a time) into more credit amongst the schools, than the most judicious and orthodox of our best new writers (Luther, Calvin, Martyr, Bucer, and the rest)" because of a preference for scholastic precision in argumentation, though the schoolmen lacked insight in the Scriptures. By the "schools" he probably refers to Cambridge and Oxford, and perhaps Harvard.

3. Norton, *The Orthodox Evangelist,* 129–163.

that Norton quoted William Pemble no less than six times, five of which are from his *Vindiciae Gratiae*.[4] Once again Cotton and Pemble do not appear to be the archenemies of preparation that Miller said they were.

In this chapter we will examine Norton's view of preparation. While many of the writers we previously studied may be considered quite scholastic in their approach, Norton extensively employs the scholastic method. Norton also gives lengthier consideration to our subject than Ames did in his scholastic treatise. Examining his writings also offers us valuable insights about his interactions with previous writers.

Norton's Disputation for Preparation

Norton stated, "There are certain preparatory works coming between the carnal rest of the soul in the state of sin, and effectual vocation."[5] Note that he did not teach that there was a state of preparation between the state of sin and effectual calling, for preparation is not a distinct spiritual *state* but a subjective *work* in the soul, which is still under the power of sin and death but is no longer permitted to lie in "carnal rest" in that state. This preparatory work is done in the season when men are still under condemnation but before they trust in Christ, and shakes them out of their "ease in sin."[6]

Norton elaborated this position, saying, "Christ in his ordinary dispensation of the gospel, calleth not sinners, as sinners, but such sinners, i.e. qualified sinners, immediately to believe."[7] In saying this, Norton meant that such sinners have no other duties that must be done "before we can believe." These "inherent qualifications" are "wrought in the ministry, both of the law, and gospel; by the common work of the Spirit concurring."[8] These qualifications are necessary for a sinner to be "invited immediately to believe," because he must first be "sensible of sin" and "sensible of his misery, and of his being destitute of any remedy."[9] We will examine what he meant by "qualification" later.

God's way is to give people a sense of their need and powerlessness before He delivers them by His grace. Norton used biblical typology to

---

4. Norton, *The Orthodox Evangelist*, 162, 166, 256, 264, 298, 326.

5. Norton, *The Orthodox Evangelist*, 129; cf. p. 141.

6. Norton, *The Orthodox Evangelist*, 137.

7. Norton, *The Orthodox Evangelist*, 129.

8. Norton, *The Orthodox Evangelist*, 130.

9. Norton, *The Orthodox Evangelist*, 130–31.

support his case for preparatory grace. Sarah had to endure years of barrenness before supernaturally giving birth to Isaac. That typifies our regeneration (Gal. 4:28–29), Norton said. Likewise, Israel suffered slavery prior to the exodus from Egypt, and exile prior to returning to the Promised Land, which are both types of salvation, Norton said, for Christ, "by the common work of the Spirit he maketh them sick, before by the saving work of the Spirit he maketh them well."[10] God does this preparatory work so that we may glorify Him. Sinners must learn to condemn themselves so they can declare God and His law to be just. Men must sense their nothingness so they may honor Christ as their all in all.[11] Norton wrote, "We cannot acknowledge the justice of God, if we do not acknowledge sin.... We cannot acknowledge grace, if we do not acknowledge both sin and justice."[12]

By viewing preparation as a common work of the Spirit of Christ, Norton indicated that preparation was a mercy from God but one that did not include or belong to salvation. Though the Spirit works preparation through the law, it is not, strictly speaking, a work of justice but an expression of mercy to awaken the sinner. Preparation does not satisfy justice, for it is not meritorious. Parker is confused when he says that Norton and "the stricter preparationists" viewed humiliation as the work of divine justice and is not "more immediately associated with God's mercy and the redemptive offer of the Gospels [*sic*]."[13] Preparatory humiliation springs from a view of divine justice, but the Spirit works it out of mercy to prepare the heart in conjunction with God's free offer in the gospel. Sheer justice would simply damn sinners, not awaken them to their danger. Pettit's comment on Hooker also applies here, "Yet if the process [of humiliation] itself is long and tedious, it must nevertheless be centered on mercy or the promise of divine love."[14]

---

10. Norton, *The Orthodox Evangelist*, 135.

11. Norton, *The Orthodox Evangelist*, 136.

12. Norton, *The Orthodox Evangelist*, 150.

13. Parker, "Edward Taylor's Preparationism," 265. Therefore Taylor's attribution of humiliation to God's mercy does not contradict the views of preparatory grace of Norton and others like him. In fact, Taylor depicted preparation as a cooperative effort of mercy and justice. For his poetic views on preparation, see "God's Determinations," lines 97–210, in *The Poems of Edward Taylor*, ed. Donald Stanford (Chapel Hill: University of North Carolina Press, 1989), 270–74.

14. Pettit, *The Heart Prepared*, 98.

Later in his treatise, Norton offered a detailed explanation of preparation through the law and the gospel. He said the Spirit of God uses the law to work (1) conviction of the holiness of the law as the will of God; (2) conviction of sin as a transgression of the law, including Adam's sin imputed to us all, our original sin or corruption inherited from Adam, and our actual sins of omission and commission; (3) conviction of guilt or the binding of the sinner to punishment; (4) imprisonment of the sinner under a sense of the power and guilt of sin; (5) conviction of the righteousness of God in punishing us for sin; and (6) destruction of the sinner's excuses and self-defenses so that he is silenced before the Judge.[15]

The Spirit uses the gospel to give men (1) revelation of the historical facts of the gospel of Christ for the salvation of sinners, (2) preparatory repentance (as distinct from evangelical repentance) resulting in an external conformity to the principles of Scripture, (3) further sense of one's lost estate because one lacks the righteousness of Christ and lacks the ability to turn to Christ, (4) acknowledgment of God's sovereignty in showing grace or not showing grace as He pleases, (5) understanding the command of the gospel to believe in Christ and the power of the gospel to create faith, and (6) waiting on the Lord by actively receiving the Word in hearing, reading, meditating, discussing, and praying.[16]

Norton listed a dozen different points of preparation, yet he denied that a person must have a "distinct experience of the several heads of preparatory work.... Yet the more distinctness, the better."[17] Norton also said that a "sincerely converted" man might not remember experiencing all the specific parts of preparation, perhaps through a lack of "light" in the preaching he had heard or in his own mind.[18] Thus, in preparation he spoke of an ideal spiritual situation rather than one that every person should experience in specific steps. He also taught converts with a weak or confused experience of preparation to expect that they might be unsettled and struggle with assurance of salvation as God worked to reduce their "carnal confidences" and taught their souls "to magnify the law, to condemn sin, to judge itself, and exalt grace" in a greater degree.[19] In other words, rather than injuring the soul with a low self-image, he said a

15. Norton, *The Orthodox Evangelist,* 142–52.
16. Norton, *The Orthodox Evangelist,* 152–59.
17. Norton, *The Orthodox Evangelist,* 160.
18. Norton, *The Orthodox Evangelist,* 161.
19. Norton, *The Orthodox Evangelist,* 162.

solid preparatory work lays a foundation for humility and maturity after the Spirit comes to dwell in the soul.

As to what degree of preparation was necessary, Norton offered the standard Puritan answer that what counts is the reality of humiliation, not its depth or duration. He said, "As the greatest measure hath no necessary connection with salvation, so the least measure puts the soul into a preparatory capacity.... There is not the like degree of humiliation in all those that are converted; for some feel a greater measure of trouble, other a lesser. But all that are truly converted are truly humbled."[20]

For Norton, preparation was such a normative pattern that he believed not a single example of adult conversion in the Bible could be cited to prove the lack of some degree of preparation.[21] He also rejected arguments from conversion accounts that did not speak of preparation as arguments from silence.[22]

Man's Preparation and God's Freedom

Norton defined preparatory grace in a way that fit with the Reformed doctrine of the sovereignty of God. Some of the confusion we have observed in recent scholarship rises from the failure to note the differences between Roman Catholic or Arminian notions of preparation and Reformed preparation. Norton made this distinction very plain, saying: "Preparatory work is said to be so; either by way of mere order, asserted by the Orthodox, according to the Scriptures: or by way of causation, merit, and congruity; asserted by the Papists, and Arminians; contrary to the Scriptures."[23] In so doing, he made the same distinction as Ames had before him.[24]

Against the objection that God's omnipotence means "there is no use of preparatory work," Norton responded that God's providence ordinarily does not operate by mere operations of absolute power but through the "second cause" of creatures working according to His will.[25] This resembles Burroughs's argument that God prepares the mind for conversion

20. Norton, *The Orthodox Evangelist,* 160–61.
21. Norton, *The Orthodox Evangelist,* 138.
22. Norton, *The Orthodox Evangelist,* 139.
23. Norton, *The Orthodox Evangelist,* 130.
24. Ames, "The Preparation of a Sinner for Conversion," theses 1–2.
25. Norton, *The Orthodox Evangelist,* 138–39.

because He has created men to be rational. Norton was applying the Reformed doctrine of God's will operating powerfully and effectively through the means of human activity.[26] Cohen writes, "God's use of second causes as the instruments of His efficiency does not violate their integrity as actors.... It does not disturb the normal functioning of the human faculties; consequently, people can exercise their free choice."[27] Against the objection that "preparatory work seemeth to darken the freeness of grace," Norton said, "Preparatory works precede vocation in way of order, not in way of causality.... Preparatory work is the effect of free common grace: as saving work is the effect of free special grace."[28] He also said all is of grace, not of merit, and common grace does not cause saving grace.

Norton taught that "the soul is passive in vocation," that is, in "the infusion of a principle of life...by the Spirit into the lost soul."[29] He anticipated the objection that the soul is active in using the means of grace prior to and in receiving saving grace. He also clarified the process by saying that the soul is active in the use of means, yet passive in regard to the saving power which God sends through the means. He said, "God doth not work savingly upon us, as upon stocks or senseless creatures."[30] Norton then made the same point as Burroughs in bringing together the doctrines of creation and redemption:

> We on the one hand against the Enthusiasts affirm not only the power to use, but the duty of using the means; and on the other hand, against the Arminians, deny that man before grace can do anything, having the power of a cause (so far forth as cometh from them) in order to life; because we are reasonable creatures God proceeds with us in the use of means; because we are dead creatures, in respect to the efficacy of the means, we depend wholly and absolutely upon God.[31]

Both preparation and regeneration have their place. Norton cited the illustration of Ezekiel's vision to say there can be no resurrection unless the bones and flesh of the dead are collected and assembled together. But

---

26. Stoever, "Nature, Grace and John Cotton," 25–27.
27. Cohen, *God's Caress*, 93.
28. Norton, *The Orthodox Evangelist*, 139.
29. Norton, *The Orthodox Evangelist*, 257.
30. Norton, *The Orthodox Evangelist*, 270.
31. Norton, *The Orthodox Evangelist*, 271.

until the Spirit of life comes, those reassembled bones, covered with flesh, remain lifeless corpses, unable to give themselves life.[32] Pettit mistakenly attributes a new approach to preparation by Norton when he says, "In Norton, as in none other, we find a new and significantly different attitude towards the function and purpose of preparatory motions," by asserting that during preparation the soul remains dead and passive.[33] On the contrary, Norton's combination of the doctrines of preparation and regeneration has a clear precedent in William Ames, as is evident in Norton's borrowing of Ames's metaphor of the bones taken from Ezekiel's vision.[34]

Preparation and Qualification

Let us now address some questions about Norton's definition of preparation. He wrote, "By preparatory work, we understand certain inherent qualifications...wrought in the ministry, both of the law, and gospel.... Before sinners are invited immediately to believe, they must be such sinners, qualified sinners."[35] What does Norton mean by "inherent qualifications"?

Norton said, "Qualifications are gracious dispensations whereby the soul is in some measure rendered a more capable subject of faith, or conversion."[36] These qualifications might refer to "the remainders of the image of God in man after the fall," which is "the grace of nature." Or, more properly, they might refer to "the common work of the Spirit, by ministry of the law and gospel...common supernatural grace" consisting of "preparatory works."[37]

Qualification: A Warrant to Believe or Capacity for Faith?

Still, why did Norton call preparation a qualification? Was he saying that the sinner has no warrant to believe in Christ until he has acquired certain inner qualifications? His language might lead us to think so. Or was he merely saying that a sinner without these qualities, while called and

---

32. Norton, *The Orthodox Evangelist,* 270–71.
33. Pettit, *The Heart Prepared,* 182.
34. Ames, "The Preparation of a Sinner for Conversion," theses 16–17, objections 4–5.
35. Norton, *The Orthodox Evangelist,* 130; cf. p. 141.
36. Norton, *The Orthodox Evangelist,* 163.
37. Norton, *The Orthodox Evangelist,* 163–64.

obligated to believe, has no proper frame of heart and mind in which faith could exist?

Norton wrote about God's "command to believe" as well as "our duty to believe" (1 John 3:23).[38] Although God made an absolute decree as to whom He would save, He has revealed the gospel of salvation with the condition of faith. Thus Norton said, "All men may be admonished of their duty to believe, whether they are elected or not elected."[39] He said of convicted unbelievers, "Though they that have not faith and cannot seek Christ as they ought, but their very prayer is sin; yet it is their duty to pray and to seek after Christ (Ps. 79:6; Jer. 10:25)."[40] He then distinguished between moral ability and moral duty, saying that God commanded Judas to believe, revealing his duty to believe, but God chose not to give him faith. God's decree determines what God will do, and God's command determines what man should do. God commanded Abraham to sacrifice Isaac, placing him under the duty of taking up the knife, but God also decreed that Abraham would not actually slay his son.[41]

Therefore Norton's language of qualification does not mean that man cannot be outwardly called to trust in Christ until he experiences preparatory conviction of sin. He repeatedly said that it is the "duty" of everyone who hears the preaching of the gospel of Christ to believe.[42]

Imprecision at the point of man's duty leads to great confusion about preparation for faith. Evangelistic preaching in the Reformed tradition pressed upon men their duty to trust in Christ, repent of sin, and offer themselves up to God in new obedience. But in so addressing the unconverted, the Reformed preacher distinguished between moral duty and moral ability. He was not making a statement about the ability of fallen men to prepare themselves. He was issuing the gospel call, through which it may please God to send His effectual call, empowering the sinner to believe, repent, and walk in newness of life. If we interpret Puritan theology under the assumption that *in their belief system* responsibility implies ability, we will misunderstand them as attributing powers to fallen men that they do not have.

---

38. Norton, *The Orthodox Evangelist,* 158.
39. Norton, *The Orthodox Evangelist,* 86.
40. Norton, *The Orthodox Evangelist,* 159.
41. Norton, *The Orthodox Evangelist,* 92; cf. p. 67.
42. Norton, *The Orthodox Evangelist,* 17, 81, 84, 158, 162, 171, 191–92, 194, 199, 202, 231.

Furthermore, one can see how the very preaching of the Puritans could create such confusion. While exhorting the lost to do works of preparation, preachers could also impress upon sinners their duty to believe in a way that suggested conversion was part of preparation. The goal of such sermons was that sinners would come to Christ. Since many of the Puritan documents on preparation consisted of evangelistic sermons, one can see how exhortations to duty could be misunderstood as descriptions of preparation, whereas some of those duties are actually fulfilled in conversion itself. So, when interpreting Puritan theology, we must ask whether the writers are addressing the duty or ability of their hearers, and if it is the duty, whether it is a duty fulfilled in preparation or in conversion and sanctification. Norton was clear that though unconverted sinners do not have the ability to convert themselves, all men have the gospel duty of faith and repentance.

What then should we make of Norton's statement that "Before sinners are invited immediately to believe, they must be such sinners, qualified sinners"?[43] The key word here is *immediately*. On the same page Norton distinguished between a "mediate" calling to believe versus an "immediate" calling. A mediate calling meant that "some other duty, or duties, are to be done before we can believe." The word *can* indicates this is a matter of ability, not duty. To use a modern illustration, if I command you to fly to Heidelberg, this also implies that you must first go to an airport to board an airplane, not attempt to fly like Superman. In the same way, Norton taught that God commands all men through the gospel to believe in Christ, but they cannot do so unless they first acknowledge their sinfulness, condemnation, and need for Christ. That is what it means to be a "qualified sinner."

Norton was not wise to refer to humiliation as a qualification. Preston had written, "Humiliation is not required as a qualification."[44] The use of the term *qualifications* could confuse people and discourage them from coming to Christ by making preparation necessary to conversion after all. It might push them toward morbid introspection to search for such qualifications. Though sanctification has an important role as evidence for one's justification, it does not seem wise to describe preparation as

---

43. Norton, *The Orthodox Evangelist*, 130.

44. John Preston, *The Breast-plate of Faith and Love* (1634; facsimile repr., Edinburgh: Banner of Truth, 1979), 1:11.

qualification for calling people to faith. For we then make it sound like we should only offer Christ to the class of the duly prepared, and therefore duly qualified sinners. If that is what Norton is saying, he was simply wrong. If, however, he only meant that humiliation is a qualification in the sense that this is the way that the Holy Spirit ordinarily works so that sinners feel a need to flee to Christ, he is right. We believe that this latter interpretation is indeed Norton's view. We must also remember that his treatise was not a series of sermons preached to ordinary people, but a scholastic, theological disputation adorned with Latin quotations from other theologians. In such a genre, the reader was expected to grasp precise terminology and fine distinctions. As Norton himself recognized, this was not milk for babes but strong meat for men.[45]

Is Preparation a Mark of Election?
Another danger inherent in the use of *qualifications* was that it might encourage people to count themselves as elect before trusting in Christ. They could emphasize their preparation as a qualification that allowed them to rest in their humiliation instead of resting in Christ. Norton devoted an entire chapter of his book to refuting this error.[46] He said while it is "our duty" to encourage men to believe in Christ, "and to hold forth the increase of hope, according as the preparatory work doth increase: yet, not so far as certainly to promise faith or salvation."[47] Until a sinner trusts in Christ, Scripture teaches that he remains under God's wrath (Mark 16:16; John 3:36; Heb. 11:6).[48] Norton also wrote, "In an elect person, yet not a believer, there is no other qualification than what may be found in a reprobate...than what is the effect of common grace."[49] No quality or quantity of preparation marks an unbeliever as one of God's chosen. Only faith in Christ can do that.

Earlier we observed that both Hooker and Shepard taught that prior to being engrafted into Christ by faith, an elect person must be cut off from the root of Adam.[50] That suggests there is a unique quality in the elect

45. Norton, "The Epistle Dedicatory," in *The Orthodox Evangelist*, [no pagination].
46. Norton, *The Orthodox Evangelist*, 163–93.
47. Norton, *The Orthodox Evangelist*, 166.
48. Norton, *The Orthodox Evangelist*, 166–67.
49. Norton, *The Orthodox Evangelist*, 170.
50. Shepard, *The Sound Beleever*, 97–116; Hooker, *The Application of Redemption... The Ninth and Tenth Books*, 673–79.

prior to faith in Christ. In chapter eight, Norton addressed the question, "whether there be any saving qualification, before the grace of faith."[51] By "saving qualification," he meant an effect of grace that has a "necessary and infallible connection with eternal life."[52] Norton recognized that some "reverend, learned, judicious, and pious" men, who were not in the same category as Pelagians, Papists, or Arminians, nevertheless "seemed to teach that there are some qualifications before faith that are saving."[53] This was an internal debate within the Reformed church.

Norton expressed his opponents' objection by saying, "If in the order of our spiritual marriage the soul is dead unto the law before it be married to Christ, then there is a parting with all, a cutting off from, or dying unto sin, and consequently a saving qualification before faith" (Rom. 7:4; cf. Gal. 2:19).[54] Hooker and Shepard had already asserted there was such a cutting off before faith. It also seems likely that Cotton opposed such an idea when he denied that there were any "saving qualifications" prior to union with Christ by faith.[55] It was not a debate between Cotton and preparationists but a debate among men who all affirmed preparation. Norton argued against Hooker and Shepard by saying this grace of dying to sin and law was "grace given in vocation, and is called habitual mortification."[56] While the soul under preparation may part with sin in external obedience and inward restraint, only through faith does it part with sin in habitual, Spirit-worked mortification, evangelical obedience, and ongoing sanctification.[57]

To Hooker's credit, he did say, "The Spirit never doth give, nor can there be any evidence that God will work the first condition of grace, or the first grace in the soul before it is wrought."[58] But Norton rightly corrected Hooker and Shepard for allowing preparation to intrude into the realm of regeneration. Though they may not have intended to do so, the early New England theologians opened the door for people to ground their hope of salvation upon the evidence of preparation alone.

51. Norton, *The Orthodox Evangelist,* 163.
52. Norton, *The Orthodox Evangelist,* 165.
53. Norton, *The Orthodox Evangelist,* 166.
54. Norton, *The Orthodox Evangelist,* 180.
55. Cotton, *The New Covenant,* 52–54.
56. Norton, *The Orthodox Evangelist,* 181.
57. Norton, *The Orthodox Evangelist,* 182–83.
58. Hooker, *The Application of Redemption... The First Eight Books,* 36.

In addition to quoting and interpreting Scripture, Norton quoted many Puritan and Reformed writers to show that he was not deviating from an orthodox position nor from the general Puritan doctrine of preparation. He cited Ames's disputation on preparation as saying,

> Preparatory works are not dispositions, having always a necessary or certain connection with the form to be introduced; they are not so proportioned unto regeneration, as any degree of heat produced by the fire in the wood hath itself unto fire, but they are material dispositions, which maketh the subject more capable of the form to be introduced; as the dryness of the wood hath itself unto the fire.[59]

Norton also quoted Preston as saying, "The promise is not made to preparation, but to coming."[60]

Preparation and the Soul's Capacity

Ames's statement just cited implies that preparation gives sinners more capacity for faith. Norton also used such language, saying that preparatory work is "wrought in the ministry, both of the law, and gospel; by the common work of the Spirit concurring, whereby the soul is put into a ministerial capacity of believing immediately; i.e. of immediate receiving of the Lord Jesus Christ."[61] Elsewhere he also spoke of preparation producing "ministerial capacity" in the context of the "ministry" of the law and the gospel.[62]

So "ministerial capacity" refers to how God works to prepare and enlarge the heart for faith, through the means of grace, such as the ministry of the Word. Norton wrote of "a preparatory capacity, or ministerial next-disposition to the receiving of Christ. So in the order of God's dispensation, a soul who is being called to believe will not then object to its believing."[63] However, this "ministerial capacity…is common both to the elect and reprobate."[64] It is not a saving grace, nor a saving qualification. But it is a capacity for faith in Christ that is formed in the soul by preparatory common grace. Though the soul does not yet have the grace to

59. Norton, *The Orthodox Evangelist*, 177.
60. Norton, *The Orthodox Evangelist*, 188.
61. Norton, *The Orthodox Evangelist*, 130.
62. Norton, *The Orthodox Evangelist*, 141, 164.
63. Norton, *The Orthodox Evangelist*, 160–61.
64. Norton, *The Orthodox Evangelist*, 198.

exercise faith, it now has the capacity to receive such grace, if God should be pleased to bestow it as the next step in His ordinary way of saving sinners through the preaching of the Word.

Remember that Norton taught, "The soul is passive in vocation," that is, in "the infusion of a principle of life...by the Spirit into the lost soul."[65] What capacity did he speak of here, given that he affirmed man's depravity and passivity in regeneration? He wrote, "The passivity of the soul, is the obediential subjection of a soul ministerially prepared, wherein being unable to act, it only receiveth the impression of the agent."[66] Preparation does not form an active capacity or the ability to act spiritually towards God. Rather, it forms a *passive* capacity, a fitness for God to act spiritually upon it.

Norton illustrated this with "the lifeless body of Adam when it was made alive."[67] Genesis 2:7 says, "And the LORD God formed man of the dust of the ground, and breathed into his nostrils the breath of life; and man became a living soul." Before God formed man's body out of the earth, there was no appropriate framework in which the spirit of life could dwell. So God first made the body, then breathed life into it. Without the divine "breath of life," Adam's body could not have animated itself; nonetheless, it was formed with the capacity to receive that breath. Likewise, God prepares dead sinners by forming knowledge and grief in their minds, then breathes faith into them. Without preparatory conviction, there is no way in which faith can dwell in hearts and minds that are framed agreeably to it, rationally, emotionally, and volitionally. Still, preparatory conviction cannot give sinners life.

What did Norton mean by *obediential subjection*? This term might suggest that the prepared sinner becomes obedient to God prior to conversion. Here again, with scholastic precision, Norton defined his terms, saying: "Obediential subjection is that capacity in the subject to receive an impression from the agent, whereby as it remains without ability in itself, to put forth any causal virtue, in order to such effect."[68] The unregenerate soul still has no power to obey God or to bring itself to a position to obey God. Rather, it merely has the fitness to receive, like an empty bucket can

65. Norton, *The Orthodox Evangelist*, 257.
66. Norton, *The Orthodox Evangelist*, 258.
67. Norton, *The Orthodox Evangelist*, 257.
68. Norton, *The Orthodox Evangelist*, 258.

receive water but has no ability to fill itself or even to move itself under a faucet. Norton's term "obediential subjection" might also echo Ames's teaching that the soul is passive in regeneration. Ames wrote, "Yet the will in this first receiving plays the role neither of a free agent nor a natural bearer, but only of an *obedient subject.*"[69] By this he meant that though the will becomes active in trusting Christ upon regeneration, it is not active in regeneration itself but is only the passive subject of God's grace.

Certainly Norton's simile of Adam's body was rooted in Ames. Norton said, "The soul in this passive reception acteth not, only it receiveth the impression of the Agent; as Adam's body was a passive receiver of life, inspired by God thereinto (Gen. 2:17 [*sic*]) formed, and organized, but yet lifeless, and breathless."[70] John Owen later used the same metaphors for preparation in his treatise on the Holy Spirit (1674), writing,

> In reference unto the work of regeneration itself, positively considered, we may observe, that ordinarily there are certain previous and preparatory works, or workings in and upon the souls of men, that are antecedent and dispositive unto it…. So the body of Adam was formed before the rational soul was breathed into it; and Ezekiel's bones came together with a noise and shaking before the breath of life entered into them.[71]

Therefore when Norton spoke of preparation as increasing the soul's "capacity," he was not granting any holiness or spiritual ability to the unconverted, any more than a fully intact corpse is alive. This point is crucial in distinguishing Reformed preparation from Roman Catholic or Arminian preparation. Bozeman overlooks this distinction when he says Puritan preparatory teaching "offers a limited but striking recurrence of the age-old Catholic theological premise that likes attract and opposites repel, or more specifically that a human being must be likened to God to become acceptable to him."[72] Preparation does not make a sinner any more like God, nor does it make him acceptable to God. God works these effects only in justification and sanctification, as the Puritans understood them.

---

69. Ames, *The Marrow of Theology*, 1.26.25, emphasis added. The Latin reads "obedientialis…subjectionis" (Gulielmi Amesii, *Theologiae Medullae, Liber Primus*, ed. James S. Candlish [London: James Nisbet, 1874], 131).
70. Norton, *The Orthodox Evangelist*, 259.
71. Owen, *Pneumatologia*, 3:228–29.
72. Bozeman, *The Precisianist Strain*, 109.

Conclusion: Lost, Helpless, but Not Utterly Hopeless

John Norton, a friend of Cotton who wrote almost two decades after the Antinomian Controversy erupted, crafted a doctrine of preparation with the precise instruments of scholastic theology. Whereas Perkins had identified four steps of preparation, Norton listed twelve. However, Norton also acknowledged that assurance did not depend on a distinct experience of each of those steps. Rather he aimed at identifying an ideal preparation that would lay the best foundation for the Christian life after the Spirit granted faith.

Norton positioned his doctrine of preparation in opposition to Roman Catholics and Arminians on the one hand and the Enthusiasts on the other. Against the former he taught that preparation is a matter of order in God's way, not an ability in a sinner to merit or cause salvation. Against the latter he taught that God works through means and people have a duty to use the means of grace, not simply to wait passively for God to seize them.

Leaning on Ames, Norton taught that preparation forms in the soul a passive capacity to receive God's gift of faith, just as Adam's body was formed before God breathed life into it. Such a preparative capacity does not give the sinner the ability to animate or quicken himself. Nonetheless, it is the way that God normally begins a work of conversion in His rational creatures by means of His Word.

Though he described preparation with the language of "qualification," Norton did not mean that a sinner has no right to come to Christ until he has been prepared. He repeatedly taught that the gospel calls all men to trust in Christ. But without the "qualification" of a heart that is convicted of sin, no sinner will trust in Christ. So Norton's theology was sound regarding the free offer of the gospel even though his terminology could be a bit clearer.

Though he spoke of preparation as "qualification," Norton denied that it was a "saving qualification," or a mark that one would be saved. Like Cotton, Norton opposed the concept of Hooker and Shepard that sinners had to be cut off from the old Adam prior to their engrafting into Christ. However, Norton did not regard Hooker and Shepard as Arminians, but recognized the dispute with them as a debate among Reformed advocates of preparation by grace.

Sinners without faith have no right to the assurance of their election; however, those "under the ministry, or preparatory work" should be

"encouraged in their ministerial and preparatory hope of effectual calling, and salvation,"[73] Norton said. Seeing salvation as a process effected
by the ministry blessed by the Spirit, he said that preparation positioned
the sinner for the next step of faith in Christ. More conscious now of their
condition as lost sinners under wrath, they need not despair but should be
motivated to keep using the means of grace by glimmers of hope, which
Norton called "ministerial" and "preparatory" hope.[74] "Ministerial hope"
arises from living under the "ministry" of the gospel, as the primary
means of grace, whereas "preparatory hope" comes from experiencing
God's work of preparation through the use of that means.[75] Sinners in
such a condition are like people hoping for an audience with a king. They
are trembling in the courtyard yet encouraged by knowing that the palace
guard has permitted them to speak with one of the king's servants.

Norton developed the doctrine of preparation to keep unbelievers
from false assurance but also to encourage the convicted to keep seeking
God. The preparation he described was not an intermediate state between
the domain of darkness and the kingdom of light. But it was an intermediate experience in which the blind, long content in darkness, now begin
to cry out to the Son of David for restoration of sight. He wrote,

> Notwithstanding preparatory repentance worketh not any change
> of heart, yet there are in it, and accompanying of it, certain inward
> workings, that do dispose to a change. Ignorance is taken away by
> illumination; pleasure in sin is abated by sorrow for sin, that is,
> trouble of conscience: boldness in sinning is abated by the fear of
> punishment: whence followeth a kind of abating the contumacy of
> the will, like a stone that is broken, though it yet remains a stone.
> Conceitedness in our own strength is diminished by the sense of
> our lost condition, false confidence by the conviction of the righ-
> teousness of Jesus Christ. Ministerial, and preparatory hope of the
> change of the heart by grace, is increased by our restlessness in our
> present condition, and occasioning an application of ourselves to the
> obtaining of mercy in the use of means.[76]

73. Norton, *The Orthodox Evangelist*, 86.
74. Norton, *The Orthodox Evangelist*, 86, 152, 154.
75. Norton, *The Orthodox Evangelist*, 192.
76. Norton, *The Orthodox Evangelist*, 154.

CHAPTER TEN

Preparation and Subsequent Puritan Critiques: Thomas Goodwin and Giles Firmin

A man may be held too long under John Baptist's water.
—Thomas Goodwin[1]

The teachings of Thomas Hooker were favorably received by many Puritan leaders on both sides of the Atlantic. Isaac Ambrose (1604–1664) was an English Puritan pastor best known for his devotional meditations on Christ, *Looking unto Jesus*. In considering the human side of conversion in his treatise on regeneration, Ambrose asked, "What man hath writ more on this subject, than T. Hooker?"[2] For the next thirty-five pages, Ambrose gave his readers a condensed version of Hooker's books on preparation and conversion. Evidently he had much respect for Hooker as an authority on the application of redemption.

The doctrine of preparation for conversion was also widely accepted by leaders among the English Reformed. Theologians as different as Richard Baxter (1615–1691) and John Owen (1616–1683) both taught that God's Spirit uses the law to give men a sense of their sin and misery before saving them.[3] If this book were to give an exposition of every Puritan's teaching of preparation, it would be several volumes in length.

---

1. Thomas Goodwin and Philip Nye, "To the Reader," in Thomas Hooker, *The Application of Redemption, By the effectual Work of the Word, and Spirit of Christ, for the bringing home of lost Sinners to God, The First Eight Books* (1657; facsimile repr., New York: Arno Press, 1972), [no pagination].

2. *Works of Isaac Ambrose* (London: Thomas Tegg and Son, 1829), 40.

3. Timothy K. Beougher, *Richard Baxter and Conversion* (Ross-shire, U.K.: Christian Focus Publications, 2007), 82–89; J. I. Packer, *The Redemption and Restoration of Man in the Thought of Richard Baxter* (Vancouver, B.C.: Regent College Publishing, 2003), 337; Craig, "The Bond of Grace and Duty in the Soteriology of John Owen"; Sinclair B. Ferguson, *John*

However, that does not mean Hooker's views were accepted uncritically by others. The Puritans, who sought to weigh all things in the balance of the sanctuary,[4] in some respects found Hooker and Shepard's preparation wanting. In this chapter we will consider two Puritan responses to Hooker, those of Thomas Goodwin and Giles Firmin.

Thomas Goodwin: Cautious Preparation

Thomas Goodwin (1600–1679) was influenced by Sibbes and Preston during his years of study at Cambridge. For a time he sought popularity as a preacher through rhetoric and style. But he came to a tremendous conviction of sin through a funeral sermon by Thomas Bainbridge and was converted. He then aligned himself with the theology and plain style of preaching of the Puritans. John Cotton convinced him of the soundness of Congregational polity. Soon, however, Goodwin's Independent principles forced him to take refuge in the Netherlands. In 1641 he was able to return to England, where he participated in the Westminster Assembly. Goodwin also worked alongside John Owen as a teacher and president of Magdalen College at Oxford during the protectorate of Oliver Cromwell. He left Oxford when Charles II ascended to the throne in 1660, but continued to minister to an Independent congregation in London throughout the rigors of persecution and plague. He published the works of other Puritans, such as Preston and Sibbes, and wrote many books himself.

Goodwin and Philip Nye wrote a preface to their edition of Hooker's *Application of Redemption,* saying, "It hath been one of the glories of the Protestant religion, that it revived the doctrine of saving conversion, and of the new creature brought forth thereby." They went on to say,

> God...may have had this in the eye of all wisely designing providence to set out this great author's works and writings...to bring back, and correct the errors of the spirits of professors of these times (and perhaps by urging too far, and insisting too much upon

---

Owen on the Christian Life (Edinburgh: Banner of Truth, 1987), 45–54. For Owen's view of preparation, see Owen, *Pneumatologia,* 3:228–42, 345–62; *The Doctrine of Justification by Faith Alone,* in *Works,* 5:74–80. Owen's treatment of preparation is helpful, but appears to repeat the mainstream views of Puritanism, and so we have not given him a distinct section in this book.

4. I.e., to examine them to determine whether they agree with the witness and teaching of Holy Scripture.

that as preparatory, which includes indeed the beginnings of true faith—and a man may be held too long under John Baptist's water) to rectify those that have slipped into profession, and leaped over all both true and deep humiliation for sin, and sense of their natural condition; yea and many over Christ himself too, professing to go to God without him…. If any of our late preachers and divines came in the Spirit and power of John Baptist this man did.[5]

These later English Puritans viewed Hooker with some degree of reservation about his doctrine of humiliation. They had two basic criticisms. First, they thought Hooker's preaching held his congregation "too long" under preparation. They might have been referring to Hooker's lengthy expositions about conviction of sin with few references to Christ and His grace. For example, Hooker's ninth and tenth books in *The Application of Redemption* devote more than seven hundred pages to the evil of sin and how to meditate on it as preparation for conversion.

Richard Bauckham writes, "This theology was Reformed in that it wished to stress at every point the divine initiative in man's salvation, but it was also primarily an experiential theology and excessively introspective." It became "imbalanced" by losing its center "in the facts and proclamation of the Gospel."[6] As we noted earlier, Packer offered a similar criticism, saying that "by concentrating attention on this preliminary work of grace, and harping on the need for it to be done thoroughly, these writers effectively discouraged seeking souls from going straight to Christ in their despair…. This naturally led to much morbidity."[7]

There is truth in this criticism. If a preacher dwells on any one doctrine too long, other doctrines necessarily recede into the background. Such an imbalance opens the door for fallen people to abuse a particular doctrine in ways that the larger theological system holds in check. Yet we must also be careful not to judge the Puritans too harshly here, particularly according to contemporary expectations. The seventeenth century had no microwave ovens or fast-food restaurants; instant gratification

---

5. Goodwin and Nye, "To the Reader," in Hooker, *The Application of Redemption… The First Eight Books,* [no pagination]. There is an irregular use of parentheses in the original text; we have replaced a second open parenthesis, "(and a man," with a dash, "—and a man," to correct it.

6. Richard J. Bauckham, "Adding to the Church—During the Early American Period," in *Adding to the Church* (London: The Westminster Conference, 1973), 46.

7. Packer, *A Quest for Godliness,* 172.

and the demand for immediate results were not so imperative. Puritan preachers served churches for decades and were committed to a long-term exposition of the whole counsel of God. Before giving 702 pages to discuss contrition and humiliation, Hooker spent 451 pages developing a Christ-centered theology of the application of redemption in Books One through Eight of *The Application of Redemption*. Any imbalance in Hooker's teaching appears less severe when viewed against the entire body of his preaching.

Second, Goodwin and Nye believed that Hooker sometimes confused preparation with true faith. That also might hold listeners "too long under John Baptist's water," by keeping them from attaining assurance because they mistook faith and repentance for mere preparation. For example, Hooker included under preparation a sincere hatred of sin which moved the soul to search out all sin and kill it while praising the Lord.[8] Surely this description indicated that he had passed from preparation to faith in Christ and evangelical repentance.

Goodwin disagreed with Hooker on certain matters, but we are surprised by Winship's statement that Goodwin "bitterly attacked Hooker's distended conception of preparation in the 1630s."[9] If that is so, Goodwin's perspective must have changed a great deal in two decades. Goodwin wrote a preface to Hooker's book, implying his fundamental approval of and respect for Hooker's teachings in the book. Preparation was a necessary antidote to those who would "leap over" contrition and humiliation and enter immediately into a superficial profession of faith. He did not view Hooker as a harmful extremist but as an instrument in God's hand to meet the need of the hour. Bauckham comments,

> The concept of preparation—the preparation of the heart to receive Christ—which characterized most New England theology of conversion, has been understood by some as a way of making salvation easier, a sort of theological subterfuge in the face of an unpalatably severe doctrine of divine sovereignty, a means by which man could on his own part make some approach toward salvation. In reality, the 'Preparationists' were mostly concerned that salvation should not appear too easy, to keep men from claiming God's promises of

---

8. Hooker, *The Soules Preparation for Christ*, 218–22.
9. Winship, *Making Heretics*, 71. Winship does not cite any works by Goodwin at this point, but the diary of Samuel Hartlib (c. 1600–1662), a friend of Goodwin.

mercy before they could conceivably be applicable to them, before they had been through the depths of humiliation, the 'prostration of the heart' as John Cotton called it.[10]

Goodwin certainly did not reject preparation; rather, he taught his own doctrine of "humiliation preparatory."[11] Paul Blackham writes, "In the Puritan tradition, Goodwin describes the work of the law in preparing the sinner for faith in Christ."[12] Goodwin viewed John 16:7–11 as a description of the Holy Spirit's three-fold work of converting the elect in the world. He followed the same pattern as the Heidelberg Catechism of "misery, deliverance, and thankfulness," stating "unto which three heads our divines have reduced their catechisms and systems of theology."[13] He wrote,

1) "The Spirit will 'convince of sin,' that is, of that miserable and sinful estate which men live in by nature, and which, without belief in him, will prove matter of condemnation to them."

2) "He will convince them of 'righteousness, because I go to my Father,' says Christ; that is, the Spirit shall by faith reveal unto them the righteousness of me, who am to ascend up to heaven to be the only true means by whom to be justified and saved."

3) "He will convince of 'judgment, because the prince of this world is judged.'" Goodwin compared this to John 12:31–32 and the use of the term *judgment* in Matthew 12:18, 20. He concluded that it referred to the conquest of Satan and the reformation of men's lives by repentance and obedience to Christ's laws.[14]

Goodwin also argued that conviction of sin involves the Holy Spirit's use of God's law, just as John the Baptist prepared the way for Christ's coming.[15] The apostle Paul devoted considerable space in his Epistle to the Romans to the themes of wrath, law, sin, and death (chaps. 1–3, 5, 7), yet the epistle is mostly about the gospel.[16] The apostle lays out his

---

10. Bauckham, "Adding to the Church—During the Early American Period," 41–42.

11. Thomas Goodwin, *The Work of the Holy Ghost in Our Salvation*, in *The Works of Thomas Goodwin* (1861–1866; repr., Grand Rapids: Reformation Heritage Books, 2006), 6:362.

12. Paul Blackham, "The Pneumatology of Thomas Goodwin" (PhD Dissertation, University of London, 1995), 230.

13. Goodwin, *The Work of the Holy Ghost in Our Salvation*, 6:359–60.

14. Goodwin, *The Work of the Holy Ghost in Our Salvation*, 6:361.

15. Goodwin, *The Work of the Holy Ghost in Our Salvation*, 6:362–63.

16. Goodwin, *The Work of the Holy Ghost in Our Salvation*, 6:364–65.

presentation of the gospel in this way because the work of humiliation takes away a person's ability to find comfort in anyone but God, and righteousness in anyone but Christ.[17]

Though Goodwin had reservations about some aspects of Hooker's doctrine of preparation, he was not half-hearted about preparation. He defended it against the charges of others that it led to despair, saying rather that it led men to Christ. He said humiliation demanded no "deeply vexing gashes and impressions of wrath" any more than faith required "ravishing joy."[18] Goodwin blamed despair and suicidal impulses not on humiliation but on the sinner's "stubbornness of heart not to go out to Christ," and on Satan's entering into God's work to spoil and discredit it.[19]

Yet Goodwin also taught men to despair of *themselves*. He said more than a twinge of conscience is required before sinners will trust in Christ alone. Sinners must see their "utter helplessness and hopelessness" before they may rest in Christ for both justification and sanctification, indeed for their very faith.[20] Goodwin offered this illustration,

> A man that hath no money in his purse, yet whilst he hath hands to work, he makes no such reckoning of want [need]; and so men, when they want [lack] all good for the time past, yet they hope to work it out; they have hands left, and with them they fall to work; but when a man shall see hands cut off too, and nothing but stumps left, which are as unfit and unable to lay hold on Christ, as a man's arm without hands is upon a rope to save him; and God must not only find him Christ, but his grace must give him hands to lay hold on him also: that the apprehension of this serves both to drive him out of himself, and to magnify God's free grace in working faith.[21]

From these words, we can begin to see why so many Reformed Christians value the doctrine of preparation. They believe both in fallen man's stubborn self-confidence and in salvation by faith in Christ alone. To guard the glory of God's grace as the sole cause of salvation, they see the need to humble sinners with not only a sense of their guilt but also their inability to believe. The Puritans did not believe the doctrine of sovereign grace opposed preparation. Rather, they believed preparation

17. Goodwin, *The Work of the Holy Ghost in Our Salvation*, 6:382.
18. Goodwin, *The Work of the Holy Ghost in Our Salvation*, 6:386.
19. Goodwin, *The Work of the Holy Ghost in Our Salvation*, 6:387–88.
20. Goodwin, *The Work of the Holy Ghost in Our Salvation*, 6:383–84.
21. Goodwin, *The Work of the Holy Ghost in Our Salvation*, 6:384–85.

brings proud sinners to look to sovereign grace as their only hope. Furthermore, the Puritans did not view preparation as man's attempt to meet God halfway. They said the whole process is God's work. Goodwin said, "It is a mighty work of the Spirit to convince."[22] The Spirit's work is to bring men to Christ. Goodwin thus said that to trust in one's own preparation is to sit down in sorrow beside Christ instead of coming to Christ for rest.[23]

Giles Firmin: Critical Preparation

Giles Firmin (1614–1697) came to New England around 1630–1632 and joined First Church of Boston, where John Cotton was minister. He was present during the Antinomian Controversy and later wrote in defense of the ministers. In the latter part of the 1630s, Firmin married and became a landowner in Ipswich, where he practiced medicine. In 1644, Firmin left his wife and children in New England and sailed across the Atlantic. His ship was wrecked off the coast of Spain, but he survived. He returned to England and became a parish minister. His family joined him there in 1646 or 1647. While in England, Firmin preached before Parliament and published at least fifteen works. He later lost his ministerial position for refusing to conform to the liturgy and order of the Church of England in 1662, but he continued to serve a group that met in his home while supporting himself once more as a physician. His medical services to both the poor and the gentry protected his meetings from persecution. He never returned to New England.[24]

Firmin published a book in 1670 with the lengthy title: *The Real Christian, Or a Treatise of Effectual Calling. Wherein the work of God in drawing the soul to Christ being opened according to the holy Scriptures, some things required by our late divines as necessary to a right preparation for Christ and true closing with Christ, which have caused, and do still cause much trouble to some serious Christians, are with due respects to those worthy men, brought to the balance of the sanctuary, there weighed, and accordingly judged.* The book was highly esteemed by other Puritan leaders. Cotton Mather wrote, "Among the rest of his books, that golden one, which is entitled, 'The Real Christian,'

---

22. Goodwin, *The Work of the Holy Ghost in Our Salvation*, 6:389.
23. Horton, "Christ Set Forth," 305.
24. John W. Dean, *A Brief Memoir of Rev. Giles Firmin* (Boston: David Clapp & Son, 1866).

does really prove the title to be his own character; and the rest, as well as that, prove him to be an able scholar, as well as a real Christian."[25]

James W. Jones regards Firmin's view as "anti-preparation" and a prelude to the rise of anti-supernaturalism in New England. In Firmin, Jones claimed to find the first steps of turning away from the doctrine of divine regeneration unto conversion to embrace a more "rational" religion of morality. Jones wrote, "In those who began to adopt Firmin's outlook, one can find the seeds of the antirevivalist party of the eighteenth century."[26] Firmin was said to have been a precursor of Charles Chauncy. If that was truly the case, it is hard to understand why Cotton Mather regarded Firmin's book as "golden." Let us take our own look at what Firmin wrote.

Firmin's Doctrine of Preparation

Firmin said that whereas in ancient times persecutions made the name *Christian* a mark of death, in contemporary England "they profess they are born Christians" who are but "nominal Christians." Thus, he said the early church "labored to convert heathens, we to convert Christians." Such a situation called for a discriminatory ministry of the Word. However, Firmin also observed that "some eminent divines" set such strict requirements for conversion that they "trouble many, and cut off most of the sound with the unsound Christians."[27]

Firmin did not deny the truth of either preparatory grace or preparatory preaching. He wrote, "That the preaching of the law is necessary to make men know their sins, and their woeful condition by sin, that thereby they may be glad to listen after, and embrace the gospel, I think this cannot be denied by any judicious divine."[28] Pettit therefore goes too far in saying that Firmin accepted preparation "so long as all anxiety is eliminated."[29] It is hard to come to a conviction of sin and one's lost estate without some anxiety. Firmin thus recommended a "searching" ministry that warned people that few are saved, though he knew this

---

25. Cotton Mather, *Magnalia Christi Americana*, 3:214.

26. James W. Jones, *The Shattered Synthesis: New England Puritanism before the Great Awakening* (New Haven: Yale University Press, 1973), 34.

27. Giles Firmin, "The Epistle Dedicatory," in *The Real Christian, or A Treatise of Effectual Calling* (London: for Dorman Newman, 1670), [no pagination]. On nominalism and a searching ministry, see also pp. 227ff.

28. Firmin, *The Real Christian*, 51–52.

29. Pettit, *The Heart Prepared*, 188.

emphasis would prompt critics to say he was one of those "peevish and censorious Puritans."[30]

He went on to clarify his understanding of preparation by stating the following positions. First, everyone who listens to the gospel has the duty to trust and receive Christ "be they prepared or not prepared" (1 John 3:23; John 6:29; 3:16, 18, 36).[31] This is crucial for evangelism, for it enables the preacher to press upon listeners the call to believe in Christ, and to guard the church from hyper-Calvinism.

Second, an adult natural person is not "fit or disposed to receive Christ" until there is "some work of the Spirit upon him, to prepare him."[32] Firmin explained, "So blind are we…that did not the Spirit of the Almighty set his power to work, open our eyes to see ourselves, sin, and creatures, and filthiness that is in our righteousness," we would rest in sin like Samson in Delilah's lap.[33] Illumination is necessary because natural man lies in darkness and cannot see the truth apart from the Spirit, and also because God "works upon a rational creature" whose will follows the perceptions of the mind.[34] Illumination enables men to recognize some of God's glory. Echoing Calvin, Firmin said, "Sin and the creature are never known as *they are*, till God be known in some measure as *he is*."[35] He wrote, "Eternal purpose towards the elect now breaking forth…some beams of that Majesty are let in, and now take that wanton heart which played with sin before, what sayest to sin now? Dost thou see him against whom this sin rebels?"[36] Thus the illumination of God's glory brings about the conviction of sin in a sinner.

Third, Firmin said, "The ways of God in converting, or drawing the soul to Christ, are very secret, and in preparatory works very various."[37] We have noted this point in other writers, but Firmin developed it at greater length. He said that while some believers know the time of their conversion, others do not; some have a lengthy birth process, while others have a short one; some experience preparation by legal terrors,

---

30. Firmin, *The Real Christian*, 229; cf. p. 236.
31. Firmin, *The Real Christian*, 2.
32. Firmin, *The Real Christian*, 6.
33. Firmin, *The Real Christian*, 10.
34. Firmin, *The Real Christian*, 28–30.
35. Firmin, *The Real Christian*, 38, emphasis original.
36. Firmin, *The Real Christian*, 41.
37. Firmin, *The Real Christian*, 11.

while others have alternating experiences of law and gospel hope. God drenches some sinners in sorrow and humblings, while He only sprinkles others, and not necessarily in proportion to their morality before conversion. Some sinners continue in preparation until conversion, while others experience seasons of conviction interspersed with times of complacency. Sometimes the Lord comes to sinners in a thunderstorm; at other times He comes in a still, small voice.[38] Similarly, the Spirit convicts sinners in various ways, putting His finger upon one particular transgression for one sinner, and other transgressions for other sinners. Firmin said the Holy Spirit does not always reveal a man's original sin (inherited corruption) at "the first stroke," though He always reveals it to the elect at some point.[39] His emphasis on variety warns against a scheme or "morphology" of conversion that is too detailed or standardized.

Fourth, it is "tyranny" to make God's way of dealing with one person the standard by which to judge others. Fifth, though God's preparations vary, His work of regeneration is essentially the same in all the elect. Sixth, "To say of a man under God's working, that he is but under a preparatory work, and no more, is a difficult thing. Who can say there is no more but preparation in such a person?"[40]

Seventh, one must not require those under preparation to be as good as those who are united with Christ. Firmin wrote, "When Mr. Hooker preached those sermons about the soul's preparation for Christ and humiliation, my father-in-law, Mr. Nathaniel Ward, told him, 'Mr. Hooker, you make as good Christians before men are in Christ, as ever they are after,' and wished, 'Would I were but as good a Christian now, as you make men while they are but preparing for Christ.'"[41]

Eighth, most preparatory works abide in the soul after union with Christ, such as sorrow over sin and humility, but now without legal terrors. Ninth, whereas a minister can only describe one work at a time, "in order of time they may go all together."[42] This point supports what we have previously said that the Puritans' analysis of preparation should be taken less as a chronological morphology and more of a pedagogical explanation in logical order. In conclusion, Firmin wrote, "Let the

---

38. Firmin, *The Real Christian*, 13–17, 75–77.
39. Firmin, *The Real Christian*, 47, 49.
40. Firmin, *The Real Christian*, 17–18.
41. Firmin, *The Real Christian*, 19.
42. Firmin, *The Real Christian*, 24–25.

Lord begin when he please, let him work how he please," for over time God will show every elect soul the wonders of His saving grace. Firmin remembered that his teacher Thomas Hill used to lay his hand on his heart and say, "Every true convert hath something here that will frame an argument against an Arminian."[43]

So though Firmin criticized some aspects of other men's doctrines of preparation, he was firmly committed to a Reformed doctrine of preparation and taught men to seek this preparatory grace. He asked, "If this be the way of the Spirit in drawing the soul to Christ, how rational and necessary is it for those who indeed would have Christ, and would have a sound work, to beg this light and conviction from God?"[44] Firmin even defended Shepard's doctrine of preparatory separation of the soul from sin *before* union with Christ, though Norton had argued against it.[45]

Firmin also had much respect for Hooker. He said his father-in-law visited James Ussher when the bishop was sick and heard Ussher say, "I wish that Mr. Hooker were here to preach the law home to my conscience." Firmin considered this was the spirit of a "godly and judicious Christian" to delight in a convicting ministry "to gospel-ends."[46] So we cannot say Firmin's criticisms of others on preparation were so severe that they merit the title "Firmin against the Preparationists."

Firmin's Major Criticism: Humiliation Not Contentment to Be Damned
Firmin believed that if a person's self-righteousness has been destroyed, his hope in his ability demolished, his soul heavily burdened with the guilt of sin, and his ears opened to listen to the gospel, "the soul now is rightly prepared for Christ."[47] But he also noted that "holy Hooker and Shepard" would assert that something more is necessary: the properly humbled soul must be so submissive to God as to be satisfied to be damned if that be His will.[48]

Firmin rejected this last point because such submission would require inward saving grace (which all Reformed believers believed does not

---

43. Firmin, *The Real Christian*, 26. Cf. Dean, *Memoir*, 6.
44. Firmin, *The Real Christian*, 55.
45. Firmin, *The Real Christian*, 87–93. Norton, *The Orthodox Evangelist*, 180.
46. Firmin, *The Real Christian*, 51.
47. Firmin, *The Real Christian*, 104–106.
48. Firmin, *The Real Christian*, 107. See chapter 4 on Hooker and Shepard's views of humiliation.

exist in the lost).[49] Firmin also said the Scriptures do not place any such requirement on men, whether sinners or saints.[50] He argued that Moses (Ex. 32:32–33) and Paul (Rom. 9:3) offered themselves up not for eternal damnation but for temporal loss, such as separation from the people of God or death.[51] Regardless of how we interpret Moses and Paul's prayers, Firmin said, "I have not met one divine who will maintain that all Christians are bound to come up to Moses and Paul in their wish: but both Mr. Hooker and Mr. Shepard have made that whereof we now treat, a part of the soul's humiliation and preparation for Christ, and therefore must be found in all."[52] Firmin disputed this need for contentment in damnation in almost fifty pages of text.[53] He said this teaching was one of the biggest obstacles holding back awakened sinners from fleeing to Christ.[54]

This teaching of becoming "content to be damned" offended other Puritans besides Firmin. Richard Baxter (1615–1691) wrote, "I know no warrant for putting such a question to ourselves, as some do, Whether we could be content to be damned, so God were glorified? Christ hath put no such question to us, nor bid us put such to ourselves. Christ had rather that men would inquire after their true willingness to be saved, than their willingness to be damned."[55] John Flavel (1628–1691) wrote of "the very fundamental law of our creation, which inclines and obliges all men to seek their own felicity. And on this account, not only our Antinomians are blame-worthy, but others also, who urge humiliation for sin beyond the Scripture requirement; teaching me, they are not humbled enough till they are content to be damned."[56]

The Scotsman Thomas Halyburton (1674–1712) wrote, "Those whom the Lord deals with, in order to their conversion, will all subscribe to the justice of God, should he damn them eternally. I do not say that they will

---

49. Firmin, *The Real Christian*, 108–109.

50. Firmin, *The Real Christian*, 138–39.

51. Firmin, *The Real Christian*, 19–24.

52. Firmin, *The Real Christian*, 24.

53. Firmin, *The Real Christian*, 19–24, 107–149.

54. Firmin, *The Introduction*, in *The Real Christian*, [no pagination].

55. Richard Baxter, *The Saints' Everlasting Rest*, in *The Practical Works of Richard Baxter* (London: George Virtue, 1837), 3:13. See also *The Reasons of the Christian Religion*, in *The Practical Works of Richard Baxter* (London: James Duncan, 1830), 21:399.

56. John Flavel, *A Blow at the Root of Antinomianism* (Philadelphia: Presbyterian Board of Publication, 1830), 113. Cf. *The Works of John Flavel* (1820; repr.: Edinburgh, Banner of Truth, 1997), 3:587.

be content to be damned; but they will own that God were most just should he deal so by them."[57] Norton wrote in 1654, "But we are not hence to infer, that we ought to be content to be damned; to justify God is our duty, but to be contented to be damned is nowhere commanded; nay if taken without limitation, it is prohibited; because to be contented to be damned, is to be contented to be an enemy, and to sin against God, and that forever."[58] The same point was made by Oliver Heywood (1630–1702),[59] John Howe (1630–1705),[60] and later by the Scottish preacher Ralph Erskine (1685–1752).[61]

Firmin's rebuttal to Hooker particularly affected the Reformed community outside of England. Jacob Koelman (1631–1695), a leader in the Dutch Further Reformation which paralleled English Puritanism in many ways, translated many Puritan works into Dutch, especially those of Christopher Love and Thomas Goodwin. One of them was Hooker's *The Soul's Humiliation*, which Koelman subtitled, "Wholesome Desperation." Though he saw much value in this book, Koelman also wrote a critical preface to it, devoting twenty pages to refute the idea of being content to be damned. He drew much of his material from Firmin's book.[62]

Therefore Hooker's idea of contentment with damnation never became part of either the mainstream Puritan doctrine of preparation or the broader Reformed tradition. Most Puritans denied that a sinner must become content or satisfied to be damned, as part of preparation for conversion or as a fruit of regeneration by the Holy Spirit. But there was general agreement that a sinner must bow before the justice of God and acknowledge that God would be just to damn him.

Questions about the Doctrine of Preparatory Contentment to be Damned
Why would such holy and scholarly men, as Firmin referred to them, propose such an extreme teaching? Firmin said that he wrote to Shepard about

57. Thomas Halyburton, *The Great Concern of Salvation*, in *The Works of the Rev. Thomas Halyburton* (London: Thomas Tegg & Son, 1835), 71.

58. Norton, *The Orthodox Evangelist*, 151.

59. "Baptismal Bonds," in *The Whole Works of the Rev. Oliver Heywood* (Idle: by John Vint, for F. Westley et al., 1826), 4:154.

60. *The Works of the Rev. John Howe* (New York: John P. Haven, 1838), 1:407.

61. Ralph Erskine, *Sermons and Other Practical Works* (Falkirk: by Patrick Mair for John Stewart, Peter Muirhead, and Hugh Mitchell, 1795), 2:272.

62. Pieter Rouwendal, "Jacob Koelman on Thomas Hooker's *The Soules Humiliation*," *Puritan Reformed Journal* 2, no. 2 (July 2010): 174–86. See Thomas Hooker, *Zielsvernedering en heylzame wanhoop*, trans. Jacobus Koelman (Amsterdam: J. Wasterlier, 1678).

this matter, objecting that such an act of obedience is strangely ascribed to men outside of Christ. He said that Shepard's reply was that such a level of submission is not "the highest measure of grace (as you hint)" but "is far different from that readiness of Paul and Moses, out of a principle of love to Christ, to wish themselves anathematized for Israel's sake."[63]

Shepard's reply is intriguing. He said such preparatory contentment did not arise out of love for God and His glory (as de Sales had taught). It must therefore be forced upon the soul by an inescapable sense of God's justice and glory. In this pre-Judgment Day experience, the mouth is stopped in its self-justification and the soul knows such profound guilt that it is compelled to bow and confess that God is the Lord, even if He damns us (Rom. 3:19; Phil. 2:10–11). This suggests the instincts behind this doctrine were biblical, though the doctrine itself was wrong. How can a sinner be prepared to trust in Christ to save him from God's wrath if he believes God's wrath is unjust? How can he be prepared to trust in grace alone if he thinks he has merit?

Firmin said both Shepard's book and letter repeatedly fell back on this statement: "The soul seeth itself worthy of no mercy."[64] That is truly an evangelical instinct. But how can a sinner be prepared to receive the Savior if he is truly content not to receive Him? Therefore, Hooker and Shepard's use of words such as *content* and *satisfied* was not wise. It would have been better for them to have said that in preparation the sinner must bow before God's just condemnation but must passionately and persistently seek God's merciful salvation. Their error was an outgrowth of attempting to specify just how deep conviction of sin had to be experienced.

Thus the so-called *contentment to be damned* actually refers to submission based on hope in God's saving love. Shepard seemed to imply as much when he wrote to Firmin, "I do not think that any man in humiliation for sin is to be carelessly content and quiet…that God should dispose of him how he will, as caring for nothing, but humbly and meekly, quiet and content he should, as unworthy of anything…which latter may well stand with earnest seeking after God's love."[65] Hooker depicted the

---

63. Firmin, *The Real Christian*, 19.

64. Firmin, *The Real Christian*, 129.

65. Firmin, *The Real Christian*, 145. The ellipses omit Firmin's parenthetical comments, not Shepard's words.

prodigal son as "content to be at his father's disposing" as long as he could return to his father's house. He said, "Father, I am not worthy to be thy son, make me as a hired servant, if I can but get into my father's house again; I will die rather than go away any more: he is content to be anything, so his father will but receive him into his family, though it were but a drudge [menial servant] in the kitchen."[66] The doctrine that Hooker derived from this part of the parable was, "The distressed sinner that despairs of all supply and succor [help] in himself, is driven to submit himself to the Lord God *for succor and relief.*"[67] This is not contentment to be damned but contentment to be saved by God on any terms that God may see fit to impose. It appears, then, that there is contradiction within Hooker's own presentation of the topic.

It is also possible that the words of printed books did not always precisely represent the preached words of Hooker and Shepard. Increase Mather (1639–1723) wrote a preface to Solomon Stoddard's *Guide to Christ*, in which he affirmed preparation, yet his words say,

> There have been some, who have maintained, that a man is not sufficiently prepared for Christ, except he be brought to that pass, as out of respect to the will and glory of God, to be content to be damned eternally. An horrid assertion, justly disclaimed by the author of this discourse, and refuted by the [John Norton's] *Orthodox Evangelist*, yet there are some unhappy passages of that nature, in a book of humiliation, which goes under Mr. Hooker's name, by which, incredible wrong has been done to that author.[68]

Mather went on to quote Thomas Goodwin to make the point that the words of some books published under Hooker's name were carelessly taken down by his hearers, published without his review, and so distorted Hooker's meaning. Mather believed the same thing had happened with some of Shepard's books.[69] Fulcher writes,

> A review of Hooker's works calls for some distinction in the levels of their reliability. Sermons preached in England before his departure, which were taken down and later published without his knowledge

---

66. Hooker, *The Sovles Humiliation*, 79.

67. Hooker, *The Sovles Humiliation*, 80.

68. Increase Mather, "To the Reader," in Solomon Stoddard, *A Guide to Christ* (Northampton: Andrew Wright, 1816), viii.

69. Mather, "To the Reader," in Stoddard, *A Guide to Christ*, ix.

or consent, should not be considered on the same level as those sermons which were prepared for the press from his own writings and
by his colleagues in England. The normative expression of his theological views may be found in the posthumous edition of his sermons,
collected under the title, *The Application of Redemption*, by Thomas
Goodwin and Philip Nye, Congregational Puritans in England.[70]

Sadly, the part of *The Application of Redemption* that pertains to humiliation was never completed.

Thus there is some question about what these men actually taught
on this subject. Given that Hooker and Shepard lived on the other side of
the ocean from the publishing presses at that time, it is entirely possible
that books were published in their name that did not accurately reflect
their teaching on all points. The same ocean separated Firmin from New
England when he published *The Real Christian*. One wonders whether
Hooker and Shepard might have agreed more with Firmin than he realized, especially since he wrote more than two decades after their deaths,
and it had been even longer since he had been in New England.

On the other hand, as we have already noted, Firmin said he cor-
responded with Shepard on this matter: "I wrote to him about it, and
have his letter in answer by me."[71] That makes it likely that Firmin had
some access to Shepard's opinion on this question, though we wish that
we also had his letter. We do have the conversion testimony of Elizabeth
Cutter (c. 1576–1663), who said that under Shepard's ministry, "I thought I
had no repentance, yet I was encouraged to seek the Lord and to be content with his condemning will to lie at [the] Lord's feet."[72] Yet even then
she lay down at Christ's feet trusting His promise "that he that comes to
me I'll not cast away."[73]

Conclusion

Thomas Goodwin commended the publication of Hooker's writings, but
with some caveats. He believed that Hooker held people too long under
preparation, both by dwelling on the subject for an overly extended period

---

70. Fulcher, "Puritan Piety in Early New England," 203–204.

71. Firmin, *The Real Christian,* 107. We already noted his quotation from the letter (p. 19
of Firmin's book).

72. McGiffert, ed., *God's Plot,* 196.

73. McGiffert, ed., *God's Plot,* 197. Cf. John 6:37.

of time in his preaching, and in requiring preparatory works that properly belonged to regeneration, thus hindering assurance. Yet Goodwin taught and defended the doctrine of preparation for faith as part of the three-fold structure of misery, deliverance, and gratitude found in Paul's letter to the Romans, Christ's description of the work of the Holy Spirit in John 16:8–11, and the Heidelberg Catechism of the Reformed churches. Far from undermining the Reformed faith, Goodwin viewed preparation as a formative experience of man's total inability to save himself.

Giles Firmin faulted Hooker and Shepard (and others) for setting up unnecessary obstacles between sinners and Christ. However, he did not regard preparation as an obstacle to faith but as the divine remedy to the obstacles of ignorance and complacency in the sinner. He said that legal preparation assisted the free offer of the gospel so long as one recognizes the variety of depth and duration in preparation, and does not demand that sinners become sanctified before conversion. He even supported Hooker and Shepard's peculiar doctrine of preparatory separation of the soul from sin prior to union with Christ.

Firmin's greatest objection to the teaching of the two New England divines was their doctrine that humiliation is only complete when a sinner becomes content to be damned. Similar objections can be found in the writings of Baxter, Flavel, Halyburton, Norton, Heywood, Howe, Koelman, and Ralph Erkine. The Puritan movement as a whole believed that preparatory humiliation must include the recognition that God could in all justice damn us to hell, but they firmly rejected the idea that one must become content to be damned. Shepard's correspondence with Firmin reveals that Shepard did not regard such contentment to spring from love for God but was a confession forced from the sinner's conscience by a view of God's justice. Indeed, Hooker's own writings suggest that this submissive contentment comes from the hope that one will nevertheless somehow be saved. Thus it appears there is contradiction within Hooker and Shepard's writings, at least as they were recorded and passed down to us today.

The cautious and critical views on preparation by Goodwin and Firmin exemplify how later Puritans embraced the doctrine of preparation but sought to make it more biblical and consistent—*reformata et semper reformanda secundum verbum Dei.*

CHAPTER ELEVEN

Later Puritan Preparation:
John Flavel and John Bunyan

A light from God enters the soul, to discover the nature of God, and of sin.

—John Flavel[1]

Preparation for faith was part of seventeenth-century Reformed orthodoxy in England. The same year that Norton published *Orthodox Evangelist* (1654), Edward Leigh (1602–1671) published his *Body of Divinity*, which is a lengthy statement of Reformed orthodoxy in which "most of the controversies between us, the Papists, Arminians, and Socinians [are] discussed."[2] Leigh said one mark of effectual calling is that "God breaks the heart by some preparatory conviction to make the soul fit to receive the grace of God." This "work of the law" for conviction "hath not the like effects in all, in some anxiousness, in others horror, [though] all see themselves in a wretched condition."[3] Like Hooker, Leigh offered sinners the motives to be converted and its means, which include paying attention to their sins; acknowledging their inability to convert themselves; praying for God to turn them back to Himself; getting rid of bad company and occasions of temptation; resisting the love of earthly things; battling the extremes of presumption, despair, and hardness of heart; and making use of good company, church meetings, reading, and meditation.[4]

---

1. John Flavel, *The Method of Grace*, in *The Works of John Flavel* (1820; repr.; Edinburgh: Banner of Truth, 1997), 2:311.

2. Edward Leigh, *A Systeme or Body of Divinity: Consisting of Ten Books. Wherein the Fundamentals and main Grounds of Religion are Opened: the Contrary Errours Refuted: Most of the Controversies between Us, the Papists, Arminians, and Socinians Discussed and Handled* (London: by A. M. for William Lee, 1654).

3. Leigh, *Body of Divinity*, 491.

4. Leigh, *Body of Divinity*, 495.

The doctrine of preparation had its greatest impact, not in theological tomes, but in the popular sermons, devotional books, poetry, and literature of the Puritans. In this chapter we will explore the work of two popular preachers, John Flavel and John Bunyan, on preparation in the books they wrote in the later part of the seventeenth century.

John Flavel: The Savior's Method

John Flavel (1628–1691) was pastor of a church in the English seaport of Dartmouth. He continued to minister secretly after he was ejected from the pulpit in 1662 for nonconformity. His commitment to preach Christ led him to preach nightly in the woods and to travel in disguise. He wrote books with spiritual truths to reach out to sailors and farmers. One of his parishioners said that a man must have either a very soft head or a very hard heart not to be affected by Flavel's preaching. Another man was converted by a sermon he had heard Flavel deliver some eighty-five years earlier.

Clifford Boone says Flavel taught a form of preparatory grace resembling Firmin's cautious doctrine of preparation, quoting Firmin several times in his works.[5] Let us take a closer look at Flavel's teaching on preparation.

The Ordinary Need for Preparatory Conviction
In *Method of Grace* (1681), Flavel said that in Romans Paul taught us two key truths about the law of God: he was "denying to it a power to justify us," but he was also "ascribing to it a power to convince us, and so prepare us for Christ."[6] Flavel believed such legal preparation was necessary because "unregenerate persons are generally full of groundless confidence and cheerfulness, though their condition be sad and miserable."[7]

Under the power of Satan, these sinners are at peace in "carnal security" (Luke 11:21), Flavel said; they have a "presumptuous hope" (John 8:54–55) and hear the Word with "false joy" (Matt. 13:20). This illusory confidence is bolstered by ecclesiastical privileges, ignorance, and self-deceit, allowing them to claim signs of grace in external mercies, superficial

---

5. Clifford B. Boone, "Puritan Evangelism: Preaching for Conversion in Late-Seventeenth Century English Puritanism as Seen in the Works of John Flavel" (PhD Dissertation, University of Wales, 2009), 194–95.

6. Flavel, *Method of Grace*, 2:287.

7. Flavel, *Method of Grace*, 2:288.

responses to the gospel, self-evaluations biased by self-love, and comparing themselves to worse sinners. This powerfully blinds them under the hand of Satan.[8] Flavel thus came to the grim conclusion, "Hence it follows that the generality of the world are in the direct path to eternal ruin."[9]

It is impossible for fallen men to come to Christ without a supernatural work of God. The Puritan doctrine of conversion is incomprehensible without the Reformed doctrine of human depravity. Sinners' minds are full of "errors, by which they are prejudiced against Christ." Flavel wrote, "The natural mind of man slights the truths of God, until God teach them; and then they tremble with an awful reverence of them."[10] Sin has such a firm grip on the hearts of men that "no human arguments or persuasions whatsoever can divorce or separate them."[11]

Nor can the Scriptures penetrate the fallen human soul without divine assistance. Flavel said in *England's Duty* (1689) that God's law makes no more impression on the hearts of fallen men than a tennis ball thrown against a stone wall.[12] To men untouched by the Spirit, the gospel of free grace is nothing more than a sweet song lulling them to sleep in their sins.[13]

Therefore sinners must hear the preaching of the Word in the power of the Spirit. Flavel said, "There is a mighty efficacy in the word or law of God, to kill vain confidence, and quench carnal mirth in the hearts of men, when God sets it home upon their conscience."[14] By "word," Flavel wrote not merely of the law but of the combined ministry of the law and gospel: "The law wounds, the gospel cures."[15] He ascribed converting power not to the law alone, but to the law and gospel together.

As Flavel said in *England's Duty*, the convictions of the law and the sweet allurements of the gospel together are Christ knocking at the door

---

8. Flavel, *Method of Grace*, 2:289–91.

9. Flavel, *Method of Grace*, 2:294.

10. Flavel, *Method of Grace*, 2:320.

11. Flavel, *Method of Grace*, 2:321.

12. In the seventeenth century, tennis was played in an area enclosed by walls, not an open lawn.

13. Flavel, *England's Duty*, 4:48. Also known as *Christ Knocking at the Door of Sinners' Hearts*.

14. Flavel, *Method of Grace*, 2:295.

15. Flavel, *Method of Grace*, 2:297. Many of the Scriptures he cited on this and the previous page to prove the power of the "word or law" refer to the preaching of the gospel (Acts 2:37; Rom. 1:16; Phil. 3:7–9; 2 Cor. 4:6; 1 Pet. 1:23; 1 Thess. 1:9).

of the sinner's heart. Without the gospel, "no heart would ever open to Christ." Flavel explained, "It is not frosts and snow, storms and thunder, but the gentle distilling dews and cherishing sun-beams that make the flowers open in the spring. The terrors of the law may be preparative, but the grace of the gospel is that which effectually opens the sinner's heart."[16]

Nevertheless, the law has its own function in the hand of the Spirit: it has "an awakening efficacy" on sleepy sinners and "an enlightening efficacy" on blinded sinners.[17] The law has "a convincing efficacy" that draws up one's sins like a vast and terrifying army besieging the soul "so that the soul stands mute, and self-condemned at the bar of conscience."[18] The law also has "a soul-wounding, heart-cutting efficacy; it pierces into the very soul and spirit of man."[19]

Given the presence of Christ in the means of grace, Flavel exhorted sinners "to attend and wait assiduously [diligently] upon the ministry of the word, and to bring all that are capable, there to wait upon Christ with you."[20] God is free to act as He pleases by the Word (John 3:8), but the ministry of the Word is "the way of the Spirit" in which we hope to meet Him.[21] Though sinners cannot convert themselves, they were urged by Flavel to "strive" to the "uttermost" after salvation, for they do have the power to avoid external acts of sin or to attend external worship services ("Why cannot those feet carry thee to the assemblies of the saints, as well as to an ale-house?"), to apply their minds with more attention to the Word, to examine themselves, and to cry to God for mercy. The kingdom must be taken by force (Matt. 11:12).[22]

But sinners must not grasp the means of grace as if they could produce conversion by any inherent power of their own. Flavel said power to convert lies not in the word of law and gospel, nor in the preacher, but only in the "glorious sovereignty" of the Holy Spirit. He said the Spirit of God exercises sovereignty over the Word, the soul, and the times of conviction and conversion (Isa. 55:10–11; Ezek. 36:26; John 16:8–9).[23] Sinners

---

16. Flavel, *England's Duty*, 4:95.
17. Flavel, *Method of Grace*, 2:296–97.
18. Flavel, *Method of Grace*, 2:297.
19. Flavel, *Method of Grace*, 2:297.
20. Flavel, *England's Duty*, 4:39.
21. Flavel, *England's Duty*, 4:40.
22. Flavel, *England's Duty*, 4:52–53.
23. Flavel, *Method of Grace*, 2:298–99.

must be taught by the Father through the Holy Spirit (John 6:45) to be converted—not by a vision or immediate revelation, but through the Word, and the preaching of the Word, illuminated by the Spirit.[24]

The Holy Spirit uses the law to draw sinners to Christ "in the due method and order of the gospel." Flavel wrote, "In this order, therefore, the Spirit (ordinarily) draws souls to Christ, he shines into their minds by illumination; applies that light to their consciences by effectual conviction; breaks and wounds their hearts for sin in compunction [pricking or grief]; and then moves the will to embrace and close with Christ in the way of faith for life and salvation."[25]

Boone notes that Flavel varied somewhat in describing this process in other writings, but he generally followed the same pattern of the illumination of the mind, conviction of the conscience and compunction of the affections through the mind, and the renewal of the will with further illumination of the mind with knowledge of Christ.[26] Flavel's understanding of conversion was shaped by his analysis of the soul in the faculties of mind, affections, and will. Boone writes, "The faculty psychology of Flavel was inextricably linked with his view of the effectual call. Each step was related to certain faculties. Effectual grace overcame the effect of sin on the faculties."[27] In the preparative stages of calling, the Lord wounds the soul to make way for healing in Christ alone, Flavel said. God plows the soil to make way for planting the seed which alone can produce the harvest.[28]

Flavel did not prescribe a set pattern of conversion to which all sinners must conform as much as to describe God's dealings with sinners in general. He said,

> These several steps are more distinctly discerned in some Christians than in others; they are more clearly seen in the adult convert, than in those that were drawn to Christ in their youth; in such as were drawn to him out of a state of profaneness, than in those that had the advantage of a pious education; but in this order the work is carried

24. Flavel, *Method of Grace*, 2:309.

25. Flavel, *Method of Grace*, 2:71. See also Stephen J. Yuille, *The Inner Sanctum of Puritan Piety: John Flavel's Doctrine of Mystical Union with Christ* (Grand Rapids: Reformation Heritage Books, 2007), 65–66.

26. Boone, "Puritan Evangelism," 156–60. Compare the Westminster Shorter Catechism (Q. 31).

27. Boone, "Puritan Evangelism," 166.

28. Boone, "Puritan Evangelism," 182, 184.

on ordinarily in all, however it differs in point of clearness in the one and in the other.[29]

As Flavel stated in *England's Duty*, Christ pounded forcefully on the heart of the Philippian jailer but knocked quietly on Lydia's door (Acts 16), thus showing that "The Spirit of God varies his method according to the temper of the soul he worketh on."[30]

In no case are such steps to be relied upon, for they are only steps toward reliance on Christ, the only Savior. Flavel warned against "a more refined way of self-righteousness" that cloaks itself in such an appearance of humility as to be nearly invincible. He explained,

> I pity many poor souls upon this account, who stand off from Christ, dare not believe because they want [lack] such and such qualifications to fit them for Christ. O saith one, could I find such brokenness of heart for sin, so much reformation and power over corruptions, then I could come to Christ; the meaning of which is this, if I could bring a price in my hand to purchase him, then I should be encouraged to go unto him. Here now lies horrible pride covered over with a veil of great humility: Poor sinner, either come naked and empty-handed (Isa. 55:1; Rom. 4:5), or expect a repulse.[31]

The inward teaching of God through the outward teaching of the Scriptures communicates various experiential lessons to the soul. Flavel cautiously stated that though the order and degree may vary, God's teaching upon the soul always includes twelve lessons: (1) an intuitive knowledge of the abundant evil of our sinful actions and nature, (2) a trembling fear of the wrath and misery threatened against sinners, (3) the concern that salvation from sin and God's wrath is the most important business in life, (4) a compelling obligation to strive after salvation yet despair of obtaining salvation by one's own will-power or worthiness, (5) a dawning hope from the general promises of the gospel that salvation is possible, and (6) satisfaction with the fullness of Christ that everyone who receives Him will be saved to the uttermost.[32]

God's teachings regarding salvation also include: (7) the firm belief that no one can benefit from the blood of Christ unless he is united with

29. Flavel, *Method of Grace*, 2:71.
30. Flavel, *England's Duty*, 4:99.
31. Flavel, *England's Duty*, 4:57.
32. Flavel, *Method of Grace*, 2:310–13

Christ by faith, (8) the inward necessity to prayerfully seek from God all the grace we need to be united to Christ, (9) an abandonment of sinful lifestyles and companions to find mercy with God, (10) a heart-engaging view of the beauty and excellence of Christ's church, (11) a resolved determination not to give up on Christ and not to turn back to sin no matter what the cost, lest one be damned, (12) a courage to venture upon Christ despite one's wickedness and fears of damnation because of the great promises of His grace.[33] These twelve lessons should not be viewed as steps of preparation but as the spiritual curriculum that God ordinarily follows in teaching sinners over the course of their conversion.

Convicting Illumination versus Saving Illumination

Boone writes that to understand Flavel correctly, we must realize that "the preparatory workings of the Spirit are not some work of God or of man in distinction from the effectual call, but rather the initial steps of the effectual call. Thus, these preparatory works do not apply to the non-elect and any apparent illumination or conviction which takes place in them."[34] That suggests a qualitative difference between the convictions of the non-elect and those of the elect. Boone says this separates Flavel's concept of preparation from that of Pettit.[35] Boone explains:

1) Flavel never speaks of the "partial conviction" or "common conviction" of someone who is later converted.

2) Flavel never speaks of the "preparatory work of the Spirit" in the non-elect.

3) Flavel differentiates between "special and common convictions," the latter having a transient nature, but the former continuing until conversion.[36]

Boone's point is enforced by the correspondence between Flavel's view and the Westminster Shorter Catechism (Q. 31), which includes "convincing us of our sin and misery" under the category of effectual calling.

However, we have already argued that the Westminster Standards recognize some works ("operations") of the Spirit that are "common" to

---

33. Flavel, *Method of Grace*, 2:313–17.
34. Boone, "Puritan Evangelism," 189–90.
35. Boone, "Puritan Evangelism," 191–92.
36. Boone, "Puritan Evangelism," 189–90.

all men (WLC Q. 68), and this category may include the conviction of sin that the Shorter Catechism identifies as part of effectual calling (SC 31).[37] That means Flavel's consideration of conviction under the category of effectual calling need not imply a distinct quality of conviction of sin in the elect.

Is partial conviction only the experience of the reprobate? Flavel appears to have used the phrase *partial conviction* in only one place in his *Works*,[38] as one of the uses (applications) in *England's Duty*.[39] We cannot argue that he never uses the phrase in certain ways, but that he only used it once. His point here seems to be warning sinners to seek a more powerful conviction unto conversion. We cannot therefore say "partial conviction" is an experience that never leads to conversion; it could be a first, albeit incomplete, step that might ultimately proceed to salvation.

"Common convictions" do not only belong to the reprobate. Flavel distinguished between common convictions that come and go, as opposed to special convictions which continue unto conversion, "for Christ is in pursuit of the soul."[40] However, the experience of transient convictions does not prove that one is reprobate. Flavel wrote, "Sometimes Christ knocks intermittingly, knocking and stopping, a call and silence, and that at considerable time and distance…. But the Lord follows his design, and at last the conviction settles, and ends in conversion."[41] If a person is one of Christ's elect, then transient convictions will give way to lasting conversion. So once again, Flavel was not setting aside a certain kind of conviction that belongs only to the reprobate. It could have been disastrous for a pastor to have taught people that their imperfect convictions signaled their unchangeable destiny to hell. Though some convictions are unsuccessful in opening the heart, Flavel said, they are still the "knocks of Christ."[42] In his use of the term of transient convictions, Flavel was simply warning people not to consider themselves converted when they had only experienced a work of the Spirit common to both elect and reprobate.

---

37. See chapter 8.

38. This statement is based on a computer search of digital image files for Flavel's *Works*, found both at Google Books and the Internet Archive.

39. Flavel, *England's Duty*, 4:202.

40. Flavel, *England's Duty*, 4:103.

41. Flavel, *England's Duty*, 4:100–101. See also *Method of Grace*, 2:75.

42. Flavel, *England's Duty*, 4:99.

Does the Spirit perform preparatory work only on the elect? Asserting that seems to overreach the evidence, given that Flavel often spoke of preparation with respect to people whose eternal destiny was presently unknown, and therefore he urged them to come to Christ.[43] Boone's distinction between "partial conviction" in the reprobate and "preparatory work" in the elect misapplies the doctrine of the eternal decree to Flavel's view of how the Spirit works in time. Though he may have been inconsistent at times, Flavel did not generally use the common/special distinction in the Spirit's work as a difference between the non-elect and the elect, but, like other Puritans, spoke of the Spirit's "common" gifts to the saved and unsaved alike, and of His "special" gifts that come only with salvation.[44] Contrary to what Boone says, Flavel viewed conviction of sin as "preparative for the new creature" and "a common work of the Spirit both upon the elect and reprobate," because, like blossoms on a tree, such conviction may either turn into fruit or wither and vanish.[45]

What then is the difference between the illumination that convicts and the illumination that converts? Flavel explained this in his sermon on the text, "Light has come into the world, and men loved darkness rather than light" (John 3:19). He said Christ's light comes to sinners in different ways. First is the light that shines in the means, or the knowledge given through preaching. Second is the light that shines in the soul, yet is "common, and intellectual only, to *conviction*." Third is the "special and efficacious light" that shines in the soul, "bringing the soul to Christ in true *conversion*."[46]

Boone faults Flavel for failing to distinguish between ineffectual conviction and saving illumination. He says Flavel describes the difference only in terms of "the various ways in which people respond to the gospel, rather than an actual explanation of those responses."[47] But Flavel *did* explain the difference. He said it is the contrast between the natural conscience's awareness of God's fearsome majesty, and a new spiritual sight

---

43. Flavel, *Method of Grace*, 2:30.
44. Flavel, *Method of Grace*, 2:68, 330–31; *England's Duty*, 4:111–12.
45. Flavel, *Method of Grace*, 2:363.
46. Flavel, *Method of Grace*, 2:440–41, emphasis original to contrast "conviction" and "conversion."
47. Boone, "Puritan Evangelism," 177.

of Christ's beauty. In this, Flavel anticipates "the new spiritual sense" taught by Jonathan Edwards.[48]

Mere conviction, or partial conviction, acts upon the natural man's understanding to impart knowledge, orthodoxy of judgment, and some "transient motions upon the affections."[49] It "may actually shine into the consciences of men by those means, and convince them of their sins, and yet men may hate it, and choose the darkness rather than light."[50] Thus mere conviction will "inform" and "rectify" the intellect and conscience, and may even "give check to the affections in the pursuit of sinful designs and courses," thus leading to moral reform.[51] It is more than the "traditional" knowledge of sin possessed by uneducated men, and more than the "discursive" knowledge of sin held by learned men; it is an "intuitive sight of sin" as different from the previous two kinds of knowledge as a living, roaring lion is to a painting on a wall.[52]

In this kind of conviction, God's greatness and holiness become vivid and real to the sinner, and Judgment Day draws near to the conscience. Flavel wrote, "But when a light from God enters the soul, to discover the nature of God, and of sin, then it sees that whatever wrath is treasured up for sinners in the dreadful threatening of the law, is but the just demerit of sin."[53] But it still does not introduce into the soul a new spiritual sense or new kind of affection towards Christ. Rather it merely energizes the natural conscience of fallen men. Indeed, such conviction of sin casts Satan out of the faculty of the understanding, but "the soul is scarcely half won to Christ" because "Satan keeps the fort-royal, the heart and will are in his own possession."[54] As a result these convicted sinners fear hell but also hate the light.

In a similar way, Perkins distinguished between the Holy Spirit's work upon the mind and His work upon the will.[55] John Owen wrote, "It may be observed, that we have placed all the effects of this work in

---

48. Jonathan Edwards, "A Divine and Supernatural Light," in *The Works of Jonathan Edwards, Volume 17, Sermons and Discourses, 1730–1733*, ed. Mark Valeri (New Haven: Yale University Press, 1999), 414–18.

49. Flavel, *England's Duty*, 4:202.

50. Flavel, *Method of Grace*, 2:441.

51. Flavel, *Method of Grace*, 2:442.

52. Flavel, *Method of Grace*, 2:310.

53. Flavel, *Method of Grace*, 2:311.

54. Flavel, *Method of Grace*, 2:449.

55. Perkins, *Exposition of the Creede*, 192–93.

the mind, conscience, affections, and conversation. Hence it follows, notwithstanding all that is or may be spoken of it, that the will is neither really changed nor internally renewed by it."[56]

Saving illumination, by contrast, is worked in "that spiritual and heavenly light, by which the Spirit of God shineth into the hearts of men, to give them 'the light of the knowledge of the glory of God in the face of Jesus Christ' (2 Cor. 4:6)."[57] Flavel quoted Edward Reynolds (1599–1676) as saying that saving illumination gives the heart "a due taste and relish of the sweetness of spiritual truth."[58] This new taste for the sweetness of revealed truth is central to Flavel's concept of saving illumination. He wrote, "No knowledge is so distinct, so clear, so sweet, as that which the heart communicates to the head"; it is a new "spiritual sense and experience" which puts Scripture in a whole new light, indeed it writes "the word of God upon the heart of man" (cf. Jer. 31:33). To view Christ by faith is to see with hearty affection His unsurpassed loveliness.[59] Christ not only "breaks in upon the understanding and conscience by powerful convictions and compunctions," but also opens "the door of the heart," that is, "the will," conquering it and making it willing "by a sweet and secret efficacy." "When this is done," Flavel said, "the heart is opened; saving light now shines in it."[60]

In much the same way, Goodwin said faith is "a spiritual sight" of Christ, the supernatural creation of a new "sense" that is as different from fallen human reason as hearing music with one's ears is different from reading music printed in a book.[61] Owen wrote,

> The effects of this [preparatory] work on the mind, which is the first subject affected by it, proceeds not so far as to give it delight, complacency, and satisfaction in the lively spiritual nature and excellencies of the things revealed unto it. The true nature of saving illumination consists in this, that it gives the mind such a direct intuitive insight and prospect into spiritual things as that, in their own spiritual

---

56. Owen, *Pneumatologia*, 3:238.
57. Flavel, *Method of Grace*, 2:309.
58. Flavel, *Fountain of Life*, 1:133. See Edward Reynolds, *Animalis Homo*, in *The Works of the Right Rev. Edward Reynolds* (1826; repr. Morgan, Pa.: Soli Deo Gloria, 1998), 4:368.
59. Flavel, "The Epistle Dedicatory" to *Fountain of Life*, 1:xviii–xx.
60. Flavel, *Fountain of Life*, 1:137.
61. Thomas Goodwin, *The Object and Acts of Justifying Faith*, 8:258–59.

nature, they suit, please, and satisfy it, so that it is transformed into them, cast into the mold of them, and rests in them.[62]

Therefore Flavel distinguished convicting illumination from saving illumination in two ways. First, he said that conviction touches the intellect and conscience but salvation alone changes the will. Second, he taught a new sense of the heart by which a man sees God's beauty and tastes His sweetness in Jesus Christ. While conviction brings to a sinner a heightened awareness of God's terrible justice and power, only saving illumination grants him the spiritual sense of Christ's heart-captivating loveliness. This view of regeneration was shared by other Puritans and later perpetuated by Jonathan Edwards.

Conviction, Conversion, Hope, and Assurance

The work of conversion may be likened to conception and birth. Some souls are utterly barren when they hear the Word and never sense its power. Others sense "some slight, transient, and ineffectual operations of the gospel on their souls." These can be "abortives and miscarriages" that never result in a living birth.[63] Yet upon others "the word works effectually and powerfully…to kill their vain hopes." These Flavel classified as either "embryos," souls under the initial workings of the Spirit, or "complete births" or souls regenerated by the Spirit.[64] This language suggests that Flavel considered the new birth to be a process that was not complete until sinners had a living hope in Christ.

But even spiritual embryos may find hopeful and encouraging signs in themselves, Flavel said, if they observe "deeper and more powerful" operations of the Word on their hearts than those who miscarry.[65] Flavel suggested three questions people should ask themselves to determine if the misery of conviction would lead them to salvation:

- Does the Word show you not just the evil of this or that sin but also the corruption and wickedness of your whole heart, life, and nature?

- Does the Word merely frighten you with hell or melt you with grief that you have sinned against a holy and good God?

62. Owen, *Pneumatologia*, 3:238.
63. Flavel, *Method of Grace*, 2:301–303.
64. Flavel, *Method of Grace*, 2:304.
65. Flavel, *Method of Grace*, 2:304.

- Does the Word only shake your hopes or does it drive you to Christ alone as your only door to salvation?[66]

In these questions Flavel hinted that distinguishing grace might actually begin prior to conscious hope in Christ. The convicted sinner who longs for Christ may not yet have grounds to consider himself saved, but he may be hopeful that he is traveling "in the way of believing." He might observe his "sensible changes" and say,

> Time was, when I had no sense of sin, nor sorrow for sin; no desire after Christ, no heart to duties. But it is not so with me now; I now see the evil of sin, so as I never saw it before; my heart is now broken in the sense of that evil; my desires begin to be enflamed after Jesus Christ; I am not at rest, nor where I would be, till I am in secret mourning after the Lord Jesus; surely these are the dawnings of the day of mercy; let me go on in this way.[67]

Flavel considered an experiential knowledge of one's sin and God's wrath to be absolutely essential in true conversion. He said that was often present when one had only a dim hope of the possibility of salvation. Yet he counted terrors part of the inward teaching of God of which Jesus Christ said, everyone that "hath learned of the Father, cometh unto me" (John 6:45). Of this divine teaching, Flavel wrote, "No man can miss of Christ, or miscarry in the way of faith, that is under the special instructions and teachings of the Father."[68]

An assured believer in Christ may thus look back to the days of his heart-rending convictions and longings after the Savior and say, "Though I did not know it for certain at the time, already the Father's saving call was upon my life." So we must view questions about preparation in light of the Puritan belief that conversion is a process in which a sinner may not always be clear about when he crosses from death to life. What initially seems to be preparation may later prove to be salvation. There is mystery in the regenerating work of the Spirit, and we must acknowledge that the wind blows where it wishes and we see it not (John 3:8). Flavel offered his readers the following poetic tribute to the skill of the great Preparer:

66. Flavel, *Method of Grace*, 2:305.
67. Flavel, *Method of Grace*, 2:317.
68. Flavel, *Method of Grace*, 2:307.

There's skill in plowing, that the plowman knows,
For if too shallow, or too deep he goes,
The seed is either bury'd, or else may
To rooks and daws become an easy prey.

This, as a lively emblem, fitly may
Describe the blessed Spirit's work and way:
Whose work on souls, with this doth symbolize;
Betwixt them both, thus the resemblance lies.

Souls are the soil, conviction is the plow,
God's workmen draw, the Spirit shows them how.
He guides the work, and in good ground doth bless
His workmen's pains, with sweet and fair success.

The heart prepar'd, he scatters in the seed,
Which in its season springs, no fowl nor weed
Shall pick it up, or choke this springing corn,
'Till it be housed in the heavenly barn.

When thus the Spirit plows up the fallow ground,
When with such fruits his servant's work is crown'd
Let all the friends of Christ, and souls say now,
As they pass by the fields, "God speed the plow."

Sometimes this plow thin shelfy ground doth turn,
That little seed which springs, the sun-beams burn.
The rest uncover'd lies, which fowls devour.
Alas! their heart was touch'd, but not with pow'r.

The cares and pleasures of this world have drown'd
The seed before it peep'd above the ground.
Some springs indeed, the Scripture saith that some
Do taste the powers of the world to come.

These embryos never come to timely birth,
Because the seed that's sown wants depth of earth.
Turn up, O God, the bottom of my heart;
And to the seed that's sown, do thou impart

Thy choicest blessing. Though I weep and mourn
In this wet seed-time, if I may return
With sheaves of joy; these fully will reward
My pains and sorrows, be they ne'er so hard.[69]

---

69. Flavel, "Upon the Plowing of Corn-land," Ch. VII, *Husbandry Spiritualized,* in *Works,* 5:66–67.

John Bunyan's Picturesque Preparation

John Bunyan (1628–1688) was given to frightful cursing and swearing in his youth. His experience in coming to God included much doubting and striving until he finally rested on the righteousness of Jesus Christ alone. After that he became a powerful preacher of Christ. However, he was repeatedly imprisoned for preaching outside of the Church of England during the 1660s and 1670s. He is most famous for his narrative of the Christian's journey from this world to heaven in *Pilgrim's Progress* (1678). What is sometimes overlooked is Bunyan's robust view of God's sovereignty in saving sinners, expressed in such works as *Come and Welcome to Jesus Christ*. Though Bunyan was not a Puritan who sought to reform the Church of England from within, his work clearly reveals a Puritan synthesis of Reformed theology and experiential piety albeit one mixed with a sectarian view of the church.[70]

Bunyan's allegory of the Christian pilgrimage includes a remarkable description of the stages of a man's conversion. There was a day when virtually everyone in English-speaking lands, and many others, knew this story. Today that has changed. Furthermore, many who read this story may overlook Bunyan's teaching on preparation. So let us consider how Bunyan described the man's journey from the City of Destruction to the Cross in terms of preparation.

Christian's Progress to Conversion and Assurance

Pilgrim's Progress begins with a man who is so frightened by a sense of his sin and the coming judgment that these fears lie like a heavy burden strapped to his back. He learned about his sin from a book ("the Book") and in response "wept and trembled" and cried out, "What shall I do?"[71] This shows how an unconverted sinner comes under the conviction of God's law and threats of His wrath against mankind and begins to make use of the means of grace. As Bunyan wrote elsewhere, such convictions are "God's ordinary dealing with sinners" when He first comes to their souls.[72]

---

70. See Brian G. Najapfour, "'The Very Heart of Prayer': Reclaiming John Bunyan's Spirituality" (ThM thesis, Puritan Reformed Theological Seminary, 2009).

71. John Bunyan, *The Pilgrim's Progress* (1678; facsimile repr., London: Elliot Stock, 1895), 1–2. Henceforth this will be referred to as Bunyan, *The Pilgrim's Progress* (1678 facsimile), to distinguish it from other editions.

72. John Bunyan, *Saved by Grace*, in *The Works of John Bunyan*, ed. George Offor (Glasgow: Blackie and Son, 1855), 1:350.

In another allegory titled *Holy War* (1682), Bunyan pictures this stage
of preparation in the sending of Captain Boanerges, Captain Conviction,
Captain Judgment, and Captain Execution to assault the rebellious city
of Mansoul before the Son of the King came to take it. Bunyan said, "For
indeed generally in all his wars he did use to send these four captains in
the van[guard], for they were very stout and roughhewn men, men that
were fit to break the ice."[73]

After being convicted of sin, the burdened man in *Pilgrim's Progress*
meets Evangelist, who tells him to flee to the wicket-gate to escape the
wrath to come (cf. Matt. 7:13–14).[74] The man cannot see the gate, which
is some distance off, but Evangelist tells him to follow "yonder shining light." Bunyan comments on this light in a marginal note, saying:
"Christ and the way to him cannot be found without the Word." Evangelist directs the man to follow the Word to the gate, which marks the way
to eternal life through Christ. The man runs ahead, crying "Life, life,
eternal life!" leaving behind his family and his town, the City of Destruction.[75] At this point, Bunyan identifies the man as Christian,[76] a man who
has broken with the world and is seeking God's grace but is not yet in the
way of salvation.

Later, in the Palace Beautiful, Christian tells the damsel Piety that
though fear of destruction drove him out of his homeland, he would
never have found the wicket-gate without Evangelist. He attributed this
"chance" meeting with Evangelist to God ("as God would have it").[77] In
this Bunyan indicated that the terrors of the law motivate a man to seek
salvation, but only the gospel can reveal the way to salvation in Christ.

Christian says that if his neighbor Obstinate had "felt what I have
felt of the powers and terrors of what is yet unseen" he would have
come along. Yet one man, Pliable, does accompany Christian, and as
they travel, Christian talks of the wonders of heaven and the infallible
truth of the Bible. But despite his belief in such things, Christian still
carries a heavy burden. The weight of this burden nearly undoes him
when he and Pliable fall into the Slough of Dispond, or the swampy

---

73. John Bunyan, *Life and Death of Mr. Badman and Holy War*, ed. John Brown (London:
Cambridge University Press, 1905), 217–18.
74. A "wicket" is a small gate.
75. Bunyan, *The Pilgrim's Progress* (1678 facsimile), 2–3.
76. Bunyan, *The Pilgrim's Progress* (1678 facsimile), 4.
77. Bunyan, *The Pilgrim's Progress* (1678 facsimile), 53–54.

mire of spiritual depression. Pliable is disgusted and returns home, but Christian struggles on to that side of the Slough "still further from his own House, and next to the Wicket-gate"; and Help comes to lift him out of the swamp.[78]

Bunyan was warning that people such as Pliable, who have not yet experienced the burdens and terrors of sin, are ill-equipped for the hardships that await those who follow the way of Christ. In another context Bunyan said coming to Christ was "a moving of the mind towards him, from a sound sense of the absolute want [need] that a man hath of him for his justification and salvation. Indeed, without this sense of a lost condition without him, there will be no moving of the mind towards him."[79]

In his allegory of the pilgrim, Bunyan was also warning us that conviction of sin is accompanied with "many fears, and doubts, and discouraging apprehensions" that threaten to swallow up would-be believers. The King has placed solid stepping-stones across the swamp, which a marginal note identifies as "the promises of forgiveness and acceptance to life by faith in Christ." The King's servants have also dumped "twenty million Cart Loads...of wholesome instructions" into the Slough to mend it, but to no avail.[80] Bunyan is observing that sound preaching by itself cannot keep men from falling into such troubles of the soul. Bunyan certainly was not accusing Puritan preachers of driving men to despair by convicting them of their sin. Rather, he saw despair as an evil consequence of man's sinful reactions to the conviction of sin.

Bunyan also did not believe that a sinner had to fall into such despondency to be saved. Later Christian meets another pilgrim, Faithful, who says he made it to the wicket-gate without falling into the slough. Instead he had to resist the temptations of an immoral woman named Wanton.[81] In this Bunyan recognized the variety of spiritual experiences. He uses Faithful to describe God's work of grace in the soul this way:

> It gives him conviction of sin, especially of the defilement of his nature, and the sin of unbelief.... This sight and sense of things worketh in him sorrow and shame for sin; he findeth moreover revealed in him the Savior of the world, and the absolute necessity

78. Bunyan, *The Pilgrim's Progress* (1678 facsimile), 7–11.
79. Bunyan, *Come and Welcome to Jesus Christ*, in *Works*, 1:247.
80. Bunyan, *The Pilgrim's Progress* (1678 facsimile), 11–13.
81. Bunyan, *The Pilgrim's Progress* (1678 facsimile), 89.

of closing with [coming to] him for life, at the which he findeth hungering and thirsting after him, to which hungering, etc the promise is made. Now according to the strength or weakness of his faith in his Savior, so is his joy and peace, so is his love to holiness, so are his desires to know him more, and also to serve him in this world.[82]

Nevertheless, Faithful concludes that a sinner often has difficulty discerning God's work of grace in his own life, whereas others see it in his confession of faith and holy life. Therefore Bunyan expected conversion to involve conviction of sin, but not everyone who was convicted had to fall into extreme humiliation.

Christian reaches the wicket-gate, which he must knock on "more than once or twice." The guard asks the pilgrim who he is. When Christian identifies himself as "a poor burdened sinner" traveling to heaven, the guard opens the gate. The guard's name, Goodwill, symbolizes the willingness of Christ to receive all who come to Him. Bunyan notes in the margin, "The gate will be opened to broken-hearted sinners."[83] Christian is now shown the narrow way of salvation.[84] But the burden remains on his back, for, as the margin note says, "There is no deliverance from the guilt and burden of sin, but by the death and blood of Christ."[85]

Bunyan seems to be teaching in this that a person can be in the way of salvation and yet not have conscious assurance of salvation. He may be through the gate and on the right path, but he has not yet received the assurance of forgiveness of sins at the cross. At the same time, Bunyan was also warning us to be cautious about too quickly counting men as saved. They may be convinced of sin, be sorry for wrongdoing, ask for the prayers of the church, attempt to make restitution for their wrongs, be engaged in Christian service, and listen to preachers with reverence and joy, yet still be outside the covenant of grace.[86]

Christian comes next to the house of the Interpreter, who shows him spiritual truths by the light of a candle (marginal note: "illumination").[87] The Interpreter represents the Holy Spirit in His office of interpreter of

82. Bunyan, *The Pilgrim's Progress* (1678 facsimile), 115.
83. Bunyan, *The Pilgrim's Progress* (1678 facsimile), 14.
84. Bunyan, *The Pilgrim's Progress* (1678 facsimile), 35.
85. Bunyan, *The Pilgrim's Progress* (1678 facsimile), 17–18.
86. Bunyan, *The Doctrine of the Law and Grace Unfolded*, in *Works*, 1:511–12.
87. Bunyan, *The Pilgrim's Progress* (1678 facsimile), 19.

the Word of God and illuminator of the soul.[88] One room of the Interpreter's house especially concerns us here. In it a man sweeps a dusty
floor, stirring up clouds of dirt. A maid then sprinkles water on the floor
and easily sweeps it clean. The Interpreter explains that the law cannot
cleanse original sin and inward corruptions but only stirs them up. Only
"when the Gospel comes in the sweet and precious influences thereof to
the heart" is sin subdued.[89] The preparatory work of the law cannot save
sinners but only aggravates sin until saving grace comes.

In a later edition of the book, Bunyan added a similar point about
the weakness of the law by describing a detour that Christian takes after
escaping the swamp but before reaching the wicket-gate. Worldly-Wise-
man persuades the pilgrim to turn aside to the village of Morality, where
Legality and his son, Civility, reportedly can remove men's burdens. The
pilgrim turns aside to go there, but he is stopped by a huge hill (margin:
"Mount Sinai"), which threatens to fall upon him, makes his burden feel
heavier, and flashes with fire.[90] Evangelist meets him there and explains
that the wisdom of this world sends us to the law for justification, which
it cannot afford us. As Evangelist speaks, Mount Sinai bursts into flames
and a voice says, "As many as are of the works of the law are under the
curse: for it is written, Cursed is every one that continueth not in all
things which are written in the book of the law to do them" (Gal. 3:10).[91]
Christian speedily goes away from the hill to the gate, and from there to
the house of the Interpreter.

Bunyan said this teaches that on one hand, the world abuses the law
by turning men away from seeking justification by faith alone to trust
in their own works. This is legalism. On the other hand, the law assists
the gospel preacher. The law's fearful declarations of wrath against sinners should rather stop men from proceeding in legalism, and, joined
with the gospel, drive them to faith in Christ. In this respect the law is
the tool of the Holy Spirit to convince sinners of sin and awaken them

---

88. Interpreter's last words to Christian promise the ministry of the Comforter to
continue to do what Interpreter had begun: "The Comforter be always with thee good
Christian, to guide thee in the way that leads to the city" (Bunyan, *The Pilgrim's Progress*
[1678 facsimile], 34).

89. Bunyan, *The Pilgrim's Progress* (1678 facsimile), 21–22.

90. John Bunyan, *The Pilgrim's Progress* (London: by A. W. for J. Clarke, 1738), 14–15. The
first complete version of Bunyan's tale, as it stands today, was actually the third edition,
published in 1679 (John Brown, preface to Bunyan, *The Pilgrim's Progress* [1678 facsimile], ii).

91. Bunyan, *The Pilgrim's Progress* (1738), 20–21.

to flee damnation.[92] In this Bunyan revealed a remarkably sophisticated doctrine of uses of the law.

Leaving the house of the Interpreter, Christian ascends another hill where he sees a cross and below it, an open tomb. As he looks at the cross, his burden falls from his back and rolls down into the tomb. Angels speak peace and forgiveness to him. They give him new clothes in place of his rags, and seal him for heaven. Christian weeps with wonder and joy, and sings,

> Thus far did I come loaded with my sin;
> Nor could ought ease the grief that I was in,
> Till I came hither: what a place is this!
> Must here be the beginning of my bliss?
> Must here the burden fall from off my back?
> Must here the strings that bound it to me crack?
> Blessed Cross! Blessed Sepulchre! Blessed rather be
> The Man that there was put to shame for me.[93]

This culminates the conversion process for Bunyan's pilgrim up to the experience of assurance, though his subsequent journey to the city of God includes many dangers and temptations.

The Salvation of Christiana and Mercy

Bunyan wrote a second part of *Pilgrim's Progress* (published in 1684), which describes the journey of Christian's wife, Christiana, and their children on their way to salvation. After Christian leaves, his wife grieves over the loss. She and the children weep because they have not followed Christian in the path of life.[94] Bunyan alludes here to Hosea 13:8, in which the Lord says of Israel, "I will meet them as a bear that is bereaved of her whelps, and will rend the caul of their heart, and there will I devour them like a lion: the wild beast shall tear them."

God reveals to Christiana the blackness of her sins and the willingness of God to forgive her. So she, her sons, and her young neighbor Mercy pack up and leave the City of Destruction. Mercy has doubts that God will accept her, but resolves to go ahead, praying both for herself and her hard-hearted relatives.[95]

---

92. Bunyan, *The Fear of God*, in *Works*, 1:449.
93. Bunyan, *The Pilgrim's Progress* (1678 facsimile), 35–36.
94. John Bunyan, *The Pilgrim's Progress… in Two Parts* (London: for W. Johnston, 1757), 2:7.
95. Bunyan, *The Pilgrim's Progress… in Two Parts*, 2:7, 9, 17, 19.

When the ladies and children came to the Slough of Despond, they find it worse than before. Bunyan wrote, "For many there be, that pretend to be the King's laborers, and say, They are for mending the King's highway, that bring dirt and dung instead of stones, and so mar instead of mending."[96] Here Bunyan finds fault with preachers who substitute the wisdom of men for the "wholesome instructions" of God's Word.

Despite this miry obstacle, Christiana and the youth cross the swamp without falling in—though she almost fell "and that not once or twice." Again, as he did with Faithful, Bunyan uses the case of Christiana to communicate that all sinners need not experience the same depths of despair when coming to Christ. As Christiana quipped to Mercy, who still doubted she would be accepted at the gate, "You know your sore, and I know mine; and, good friend, we shall all have enough evil before we come to our journey's end."[97]

When the group arrives at the gate, Christiana knocks and knocks. But then a large dog begins barking. The margin says: "The dog, the devil, an enemy to prayers." The devil thus aggravates the fears of convinced sinners and tries to drive them away from Christ. This barking frightens the pilgrims, who step back. But then Christiana knocks again, this time harder. The gate-keeper opens the door, and upon learning that it is Christian's wife, immediately lets her and the children in.[98]

Meanwhile, poor Mercy stands outside, "trembling and crying, for fear that she was rejected." She has not received the revelation that Christiana has of the King's summons and thus fears she came presumptuously. Yet she cannot stand being left outside, so she starts knocking loudly.[99] Later Christiana tells her, "I thought you would come in by a violent hand, or take the kingdom by storm" (Matt. 11:12).[100] When the guard opens the gate, he discovers that Mercy has fallen down in a faint. Bunyan writes, "Then he took her again by the hand and led her gently in, and said, I pray for all them that believe on me, by what means soever they come unto me."[101] This tender passage reminds us that people do not need to have the same experiences, or even the same degree of knowl-

---

96. Bunyan, *The Pilgrim's Progress... in Two Parts*, 2:19–20.
97. Bunyan, *The Pilgrim's Progress... in Two Parts*, 2:20.
98. Bunyan, *The Pilgrim's Progress... in Two Parts*, 2:21–22.
99. Bunyan, *The Pilgrim's Progress... in Two Parts*, 2:22–23.
100. Bunyan, *The Pilgrim's Progress... in Two Parts*, 2:25.
101. Bunyan, *The Pilgrim's Progress... in Two Parts*, 2:24.

edge or faith, as others to be truly converted. The guard's words, "I pray for all them that believe on me," also reminds the readers that Christ Himself meets pilgrims at the wicket-gate.

Unlike Christian, Christiana and the young people receive promises of pardon at the gate. The guard takes them to the top of the gate, where they see Christ crucified from afar off.[102] At Interpreter's house, they receive a bath (margin: "the bath of sanctification"), a seal, and new garments—Christian did not get the seal and new garment until reaching the cross.[103] A man named Great-heart then brings them to the cross, where he teaches them about justification by the imputed righteousness of Jesus Christ. Christiana comments that it was here that her husband's burden fell off. She adds, "Though my heart was lightsome and joyous before, yet it is ten times more lightsome and joyous now."[104]

Bunyan thus laid out a pattern of conversion that allowed for variation. The conversions of Christian, Faithful, Christiana, and Mercy all involved conviction of sin, revelation of the gospel, passing through the wicket-gate, and finding peace through the cross. But the intensity of their experience, the manner of their entry through the gate, and the timing of their assurance differed. Christian's profound burden fell off at once at the cross, while Christiana's guilt gradually turned to joy. The sight of the cross gave Christian assurance of pardon, while the cross brought his wife a deeper understanding of how God's promise of forgiveness was accomplished by Christ's great work.

The varied experiences of Christian and Christiana allow us to answer the criticism that Spurgeon made against Bunyan, namely, that he should have put the cross at the wicket-gate, not further on in the way.[105] We say that all of Bunyan's pilgrims meet Christ at the gate of conversion. In Bunyan's allegory, the cross does not represent conversion to faith in Christ but assurance of pardon through faith in Christ. Bunyan understood that for some people assurance dawns at conversion, while others must walk for a time before their burdens fall off due to a clearer view of the gospel. He represented the latter experience through Christian, and the former through Christiana.

---

102. Bunyan, *The Pilgrim's Progress… in Two Parts*, 2:24.
103. Bunyan, *The Pilgrim's Progress… in Two Parts*, 2:47–48.
104. Bunyan, *The Pilgrim's Progress… in Two Parts*, 2:50–54.
105. Charles H. Spurgeon, *Pictures from Pilgrim's Progress* (1903; repr. Grand Rapids: Baker, 1982), 24–25.

Conclusion

John Flavel brought the doctrine of preparation down to the grass-roots level. He warned that men's heart are so naturally opposed to God's Word that the law bounces off them like a tennis ball off a stone wall, and the gospel lulls them to sleep like a love song. So Christ knocks on the doors of their hearts with the Spirit-energized law and gospel. He draws their sins against them like an army besieging a city.

Though Flavel listed twelve lessons God inwardly teaches the soul to save a sinner, he also said that God works in a variety of ways. He warned against trusting in one's preparations as worthiness to come to Christ. Such self-righteousness is the secret root of standing back from Christ because you do not feel you are humble enough.

Flavel carefully distinguished between the illumination that convicts one of sin and the illumination that saves the soul through faith. In conviction of sin the light of God's glory shines into the mind and conscience. It gives sinners a sense of God's majesty and justice, leading them to guilt and fear. But saving illumination penetrates beyond the mind to the will. It gives sinners a sense of Christ's loveliness and sweetness, leading them to faith and love.

If Flavel made Puritan preparation understandable to the mind of ordinary readers, Bunyan made it engaging to their imagination. The vivid figures of Christian, Christiana, and their companions on the road to the Celestial City brought to life the Puritan view of preparation. Through these characters, Bunyan taught that conviction of sin drives men to seek a way of escape through the diligent use of the means of grace, but only the gospel of Christ can lead them to salvation. The degree of humiliation varies from person to person. Some nearly drown in a swamp of despair as they are convicted of sin, but Bunyan blamed that on man's sinfulness, not godly preachers—though he did speak strongly against teachers who claimed to help despairing sinners but only made matters worse.

The law awakens the sinner to seek salvation, but the world abuses the law by making it a means of justification. The law can only stir up sin until grace comes through faith, to justify the sinner. Indeed the explicit declarations of the law should serve the evangelist well in driving men away from legalism and towards grace.

Though people may have to knock on heaven's doors repeatedly before entering the way of true Christianity, the door will open to broken-hearted sinners. Yet even after entering the narrow gate, and beginning to walk in the salvation road, they may not enjoy full assurance until they gain a clearer view of Christ crucified. Bunyan showed through the varying experiences of Christian, Faithful, Christiana, and Mercy that God chooses a variety of ways to convert sinners.

Bunyan's view of preparation is especially interesting given that he stood outside of mainstream Puritanism on some points of doctrine. He did not feel compelled to follow the teachings of men such as Perkins in all respects. But Bunyan was above all a man of the Scriptures. Therefore his embrace of the Puritan idea of preparation is even more significant. Modern readers may be surprised to discover that Bunyan was a "preparationist," but he was—in the best sense of the term. He appealed to his readers, "Dost thou love thine own soul? Then pray to Jesus Christ for an awakened heart...that thou mayest be allured to Jesus Christ."[106]

---

106. Bunyan, *The Strait Gate*, in *Works*, 1:390.

CHAPTER TWELVE

Jonathan Edwards and
Seeking God

When sinners are the subjects of great convictions of conscience, and
a remarkable work of the law; 'tis only a transacting the business of
the day of judgment, in the conscience beforehand.

—Jonathan Edwards[1]

In the preface to Solomon Stoddard's *Guide to Christ* (1714), Increase
Mather wrote, "That preparation for Christ is necessary, before the soul
can be united to him by faith, is an undoubted truth."[2] Passing over the
standard Puritan qualifications that preparation is God's *usual* manner
of working with the conversion of *adults*, Mather's confident statement
reminds us that the famous grandson of Stoddard was born into an ecclesiastical setting soaked in the doctrine of preparation for conversion.

In 1697 in Boston, Samuel Willard had preached a carefully nuanced
view of conviction of sin and misery prior to faith (published in 1726).[3]
He called preachers to nurture such conviction in sinners, and urged sinners to inquire after salvation and pursue it rather than sitting still and
perishing in their neglect.[4] Even in controversies over the Great Awakening during Edwards's life, both New Light (pro-revival) and Old Light
(anti-revival) ministers agreed that God ordinarily prepares sinners with

1. "True Grace, Distinguished from the Experience of the Devils," in *The Works of
Jonathan Edwards, Volume 25, Sermons and Discourses, 1743–1758*, ed. Wilson H. Kimnach
(New Haven: Yale University Press, 2006), 621. The Yale edition of Edwards's works may
be viewed online at http://edwards.yale.edu/ (accessed July 15, 2011).

2. Mather, "To the Reader," in Stoddard, *Guide to Christ*, iii.

3. Willard, *A Compleat Body of Divinity*, 435–36, 441–49.

4. Willard, *A Compleat Body of Divinity*, 449, 249.

conviction prior to conversion, though the Old Lights did not emphasize to the same degree the awakening of sinners.[5]

Robert Middlekauff says that Increase Mather's son, Cotton Mather (1663–1728), far from being a "leading exponent of preparation," actually rejected preparation with "distaste."[6] As evidence he cites Mather's warnings against pride in one's convictions and preparations. But Middlekauff appears to have misunderstood Mather, who commended the works of Shepard and Flavel, both of whom issued the same warnings even while advocating preparation.[7] Mather also highly commended Hooker's efforts in "the grand concerns of a sinner's preparation for, implantation in, and salvation by, the glorious Lord Jesus Christ."[8] Holifield says the following about Cotton Mather: "Like his father, he emphasized that the Spirit's preparation of the elect could occur in various ways, but he still assumed that the contrition and humiliation it normally produced as a prelude to conversion came as a gift of the sovereign Spirit."[9]

Stoddard's son-in-law and Jonathan Edwards's father, Timothy Edwards, preached the standard Puritan view of conversion as generally preceded by conviction or awakening to sin and judgment, followed by humiliation stripping a person of his sense of worthiness, which then set the stage for God's gracious gift of saving light and life.[10] Thus the Edwards family grew up with the doctrine of preparation as part of their orthodoxy and church experience.

Jonathan Edwards (1703–1758), however, while heir of his grandfather's and father's Puritanism, lived in a world of theological ferment, in which religious rationalism challenged the confessional stance of Reformed churches. His defense of justification by faith alone for his master's degree at Yale, given right after the great defection of Yale's faculty to Anglicanism, demonstrated that even in the hallowed halls

---

5. Holifield, *Theology in America,* 98. One of the major issues beween the New Lights and the Old Lights was the debate over conversion as a gradual process or as a sudden event. The Old Light ministers regarded claims to sudden conversion as dangerous enthusiasm.

6. Robert Middlekauff, *The Mathers: Three Generations of Puritan Intellectuals, 1596–1728* (Berkeley: University of California Press, 1999), 233.

7. Shepard, *The Sincere Convert,* 238–39; *The Sound Beleever,* 86; Flavel, "England's Duty," 4:57.

8. Mather, *Magnalia Christi Americana,* 2:65.

9. Holifield, *Theology in America,* 69.

10. George M. Marsden, *Jonathan Edwards: A Life* (New Haven: Yale University Press, 2003), 26–29.

of Puritan-founded colleges the old ideas were being challenged.[11] Edwards's brilliant intellect and revival experiences led him to probe his inherited beliefs as part of his life-long quest to search the Holy Scriptures for truth.

Though Edwards technically did not belong to the Puritan era (the late sixteenth through seventeenth centuries), his theology and spirit so closely reflect Puritanism that he should rightly be included in our study of Puritan preparation. As Perry Miller quipped, "Puritanism is what Edwards is."[12] D. Martyn Lloyd-Jones also said, "In Edwards we come to the very zenith or acme of Puritanism, for in him we have what we find in all the others, but in addition, this spirit, this life, this additional vitality."[13] Furthermore, Edwards bridges the gap between the evangelicalism of the Reformers and Puritans and later forms of Evangelical Christianity that arose during and after the Great Awakening in England and its American colonies. Therefore, let us explore Jonathan Edwards's teaching on the preparatory work of the Spirit.

Edwards's Basic Doctrine of Preparation

From Miller onward, some scholars have viewed Edwards as a champion of sovereign grace against the supposedly self-contradictory theories of predestinarian "preparationists." They say that since preparation cannot coexist with "grace alone" (*sola gratia*) and "by faith alone" (*sola fide*), two Reformation principles that Edwards proclaimed, he should thus be seen as an anti-preparationist who viewed conversion as "a divine seizure" in which "God sent his Spirit like a thunderbolt to electrify the helpless soul."[14] Lloyd-Jones, who wrote from a different perspective than Miller, nevertheless came to a similar conclusion, saying: "Jonathan Edwards would have nothing to do with the teaching of preparationism.... He believed in a direct and immediate influence of the Spirit, and in a

---

11. Kenneth P. Minkema, editorial introduction to *The Works of Jonathan Edwards, Volume 14, Sermons and Discourses 1723–1729* (New Haven: Yale University Press, 1997), 17.

12. Perry Miller, *Jonathan Edwards* ([New York]: William Sloane Associates, 1949), 194.

13. D. M. Lloyd-Jones, *The Puritans: Their Origins and Successors* (Edinburgh: Banner of Truth, 1987), 351.

14. David Laurence, "Jonathan Edwards, Solomon Stoddard, and the Preparationist Model of Conversion," *Harvard Theological Review* 72, no. 3–4 (July-October 1979): 277–78.

sudden and dramatic conversion."[15] But according to David Laurence, Edwards's disagreements with the preparation doctrine that he inherited from his forefathers "had nothing to do with problems raised by predestination."[16] Rather, he taught what Robert Caldwell calls "moderate preparationism."[17]

In a series of sermons preached in the fall of 1730,[18] Edwards argued, "'Tis God's manner to make men sensible of their misery and unworthiness before he appears in his mercy and love to them."[19] He derived this truth from Hosea 5:15 and the history of God's dealings with the patriarchs and Israel (e.g. Deut. 8:2–3, 15–17; Judg. 10:10–16).[20] That is particularly true of the way God leads sinners into His greatest mercy, viz., salvation from sin. In his "Miscellanies," Edwards asked if it is reasonable to think that God would save a man out of his life-long course of sin without any thought or concern on the person's part to introduce his conversion.[21] He argued, rather, that God's "ordinary method" is to make men concerned for salvation, then they seek it earnestly, after which God gives it to them.[22]

The work of the Spirit is to convict the world of sin (John 16:8),[23] Edwards said. In a seven-part sermon series preached in the spring of 1729, Edwards elaborated upon "The Threefold Work of the Holy Ghost."[24]

---

15. Lloyd-Jones, *The Puritans*, 350.

16. Laurence, "Jonathan Edwards, Solomon Stoddard, and the Preparationist Model of Conversion," 278.

17. Robert W. Caldwell, III, "Pastoral Care for the Converting: Jonathan Edwards' Pastoral Cure of Soul in Light of the Puritan Doctrine of Preparation" (MA Thesis, Trinity Evangelical Divinity School, 1997), iv and *passim*.

18. Mark Valeri, editorial introduction to "God Makes Men Sensible of Their Misery Before He Reveals His Mercy and Love," sermon on Hos. 5:15, in *The Works of Jonathan Edwards, Volume 17, Sermons and Discourses 1730–1733* (New Haven: Yale University Press, 1999), 139. We refer to this as a sermon series (though it is commonly called a single sermon) because its delivery required more than one occasion.

19. Edwards, "God Makes Men Sensible of Their Misery," 17:143. On Edwards's epistemology of "speculative" knowledge and "sensible" knowledge (i.e. the "sense of the heart"), see "Miscellanies," no. 782, in *The Works of Jonathan Edwards, Volume 18, The "Miscellanies" 501–832*, ed. Ava Chamberlain (New Haven: Yale University Press, 2000), 452–66.

20. Edwards, "God Makes Men Sensible of Their Misery," 17:142–46.

21. "Miscellanies," no. r, in *The Works of Jonathan Edwards, Volume 13, The "Miscellanies," a–500*, ed. Thomas A. Schafer (New Haven: Yale University Press, 1994), 173.

22. "Miscellanies," no. 116b, 13:282–83.

23. Edwards, "God Makes Men Sensible of Their Misery," 17:158.

24. Minkema, editorial introduction to "The Threefold Work of the Holy Ghost," 14:371.

He said that in the saving economy of the Trinity, the Holy Spirit is the messenger of Christ who applies the redemption of Christ.[25] He does so in the three-fold work of convincing men of sin, righteousness, and judgment. Righteousness here refers to the righteous obedience of Christ by which He reconciles men to God as our exalted Priest, or, in the words of Christ, "because I go to my Father" (John 16:10).[26] Judgment here refers to Christ's powerful conquest of Satan and the establishment of His rule over men. As John 16:11 says, "The prince of this world is judged."[27] Therefore the Spirit's conviction of righteousness and judgment in the sinner leads to faith in Christ as mediatorial Priest and King.

Regarding conviction of sin, Edwards wrote, "That work of the Holy Ghost is only preparatory to the two acts that follow: convincing men of righteousness and of judgment. These two latter comprehend those convictions and saving light that are given in conversion, when the soul is first [brought] out of a state of sin, is brought to Jesus Christ the Savior."[28] Edwards's interpretation of John 16:8–11 followed the same basic pattern proposed by Thomas Goodwin.[29]

This Spirit-wrought preparatory conviction of sin first includes a sense of one's guilt, danger, and helplessness in sin. Edwards wrote, "God makes men to consider and to be sensible what sin they are guilty of."[30] God then reveals to sinners their acts of sin and their sinful nature. Edwards wrote, "Sin, as it were, lies hid while sinners are unconvinced. They take no notice of it, but God makes the law effectual to bring man's own sins of heart and life to be reflected on and observed (Rom. 7:9)."[31]

Second, Edwards said, "God convinces sinners of the dreadful danger they are in by reason of their sin," that is, "the relation that their sin has to misery."[32] The Lord gives sinners a sense of how dreadful God's anger is against sin (Isa. 33:14). He also enables them to see the connection between their sins and God's wrath so that they fear judgment. And

25. Edwards, "The Threefold Work of the Holy Ghost," 14:377–78.
26. Edwards, "The Threefold Work of the Holy Ghost," 14:392–94.
27. Edwards, "The Threefold Work of the Holy Ghost," 14:418.
28. Edwards, "The Threefold Work of the Holy Ghost," 14:391.
29. Goodwin, *The Work of the Holy Ghost in Our Salvation*, 6:359–62.
30. Edwards, "God Makes Men Sensible of Their Misery," 17:147.
31. Edwards, "God Makes Men Sensible of Their Misery," 17:149.
32. Edwards, "God Makes Men Sensible of Their Misery," 17:149.

He makes them see that their sins deserve this divine judgment by giving them a sense of their guilt (Rom. 3:20).[33]

Third, God makes sinners realize their inability to save themselves. People generally respond to conviction of sin by trying to be
better people so that God will give them the grace to become believers.
But God teaches them to despair of such efforts by realizing they are
prisoners locked up in a place from which they cannot escape (Luke
4:18; Gal. 3:23). He may do this by opening their eyes to sin. Or He may
soften their hearts despite all their efforts to convert themselves. Or He
may work with their understanding to perceive the deadness of their
hearts.[34] This sense of helplessness and self-despair is much like the
experience the Puritans called "humiliation."[35] Later in this chapter we
will see how Edwards differed from Hooker and Shepard on the aspect
of humiliation.

The Dynamics of a Soul's Awakening

How can natural man know that he deserves God's wrath when he
remains blind to the beauty of God and the true evil of sin? Edwards
answered this question by speaking of a natural principle in fallen men,
which a supernatural agent aids by ordinary means. That principle is
the conscience created by God, which continues, even after the fall, to
teach people the difference between right and wrong, and to accuse and
condemn them for wrong. However, the conscience largely becomes stu-
pefied in most sinners.[36] Edwards wrote, "So dull and stupid are the souls
of men naturally, so under the power of that blinding, stupefying thing
sin, that even natural conscience is lulled asleep and the natural reason is
kept from a free exercise by it, so that they will not be sensible."[37] As we
have already seen, conscience, or "the light of nature," plays a large role
in the theology of Calvin and the Puritans.

---

33. Edwards, "God Makes Men Sensible of Their Misery," 17:149–52.
34. Edwards, "God Makes Men Sensible of Their Misery," 17:156–58. Edwards followed the same three-part analysis of preparatory conviction into conviction of guilt,
danger, and helplessness in "The Threefold Work of the Holy Ghost," 14:381–83.
35. Edwards, "Miscellanies," no. 317, 13:397.
36. Edwards, "God Makes Men Sensible of Their Misery," 17:152–54.
37. Edwards, "The Threefold Work of the Holy Ghost," 14:381.

The Holy Spirit assists the natural conscience by revealing God's terrifying greatness to the sinner. Natural men cannot see God's loveliness, but they can sense God's awful majesty today, as they will on Judgment Day and in hell.[38] In convicting people of sin; the Holy Spirit awakens the natural conscience to God's might without yet enabling the soul to see God's loveliness. Edwards said, "Before, they did not think with themselves what it is to slight [despise] the commands of so great and mighty a God.... Unawakened men don't regard those threatenings nor their danger. Sinners are in exceeding great danger. Awakened sinners see it, see God's anger flaming, they themselves hanging over the pit, God's sword drawn, his bow bent."[39] Unregenerate men still have a disposition to enmity against God and self-righteousness, but the Spirit suppresses this enmity (without conquering it) when "God convinces men against their nature and inclination."[40]

Edwards considered this work of the Spirit upon unconverted men as fundamentally different from His work in the saints. Certainly the Holy Spirit acts upon unsaved sinners, but they resist this work (Acts 7:51; Heb. 6:4). But when the Holy Spirit dwells in believers (1 Cor. 3:16), He "is in them as a principle [or source] of life and principle of action" (John 4:14; Gal. 5:25). His work becomes part of their very nature, while upon the unconverted the Spirit acts only as "an external agent."[41]

Edwards carefully distinguished between the common, preparatory operations of the Spirit and His saving operations. The convictions of natural men come when the Spirit assists the natural principles of conscience and self-love in them, whereas saving grace infuses and then excites supernatural principles.[42] In the regenerate alone, the Spirit shares His own nature of "divine love."[43]

Edwards wrote, "There is no necessary connection in the nature of things, between anything that a natural man may experience, while in a state of nature, and the saving grace of God's Spirit.... God has revealed

38. Edwards, "God Makes Men Sensible of Their Misery," 17:154–55; "Miscellanies," no. 317, 369, 13:397, 439.

39. Edwards, "The Threefold Work of the Holy Ghost," 14:382–83.

40. Edwards, "Miscellanies," no. 317, 13:397–98.

41. Edwards, "The Threefold Work of the Holy Ghost," 14:384.

42. Edwards, "Miscellanies," no. 626, 18:155. See John Gerstner, *Steps to Salvation: The Evangelistic Message of Jonathan Edwards* (Philadelphia: Westminster Press, 1960), 42, 64.

43. Edwards, "Miscellanies," no. 471, 13:513.

no certain connection between salvation, and any qualifications in men, but only grace and its fruits."[44] Like Cotton and Norton before him, Edwards denied that there were any saving qualifications before faith in Christ that marked the sinner as elect. Rather, he said, God makes "no promises to unconverted men's seeking salvation.... God makes promises of grace only to grace."[45]

The primary means the Holy Spirit uses to awaken the conscience is God's law (Gal. 3:24; Rom. 3:19–20).[46] Edwards wrote, "It shows God's sacred authority and terrible majesty. When, therefore, the law is improved [applied] by God's Spirit and is set home upon the heart to make men sensible of God's fearful anger, it has a tendency to bring men to a sight of the heinousness of their sins and so of their desert of hell."[47] He said, "Other means are used, as providences, etc. But they work by the law in subordination."[48] The law is the electrical cable by which the Holy Spirit charges the consciences of men.

Edwards's Zealous Advocacy of Puritan Preparation

Edwards consciously operated within the Reformed and Puritan tradition. In *Religious Affections* (1746), he supported Perkins, Shepard, and Stoddard on their views of preparatory convictions.[49] He also defended this tradition from Scripture and reason. He offered the following arguments to support the doctrine of preparation.

First, he said, preparation expresses the plain teachings of the Bible about "God's ordinary manner in working salvation for the souls of men."[50] In one parable of Christ, a servant who owes his master ten thousand talents is called to account. He experiences great terror before he is forgiven (Matt. 18:23–27). The prodigal son in another parable comes to a very low condition and admits his unworthiness before he goes home to feast at his father's house (Luke 15:14–24). The Scriptures say

44. *The Works of Jonathan Edwards, Volume 2, Religious Affections,* ed. John E. Smith (New Haven: Yale University Press, 1959), 160. See "Miscellanies," no. 481, 13:523.
45. Edwards, "Miscellanies," no. 522, 18:67.
46. Edwards, "God Makes Men Sensible of Their Misery," 17:152–56.
47. Edwards, "God Makes Men Sensible of Their Misery," 17:170.
48. Edwards, "The Threefold Work of the Holy Ghost," 14:384.
49. Edwards, *Religious Affections,* 2:156–57.
50. Edwards, *Religious Affections,* 2:154.

that Christians are people "who have fled for refuge" to Christ, which implies that they have first experienced fear and a sense of danger (Heb. 6:18). God dealt with Israel through the thunders of the law to prepare His people for Christ (Gal. 3:24). John the Baptist prepared men for Christ by showing them their sins, declaring them to be vipers, and worthy of the wrath to come (Luke 3:1–14). Peter's preaching so pierced the hearts of men in Jerusalem that they cried out, "What shall we do?" (Acts 2:37). Paul trembled and was astonished by Christ's glory before he found comfort (Acts 9:6). The jailer of Philippi trembled and fell down before Paul and Silas, saying, "What must I do to be saved?" (Acts 16:29–30). The very meaning of the word "gospel" or good news implies that "it is news of deliverance and salvation, after great fear and distress."[51] Elsewhere Edwards cited other Scriptures on conviction and humiliation (such as 1 Kings 8:38; Isa. 61:1; Ezek. 20:33–37; Hos. 5:15; Matt. 11:28; 15:22–28; John 16:8; Rom. 3:19–20; 7:9; Gal. 2:19; 3:22–24; 2 Cor. 10:4).[52]

Second, God's preparatory grace assumes that man is a rational creature. Edwards wrote, "Surely it can't be unreasonable to suppose, that before God delivers persons from a state of sin and exposedness to eternal destruction, he should give them some considerable sense of the evil he delivers from; that they may be delivered sensibly, and understand their own salvation, and know something of what God does for them.... God in the work of the salvation of mankind, deals with them suitably to their intelligent rational nature."[53] God could plant "a principle of grace" in men without preparatory convictions; indeed He could do it without the gospel. But then men could not exercise this grace in a proper manner, "which is to desire Christ, to love him, to give himself to him, humbly and thankfully to rejoice in him, and trust in him as a savior from destruction and great misery."[54] In theory God could save such a man, but the person would not know why he was saved, or how, or from what danger. That would hinder the goal of salvation, which is to manifest God's glory. Edwards wrote, "God won't force men into heaven that don't seek to go there.... Though 'tis true God does all but if he ever does

---

51. Edwards, *Religious Affections*, 2:154–55. On Paul's Damascus road experience as a physical picture of spiritual preparation, see "Miscellanies," no. 645, 18:176.

52. Edwards, "Miscellanies," no. 317, 328, 369, 13:399–400, 406–407, 441.

53. Edwards, *Religious Affections*, 2:152. See "Miscellanies," no. 354, 13:428.

54. Edwards, "Miscellanies," no. 325, 13:404.

anything that ends in salvation the first thing he does is to stir men up earnestly to seek their salvation."[55]

Third, God's preparatory grace encourages saints to pray for unbelievers. The doctrine of preparatory grace actually gives us hope, for no matter how wicked and foolish an individual is because of sin, the Holy Spirit has the power to convince him of sin. Edwards said the "prayers of God's people should therefore be encouraged."[56]

Fourth, preparatory preaching spurs on lazy, complacent sinners. In his 1735 sermon "Pressing into the Kingdom of God," Edwards anticipated the objection from sinners that they do not have the power to strongly desire and resolve to seek salvation. Edwards replied, "'Tis true, persons will never be thoroughly engaged in this business, unless it be by God's influence; but God influences persons by means."[57] Sinners thus have the responsibility to consider their need for salvation, the difficulty of conversion, and the shortness of life—for by such considerations God works. Sinners may also strive to keep God's commands and fight their sins, diligently attend the meetings of the church, read the Bible, and pray in private.[58] In another place Edwards, while acknowledging that the unsaved cannot exercise faith or true humility, pressed upon them ten things they could do and should do:

- "abstain from the outward gratification of their lusts,"

- "in many respects, keep out of the way of temptation,"

- "perform duties of morality towards their neighbors,"

- "search the Scriptures,"

- "attend the ordinances" (church meetings and preaching),

- "use their tongues to the purpose of religion,"

- think carefully, for "in a great measure the command of their thoughts" is theirs,

---

55. Sermon #074 on 2 Kings 7:3–4, in *The Works of Jonathan Edwards Online, Volume 43, Sermons, Series II, 1728–1729,* Jonathan Edwards Center at Yale University, http://edwards.yale.edu/archive?path=aHR0cDovL2Vkd2FyZHMueWFsZS5lZHUvY2dpLWJpbi9uZXdkaGlsby9nZXRvbmplY3QucGw/Yy40MToxNi53amVv (accessed July 18, 2011).

56. Edwards, "The Threefold Work of the Holy Ghost," 14:385.

57. "Pressing into the Kingdom of God," in *The Works of Jonathan Edwards, Volume 19, Sermons and Discourses 1734–1738,* ed. M. X. Lesser (New Haven: Yale University Press, 2001), 283.

58. Edwards, "Pressing into the Kingdom of God," 19:283–84.

- "set apart a suitable proportion of their time for these things,"

- "lay out their strength in these things as well as in other" things.[59]

John and Jonathan Gerstner thus say, "It is perfectly clear that this answers the criticism that Edwards capitulates to Arminianism in his preparation doctrine. As much as he gives the sinner to do, all of it could be done by natural ability."[60]

Fifth, preparatory striving undermines self-righteousness. Edwards anticipated another objection that if men make earnest efforts to seek God, they will trust in those efforts. He responded that anyone who is not thoroughly humbled will trust in his own righteousness. That is what fallen man's nature does. Furthermore, this self-righteousness is generally strengthened by being "slack and dull" in one's religion, for most people live peacefully under the delusion of being better than they are. But earnest pressing forward in religious duties makes men restless about themselves—they have more experience of their weakness.[61]

Sixth, preparatory conviction is needed because of the depth of our sin. Edwards developed a medical metaphor from Scripture to illustrate this:

> Bad wounds must be searched to the bottom; and oftentimes when they are very deep they must be lanced, and the core laid open, though it be very painful to endure, before they can have a good cure. The surgeon may skin them over, so that it may look like a cure without this, without much hurting the patient, but it will not do the patient much good. He does but deceive him for the present, but it will be no lasting benefit to him; the sore will break out again. This figures forth to us the case of our spiritual wound. The plague of our hearts, which is great and deep and must be searched, must be lanced by painful conviction. The core must be laid open. We must be made to see that fountain of sin and corruption there is, and what a dreadful state we are in by nature, in order to [find] a thorough and saving cure. Jeremiah 8:11, speaking of the teachers of Israel, their prophets and priests, [says], "They have healed the hurt

59. Sermon #307 on Eccles. 9:10, in *The Works of Jonathan Edwards Online, Volume 48, Sermons, Series II, 1733,* Jonathan Edwards Center at Yale University, http://edwards.yale. edu/archive?path=aHR0cDovL2Vkd2FyZHMueWFsZS5lZHUvY2dpLWJpbi9uZXdwaGls by9nZXRvbylpY3QucGw/Yy40NjozOS53amVc (accessed July 19, 2011).

60. Gerstner and Gerstner, "Edwardsean Preparation," 24.

61. Edwards, "Pressing into the Kingdom of God," 19:284–85.

of the daughter of my people slightly, saying, peace, peace, when there is no peace."[62]

Seventh, God's preparatory grace glorifies God. Edwards extolled the wisdom of God in giving men a sense of their sin and misery prior to a saving revelation of Christ. God's glory consists of His attributes of both infinite mercy and terrifying majesty, both gentle love and awful justice in perfect harmony (Ex. 34:6–7). To reveal God's mercy without holiness would reflect poorly on God and promote irreverence. But knowing God's wrath prior to His love shows sinners that God's grace is free, sovereign, and wonderful. This divine manner of dealing with sinners also prepares men to depend on a mediator. Sinners who are thus convinced will greatly prize the mercy and love of God once He reveals it to them, and as a result will praise God for His love.[63] So in God's wisdom and for God's glory, "the heart is prepared."[64]

Mark Valeri says of Edwards's apologetic for preparation,

> His approach is both theological and christological. Sinners cannot apprehend the glory of God, he contends, without grasping the divine majesty that condemns sin and therefore threatens the sinner. Without such a sense, God's love appears unworthy and the mediatorial work of Christ as unnecessary. But with such a sense, God's willingness to be merciful appears as an act of divine freedom, all the more loving in that it derives not from any virtue in the sinner but solely from sovereign grace. This truly glorifies God and points the sinner to Christ.[65]

Edwards's Cautious Appropriation of Puritan Preparation

Edwards defended the doctrine of preparatory grace, yet he also sought to define it biblically. He accepted the Puritan heritage of his forefathers but examined it with a critical eye and a careful pen. Thus we find in Edwards's view of preparation both affirmation and reformation. Let us

62. Edwards, "Miscellanies," no. 635, 18:161.
63. Edwards, "God Makes Men Sensible of Their Misery," 17:158–63. See "Miscellanies," no. 255, 286, 337, 360, 468, 13:365, 381, 412, 433–34, 509–10.
64. Edwards, "God Makes Men Sensible of Their Misery," 17:162, 163.
65. Mark Valeri, editorial preface to "God Makes Men Sensible of Their Misery," 17:140.

now look at two ways in which Edwards differed from his forefathers, such as Hooker and Shepard.

Humiliation Preparatory and Evangelical
Some Puritans said humiliation included submission to the sovereignty of God. This submission was emphasized and taken to unbiblical extremes by Hooker and Shepard. But Edwards viewed submission to God's sovereignty as one of the first dawnings of saving faith. He wrote,

> The soul, while in a natural condition, is brought to such a conviction of danger, that he sees he can't deliver himself by any strength or contrivance, and that except God helps him he shall not be helped, and that God will do with him as he pleases: *thus far a natural [man] may go.* And then they are brought to an acknowledgment of the sovereignty of God, and that he may do with them what he pleases, and quietly to own that it would be just with God so to do; and then there is a discovery of the mercy of God in Christ, whereby he becomes justified in his conscience, and acquires a sense of his own justification.[66]

Edwards included submissiveness to divine sovereignty in the poverty of spirit that Isaiah and Christ pronounced blessed (Isa. 66:2; Matt. 5:3). He reasoned that calmness under divine sovereignty expresses hope and implies a secret "discovery of a sufficiency of mercy" for one's salvation. The unconverted continue to resist and resent God's sovereignty because they do not yet see the excellence and loveliness of God.[67] True submission to the sovereign Savior requires faith in Him. David Laurence writes, "Edwards made of humiliation the exercise of faith in which Christ's presence was not explicitly manifested in consciousness but only implied."[68] In this manner Edwards relocated Hooker and Shepard's nadir of preparatory humiliation to the category of evangelical humility by faith. It is interesting to note that Edwards experienced deep struggles with the doctrine of God's sovereignty, and his conversion experience consisted of a new sense of sweet delight in the sovereignty of God, crystallized in Paul's doxology in 1 Timothy 1:17, "Now unto the King eternal, immortal, invisible, the only wise God, be honour and glory for ever and

---

66. Edwards, "Miscellanies," no. 393, 13:458, emphasis added.
67. Edwards, "Miscellanies," no. 393, 470, 13:455–58, 511.
68. Laurence, "Jonathan Edwards, Solomon Stoddard, and the Preparationist Model of Conversion," 272.

ever. Amen."[69] For Edwards, humble submission to the holy Sovereign
was part of the essence of saving conversion.

Similarly, some Puritans believed that a sinner must forsake this
world and their own righteousness as preparation for trusting in Christ.
In Hooker and Shepard this idea took the form of a preparatory cutting off from the old Adam prior to implantation into Christ.[70] Edwards
agreed that to have union with Christ, the second Adam, we must first
"be taken out of the old Adam, which is done by these two things, viz.
weaning from the world, and weaning from our own righteousness."[71]
But Edwards also said that this weaning and cutting off is not complete
until conversion brings faith and repentance. He wrote, "In conversion
a man is cut off from his own stock to be engrafted into Christ."[72] He
also explained,

> There is a twofold weanedness from the world. One is a having the
> heart beat off or forced off from the world by affliction, and espe-
> cially by spiritual distresses and disquietudes of conscience that the
> world can't quiet; this may be in men, while natural men. The other
> is a having the heart drawn off by being shown something better,
> whereby the heart is really turned from it. So in like manner, there
> is a twofold bringing a man off from his own righteousness: one is
> a being beat or forced off by convictions of conscience, the other is a
> being drawn off by the sight of something better, whereby the heart
> is turned from that way of salvation by our own righteousness.[73]

The heart's separation from sin requires more than conviction and
humiliation; it requires "the sight of something better," namely Christ in
His righteousness and glory. The vision of Christ's loveliness and taste
of His sweetness is what the Spirit gives as the gracious foundation of
saving faith. Thus Edwards did not deny a partial preparatory cutting
off but insisted that effective cutting off accompanies faith. He sided with

69. Edwards, "Personal Writings," 16:792.

70. Shepard, *The Sound Beleever,* 97–116; Hooker, *The Application of Redemption... The Ninth and Tenth Books,* 673–79.

71. "Miscellanies," no. 862, in *The Works of Jonathan Edwards, Volume 20, The "Miscellanies" 833–1152,* ed. Amy Plantinga Pauw (New Haven: Yale University Press, 2002), 90.

72. Edwards, "Miscellanies," no. 862, 20:87.

73. Edwards, "Miscellanies," no. 862, 20:90–91. See also "Miscellanies," no. 1019, 20:350–51.

Norton in this matter,[74] adding his own insights into the attractive power of a spiritual sense of Christ.

Assurance and the Method of Preparation

Puritan theologians divided the process of drawing sinners to Christ into preparation and conversion. They also subdivided each of those parts, resulting in a series of steps one must take to be converted. For example, Perkins identified four steps of preparation and six steps of faith.[75] And Robert Caldwell observes that "Hooker's fine-tuning of preparationist theology by means of Ramist logic" strongly impressed his audience that "his detailed, eight-step unfolding of the preparation process" came to be regarded as the only biblical pattern for conversion.[76]

Edwards struggled with such schemes of salvation. On December 18, 1722, the young Edwards had written in his diary, "The reason why I, in the least, question my interest [share] in God's love and favor, is, 1. Because I cannot speak so fully to my experience of that preparatory work, of which divines speak; 2. I do not remember that I experienced regeneration, exactly in those steps, in which divines say it is generally wrought."[77] This led Edwards to carefully examine this doctrine in the light of Scripture and experience.

Edwards did not object to breaking down preparation into its component parts. As we saw earlier, he himself wrote of the "threefold work" of the Spirit in saving sinners, explaining the first element, conviction of sin, in terms of the three dimensions of conviction of guilt, danger, and helplessness.[78] His objection was rather to the implicit expectation that all people will have distinct experiences of each one of these steps in a set order.[79]

---

74. Norton, *The Orthodox Evangelist*, 180–83.

75. Perkins, *Cases of Conscience*, 15.

76. Caldwell, "Pastoral Care for the Converting," 42–43. The steps which Caldwell identifies are: first, contrition, consisting of the steps of the sight of sin, sorrow for sin, detestation of sin, and sequestration of sin; second, humiliation, consisting of the steps of self-reliance, self-examination, despair, and contentedness (pp. 31, 39).

77. "Personal Writings," in *The Works of Jonathan Edwards, Volume 16, Letters and Personal Writings,* ed. George S. Claghorn (New Haven: Yale University Press, 1998), 759. Edwards also questioned his salvation because he did not feel his inward graces strongly, and he saw sins in his life, especially speaking evil.

78. Edwards, "The Threefold Work of the Holy Ghost," 14:381–83; "God Makes Men Sensible of Their Misery," 17:147–58.

79. Edwards, *Religious Affections*, 2:415–18.

Furthermore, a prescribed method of preparation, followed by a sense of comfort, is no guarantee of true conversion. The devil is able to counterfeit the operations of the Spirit preparatory to saving grace. Satan can also put them in whatever order he desires. Edwards therefore appealed to the experience of seasoned ministers to prove that "persons seeming to have convictions and comforts following one another in such a method and order" often are not truly converted.[80]

On the other hand, failing to experience a prescribed method of preparation does not prove that a person is unconverted. Edwards argued that it is one thing to prove from Scripture that certain principles must be true about a person before he can heartily receive Christ, but another, to prove that each one of these things must be "plain and manifest" in every conversion experience. Edwards said Shepard wrote that conversion sometimes comes in "a confused chaos...exceeding mysterious and unsearchable." If we do not understand the formation of a child in the womb, how much less can we understand the new birth by the Spirit (Eccl. 11:5)?[81] Pemble had made a similar observation, and Hooker had used the same comparison of conversion to the mystery of the womb.[82] John Owen wrote, "The substance of these things is ordinarily found in those who are converted unto God when grown up unto the use of reason.... But yet no certain rule or measure of them can be prescribed as necessary."[83]

Thus Edwards remained grounded in the tradition while finding fault with the tendency of some within that tradition to over-schematize God's work. He said, "'Tis to be feared that some have gone too far towards directing the Spirit of the Lord, and marking out his footsteps for him, and limiting him to certain steps and methods."[84] This emphasis naturally would degenerate into legalism and mysticism, since it would draw attention away from justification by faith in Christ alone, and focus upon inward experiences as steps toward God.

---

80. Edwards, *Religious Affections*, 2:158–60.

81. Edwards, *Religious Affections*, 2:160–61. See also "Miscellanies," no. 899, 20:156, where Edwards alluded to "Charnock, 2nd volume of his *Works*, p. 217 or the next following."

82. Pemble, *Vindiciae Gratiae*, 26; Hooker, "To the Reader," in Rogers, *The Doctrine of Faith*.

83. Owen, *Pneumatologia*, 3:360.

84. Edwards, *Religious Affections*, 2:161–62.

Caldwell argues that Edwards balanced the rational description of preparation and the mysterious hiddenness of God's ways, both of which are revealed in Scripture. It is true that Edwards's concept of awakening is very similar to that of Hooker and his other New England Puritan predecessors. Yet Edwards gave more weight than they did to the doctrine of divine mystery, thereby protecting him from trying to direct and limit the Spirit of the Lord.[85]

Setting up a normative order of experiences also fails to recognize the mystery of the timing of regeneration, which may take place earlier in the process than we realize. Edwards said that "grace is sometimes given with the first awakenings of conscience, before comfort in a sense of the pardon of sin, and that the work of humiliation to fit for this comfort is afterwards, after grace is truly infused."[86]

Edwards, who was a careful student of human nature, also said, "A scheme of what is necessary, and according to a rule already received and established by common opinion, has a vast (though to many a very insensible) influence in forming persons' notions of the steps and method of their own experiences."[87] Expectations interpret experiences, he said. Therefore there is the danger that the church will become defined by outward conformity to a learned formula of experiences instead of the inward reality of broken-hearted trust in Christ. We remember here that the narratives of people who applied for membership in Shepard's church did not fit a prescribed pattern, so this tendency was at least partly corrected in Puritan pastoral practice.

Edwards believed that assurance of salvation could not be based on a set pattern of preparatory experiences. George Claghorn says, "Having been the pastor of Northampton for more than a decade and seen two awakenings, he [Edwards] had learned much. The order or structure of experience, he had come to realize, was not as important as the 'indwelling principle' and the 'nature,' or guiding disposition, of the soul. Descriptions of conversion relations…were not as reliable as the fruits of faith."[88]

In addition, Caldwell writes, "Though he [Edwards] did retain the importance of preparationism in his theology and ministry, of greater

---

85. Caldwell, "Pastoral Care for the Converting," 80–82.
86. "Miscellanies," no. 1165, in *The Works of Jonathan Edwards, Volume 23, The "Miscellanies" 1153–1360*, ed. Douglas A. Sweeney (New Haven: Yale University Press, 2004), 86.
87. Edwards, *Religious Affections*, 2:162.
88. Claghorn, editorial introduction to "Personal Writings," 16:748.

importance was the discernment of true grace and evangelical fruit in the life of the person."[89] The great thrust of Edwards's evidence of true conversion was holy practice inspired by faith working through love.[90]

The Practical Application of Preparation

On the basis of his doctrine of preparation, Edwards pressed upon unconverted sinners the duty of preparation. To those who had not yet experienced the convictions of an awakened conscience, he said, "If it be that you do not suffer eternal damnation, you have a great work to do before you die. It ordinarily is a very difficult work, especially to those that have gone on for a considerable time in ways of wickedness under means of grace. If ever you are truly comforted, you must be convinced of your misery and unworthiness."[91] To seek those convictions, sinners must avoid provoking God by great sins, cut off sensual lusts, beware of preoccupation with the world's cares, and set their minds to think often on sin, the shortness of life, and the horror of hell.[92] As Edwards wrote in a different context, "Time is a thing that is exceedingly precious"; "eternity depends on it," but "time is very short."[93] He admonished "unawakened sinners" to consider that God angrily condemns them already (Ps. 7:11), they belong to the devil (John 8:44) and hang over hell "by a slender thread." He said it is "one of the most uncertain things in the world whether ever you will get into a better state," and every day of complacency will harden their hearts more: "You can't be saved without convictions, and you fortify yourself against them."[94]

When convictions do come to a sinner by the Spirit, they must be cherished so they are not lost. The sinner must then persevere in "seeking and striving for salvation."[95] Edwards warned convicted sinners of several ways they might lose convictions, such as giving in to temptations that prevail in lust or anger or quarrelling with God, distractions by worldly

89. Caldwell, "Pastoral Care for the Converting," 92.
90. Edwards, *Religious Affections*, 2:383–461.
91. Edwards, "God Makes Men Sensible of Their Misery," 17:164.
92. Edwards, "God Makes Men Sensible of Their Misery," 17:164.
93. Edwards, "The Preciousness of Time," 19:247–48.
94. Edwards, "The Threefold Work of the Holy Ghost," 14:386–87. There are striking similarities of language between this sermon on conviction and Edwards's famous "Sinners in the Hands of an Angry God."
95. Edwards, "God Makes Men Sensible of Their Misery," 17:165.

entertainments or business, discouragements, and false hopes.[96] He urged sinners "to seek earnestly that their convictions may be thorough: that is, that you be brought to see your helplessness and that you deserve God's eternal wrath."[97] The law of God provides special ammunition for this battle, for a key activity in seeking salvation is to meditate on this law and one's violations of it. Edwards said, "Keep a catalogue of your sins in your mind and be often reading of it and often spreading it before God."[98]

John Gerstner lists twelve ways to maintain conviction from Edwards's sermon on Proverbs 5:11–13, "Act conscientiously in the light; avoid stupefying the conscience; heed conscience and follow it; cherish its intimations; don't accustom yourself to a great deal of doctrinal disputing; assist conscience and promote its convictions; be thorough in strivings, never hide from the truth; do not be discouraged; do not quench conscience; converse with the godly; cry to God for awakening."[99]

Another application of Edwards's doctrine of preparation is to earnestly "strive in a way of religion" (Luke 13:24).[100] By this Edwards meant that a convicted person must put forth concentrated effort in religious duty by striving in prayer, striving against sin, and striving against laziness. One of the paradoxes of preparation is that by striving in religion, a sinner discovers how weak and helpless and enslaved he truly is, and so is prepared for salvation by grace alone.

Edwards saw encouraging signs in the process of despairing of self. He said that though God makes no promises to unconverted seekers of grace, their position is more hopeful and salvation more probable than that of those who completely neglect salvation, for seekers make use of the means which God uses to give grace, whereas the negligent provoke God more.[101] He wrote,

> When God's Spirit is striving, then God is nigh. Isa. 55:6, "Seek the Lord while he may be found, call upon him while he is near." Then it's an acceptable time, a day of salvation. 2 Corinthians 6:2, "Behold, now is the accepted time; behold, now is the day of salvation." God

---

96. Edwards, "God Makes Men Sensible of Their Misery," 17:169–70.
97. Edwards, "God Makes Men Sensible of Their Misery," 17:170.
98. Edwards, "God Makes Men Sensible of Their Misery," 17:171. See also "Conviction and the Uses of Order," 19:267–68.
99. Gerstner, *Steps to Salvation,* 43.
100. Edwards, "God Makes Men Sensible of Their Misery," 17:171.
101. Edwards, "Miscellanies," no. 538, 18:83–84.

now stands at the door and knocks. 'Tis matter of great encourage-
ment for you to strive while God is striving with you. Draw up no
dark conclusions against yourself. Don't give yourself over when
God has not given you over.[102]

In spite of this despair, convicted sinners must be "pressing into the
kingdom of God," Edwards said. He gave this title to his sermon on Luke
16:16.[103] Pressing into the kingdom involves more than just a vague desire
to go to heaven and not hell, and more than a measure of spiritual awakening. This pressing implies strong desires, firm resolutions, great efforts,
a refusal to be side-tracked by doctrinal controversies, and breaking
through opposition.[104] It is more than just "seeking," it is "pressing."[105]

The last application of *God Makes Men Sensible of Their Misery* is self-
examination, Edwards said. This involves asking oneself questions such as:
Did your experiences of God's love and mercy come with convictions of sin?
Have you trusted in God's grace as a poor, helpless sinner? Do you know
that you need sovereign grace through the Mediator Christ? Do your comforts increase your humility and sense of your own unworthiness? Edwards
warned, "The comforts of hypocrites, they very commonly have this defect:
they think that God loves them and delights in them, but they have not a
becoming sense of the awfulness, terribleness, and justice of God."[106]

In *The Threefold Work of the Holy Ghost*, Edwards also urged people to
be wary of false convictions and impressions. People have a natural fear
that does not come from the Spirit's ministry, while the damned in hell
experience terror with no benefit. People must also remember "that at
the same time that the Spirit of God is at work with men, awakening and
convincing of them, commonly Satan also is very busy."[107]

A grave danger for people under conviction is that they will harden
themselves against the work of God's Spirit. As sinners, their natural
reaction to the Spirit's work is to become even more hostile to God and
run farther from Him into sin.[108] Edwards said it is a great sin to resist the

---

102. Edwards, "The Threefold Work of the Holy Ghost," 14:388.
103. Edwards, "Pressing into the Kingdom of God," 19:276.
104. Edwards, "Pressing into the Kingdom of God," 19:276–79.
105. Edwards, "Pressing into the Kingdom of God," 19:282.
106. Edwards, "God Makes Men Sensible of Their Misery," 17:172.
107. Edwards, "The Threefold Work of the Holy Ghost," 14:388.
108. Gerstner, *Steps to Salvation*, 46–48.

Spirit of God when He works by conviction, whether by giving in to evil desires, or by suppressing the voice of conscience that the Spirit assists.[109]

When the Spirit awakens men to fear hell, Satan injects discouragements and hard thoughts in them against God. When the Spirit encourages sinners, Satan tries to tempt them into complacency and laziness. When God's Spirit moves men to diligence, Satan tries to turn that diligence into self-righteousness. Satan also opposes the Spirit's work by temptations that stir up men's inward corruptions. The devil can even use Scripture to tempt people, as he did with Christ (Matt. 4:6), so a Scripture passage that spontaneously comes to mind could actually become a demonic temptation. For example, the devil might accuse a person's soul of committing the unpardonable sin or of having no hope of salvation. He might try to convince a sinner that the day of salvation has passed. He might argue that his experiences do not match those of other believers. To guide such troubled souls, Edwards proposed three tests to determine whether convictions are of the Spirit of God: (1) Are they grounded in the truth of the Word of God? (2) Do they make men more serious about avoiding sin? (3) Do they motivate men to use the means of grace?[110]

For Edwards, preparation was not mere emotionalism but a reasonable response to the spiritual truths described in the Bible. Thus a person's experiences of great terrors followed by peace and joy are not evidence that God's grace has saved him. Likewise, people's imaginings about hell can inspire much terror without a true conviction of sin. Some people have psychological problems that cause their imaginations and emotions to become so entangled, "till their affection is raised to a vast height, and the person is swallowed up, and loses all possession of himself."[111] But real conviction comes from a true understanding of God. As Edwards said, "Convictions of conscience, through the influences of God's Spirit, consist in conviction of sinfulness of heart and practice, and of the dreadfulness of sin, as committed against a God of terrible majesty, infinite holiness and hatred of sin, and strict justice in punishing of it."[112]

---

109. Sermon #355 on Acts 7:51, in *The Works of Jonathan Edwards Online, Volume 50, Sermons, Series II, 1735*, The Jonathan Edwards Center at Yale University, http://edwards. yale.edu/archive?path=aHR0cDovL2Vkd2FyZHMueWFsZS5lZHUvY2dpLWJpbi9uZXdw aGlsby9nZXRvYmplY3QucGw/Yy40ODo2LndqZW8=#nlink3 (accessed July 20, 2011).

110. Edwards, "The Threefold Work of the Holy Ghost," 14:388–91.

111. Edwards, *Religious Affections*, 2:155–57.

112. Edwards, *Religious Affections*, 2:156.

Edwards did not promote hysterics for the sake of revival. On the contrary, he said that preparatory grace inspires emotion based on biblical truth and motivates action directed by biblical commands. Therefore all things, including preparation, must be tested by the Bible.

Conclusion

Jonathan Edwards taught a vibrant doctrine of preparation for conversion. He accepted the Puritan tradition of preparation and defended it against objections. In a manner reminiscent of Flavel, Edwards explained how the Spirit's work upon natural conscience differs from His work in renewing the heart with a ravishing sense of God's loveliness. He carefully distinguished between "preparatory humiliation" and "evangelical humility." He avoided turning conversion into a defined sequence of experiences, and grounded assurance upon the evidence of a life transformed by divine love. In the midst of this theological precision, Edwards preached warm, evangelistic sermons, calling sinners to seek God's converting grace so they could fulfil their saving duty of trusting in Christ alone.

William Henard concludes on the basis of his doctoral research, "Edwards did not espouse preparation as a guarantee of conversion, nor did he set aside specific steps as legalistic requirements that would prevent one's conversion if that person missed a single step. Edwards believed in preparatory steps and seeking for two specific reasons."[113] The first is, in Edwards's words, "True conversion is not suddenly wrought commonly."[114]

---

113. William D. Henard III, "Waiting on God: The Doctrine of Seeking in Jonathan Edwards's Conversion Theology" (unpublished manuscript), 238. See William D. Henard, "An Analysis of the Doctrine of Seeking in Jonathan Edwards's Conversion Theology as Revealed through Representative Northampton Sermons and Treatises" (PhD Dissertation, Southern Baptist Theological Seminary, 2006).

114. Sermon #577 on Matt. 13:5–6, in *The Works of Jonathan Edwards Online, Volume 56, Sermons, Series II, July–December 1740,* The Jonathan Edwards Center at Yale University, http://edwards.yale.edu/archive?path=aHR0cDovL2Vkd2FyZHMueWFsZS5lZHUvY2dp LWJpbi9uZXdwaGlsby9nZXRvYmplY3QucGw/Yy41NDoxMy53amVuLjY4MTYyNy42O- DE2MzEuNjgxNjQ2 (accessed August 5, 2011). Edwards believed that the work of bringing a person from "a state of total corruption" to "a state of grace" to be instantaneous, but "reformation and conviction that is preparatory to conversion may be gradual" ("Treatise on Grace," in *The Works of Jonathan Edwards, Volume 21, Writings on the Trinity, Grace, and Faith,* ed. Sang Hyun Lee [New Haven, Yale University Press, 2002], 161).

The second is that though seeking is not necessary to merit salvation, it is necessary for receiving salvation.[115]

Edwards preached preparation through conviction and humiliation throughout his life.[116] In 1752 Edwards was asked to preach before the Presbyterian Synod of New York meeting in Newark, New Jersey. He selected a sermon he had written in 1746, *True Grace, Distinguished from the Experience of the Devils*. In it he maintained that conviction of sin is not necessarily saving grace, for it is fundamentally the same experience as that of the wicked on Judgment Day.

We end this chapter with Edwards's description of preparatory conviction as an intrusion of the Day of the Lord into the consciences of men. He said,

> When sinners are the subjects of great convictions of conscience, and a remarkable work of the law; 'tis only a transacting the business of the day of judgment, in the conscience beforehand: God sits enthroned in the conscience, as at the last day, he will sit enthroned in the clouds of heaven; the sinner is arraigned, as it were, at God's bar; and God appears in his awful greatness, as a just and holy, sin-hating and sin-revenging God, as he will then.[117]

Thus the Judge appears in the conscience. The book of God's holy law is opened and the conscience bears witness of one's sins. The law pronounces its sentence, God reveals His justice, and the excuses of the sinner are silenced (Rom. 3:19). While this proleptic experience of divine judgment is in itself "no certain sign" of "true faith," Edwards also said that we will never accept a Savior from punishment "which we think we don't deserve."[118]

---

115. Henard, "Waiting on God," 238.
116. See Edwards, *Works*, 25:435, 572.
117. Edwards, *True Grace, Distinguished from the Experience of the Devils*, 25:621.
118. Edwards, *True Grace, Distinguished from the Experience of the Devils*, 25:621–22.

CHAPTER THIRTEEN

Continental Reformed Perspectives: Ulrich Zwingli to Herman Witsius

A knowledge of our misery is necessary for our comfort.
—Zacharius Ursinus[1]

The doctrine of preparation is not peculiar to English Puritanism. Herman Bavinck (1854–1921), a renowned Reformed theologian of the Netherlands, wrote, "Reformed theologians have definitively rejected such a preparatory grace in an Arminian sense.... Still one can speak of 'preparatory grace.'"[2] Bavinck explained:

> For the confession of preparatory grace does not imply that, by doing what they can on their own—regularly going to church, listening attentively to the Word of God, acknowledging their sins, and yearning for salvation, and so on—people can earn or make themselves receptive to the grace of regeneration on the basis of a merit of congruity. On the contrary, it implies that God is the creator, sustainer, and ruler of all things and that, even generations before they are born, he orders the life of those on whom he will in due time bestow the gift of faith.[3]

Therefore everything in one's life, from conception and birth in a particular family to conviction of sin and the felt need for salvation, "all of this is grace preparing people for rebirth by the Holy Spirit and for the role that they as believers will later play in the church."[4]

---

1. *The Commentary of Dr. Zacharias Ursinus on the Heidelberg Catechism*, trans. G. W. Williard, 3rd ed. (Cincinnati: T. P. Bucher, 1851), 21.

2. Herman Bavinck, *Reformed Dogmatics*, ed. John Bolt, trans. John Vriend (Grand Rapids: Baker Academic, 2008), 4:39.

3. Bavinck, *Reformed Dogmatics*, 4:39.

4. Bavinck, *Reformed Dogmatics*, 4:40.

While focusing on the British Puritans, we have not given much attention to continental theologians. So let us take some time now briefly to survey their views. Richard Muller writes, "Pettit drives too much of a wedge between English Puritan and continental Reformed theology," noting that we should explore the relation of preparatory grace "to the first use of the law."[5] The first use of the law is well illustrated in Article 7 of the Bohemian Confession (1575), which states,

> For the omnipotent God was pleased to give man his eternal and unchangeable law, not only for the preservation of nobleness and a good honorable outer intercourse among all peoples in this temporal life; but first and especially to show us that we might recognize the enormity of our sin and transgressions, internal and external, and also the righteous wrath of God and eternal condemnation for our sins, whence comes despair for the wicked. So that in the sons of God by the grace of the Holy Spirit comes the true contrition of heart causing a cordial fear of God, also a constant and genuine hatred of all sin as well as inner and outer deficiency. And besides that, there comes a hearty desire to attain salvation secured by the Lord Christ the Redeemer, that is the forgiveness of sins, deliverance from the condemnation of the law and the wrath of God, from eternal death and the power of the devil, reconciliation with God, justification and sanctification, which is the communion of the Holy Spirit and inheritance of eternal life.[6]

This statement reveals a progression from recognizing the greatness of one's sin and God's wrath, to saving conversion in the fear of God and desire for salvation.

Continental Reformed theologians said much about the role of the law in preparing sinners to trust in Christ. In addition to John Calvin, whom we have already reviewed, let us proceed to what other teachers had to say on this matter.

---

5. Richard A. Muller, "Covenant and Conscience in English Reformed Theology," *Westminster Theological Journal* 42, no. 2 (Spring 1980): 310n7.

6. "Of the Law of Divine Commandments," in *The Confession of Holy Christian Faith of All Three Estates (Bohemian Confession of 1575)*, translated from the Lissa Folios of the Unitas Fratrum, article 7, http://www.moravianarchives.org/images/pdfs/Bohemian%20 Confession,%201575.pdf (accessed August 1, 2011).

Zwingli, Bullinger, Beza, van Mastricht

Ulrich Zwingli (1484–1531) was a first-generation leader of the Reformed movement in Switzerland. He served as a pastor in Zurich. Pettit says Zwingli allowed no period of preparation before conversion, only a sudden, violent seizure by divine grace.[7] But Zwingli's confessional statements suggest a more involved process of recognizing one's sins through the law prior to trusting in the grace of Christ.

In his *Short Christian Instruction* (1523) Zwingli wrote, "For anyone to know why he should mend his ways, it is necessary for him to recognize his guilt. Therefore it is essential in the first place to know the source of sin. After we find that, each person will judge himself to be a sinner and trust himself to the mercy of God."[8] After recounting the awakening of a sinner by the law in Romans 7, Zwingli said, "We must despair in ourselves of being able to come to God."[9] The law kills us; not because it is evil, but by showing us God's good will, which reveals that "one is justly damned according to the righteousness of God."[10] The sinner realizes that it is impossible for him to keep the law, and he "despairs of attaining salvation because of his works, and comes to the point where he surrenders himself solely to the grace of God.... He now lives in the sole comfort of the grace of God."[11]

Zwingli was succeeded in Zurich by Henry Bullinger (1504–1575), who wrote, at the request of Frederick III, the Second Helvetic Confession (1566). This confession was received by Reformed churches throughout Switzerland, Hungary, and Eastern Europe.[12] In it Bullinger wrote, "We teach that this Law was not given to men that we should be justified by keeping it; but that by knowledge thereof we might rather acknowledge our infirmity, sin, and condemnation; and so despairing of our own strength, might turn unto Christ by faith" (Rom. 4:15; 3:20; Gal. 3:21–22, 24).[13]

---

7. Pettit, *The Heart Prepared*, 16, 41.

8. James T. Dennison, Jr., ed., *Reformed Confessions of the 16th and 17th Centuries in English Translation, Volume 1, 1523–1552* (Grand Rapids: Reformation Heritage Books, 2008), 12.

9. Dennison, *Reformed Confessions*, 1:17.

10. Dennison, *Reformed Confessions*, 1:25.

11. Dennison, *Reformed Confessions*, 1:26.

12. James T. Dennison, Jr., ed., *Reformed Confessions of the 16th and 17th Centuries in English Translation, Volume 2, 1553–1566* (Grand Rapids: Reformation Heritage Books, 2010), 807.

13. Dennison, *Reformed Confessions*, 2:832.

Theodore Beza (1519–1605) succeeded Calvin in Geneva. He wrote a chapter in his confession (1560) on the topic, "To What End the Holy Ghost is Served by the Preaching of the Law." Beza said, "As the color of black is never better set forth than when white is set beside it, so the Spirit of God begins by the preaching of the Law (Rom. 3:20; 7:13), in which we may see what we owe and what we are not able to pay, and consequently how near we are to our condemnation, if there is no remedy found in any other way."[14]

The Hungarian *Confessio Catholica* (1562) said that the law is the "mirror" in which men see "how much they are made ugly through sin."[15] The law commands things impossible for fallen men to perform "to put to shame the strength and arrogance of men" and "to lead us to Christ as our cure."[16] So the first use of the law was prominent in the doctrine of conversion of the European Reformed confessions.

Peter van Mastricht (1630–1706) was a Dutch theologian highly respected by both Cotton Mather and Jonathan Edwards.[17] He made some distinctions in "preparation for regeneration." He rejected any idea of preparation whereby a spiritually dead sinner prepares himself by the power of his free will to be more disposed to regeneration than others. But he wrote,

> If, however, you choose to admit here some kind of preparation in those, who are to be made subjects of this spiritual life, such, for instance, as in drying wood, which is to be set on fire, such also as God used in the work of creation, when he created on the first day a shapeless mass, which he formed and modified in the following days, and such as he peculiarly used in the creation of man, forming first the body of clay, or the rib, into which he afterwards breathed the breath of life, I say, if in this sense you choose, with many orthodox divines, to admit some preparation, which is the work of God, I have no great objection thereto.[18]

The illustrations of drying wood and Adam's body are reminiscent of the Puritan tradition rooted in Ames.

---

14. Dennison, *Reformed Confessions,* 2:276.

15. Dennison, *Reformed Confessions,* 2:464

16. Dennison, *Reformed Confessions,* 2:473.

17. Peter van Mastricht, *On Regeneration* (New Haven: Thomas and Samuel Green, [1769]), vi; Edwards, "To the Reverend Joseph Bellamy," letter of January 15, 1746/7, 16:217.

18. Mastricht, *Regeneration,* 30.

To explore this topic in more depth, we will focus first on two major European confessional standards, the Heidelberg Catechism and the Canons of Dort, then on three major theologians, Turretin, Brakel, and Witsius.

The Heidelberg Catechism and the Synod of Dort

The Heidelberg Catechism and Zacharius Ursinus

The Heidelberg Catechism (1563) says that to live and die happily, enjoying the comfort of belonging to Christ, one must know three things: "the first, how great my sins and miseries are; the second, how I may be delivered from all my sins and miseries; the third, how I shall express my gratitude to God for such deliverance" (Q. 2). When asked, "Whence knowest thou thy misery?" the Catechism replies, "Out of the law of God" (Q. 3). Specifically, the law teaches the sinner that he is prone by nature to hate God and his neighbor (Q. 5), that he is wicked and perverse (Q. 6), with a nature so corrupt that he was conceived and born in sin (Q. 7), that he is wholly incapable of doing any good and inclined to all wickedness (Q. 8), and daily increases the debt he owes to the justice of God (Q. 13). Furthermore, the law teaches the sinner that God is just to require obedience to His law (Q. 9), that He will not suffer disobedience and rebellion to go unpunished (Q. 10), and that His justice requires the punishment of sin with everlasting punishment of body and soul (Q. 11). Great indeed is the sin and misery of the fallen sons and daughters of Adam.

Remarkably, the Catechism revisits the work of the law, in "The Third Part—Of Thankfulness," devoted to the Christian life (LD 32–52). Lord's Day 33 presents "the true conversion of man," not as an event in one's experience of grace, but as a twofold lifelong process, in which the "old man" is mortified, and the "new man" quickened, in those who are "delivered from misery, merely of grace, through Christ" (Q. 86, 88). Affirming that believers must do good works "performed according to the law of God" (Q. 86, 91), the Catechism proceeds to expound the requirements of each of the Ten Commandments. However, the Catechism warns us that "even the holiest men, while in this life, have only a small beginning" of the perfect obedience required in the law (Q. 114).

The Catechism then asks, "Why then will God have the ten commandments so strictly preached, since no man in this life can keep them? First, that all our lifetime we may learn more and more to know our sinful nature, and thus become the more earnest in seeking the remission of sin and righteousness in Christ" (Q. 115). In other words, just as it served the sinner before conversion, the law continues to serve the believer as a teacher of sin after conversion, or at least, after the process of conversion is underway.

The primary author of the Catechism was Zacharius Ursinus (1534–1583). Ursinus also wrote a commentary on the Catechism in which the doctrine of preparation is even more evident. He wrote, "A knowledge of our misery is necessary for our comfort." He gave several reasons why this is so: "First, because it excites in us the desire of deliverance…. Now if we do not desire deliverance, we do not seek it ; and if we do not seek it we will never obtain it, because God gives it only to those who seek, and knock" (Matt. 7:6; 5:6; 11:28; Isa. 57:15). He wrote, "Secondly, that we may be thankful to God for our deliverance. We should be ungrateful if we did not know the greatness of the evil, from which we have been delivered."[19] Then Ursinus said,

> Thirdly, because without the knowledge of our sinfulness and misery, we cannot hear the gospel with profit ; for unless, by the preaching of the law as touching sin and the wrath of God, a preparation be made for the proclamation of grace, a carnal security follows, and our comfort becomes unstable. Sure consolation cannot stand in connection with carnal security. Hence it is manifest that we must commence with the preaching of the law, after the example of the Prophets and Apostles, that men may thus be cast down from the conceit of their own righteousness, and may obtain a knowledge of themselves, and be led to true repentance. Unless this be done, men will become, through the preaching of grace, more careless and obstinate, and pearls will be cast before swine to be trodden under foot.[20]

Ursinus, alluding to Matthew 7:6 ("Give not that which is holy unto the dogs, neither cast ye your pearls before swine"), believed that the gospel must be preached and heard in its proper context, as God's solution to the problem of sin and death that has engulfed the human race. He said to preach deliverance without reference to misery fosters indifference and spiritual complacency, cheapens the grace and blessings of salvation, and invites wicked men to trample on the gospel.

---

19. Ursinus, *Commentary*, 21.

20. Ursinus, *Commentary*, 21. Ursinus also wrote about preparation in his treatment of conversion on pp. 470–72.

The Canons of Dort and the Dutch Annotations

At the Synod of Dort (1618–1619), delegates of Reformed churches formulated an official response to the five points of Arminianism as set forth in the Dutch Remonstrance. They also adopted the Heidelberg Catechism as one of three doctrinal standards and obligated ministers to expound the Lord's Days of the catechism in sequence, Sabbath by Sabbath, on an annual basis. It therefore is surprising that Pettit says the Canons of Dort reject the distinctions of Puritan preparatory grace,[21] for this would have involved the theologians of Dort in a serious contradiction.

Certainly the Canons of Dort (Head 3/4, Art. 3) teach that "all men are conceived in sin, and by nature are children of wrath, incapable of saving good, prone to evil, dead in sin, and in bondage thereto, and without the regenerating grace of the Holy Spirit, they are neither able nor willing to return to God, to reform the depravity of their nature, or to dispose themselves to reformation."[22] The Canons also deny that God chose to save those whom He foreknew would "use the light of nature aright" to make themselves "fit for eternal life" (Head 1, Rej. 4).[23] But the Reformed doctrine of preparation does not deny man's total depravity, nor does it ascribe to the unregenerate the will to turn from sin to God, nor does it base eternal election upon any condition in man before or after conversion. Instead it teaches that ordinarily God persuades the elect to seek salvation by a sense of guilt and fear of damnation prior to giving them faith. The aim of these teachings of Dort was not to refute preparation but the teachings of semi-Pelagianists.

The Canons of Dort (Head 3/4, Art. 5) also declare that the law "discovers the greatness of sin, and more and more convinces man thereof," but is unable to save men and so "leaves the transgressor under the curse."[24] Only the Spirit can save sinners through the preaching of the gospel (Head 3/4, Art. 6). Here Dort acknowledges a limited role for the law, not in converting sinners, but in helping them to see their misery and need for conversion.

It places a further limitation upon pre-conversion work when it says (Head 3/4, Rej. 4), "Moreover, to hunger and thirst after deliverance from

---

21. Pettit, *The Heart Prepared*, 127.
22. Beeke, ed., *Doctrinal Standards*, 106–107.
23. Beeke, ed., *Doctrinal Standards*, 101–102.
24. Beeke, ed., *Doctrinal Standards*, 107.

misery, and after life, and to offer to God the sacrifice of a broken spirit, is peculiar to the regenerate and those that are called blessed" (Ps. 51:10, 19; Matt. 5:6).[25] That might be understood as a rejection of all preparatory desire for salvation. But we have already observed that Perkins said that the desire to have Christ is the first spark of a living faith.[26] So Dort's rejection of natural man's ability to desire Christ is compatible with Perkins's doctrine of preparation.

It is better to understand the Canons as denying that the unregenerate can love God, be truly humble, or please Him, or as this same rejection said earlier: "offer the sacrifice of a contrite and broken spirit, *which is pleasing to God.*"[27] That would not exclude the longings of the awakened, unregenerate sinner to escape the wrath of God out of mere self-love. Otherwise, how could the law convince men of sin prior to conversion, as the Canons affirm? At the same time, the Canons imply that when a man sincerely begins to seek after God and not merely after salvation from hell, then he is already born again.

The Canons of Dort do not directly address the question of preparation, yet its doctrine appears to be compatible with mainstream Puritan preparation. This understanding of the Canons is confirmed by the *Dutch Annotations* (1637), the notes on the text of the new translation of the Bible that the Synod of Dort had commissioned. These notes state, "the law sets before a man what God commands and forbids, and a man's conscience convinceth him that he hath offended against it, by thoughts, words, and deeds."[28] The law "revealeth God's wrath against the transgression...by its threatenings of punishments."[29] When a sinner realizes that his desires war against God's law, he says, "I was convinced in my mind that I lay in the midst of death, and lost the confidence of being able to be saved by the obedience of the law."[30] The moral law "convinceth us of sin, and denounceth the curse; and therefore showeth us, that to be saved we must fly to Christ for refuge, who hath delivered us from sin, and from the curse."[31]

---

25. Beeke, ed., *Doctrinal Standards,* 110.

26. Perkins, *Cases of Conscience,* 15.

27. Beeke, ed., *Doctrinal Standards,* 110, emphasis added.

28. *The Dutch Annotations upon the Whole Bible,* trans. Theodore Haak (1657; facsimile repr., Leerdam, The Netherlands: Gereformeerde Bijbelstichting, 2002), on Rom. 3:20.

29. *Dutch Annotations,* on Rom. 4:15.

30. *Dutch Annotations,* on Rom. 7:7.

31. *Dutch Annotations,* on Gal. 3:24.

John the Baptist prepared the way of the Lord by casting down mountains and hills, "that is, proud and hypocritical persons shall be humbled, and be brought to the knowledge of their sins."[32] Likewise faithful ministers must preach that "all men, such as they are by nature... [are] as fading and as perishing as grass, and of no value at all; so that they must seek their salvation without [outside] themselves."[33] People in the days of John the Baptist did "with great earnestness and zeal seek after salvation."[34] Awakened sinners do the same today.

Three Continental Theologians: Turretin, Brakel, and Witsius

Francis Turretin and the Institutes of Elenctic Theology

Francis Turretin (1623–1687) taught theology at the academy of Geneva for thirty years. His masterpiece, *Institutio Theologiae Elencticae* (1679–1685), was valued by Jonathan Edwards (among others) and was required reading at Princeton Seminary from 1812 to 1872.[35] Written in Latin, it was only translated into English at the end of the twentieth century. Turretin was a precise theologian who carefully defended Reformed orthodoxy. He asserted that man is passive in his regeneration. The sinner does not actively cooperate with the regenerating grace of God but is merely the object of divine operations, which then produce active faith in Christ.[36] Turretin thus advocated the absolute sovereignty of God in saving sinners.

However, Turretin also explained that sovereign grace does not exclude preparation for faith. His words militate against the assumption that pure Calvinism excludes preparation:

> The question is not whether any dispositions are necessary in man by which he may be prepared for conversion. We confess that in spiritual no less than in natural generation, we reach spiritual birth by many preceding operations and that God (who wills to perform that work in man not by violent seizures, or enthusiastical movements, but in a way suitable to our nature; and who carries it on not in one moment, but successively and by degrees) uses various dispositions

---

32. *Dutch Annotations,* on Isa. 40:4.

33. *Dutch Annotations,* on Isa. 40:6.

34. *Dutch Annotations,* on Matt. 11:12.

35. Francis Turretin, *Institutes of Elenctic Theology,* trans. George Musgrave Giger, ed. James T. Dennison, Jr. (Phillipsburg, N.J.: P & R Publishing, 1994–1997), 3:648, 657n110.

36. Turretin, *Institutes,* 2:542 [Topic 15, Q. 5].

by which man is little by little prepared for the reception of saving grace (at least in ordinary calling). Thus there are various acts antecedent to conversion and, as it were, steps to the thing (*gradus ad rem*) before he is brought to a state of regeneration, either external, which can be done by man (such as to enter a church, to hear the word and the like), or internal, which are excited by grace in the hearts of those not yet converted (such as the reception and apprehension of the presented word, a knowledge of the divine will, a certain sense of sin, the fear of punishment, and a desire for deliverance). Rather the question is whether in the very moment of conversion and as to the steps of the thing (*gradus rei*), man has anything from himself with which he can cooperate with efficacious grace so that the work can be ascribed not only to grace, but also to free will excited by grace.[37]

Turretin explicitly denied that monergistic regeneration requires a sudden, violent seizure of the soul. On the contrary, he said that God sovereignly rules over the process of preparing a man for conversion. Yet in the moment when faith is born, man does nothing to produce it but is raised from spiritual death by the power of the living God.

Wilhelmus à Brakel and The Christian's Reasonable Service

The Dutch author Wilhelmus à Brakel (1635–1711) was a pastor in Friesland and Rotterdam for almost fifty years. Brakel's courage in opposing governmental interference in the church won him acclaim in the Netherlands. His book *De Redelijke Godsdienst* (1700) represents the mature fruit of the Dutch Further Reformation. In this book Brakel combines thoughtful covenant theology with profound experiential and practical application to the Christian life. His blend of systematic theology and personal devotion to God is unsurpassed. His book has been read in the households of pious Dutch families for centuries, and recently was translated for the first time into English as *The Christian's Reasonable Service*.

Brakel viewed regeneration, not merely as the act of spiritual "birth," but as "inclusive of all that pertains to it, such as conception, fetal growth, and the birth itself." However, he warned, "We must not be of the opinion that man possesses life prior to regeneration, as if there were a preparation for regeneration, which we would understand to be conversion. No, man is dead prior to regeneration and receives life by way

---

37. Turretin, *Institutes*, 2:542–43.

of regeneration. There is no third state between death and life, and thus also not between being converted and unconverted."[38] In regeneration God gives the sinner an entirely different nature, translating him from a state of death to a state of life through the Word of God.[39] Later, Brakel explained that "the soul in one moment passes from death unto life," but "conversion in a comprehensive and broad sense" may be a process of some time, stretching "from the first conviction until one consciously receives Christ."[40] Thus Brakel opposed all ascription of spiritual life to the unregenerate. He said regeneration is an instantaneous gift of life, yet allowed for conversion to be experienced as a process.

God may regenerate children at a very young age, even in the womb apart from the ordinary agency of the Word of God (Luke 1:41–42). However, there is no basis in Scripture to believe that the Holy Spirit dwells in the elect from the beginning of their lives, not even as a dormant seed. On the contrary, the elect are in the same state of spiritual death as other persons prior to conversion (Eph. 2:1). They are in a state of separation from Christ, the promise, and God (Eph. 2:12), and are thus objects of God's wrath (Eph. 2:3).[41] Any man, whether elect or not, must be born again through the Holy Spirit.

The experience of conversion varies greatly from person to person, Brakel said. Some are converted suddenly, like the thief on the cross, while others are converted gradually. Some are converted through great terrors and concerns, as on the day of Pentecost, while others, such as Zacchaeus, are converted with such a view of Christ's sweetness that they are swallowed up by joy. Others have a quiet conversion that comes with a new understanding of the truth that transforms them. Brakel reviewed this variety on a single page.[42] He also reminded readers that, given the variety and mystery of conversion, "no one ought to be concerned about the manner of conversion because the manner of his conversion has not been what he himself would prescribe it to be, nor agrees with the manner in which others are converted. If your conversion is a reality, all is well."[43]

---

38. Wilhelmus à Brakel, *The Christian's Reasonable Service,* trans. Bartel Elshout, ed. Joel R. Beeke (Grand Rapids: Reformation Heritage Books, 1999), 2:233.

39. Brakel, *The Christian's Reasonable Service,* 2:236–37.

40. Brakel, *The Christian's Reasonable Service,* 2:238.

41. Brakel, *The Christian's Reasonable Service,* 2:247.

42. Brakel, *The Christian's Reasonable Service,* 2:238.

43. Brakel, *The Christian's Reasonable Service,* 2:239.

He devoted five pages to describe what he considered "the common manner of conversion," the gradual process of convictions and desires leading to saving faith in Christ.[44] Clearly this was how he expected God to work most of the time. He said God's effectual calling "rarely occurs suddenly," because "the Lord generally uses some internal and external preparations."[45]

External circumstances are not necessarily means of conversion, for only the Word of God is the means of regeneration, and circumstances can only bring men to the Word and make them willing to listen.[46] Yet Brakel said God often uses tragedies and dangers to unsettle a person so that he begins to pay attention to the Scriptures. Conviction of sin grasps his life. He begins to see something of the eternal wrath of God and the way of salvation through Christ. He yearns to be saved, reads the Bible, prays, attends the gatherings of the church, and avoids the gross sins of the world. These are but "common convictions of the Holy Spirit" that both the elect and reprobate experience. However, they do not come from man's fallen nature but out of "divine operations within man." They do not bring a sinner part of the way to spiritual life or faith or freedom of the will to choose God. The Lord must still use His almighty power to regenerate the convicted sinner. But God uses these "preparatory circumstances" to "deal with man in a manner consistent with his humanity."[47]

In two places Brakel offered extended descriptions of the conversion process. The Holy Spirit begins working His common motions in the elect, producing convictions that endure or repeat, sometimes with terror of damnation, Brakel said. But this may take place with more or less emotion. Some sinners become aware of the free offer of the gospel that Christ offers specifically to them because He is offered to everyone. Peace with God and a life of glorifying God becomes desirable to them; Christ becomes precious. They give themselves to prayer, weeping, and restraining themselves from sin. But they act from wrong motives, trying by their works to move God to save them. They see, however, that as they continue in sin, they become perplexed and discouraged. Satan then tempts them with thoughts of despair. This cycle of moral effort and

---

44. Brakel, *The Christian's Reasonable Service*, 2:239–44.
45. Brakel, *The Christian's Reasonable Service*, 2:210.
46. Brakel, *The Christian's Reasonable Service*, 2:237.
47. Brakel, *The Christian's Reasonable Service*, 2:210.

discouragement may repeat itself. Through it God works to reveal to sinners their sinfulness and inability, and to focus their minds more upon Jesus Christ and the free offer of the gospel. They then may take refuge in Christ, yet at a distance, as the publican did (Luke 18:13). They may come to a point of waiting upon Christ with longing for salvation until God finally gives them the liberty to receive Christ by faith. They then surrender everything to Christ. They entrust their whole life to Him, even though they may still have fears and lack peace. This faith gradually leads them to assurance and confidence that Christ is theirs and they are Christ's. It also produces holiness.[48]

Brakel presented God's ordinary manner of converting sinners "in a sequential order," but he reminded his readers that these acts are often "intertwined" and not distinguishable in a particular sequence. The order of distinct experiences, he said, arises from pedagogical necessity, not spiritual necessity—a teacher can only talk about one thing at a time.[49] But in reality, "there is a wondrous diversity in the Lord's dealings."[50]

Within this conversion process, regeneration takes place, Brakel said. But while making it clear that "preparation" does not "refer to the initial elements of spiritual life," he wrote, "The soul receives the very first principle of life simultaneously with the first act of faith…. There is no spiritual life apart from union with Christ, who is the life of the soul."[51] Exactly when faith begins, Brakel explained:

> If one were further to ask if he must and can know the moment when he exercised faith for the first time, I would answer that he neither has to know this time nor is able to know this with certainty. If he were to begin with the first serious conviction, in all probability he did not have faith as yet. If he were to begin with the moment when, for the first time, he exercised faith consciously and in a most heartfelt manner, he would reckon too late, for in all probability he already had faith. I thus maintain that one cannot or rarely can know the precise moment when faith begins and when regeneration occurs. It is also not necessary to know this, and it is sufficient if, upon good grounds

48. Brakel, *The Christian's Reasonable Service*, 2:241–43, 286–88.
49. Brakel, *The Christian's Reasonable Service*, 2:288.
50. Brakel, *The Christian's Reasonable Service*, 2:246.
51. Brakel, *The Christian's Reasonable Service*, 2:245.

from God's Word and from a proper knowledge of one's heart and deeds, one may conclude that he believes and is regenerated.[52]

Thus Brakel agreed with the English Puritans about preparation for saving faith, while he maintained that the line between preparation and regenerate life is not easily discernible. It also appears that Brakel profited from the mistakes made by a minority of the Puritans. He does not delve too deeply into mysteries, nor does he fail to press everyone to believe and be saved.

Herman Witsius and The Economy of the Covenants
Herman Witsius (1636–1708), a student of Gisbertus Voetius (1589–1676), was a pastor in the Netherlands for almost two decades, then a professor of theology for more than three decades. Witsius affirmed that "a knowledge of divine truths, a sense of misery, sorrow for sin, hope of pardon, etc., go before anyone can fiducially [i.e., with trust] lay hold on Christ, and apply himself to the practice of true godliness."[53] He taught that a certain kind of knowledge, sorrow, and hopeful desire must precede the conscious exercise of faith and evangelical repentance. However, he wrote, "There are no preparations antecedent to the first beginning of regeneration."[54] Before God gives a sinner new birth, there is only death in the soul. Afterwards there is life; but there is "no intermediate state" between death and life.[55]

Witsius defined regeneration as "that supernatural act of God, whereby a new and divine life is infused into the elect person [who is] spiritually dead, and that from the incorruptible seed of the word of God, made fruitful by the infinite power of the Spirit."[56] He asserted this doctrine against the semi-Pelagians (Roman Catholics) and Remonstrants (Arminians), who taught that a sinner can have an initial love and desire for God before God gives him grace.[57]

If Witsius denied any preparation or intermediate state before regeneration, how then could he affirm that knowledge, a sense of misery,

---

52. Brakel, *The Christian's Reasonable Service*, 2:245.
53. Herman Witsius, *The Economy of the Covenants between God and Man*, trans. William Crookshank (1822; repr., Grand Rapids: Reformation Heritage Books, 2010), 1:364.
54. Witsius, *The Economy of the Covenants*, 1:360.
55. Witsius, *The Economy of the Covenants*, 1:357–59.
56. Witsius, *The Economy of the Covenants*, 1:357.
57. Witsius, *The Economy of the Covenants*, 1:361–62.

sorrow over sin, and hope for pardon could "go before" the exercise of saving faith? He counted such things "not preparations for regeneration, but the fruits and effects of the first regeneration."[58] Witsius recognized that he differed here from Perkins and Ames, but he said it was "more in words...than in sense and reality."[59] For the English Puritans, preparations were not produced by natural man nor were they ways by which men prompted God to save them, but were the work of the Holy Spirit preparing sinners for the way of the Lord.[60] In Witsius's perspective, the faith of God's elect included eight steps: knowledge of the truth, assent to the truth, love for the truth, hungering and thirsting for Christ, receiving Christ for justification and sanctification, resting upon Christ, surrendering to Christ as Lord, and finding assurance that Christ is yours.[61] So even before a sinner receives Christ, which Witsius called "the formal and principal act of faith," a person who believes the Word and hungers for Christ has faith.

That raises the question about what difference there is between saving faith and the faith of those who fall away because they have no root (Matt. 13:21). Witsius considered the difference from a number of angles. With respect to assent to the truth, only saving faith has "the true light of the Spirit" so that the soul can see the perfections of God shining in the truths of Christ.[62] Like Flavel and Goodwin (and later Edwards), Witsius linked saving faith to a new spiritual sense of Christ's loveliness and glory. Rather than saying that the regenerate and unregenerate share a common assent to the truth, he argued that even their acknowledgment of God's Word as truth came from a different source. With a vision of divine glory came "a sense of their own misery," "a trembling humility," and "a kind of sacred dread" which prevented the regenerate from flattering themselves of their salvation until they saw evidences of grace in themselves.[63]

God's law serves the covenant of grace by promoting this sense of misery. Witsius said, "Inasmuch as by the cooperation of the Spirit of grace it divests a man of all confidence in his own virtue and righteousness, and by the knowledge of his misery, constrains him to be humble;

---

58. Witsius, *The Economy of the Covenants,* 1:363.
59. Witsius, *The Economy of the Covenants,* 1:364.
60. Witsius, *The Economy of the Covenants,* 1:362–63.
61. Witsius, *The Economy of the Covenants,* 1:375–84.
62. Witsius, *The Economy of the Covenants,* 1:386.
63. Witsius, *The Economy of the Covenants,* 1:387.

and so leads him to Christ, exhibited in the gospel (Rom. 10:5; Gal. 3:24)."[64] Ministers should thus preach the law "in a diligent and serious manner: that the soul struck with a deep sense of sin may pant after the grace of Christ."[65] They must also preach the gospel. Witsius rebuked both:

- the preacher "who resolves, by the continual proclamation of the law for some months, to soften souls, and to prepare them for Christ, and the mean time, makes no mention of Christ," and,

- the preacher "who, for a remarkable space of time, soothes the ears with the allurements of the gospel only."[66]

The law and the gospel complement each other in evangelism and in the Christian life, Witsius said. New life does not come from the law but the gospel, which is "the seed of our regeneration." But the life infused by the Spirit generally exerts itself first in awakening the soul to its pollution and abomination before God and its inability to save itself, so that it grieves and "pants after salvation" until it discovers the fullness of Christ, taking Him and being taken by Him, and then is "inflamed with love to him" to serve Him as its Lord. "Thus again, the gospel brings us back to the law as a rule of gratitude."[67]

Witsius did not grant the right of assurance to every convicted sinner. He said that to have an inward sense of peace before God, a sinner must first confess his sins and unworthiness with grief; second, declare with sorrow that he can do nothing to atone for his sins and put his whole hope in Christ's blood; and third, humbly surrender himself to God as a beggar before the throne of grace, seeking grace but acknowledging that his damnation is just.[68] In hindsight, the sinner may recognize God's regenerating work earlier in his conversion process, but he cannot have assurance of forgiveness until he fully surrenders himself to the Savior.

In sum, Witsius taught preparation for receiving Christ but not preparation for regeneration. He embraced the same order of conversion as

---

64. Herman Witsius, *Conciliatory, or Irenical Animadversions on the Controversies Agitated in Britain under the Unhappy Names of Antinomians and Neonomians*, trans. Thomas Bell (Glasgow: W. Lang, 1807), 182.

65. Witsius, *Conciliatory, or Irenical Animadversions*, 186.

66. Witsius, *Conciliatory, or Irenical Animadversions*, 188.

67. Witsius, *Conciliatory, or Irenical Animadversions*, 190–91. See also *Economy of the Covenants*, 1:431–32.

68. Witsius, *The Economy of the Covenants*, 1:437–38.

the English Puritans did, but located regeneration earlier in the process. Most Puritans would not object too strongly to this, for they admitted there is such mystery in the new birth that our minds cannot comprehend it. Hooker agreed with John Rogers, who said, "It is hard to say at what instant faith is wrought, whether not till a man apprehends Christ and the promise, or even in his earnest desires, hungering and thirsting; for even these are pronounced blessed."[69]

Arthur Dent (1553–1607) had written in his best-selling book, *The Plain Man's Pathway*, "I am very glad that God hath opened your eyes, and given you the sight and feeling of your misery, which indeed, is the very first step to eternal life.... It is the only rare privilege of God's elect, to have the eyes of their souls opened.... Jesus Christ is yours."[70] Thus there was some precedent in the Puritans for Witsius's position of regeneration.

But in general the English and the Dutch differed about the timing of regeneration. Cor Harinck writes,

> There is a distinction between...the Puritans and the theologians of the Dutch Further Reformation [in how they] defined regeneration. The Dutch theologians define regeneration as the starting point of the life of grace; that is, at the initial moment of spiritual awakening and conviction. They view regeneration from God's perspective. The English theologians posit that regeneration occurs upon the initial act of faith in Christ. They view it from man's perspective, teaching that the Christian is born when a sinner believes for the first time. Therefore they [the English Puritans] view preparation for regeneration as preparation for believing in Jesus Christ.[71]

Conclusion

A survey of continental Reformed theologians of the sixteenth and seventeenth centuries demonstrates significant unity between them and the Puritans across the English Channel in the matter of preparation.

---

69. Rogers, *The Doctrine of Faith*, 175. See Hooker's epistle "To the Reader" at the beginning of Rogers's treatise.

70. Arthur Dent, *The Plain Man's Pathway to Heaven* (Belfast: North of Ireland Book and Tract Depository, 1859), 296. This was approximately the fiftieth edition of this popular book.

71. Cor Harinck, "Preparation as Taught by the Puritans," *Puritan Reformed Journal* 2, no. 2 (July 2010): 161.

Reformed confessions in Switzerland, Bohemia, Hungary, as well as theologians such as Zwingli, Bullinger, and Beza, acknowledged the role of the law in convicting sinners and driving them to seek salvation in Christ. Dutch theologian Peter van Mastricht could not object to the model of preparation set forth by William Ames.

The Heidelberg Catechism and the commentary on it by one of its authors, Ursinus, present misery as the first and foundational thing that we must know to gain the comfort of deliverance and live in gratitude for that deliverance. This sense of misery over our sins is a necessary preparative for a right understanding and estimation of the gospel.

The Canons of Dort rejected semi-Pelagian and Arminian preparation but affirmed the role of the law in convicting sinners. They also taught that no man can please God with broken-hearted desires for salvation unless God has already given him saving grace. This can be understood in a manner consistent with the preparation doctrine of Perkins, but may also favor the view that humiliation is the result of regeneration, not a preparation for it. The *Annotations* on the Scriptures that Dort commissioned clearly state that preachers should use the law to convince and humble sinners so they would seek after salvation.

Francis Turretin, the great champion of late Reformed orthodoxy in Geneva, simultaneously denied any active role to man in receiving the first act of regenerating grace, while affirming means and operations by which spiritually dead sinners are prepared by the grace of God, consisting of such things as conviction of sin, fear, and a desire for salvation. He explicitly denied that conversion by sovereign grace requires a violent seizure of the soul.

Wilhelmus à Brakel asserted that sinners are dead before regeneration, and there is no intermediate state between spiritual death and life. Yet he also recognized that the experience of conversion can take time and will manifest itself in various ways. He gave much attention to the way God most commonly uses to prepare sinners for conversion: cycles of guilt and self-effort leading to increasing self-despair until the sinner rests upon Christ alone. Brakel believed in a pious agnosticism regarding the first moment of regeneration, saying that it falls somewhere between the first conviction of sin and the first conscious act of faith in Christ.

Herman Witsius presented a view similar to Brakel's, but located regeneration even earlier in the conversion process. In his perspective, the first convictions and fears arising from a sense of God's glory are the fruits of regeneration. A conscious resting of faith upon the Savior follows. He knew that his view differed somewhat from that of the English Puritans, but believed it was mostly a matter of semantics.

The threefold structure of misery, deliverance, and gratitude bound together Reformed theologians from Britain to the European continent. Though we have observed some differences among these writers, most of them strikingly agree that, first, before a sinner rests peacefully upon Christ he ordinarily is convicted of sin and guilt; and second, there is a mystery concerning the exact point of regeneration in the process of conversion, broadly understood.

Puritan preparation is a theme that runs through Reformed theology, particularly in its use of the law to assist the gospel by awakening sinners to their terrible state. Far from being a betrayal of Reformed theology, the Puritan doctrine of preparation underscores the central truth of conversion, which is that God saves guilty sinners by Christ alone.

CHAPTER FOURTEEN

The Grace of Preparation
for Faith

They that are whole need not a physician; but they that are sick. I came
not to call the righteous, but sinners to repentance.
                                                              —Luke 5:31–32

When Jesus Christ said He came "not to call the righteous, but sinners to repentance," He was not suggesting that some people do not need His grace because they are already righteous. He addressed these words to the scribes and Pharisees who complained that Jesus ate and drank with "sinners." Luke says that such persons "trusted in themselves that they were righteous, and despised others" (Luke 18:9). Christ said that these Pharisees, for all their outward piety, were white-washed tombs, for "ye also outwardly appear righteous unto men, but within ye are full of hypocrisy and iniquity" (Matt. 23:27, 28). His point was that He saves sinners who know and acknowledge their sinfulness. So long as men think of themselves as self-righteous and self-sufficient, they will never respond to Christ's call for repentance.

Calvin commented, "Hypocrites, being satisfied and intoxicated with a foolish confidence in their own righteousness, do not consider the purpose for which Christ was sent into the world, and do not acknowledge the depth of evils in which the human race is plunged, or the dreadful wrath and curse of God which lies on all, or the accumulated load of vices which weighs them down."[1] Christ came to give life to the dead, to justify the condemned, to wash the filthy, and to rescue the lost from hell. If we find ourselves disgusted with other "sinners," Calvin says, "we ought immediately to descend into ourselves, and to search without

---

1. Calvin, *Commentary on a Harmony of the Evangelists,* 1:401 [Matt. 9:12; par. Luke 5:31].

flattery our own evils. Such an examination will make us willing to allow ourselves to be washed in the same fountain with the most impure, and will hinder us from rejecting the righteousness which he offers indiscriminately to all the ungodly."[2]

The Puritan doctrine of preparation was a response to a situation in which nominal Christianity abounded. Virtually everyone in the seventeenth century had a connection to a church, at least through baptism, but many showed no signs of walking with God. Rather than presuming that multitudes of people who were apathetic toward God were nonetheless His children, the Puritans preached the law of God to awaken them to their lost condition. They called sinners to self-examination. They knew that sprinkling assurance on the wicked like so much holy water would not make them holy but would be only be casting the church's pearls before swine, to be trampled under foot. Christ told hypocrites they needed to learn the true meaning of God's law, as interpreted by the prophets (Matt. 9:13; Hos. 6:6). The Puritans also used the law in preaching the gospel of Christ, who is precious only to those who are humbled enough to see their need for His blood-wrought atonement. Calvin said, "The grace of Christ is of no advantage to us, unless, when, conscious of our sins, and groaning under their load, we approach him with humility"; and yet, "we have no reason to fear that Christ will reject sinners."[3] He came to earth to die for them.

In this closing chapter, we will first review the "Calvin-versus-the-Preparationists" thesis in light of primary sources. Second, we will offer an evaluation of the Puritan doctrine of preparation.

A Review of the "Calvin-versus-the-Preparationists" Thesis

Perry Miller viewed Calvin's doctrine of conversion as "a forcible seizure, a rape of the surprised will."[4] Miller said this view of conversion logically followed from the idea that God predestined men to salvation. There could be no human activity in conversion because everything had to be from God. However, we are told that the Puritans backed away from such absolute sovereignty by softening the process with the doctrine of

---

2. Calvin, *Commentary on a Harmony of the Evangelists*, 1:403 [Matt. 9:12; par. Luke 5:31].
3. Calvin, *Commentary on a Harmony of the Evangelists*, 1:404 [Matt. 9:13].
4. Miller, *The New England Mind: From Colony to Province*, 56.

preparation for conversion, which, Miller alleged, taught that sinners could move towards God by their own power.

Miller wrote, "In many passages describing the extent to which an unregenerate man may go in the work of preparation, some of these writers passed beyond any limits that could be reconciled with Calvinism. In New England, clearly the most extreme was Thomas Hooker, who with great eloquence magnified the possibilities of a man's producing in himself a receptive frame of mind."[5] Miller said, "Even while professing the most abject fealty to the Puritan Jehovah, the Puritan divines in effect dethroned Him."[6]

Miller further argued that not all Puritans agreed with Hooker. Miller said William Pemble attacked Hooker's theology (without naming Hooker) as "a sophisticated form of Arminianism."[7] Giles Firmin attacked Hooker and his colleague, Thomas Shepard, for discouraging seekers after God.[8] Most New England Puritans supported Hooker, with the "ominous exception" of John Cotton, whose love for Calvin's theology led him to deny preparation. In that, Miller said, "Cotton was a better Calvinist."[9] Miller also viewed Jonathan Edwards as a champion who waged war against the harvest of Arminianism planted by the "preparationism" of his New England forefathers.[10] Miller's thesis was very influential among later scholars.

Norman Pettit, while offering a more thorough review of the primary sources than Miller, perpetuates the "Calvin-versus-the-Preparationists" thesis. He writes, "In orthodox Reformed theology of the sixteenth century no allowance had been made for the biblical demand to prepare the heart for righteousness. In strict predestinarian dogma the sinner was taken by storm—his heart wrenched from depravity to grace."[11] He says Puritan preparation was the struggle to find liberty from "the shadow and tyranny of the doctrine of divine coercion."[12] His underlying assumption was that "anything done on man's part diminishes God's sovereignty."[13]

---

5. Miller, *Errand into the Wilderness*, 87n154.
6. Miller, "'Preparation for Salvation' in New England," 286.
7. Miller, "'Preparation for Salvation' in New England," 265.
8. Miller, "'Preparation for Salvation' in New England," 266.
9. Miller, "'Preparation for Salvation' in New England," 266–67.
10. Miller, "'Preparation for Salvation' in New England," 286.
11. Pettit, *The Heart Prepared*, vii.
12. Pettit, *The Heart Prepared*, 217.
13. Pettit, *The Heart Prepared*, 218.

In his interpretation of various Reformed writers, Pettit constantly labors to determine which side of the chasm each writer stands on with respect to conversion: the sudden intervention of absolute sovereignty or the gradual process of human activity. For example, he writes, "Of all the preparationists [Richard] Sibbes was by far the most extreme in terms of the abilities he assigned to natural man."[14] Of William Ames, he writes regarding the natural man, "He seizes upon the Law, the Law does not seize him."[15] On the other side of the chasm Pettit places John Cotton, who he says, "carried his doctrine to such an extreme that he was unable even to accept the divine exhortations to preparation as 'useful.'"[16] Of Cotton, he writes, "Man cannot turn to God, as did Abraham, but must be seized. Man cannot willingly acknowledge God until he is wrenched, turned about, forced to believe in a new relationship which until that moment has played no part in this life."[17] By contrast, Thomas Hooker was "preaching an entirely different doctrine of conversion" than Cotton.[18] Thus the Antinomian Controversy in New England (1636–1638) revolved around the validity of preparation for conversion.[19] Pettit depicts a division among English Reformed thinkers between the "preparationists" and those loyal to Calvin's vision of God as absolutely sovereign.

R. T. Kendall, following the lead of Perry Miller and Basil Hall, popularized the "Calvin-versus-the-Preparationists" thesis, though with his own unique points. He laid the blame for the shift at the feet of Theodore Beza, Calvin's successor at Geneva, who, Kendall says, was "the architect of a system fundamentally different from Calvin's."[20] Beza's predestinarian system spread to England through the works of men such as William Perkins, replacing a gracious system with a more legalistic system that included preparation. Kendall says Calvin's perspective "rules out any preparation for faith on man's part…. There is nothing in Calvin's doctrine that suggests, even in the process of regeneration, that man must be prepared at all—including by the work of the Law prior to

---

14. Pettit, *The Heart Prepared*, 73.
15. Pettit, *The Heart Prepared*, 83.
16. Pettit, *The Heart Prepared*, 139.
17. Pettit, *The Heart Prepared*, 138.
18. Pettit, *The Heart Prepared*, 133.
19. Petitt, *The Heart Prepared*, 149.
20. Kendall, *Calvin and English Calvinism to 1649*, 38.

faith." While the law stirs men to seek salvation, for Calvin this "is but an accidental effect."[21]

In direct contrast to Calvin, all of Hooker's preaching of salvation can be summed up, according to Kendall, in the word *preparationism*.[22] Since man "initiates the process of preparation," Kendall says of Hooker, "all his pleadings about an 'effectual' calling of God are rendered meaningless by his appeal—indeed, his urgent and impassioned counsel—directly to man's will."[23] Therefore Kendall indicts Hooker as a prime example of the Puritan defection from Calvin's doctrine of salvation by sovereign grace alone.

But the "Calvin-versus-the-Preparationists" thesis fails because it imposes on the historical sources an assumption about divine sovereignty that is foreign to those sources. The assumption is that God's sovereignty is incompatible with human responsibility and activity. Against this William Stoever writes, "The Reformed doctrine of divine sovereignty was not regarded in the orthodox period as excluding human activity from regeneration [in its broader sense which includes conversion].... human activity, in the context of the ordained means for dispensing grace, is instrumental in the application of redemption."[24] God works through human means, so a writer's affirmation of human activity does not necessarily imply or involve a denial of divine sovereignty. An incorrect assumption has led scholars to misread and distort the writings of the Puritans. For example, Stoever has shown that the documents of the Antinomian Controversy do not revolve around the legitimacy of preparation, for preparation is "relatively inconspicuous" in the debate.[25] Furthermore, Hooker and other New England divines were not closet Arminians. Stoever says, "The suggestion that the elders were departing from normative Reformed doctrine, judged by the formal divinity of the period, is simply incorrect."[26] Michael Winship writes, "Historians accepted Miller's argument until William K. B. Stoever demonstrated, easily enough, that Cotton was a preparationist like the other ministers, and their debates revolved around other topics."[27]

---

21. Kendall, *Calvin and English Calvinism*, 26.
22. Kendall, *Calvin and English Calvinism*, 128.
23. Kendall, *Calvin and English Calvinism*, 132, 138.
24. Stoever, *A Faire and Easie Way to Heaven*, 195.
25. Stoever, *A Faire and Easie Way to Heaven*, 193–94.
26. Stoever, "Nature, Grace, and John Cotton," 32.
27. Winship, *Making Heretics*, 69.

Our exploration of the primary sources confirms Winship's conclusion. Rather than seeing a sharp divide between true Calvinists and nominally Calvinistic, crypto-Arminian preparationists, we note a fundamental unity among sixteenth- and seventeenth-century Reformed writers regarding both sovereign grace and preparation for faith by the convicting ministry of the law.

Calvin denied that fallen man can make even feeble motions towards God, and therefore rejected the medieval nominalist idea that man can prepare himself for salvation by his free will.[28] Man also has no merit or ability to cause or contribute to his salvation, for salvation must be entirely of God's grace. But there is gracious preparation for this grace. Calvin believed that as "preparation" for faith in His elect, "the Lord frequently communicates to them a secret desire, by which they are led to Him."[29] In this preparatory work God especially uses His law, which serves not only to direct believers in their conduct, but also to awaken the conscience of unbelievers to their guilt and need for a Savior.[30] God takes rough-hewn sinners and "prepareth our hearts to come unto him to receive his doctrine," Calvin says.[31] Thus Calvin rejected Roman Catholic preparation by meritorious acts of the will, but nonetheless taught a Reformed view of preparation for faith.

Elizabethan Puritans such as William Perkins also taught unconditional election, human inability, salvation apart from all human merit, and divine preparation of sinners by the law before faith. Contrary to Pettit's statement, Sibbes did not assign "an extreme amount" of activity to natural men in preparation. Humiliation is our duty but is impossible apart from the Holy Spirit's convicting work.[32] He said, "This bruising is required before conversion, that so the Spirit may make way for itself into the heart, by leveling all proud high thoughts."[33]

In 1633 Ames presented a paper arguing the fine points of preparation and the ways it differed from the teachings of Roman Catholics and Arminians. He compared preparation to drying wood before putting it

---

28. Calvin, *Institutes*, 2.2.27; 2.3.7; *Commentary on the Gospel according to John*, 258–59 [on John 6:45].

29. Calvin, *Commentary on a Harmony of the Evangelists*, 2:433–34 [Luke 19:1–10].

30. Calvin, *Sermons on Timothy and Titus*, 50–51; *Institutes*, 2.7.11.

31. Calvin, *Sermons on Deuteronomy*, 423.

32. Sibbes, *The Bruised Reede and Smoking Flax*, 33–35.

33. Sibbes, *The Bruised Reede and Smoking Flax*, 13.

into the fire, and to God's forming Adam's body prior to breathing life into it, and to the assembling of bodies of flesh and bone in the valley of Ezekiel's vision before they are awakened to life by the Spirit.[34] Ames's careful distinctions and gripping illustrations became the standard fare of later Puritan treatments of preparation by men such as John Norton and John Owen.

Thomas Hooker, often viewed as the arch-preparationist, certainly devoted a massive amount of time to explaining the preparation of sinners by contrition and humiliation. But contrary to Kendall, he placed his doctrine of preparation within the context of God's sovereign and particular grace in Christ, and the joy and love that men possess upon conversion.[35] Preparation itself was a work of the Holy Spirit upon unsaved men. So Hooker wrote, "The Lord by his Spirit prepares the soul."[36] He also preached the free offer of the gospel and urged all men to come to Christ.[37]

Miller presented Pemble as an opponent of preparation, but an examination of his book on salvation by grace alone proves otherwise. Certainly Pemble attacked Arminian and Roman Catholic views of self-improvement or meritorious preparation by acts of free will.[38] But he also taught that there is a good and useful preparation before conversion consisting of conviction of sin and making use of the means of grace.[39] He said, "We deny not, but that there are ordinarily many preparations whereby God brings a man to grace, and that the Word works many effects both upon the hearts and lives of men even whilst they are as yet destitute of true grace."[40]

John Cotton also proves not to be the anti-preparationist he was alleged to be. He did offer some confusing statements about union with Christ, which the antinomians abused to his great shame. However, Cotton also taught that God prepares sinners for conversion by giving them "a spirit of bondage" to convict them of sin and "a spirit of burning" to

---

34. Ames, "The Preparation of a Sinner for Conversion," theses 6, 16.
35. Hooker, *The Application of Redemption... The First Eight Books; The Soules Implantation into the Natural Olive*, 179–320.
36. Hooker, *The Sovles Preparation for Christ*, 219.
37. Hooker, *The Vnbeleevers Preparing for Christ*, 2, 19–20.
38. Pemble, *Vindiciae Gratiae*, 27–29, 56.
39. Pemble, *Vindiciae Gratiae*, 30, 76, 80–82.
40. Pemble, *Vindiciae Gratiae*, 78.

destroy their self-reliance.[41] God's ordinary way is to bring sinners under an experience of the covenant of works before bringing them into the covenant of grace.[42] He wrote,

> As a school-master driveth his scholar [student] through fear unto this or that duty…so the law of God driveth the soul through fear unto Jesus Christ…. For being once made sensible of his own inability to redeem himself, and unworthiness to be redeemed from the wrath of God; now is the soul fitted to hear the voice of the gospel, now is the news of Christ beautiful and glad tidings: and of this use is the law unto the elect of God, before they come under the covenant of the grace of God.[43]

Cotton also called unbelievers to make use of the Word and prayer. He said the blind cannot give themselves sight, but they can cry out to the Son of David until He heals them.[44] Pettit therefore errs in saying that Cotton and Hooker preached different doctrines of conversion. For all their differences, they shared the common core of Reformed theology, including preparation.

Our exploration of the teachings of John Norton, the Westminster Assembly, Jeremiah Burroughs, William Guthrie, Thomas Goodwin, Giles Firmin, John Flavel, John Bunyan, and Jonathan Edwards traces this unity through the length and breadth of the Puritan era and into the early eighteenth century. The Puritans did debate the specifics of preparation, but the idea of a division among them over predestination versus preparation is a fiction of historiography. We have shown that from Calvin to Edwards, the Reformed tradition speaks with remarkable oneness of mind regarding both *sola gratia* and the preparation of the sinner for conversion (*praeparatio peccatoris ad conversionem*).

Having reviewed and disproved the "Calvin-versus-the-Preparationists" thesis, we turn next to evaluate the teachings of the Puritans on this matter. Our intent is that this book will not only dispel illusions, but will also provide an exposition of the actual teaching of the Puritans regarding preparation for grace.

---

41. Cotton, *The New Covenant*, 21–23.
42. Cotton, *The New Covenant*, 21.
43. Cotton, *The New Covenant*, 109–110.
44. Cotton, *The Way of Life*, 184–85.

An Evaluation of Puritan Preparation

The Puritans had many admirable qualities as God-centered, warm-hearted Christians. Their teaching mined the riches of Christ in the Scriptures, laboring to draw out the best insights for the church of their day. It is not surprising, then, that their view of preparation for faith contains many gems of biblical truth that may be wisely applied to the soul. The very doctrine of sin which the Puritans preached reminds us that all Christians have remaining sin which clouds our minds and pollutes our conduct. Therefore while we offer both cautions about Puritan preparation, we also will identify some important lessons we can learn from it.

Cautions against Misunderstandings, Errors, and Imbalances
Our exposition of Puritan preparation reminds us that we must read the Puritans with discernment, as we should read any human writings. It is possible to misunderstand their exhortations to duty as affirmations of some ability to save ourselves, or to contribute to our salvation. We might assume that duty implies ability, which would then lead us into Pelagianism, or incline us to see Pelagianism where it is not to be found. Of course, in the same way, we might misunderstand Calvin, or anyone else who has ever preached the commands of the Bible. John Norton said that "because we are reasonable creatures God proceeds with us in the use of means; because we are dead creatures, in respect to the efficacy of the means, we depend wholly and absolutely upon God."[45]

Furthermore, the Puritans at times did not choose their words as wisely as they should have. For example, Norton wrote, "By preparatory work, we understand certain inherent qualifications.... Before sinners are invited immediately to believe, they must be such sinners, qualified sinners."[46] The terminology of "qualification" or "qualified sinner" suggests that evidence of preparation gives us the right to trust in Christ, or the right to consider ourselves elect. Norton used such language but plainly denied the misconceptions to which it could give rise by teaching that the duty of all men was to believe the gospel,[47] and by rejecting the idea that preparation was anything more than a gracious

---

45. Norton, *The Orthodox Evangelist*, 271.
46. Norton, *The Orthodox Evangelist*, 130; cf. p. 141.
47. Norton, *The Orthodox Evangelist*, 17, 81, 84, 158, 162, 171, 191–92, 194, 199, 202, 231.

operation of the Spirit common to both elect and reprobate.[48] It would have been better to avoid the term *qualify* entirely than to try to dispel such misconceptions.

Certain aspects of the doctrine of preparation as taught by some Puritans were rejected by most other Puritans. The classic example is the teaching of Hooker and Shepard that sinners must be humbled to the point of being content to be damned as a necessary part of preparation for receiving Christ.[49] That is an extreme idea that is contrary to Scripture and human nature as God created it. Firmin rightly took these writers to task for advancing this view.[50] Yet even in this error we recognize a grain of truth. A person cannot trust in Christ alone while clinging to his own merits, and abandoning all self-merit means recognizing that God could damn a sinner to hell in perfect justice. Norton said, "to justify God is our duty, but to be contented to be damned is nowhere commanded; nay if taken without limitation, it is prohibited; because to be contented to be damned, is to be contented to be an enemy, and to sin against God, and that forever."[51]

More subtle is the erroneous idea that Hooker, Shepard, and Firmin taught about a necessary separation of the heart from sin prior to union with Christ, a cutting off from the tree of Adam before being grafted into the tree of Christ.[52] Puritans such as Norton and Edwards rejected this idea as unscriptural,[53] since this teaching can result in the theological problem of an intermediate state between spiritual death and spiritual life, which Ames and others expressly rejected.[54]

Perhaps the greatest danger posed by some Puritan views of preparation is the lack of balance in presentation even in the context of a sound system of doctrine. By hammering away at sinners with the law over long periods of time, while withholding or ignoring the promises of the gospel, men such as Hooker sometimes neglected to mingle the sweet with

---

48. Norton, *The Orthodox Evangelist*, 163, 170.
49. Hooker, *The Sovles Humiliation*, 112–17; Shepard, *The Sound Beleever*, 147–54.
50. Firmin, *The Real Christian*, 19–24, 107–149.
51. Norton, *The Orthodox Evangelist*, 151.
52. Hooker, *The Application of Redemption... The First Eight Books*, 150–51; *The Application of Redemption... The Ninth and Tenth Books*, 673–75, 679; Shepard, *The Sound Beleever*, 97–116; Firmin, *The Real Christian*, 87–93.
53. Norton, *The Orthodox Evangelist*, 180–83; Edwards, "Miscellanies," no. 862 and 1019, 20:90–91, 350–51.
54. Ames, "The Preparation of a Sinner for Conversion," thesis 17, objection 5.

the bitter. Their readers could easily lose sight of Christ somewhere in the midst of hundreds of pages on contrition. Sibbes wisely advised, "It is dangerous...to press too much, and too long this bruising; because they may die under the wound and burden, before they be raised up again. Therefore it is good in mixed assemblies to mingle comforts, that every soul may have its due portion."[55]

Andrew Bonar (1810–1892) wrote of such imbalanced preachers, "There is, in their dealings with inquirers, a tendency to throw them in upon their own acts, or feelings, or convictions, instead of drawing them out at once to what has been finished on the cross, leading them to look for some preparatory work in themselves, before rejoicing in the gospel." Bonar also added the observation, in fairness to the men he had in mind, that, "still there are at other times full exhibitions of the Saviour, and free proclamations of his glorious gospel."[56]

We also see a lack of balance in the passion of some Puritans for doctrinal analysis as opposed to bowing before the mystery of the Spirit's work. Though they offered disclaimers along the way, they rigorously developed and painfully applied sequences of steps that could easily mislead their audiences into thinking that they were not yet saved because they were only at, say, step three of the program. Worse yet, they might think that they had no right to come to Christ as they were because they were still waiting to progress to steps four through twelve. Edwards offered a helpful corrective to this, as did the Dutch divine, Wilhelmus à Brakel, reminding us that in the mystery of the Spirit's operations in grace, we often cannot tell exactly when a person is born again.[57]

The well-known lines of John Newton (1725–1807) in "Amazing Grace" are a classic statement of the doctrine of preparation for faith:

'Twas grace that taught my heart to fear,
And grace my fears relieved;

55. Sibbes, *The Bruised Reede and Smoaking Flax*, 37.
56. Andrew Bonar, preface to John Gillies, *Historical Collections of Accounts of Revivals* (1845; repr. Edinburgh: Banner of Truth, 1981), x. It should be noted that Bonar's passing word of critique appears in the context of much praise for the Reformers and Puritans.
57. Edwards, *Religious Affections*, 2:160–62; "Miscellanies," no. 899, 20:156; Brakel, *The Christian's Reasonable Service*, 2:245.

How precious did that grace appear,
The hour I first believed.[58]

Yet Newton also wrote that,

Most New England divines I have met with have in my judgment one common fault: they abound with distinctions and refinements in experimental matters, which are suited to cast down those whom the Lord would have comforted. And in their long account of what they call a preparatory work, they include and thereby depreciate some real and abiding effects of true grace. They require such an absolute submission to the righteousness and sovereignty of God, before they will allow a person to be a believer, as I apprehend is seldom the attainment of a babe in Christ.[59]

We have a more positive view of the New England divines than Newton did, but his criticisms are valid and should be remembered by those reading the Puritans on preparation.

Positive Lessons from Puritan Preparation
Despite all these criticisms and cautions, the Puritan doctrine of preparation still offers a great deal of truth and wisdom. Here are several lessons we can learn from it.

1. Puritan preparation assists the free offer of the gospel.
It is false to portray preparation as the antithesis of an open invitation for all sinners to come to Christ. John Preston wrote, "We preach Christ generally unto all, that whosoever will, may receive Christ; but men will not receive him, till they be humbled, they think they stand in no need of Christ."[60] To be sure, preparation can be presented in a way that inhibits men from coming. The Puritans labored to avoid this error by mingling teaching on preparation with clear announcements of the gospel call.

Hooker himself preached, "Why, it is a free mercy, and therefore why mayest not thou have it as well as another?… If you will but come and take grace, this is all God looks for, all that the Lord expects and desires,

---

58. First published under the title, "Faith's Expectation and Review," *Olney Hymns* (1779).

59. John Newton, *Wise Counsel: John Newton's Letters to John Ryland, Jr.*, ed. Grant Gordon (Edinburgh: Banner of Truth, 2009), 119–20.

60. Preston, "Pavls Conversion," in *Remaines*, 187.

you may have it for the taking."[61] But Hooker also understood that "whosoever will" (Rev. 22:17) implies that sinners must be made willing to come to Christ for salvation.[62] Sinners must sense their need of Christ before they can rationally choose Him.

Regeneration is a simple and instantaneous act of God giving faith to the sinner for justification and eternal life in Christ. So the gospel call is simply, "Repent ye, and believe" (Mark 1:15). But the sinner's experience that precedes regeneration ordinarily involves thought, feeling, and activity. Thus the simple gospel call is accompanied by many subordinate and related duties such as: "hearken to my words" (Acts 2:14), "incline your ear" (Isa. 55:3), "let us reason together" (Isa. 1:19), "we ought not to think that the Godhead is like unto gold, or silver, or stone, graven by art and man's device" (Acts 17:29), "examine yourselves" (2 Cor. 13:5), and "be afflicted, and mourn, and weep" (James 4:9). When the Puritans preached such duties, they did not present an alternative to trusting in Christ without delay, anymore than Paul did when he "reasoned of righteousness, temperance, and judgment to come" with Felix (Acts 24:27). Preparatory duties are the servants of faith.

Shepard said that King Jesus commands all people to come to Him for grace, offering Himself in a great exchange.[63] But sin makes it a "wonderfully hard thing to be saved."[64] So the Westminster divines taught that the first work by which God "doth persuade and enable us to embrace Jesus Christ, freely offered to us in the gospel," is "convincing us of our sin and misery" (WSC, Q. 31). Christ is portrayed in the prophecy of Isaiah 55:1 as a merchant of salvation in the market place, crying, "Ho, every one that thirsteth, come ye to the waters, and he that hath no money; come ye, buy, and eat; yea, come, buy wine and milk without money and without price." As Guthrie said, preparation stirs our first thirst and hunger for salvation.[65]

2. Puritan preparation is thoroughly Reformed, not Roman Catholic or Arminian.
Calvin, Perkins, Pemble, Ames, Cotton, and Norton distinguished between Reformed and Roman Catholic ideas of preparation, rejecting the latter as granting partial merit to fallen men but embracing the former as revealing

---

61. Hooker, *The Vnbeleevers Preparing for Christ*, 19–20.
62. Hooker, *The Vnbeleevers Preparing for Christ*, 2–3.
63. Shepard, *The Sincere Convert*, 106–112.
64. Shepard, *The Sincere Convert*, 144.
65. Guthrie, sermons upon Isaiah 55:1–2, in *A Collection of Lectures and Sermons*, 113–14.

to men their utter lack of merit.[66] They regarded Arminian preparation as a crypto-Romanism, but put the preparation doctrine of their Reformed brothers in another category. Presbyterian theologian William G. T. Shedd (1820–1894) explained the difference:

> The term 'preparative' as used by the Augustinian and Calvinist, is very different from its use by the Semi-Pelagian and Arminian. The former means by it, conviction of sin, guilt, and helplessness.... In the Semi-Pelagian use, a 'preparative' denotes some faint desires and beginnings of holiness in the natural man upon which the Holy Spirit, according to the synergistic theory of regeneration, joins.... In the Calvinistic system, a 'preparative' to regeneration, or a 'means' of it, is anything that demonstrates man's total lack of holy desire and his need of regeneration.... It is common or prevenient grace. Man's work in respect to regeneration is connected with this. Moved and assisted by common or prevenient grace, the natural man is to perform the following duties, in order to be convicted of sin, and know his need of the new birth.[67]

Shedd also included reading and hearing the Scriptures, serious thinking about the truths of the gospel, and prayer for the Holy Spirit.

We might illustrate the difference between the Roman Catholic view of preparation and the Reformed view by asking whether a man is prepared to sell his house. The answer might depend, in part, on whether the owner is rich or poor. A rich man would say he is prepared to sell his house when he has cleaned it and decorated it so that it will attract a buyer. While no degree of such preparation could obligate a buyer to purchase the rich man's home, such preparations do increase its "merit" or market value. This corresponds to the view of preparation that the Puritans rejected as "papist." According to the Roman Catholic doctrine of congruent merit, an unsaved man cannot strictly obligate God to save him, but he can make himself as attractive as possible by doing what lies in him, and enhance his "value" or merit in God's sight.

On the other hand, a poor man is prepared to sell his house when he realizes he is completely unable to pay his bills. He once treasured his

---

66. Calvin, *Institutes*, 2.2.27; Ames, "The Preparation of a Sinner for Conversion," theses 1–2; Pemble, *Vindiciae Gratiae*, 27–29, 56; Cotton, *The Way of Life*, 182; Norton, *The Orthodox Evangelist*, 130. On Perkins, see Pettit, *The Heart Prepared*, 62.

67. William G. T. Shedd, *Dogmatic Theology* (New York: Charles Scribner's Sons, 1888), 2:511–12.

home, but now needs a buyer to deliver him from debt. Such "preparation" has nothing to do with the value of the home. As his debts mount,
the man's house decays through lack of maintenance. He is nonetheless prepared to sell it; he even prays that a buyer will have mercy on
him and take it off his hands. This corresponds to the Reformed view
of preparation that the Puritans embraced. This preparation consists not
of increased worthiness, or meritorious acts, but an increased sense of
need and helplessness. This preparation for grace leads to a conversion
by grace which excludes boasting in self, for all the glory must go to the
Redeemer of helpless and impoverished sinners.

3. Puritan preparation highlights the common work of the Holy Spirit.
Rather than viewing the Spirit's work as confined strictly to regeneration, the Puritans said the Spirit works mightily beforehand through the
preaching of the Word to convict sinners of sin. Ames quoted the British representatives at Dort as saying, "There are certain internal effects,
leading unto conversion or regeneration, which are stirred by the power
of the word, and of the Spirit, in the hearts of those not yet justified."[68]
Hooker described contrition as "an act of the Spirit of Christ, whereby
it doth fling down those strongholds" by which sin and Satan resist the
Word.[69] Both Goodwin and Edwards developed their doctrine of preparation in the context of the three-fold ministry of the Spirit promised by
Christ in John 16:8–11.[70] Puritan preparation makes a vital contribution to
the doctrine of the Holy Spirit by expanding our awareness of our depen-
dence on His work in us, and increasing our gratitude towards Him for it.

4. Puritan preparation engages sinners with the law but not with legalism.
The convicting use of the law is central to preparation for faith. Calvin
wrote, "The law summoneth all the world before God, not one except[ed]:
it condemneth all the children of Adam…. Now seeing God thundereth
against us, we must needs run to that mercy which is offered unto us in
our Lord Jesus Christ."[71] Perkins wrote, "First, the law prepares us by

---

68. Ames, "The Preparation of a Sinner for Conversion," thesis 5.
69. Hooker, *The Application of Redemption… The First Eight Books,* 151.
70. Goodwin, *The Work of the Holy Ghost in Our Salvation,* 6:359–61; Edwards, "The Threefold Work of the Holy Ghost," 14:391.
71. Calvin, *Sermons on Timothy and Titus,* 50.

humbling us: then comes the gospel, and it stirs up faith."[72] He wrote on Galatians 3:24,

> The law, especially the moral law, urgeth and compelleth men to go to Christ. For it shows us our sins, and that without remedy: it shows us the damnation that is due unto us: and by this means, it makes us despair of salvation in respect of ourselves: and thus it enforceth us to seek for help out of ourselves in Christ. The law is then our school-master not by the plain teaching, but by stripes and correction.[73]

Thus the law serves the gospel by showing that we cannot be justified by the law. Bunyan portrayed this truth in *Pilgrim's Progress* by showing that when Christian wandered off the path in search of Mr. Legality to remove his burden, the threatening of Mount Sinai held him back and spurred him on to follow Evangelist's advice to quickly go to the wicket-gate.[74] As Edwards pointed out, a superficial view of the law tends to engender self-righteousness, but the searching preaching of the law, and hard labors to keep it, tend to destroy self-righteousness.[75]

5. Puritan preparation respects the mystery of regeneration and its timing.
At the beginning of this book, we defined preparation as a prelude to conscious faith in Christ. The Puritans acknowledged that in preparation, a person may be saved by faith in Christ, but he is not yet conscious of his faith, but only of his longings for Christ and salvation.

Edwards said the new birth can come in "a confused chaos…exceeding mysterious and unsearchable." He referred to Ecclesiastes 11:5, "As thou knowest not what is the way of the spirit, nor how the bones do grow in the womb of her that is with child: even so thou knowest not the works of God who maketh all."[76] Hooker also wrote about the mystery of spiritual birth, comparing it to conception and gestation in the womb.[77] Whereas the English Puritans tended to locate regeneration closer to the soul's first conscious receiving of Christ by faith, the Dutch theologians tended to locate it in the early convictions of conscience. Brakel wisely

---

72. Perkins, *A Commentary on Galatians*, 200.
73. Perkins, *A Commentary on Galatians*, 200.
74. Bunyan, *The Pilgrim's Progress* (1738), 14–21.
75. Edwards, "Pressing into the Kingdom of God," 19:284–85.
76. Edwards, *Religious Affections*, 2:160–61.
77. Hooker, "To the Reader," in Rogers, *The Doctrine of Faith*.

observed, "If he [the sinner] were to begin with the first serious conviction, in all probability he did not have faith yet. If he were to begin with the moment when, for the first time, he exercised faith consciously and in a most heartfelt manner, he would reckon too late, for in all probability he already had faith."[78]

6. Puritan preparation honors God as Creator and Savior.
Ames said it was "crude" to treat people as nothing more than "stone."[79] The Canons of Dort likewise argue that the "grace of regeneration does not treat men as senseless stocks and blocks, nor takes away their will and its properties, neither does violence thereto" (Head 3/4, Art. 16). God created man with a mind and a will. He created a world in which He works by means. His creations are good and must be used with thankfulness. All good things did not disappear with the fall. But sin has made man dead with respect to God. Only a sovereign and undeserved act of divine grace can raise the sinner to a living faith, hope, and love in Christ. Honoring God as Creator requires us to treat people as rational and volitional beings. Honoring God as Savior also requires us to show people that they are utterly incapable of regenerating themselves. The Puritans recognized both truths in exhorting the unconverted to use their natural abilities to read, think, listen, feel, and pray, even though only a supernatural work of grace can produce faith in sinners.

Samuel Willard said that in effectual calling, "The Spirit of God, in the work of application, treats with men as reasonable creatures, and causes by counsel; not carrying them by violent compulsion, but winning them by arguments, by which they are 'made willing in the day of his power' (Ps. 110:3)."[80] Jeremiah Burroughs said, "Jesus Christ doth work upon the heart in a rational way, as a rational creature, although he doth work above reason, and conveys supernatural grace that is beyond reason."[81] Edwards wrote, "God in the work of the salvation of mankind, deals with them suitably to their intelligent rational nature."[82]

---

78. Brakel, *The Christian's Reasonable Service*, 2:245.
79. Ames, "The Preparation of a Sinner for Conversion," corollary.
80. Willard, *A Compleat Body of Divinity*, 432.
81. Burroughs, *Four Books*, 1:22.
82. Edwards, *Religious Affections*, 2:152.

7. Puritan preparation reveals the sufficiency of Christ.
Preparation reveals the sufficiency of Christ by showing that everything
that contributes to salvation, from the first stirrings of conviction of sin
to the peace of full assurance of grace and salvation, comes from Him.
Hooker said in preparation "the Lord Christ" wages a merciful war
against the power of sin.[83] Conviction of sin is Christ knocking upon the
door of the soul.[84] We must not view preparation as putting an obstacle
between Christ and the soul, for preparation is an encounter with the living God who calls out to the soul with a voice that shakes the threshold
of the heart.

Preparation also reveals the sufficiency of Christ by convincing sinners that apart from Christ they can do nothing, not even come to Christ.
Hooker said, "That soul which was cured by any other means save only
by Christ, was never truly wounded for sin.... But if the soul were truly
wounded for sin, then nothing can cure him but a Savior to pardon him,
and grace to purge him."[85] Goodwin said that until sinners are humiliated, they are like able-bodied men with no money who think they can
always get a job. Humiliation shows them to be maimed and helpless,
lacking even the hands to receive Christ, so they must look to Christ even
for the hands.[86]

8. Puritan preparation is biblical.
The Puritans based their doctrine of preparation on an array of specific
texts in the Holy Scriptures, such as: 2 Chronicles 33:12; 34:27; Job 11:12;
Isaiah 40:3–4; 42:3; 55:1; 57:15; 61:1–3; 66:2; Jeremiah 4:3; 23:29; 31:19; Ezekiel
36:31; Hosea 5:15; 6:1–2; Matthew 3:7; 11:28; Mark 12:34; Luke 15:14–18; John
4:16–18; 16:8; Acts 2:37; 9:6; 16:13–14; 29–30; 24:24–25; Romans 3:19–20; 7:7–
13; 8:15; 2 Corinthians 10:4; Galatians 3:19, 24; Revelation 3:17, 20. Patricia
Caldwell says the Puritan experience of preparation especially resonated
with the prophetic theme of Israel's sufferings in exile as God urged His
people to repent of their sins.[87]

Perhaps most fundamentally, the Puritans used the three-fold pattern of the Epistle to the Romans, which included Paul's treatment of sin

83. Hooker, *The Application of Redemption... The Ninth and Tenth Books*, 47–50, 98–99.
84. Hooker, *The Application of Redemption... The Ninth and Tenth Books*, 101, 111–12.
85. Hooker, *The Soules Preparation for Christ*, 133.
86. Goodwin, *The Work of the Holy Ghost in Our Salvation*, 6:384–85.
87. Caldwell, *The Puritan Conversion Narrative*, 172.

and wrath (1:18–3:20), salvation by faith alone in Christ (3:21–11:36), and our thankful response of obedience to God's mercies (12:1–15:13). Romans is perhaps the clearest and fullest presentation of the gospel in Scripture and arguably was the most influential book in the Reformation. It gave a definitive pattern to Reformed thinking on conversion by saying that a sense of sin and misery precedes both deliverance and having peace with God. Those who would disregard or dismiss Puritan preparation should read Romans and meditate on Paul's rationale for spending so much time on sin before explaining the good news of the gospel.

Conclusion

We can learn much from the Puritans, if we read their writings with one eye on the Bible. Their method of soul care calls the church to return to preaching the law to convict and humble the unconverted. In today's context, James 4:9 is virtually incomprehensible when it exhorts sinners and even nominal church members to "be afflicted, and mourn, and weep: let your laughter be turned to mourning, and your joy to heaviness." But sinners must be convicted of the wrath of God, and see the righteousness of it before they understand the need to repent and by faith to embrace the gospel promise. They must examine themselves and mourn over their sins. This message may not attract large crowds today apart from an extraordinary work of the Holy Spirit. But it will create a context in which the gospel makes sense and is good news indeed. It will also honor the Spirit who inspired both law and gospel and He will be pleased to honor our preaching. A comfort gained upon grieving over sin is solid and lasting comfort.

This book is far from exhaustive in explaining the Puritan doctrine of preparation. We have only briefly considered the writings of significant authors. We have almost entirely passed by the preparatory doctrines of men such as Peter Bulkeley, Samuel Rutherford, Richard Baxter, John Owen, Cotton Mather, and Solomon Stoddard. For further study, we encourage you to read Ames's disputation on preparation found in the appendix. You might also explore topics such as the relation of preparation to faculty psychology, common grace, and the conscience. The fruit of a great field of research is still waiting to be harvested. In our survey of Puritan views on this topic, we hope we have shed some needed light on a matter of great importance.

We should remember that preparation was only one part of Puritan teaching on soteriology. The Puritans also developed rich doctrines of effectual calling, saving faith, repentance unto life, assurance of salvation, and spiritual joy in Christ. It would be a mistake to think that the Puritans were obsessed with conviction of sin, contrition, and humiliation, when these preparatory works were only the beginning of the way that may lead to salvation as they understood it.

The focus of the Puritans, as with all biblical Christianity, was Christ. As William Perkins said to his student preachers at the conclusion of his *Arte of Prophecying,* "The sum of the sum: Preach one Christ by Christ to the praise of Christ."[88] Puritan preparation was just a means to an end, and the end was knowing, trusting, loving, serving, and glorifying Jesus Christ. We close with the words of Thomas Hooker:

> The Lord proclaims his mercy openly, freely offers it, heartily intends it, waits to communicate it, lays siege to the soul by his long sufferance: there is enough to procure all good, distrust it not: he freely invites, fear it not, thou mayest be bold to go: he intends it heartily, question it not: yet he is waiting and wooing, delay it not therefore, but hearken to his voice.[89]

---

88. Breward, ed., *The Work of William Perkins,* 349.
89. Hooker, *The Application of Redemption... The First Eight Books,* 362–63.

APPENDIX

William Ames's Theological Disputation on Preparation

Steven Dilday, translator

In a human sinner God provides for Himself a way.
—William Ames

William Ames wrote a work in Latin titled *Praeparatione peccatoris ad conversionem* ("On the Preparation of the Sinner for Conversion"). It was published in 1633 together with other disquisitions under the title *Disceptatio Scholastica de circulo pontificio* ("A Scholarly Discussion of the Circular Reasoning of the Pope"),[1] and reprinted in 1644 and 1658.[2] Ten pages of the book focus upon the preparation of a sinner for conversion. This disputation on preparation consists of twelve positive theses, answers to seven objections and two questions, and one corollary. Cotton, Norton, and Firmin quoted from this document, and Owen and van Mastricht alluded to it. We have already analyzed this disputation in Chapter 4 but include it here for further consideration. The translation is based upon the 1644 edition.[3]

1. William Ames, *Disceptatio Scholastica de circulo pontificio* (Lugduni Batavorum: ex officina Justi Livii, 1633). Ames's disputation, *Disceptatio Scholastica de circulo pontificio*, was originally published in 1610 and argued that the Romanists' assertion that Scripture derives its authority from the testimony of the church is circular reasoning because they base the church's authority on the promise of the Holy Spirit found in the Scripture. See Visscher, "William Ames," in *William Ames,* trans. Horton, 111, 114.

2. William Ames, *Disceptatio Scholastica de circulo pontificio* (Amstelodami: Joannem Janssonivm, 1644); *Disceptatio Scholastica de circulo pontificio* (Amstelodami: Joannem Janssonivm, 1658).

3. Ames, *Disceptatio Scholastica* (1644), 30–39. Thanks to Steven Dilday for translating this Latin treatise into English. It would be a fascinating study to compare Ames's treatise to that of Thomas Parker (1595–1677), *Theses De Traductione Peccatoris ad Vitam,* bound with this same work (pp. 84–105).

The Preparation of a Sinner for Conversion

Thesis 1: That those dispositions of justification, impetratory[4] and meritorious, whether out of condignity, or out of congruity, which dispositions the Papists imagine to proceed, either only from free will, or partly also from grace, have been justly rejected, is not to be called into question.

Thesis 2: On the other hand, to hold for that reason that very word *disposition* as hateful, so that someone, at the same time as those [impetratory and meritorious dispositions], might remove all preparatory affections and motions, without any distinction, by which in a human sinner God provides[5] for Himself a way unto his congruous conversion, and to a certain extent places him in an order tending unto regeneration. This form of argumentation is like unto the following, as if a man would simply deny good works, because meritorious works are rightly condemned.

Thesis 3: Now, we do not hesitate to assert that in the converting and regenerating of every sinner after the use of means, in succession, certain dispositions tending to that precede, although in unequal degree, according to the wisdom of the divine dispensation.

Thesis 4: We do not indicate here any natural gifts, from which something of a difference appears to proceed in an easier, or more difficult, perception, or exercise of certain things that pertain to grace. Neither do we wish to adopt for ourselves that concept of Bucer, on Matthew 12, that "in the elect, even while they live in depravity, there always lies hidden some love of justice and righteousness." We embrace only those preparations which depend upon and proceed from vocation by the word.

Thesis 5: Concerning these things nothing is more certain than what the British theologians proposed in Head 3/4 of the Canons of Dort, that "certain external works are ordinarily required of men, before they are brought to the state of regeneration or conversion. There are certain internal effects, leading unto conversion or regeneration, which are stirred by the power of the word, and of the Spirit, in the hearts of those not yet justified; of which sort is an acquaintance with the divine will, a sense of sin, a fear of punishment, a consideration of redemption, and some hope of pardon.

---

4. *Impetratoriae:* obtained by petition.
5. *Munio:* to build (a road), to fortify.

For just as in the natural generation of man there are many dispositions going before, so also in the spiritual generation, etc." Similar things are held by William Perkins, *The Whole Treatise of the Cases of Conscience,* book 1, chapter 5, where he established *four preparatory works preceding grace* (that is, habitual grace), 1. *Some breaking of obstinacy; 2. Consideration of the Law; 3. Acknowledgment of sins; 4. Legal repentance.*

Thesis 6: Belonging to this opinion is not that intention, as if works of this sort might be dispositions proportionate to regeneration, as whatever degree of heat produced in wood by fire tends to fire; or as if they have the force of ultimate disposition, having always a necessary, or certain connection with the form to be introduced; but inasmuch as they are material dispositions, which make the subject more receptive to the form to be introduced, as the dryness of wood tends to fire.

Thesis 7: Now, this is accomplished through those preparations, partly to the extent that through them various impediments (at least partly) are removed; just as formation in the truth removes ignorance, sorrow over sins removes the pleasure felt from them, fear removes audacity of sinning; and partly to the extent that they confer something, the use of which is great in conversion, like illumination, the horror of sin, the shame of its indecency, a desire (although confused) for redemption, etc.

Thesis 8: The evidence of this truth is so great, that he who resists the same, by one rash opinion, would appear to expunge the whole first part of the [Heidelberg] Catechism, with a large part of the second; and also to abrogate the entire ministry of the word in order to the conversion of sinners. For just as there is no use of the ministry with respect to those regenerated except to prepare and lead them to glory, so also there is no use of it with respect to the unregenerate except to prepare and lead them to conversion.

Thesis 9: From the Scriptures (although this doctrine is found everywhere) we proffer those two illustrious passages: "thou art not far from the kingdom of God" (Mark 12:34), and "they were pricked in heart" (Acts 2:37). From the former Calvin well observes that "we are taught that many, while they, as men confused, are yet held by error, yet approach unto the way with closed eyes, and in this manner are prepared, so that in the fullness of time they might run in the race of the Lord." From the other passage he observes also the same thing, that "sorrow over sin is the beginning of repentance, the entrance into piety."

Thesis 10: Those prior words of the Lord are not able to be thus obscured and evaded, that *by the kingdom of God is understood the church, and by approaching unto the kingdom, the profession of the truth.* For Christ was not calling anyone to the church, except through faith and repentance; neither is anyone able to approach unto the church, to the extent that it is the kingdom of God, except it be almost the case that God reigns in him. Also, all the Jews were at that time, in some manner in the visible church, and this scribe had not made a profession of any other truth than of the law.

Thesis 11: The force of the second passage is not diminished but confirmed by that response, that *that initial fear of which it treats, together with a desire of salvation and grace, etc.* (Acts 2:37 and 16:29), *is a certain part of regeneration, and an effect of the Holy Spirit.* For, just as generation ever includes all the dispositions going before, so regeneration is ever taken for the entire series of helps, by which we are moved unto it. In no other way was that fear, concerning which those passages speak, able to be called a part of regeneration than because it was preceding faith and repentance, as from the context it manifestly appears.

Thesis 12: That which is opposed has a certain appearance of difficulty here: *that fear, which arises from the law in the unregenerate, is servile, and to that extent does not lead to God, but is rather a cause of turning from God.* But it is to be observed: 1. that some servile fear is a gift of the Holy Spirit; as nearly all interpreters gather from Romans 8:15, "the spirit of bondage again to fear," and it was only now conceded (in the preceding thesis), and more even when, *that fear, which was treated in* Acts 2 *and* 16, *is established as the initial part of regeneration and an effect of the Holy Spirit.* Now, no gift of God, especially not what is part of regeneration, as such, and of itself, turns a man from God. 2. That which in any respect turns from God is able by circumstance[6] to lead to God, just as afflictions of themselves tend to evil, yet by circumstance[7] work together for good. 3. He who speaks of servile fear speaks of two things, that is, of the affection itself, by which someone is disposed unto God as the avenger of sin worthy to be feared, and of

---

6. *Per accidens.*
7. *Per accidens.*

that servile deformity, which he has annexed. The former is good in itself, and it abides in the regenerate. Just as, therefore, in servile fear, there is a material substrate; so also the material disposition is to filial fear and conversion; and thus it leads unto God, although that deformity which he has annexed inclines to a turning away from God. Hence that saying of Calvin on Acts 20 and 21 and in *Institutes* 3.3, "Legal attrition is the beginning of repentance, and a preparation unto faith. I call it our displeasure a beginning, which displeasure by fear of the anger of God, drives us, having been gravely touched, to seek the remedy." And that of Chamier: "Thus the law is wont to serve the Gospel, inasmuch as, with a most certain condemnation by works indicated, it prepares a man to seek grace (volume 3, book 15, chapter 4 [of *Panstratiae Catholicae*]); and he wrote, "We indeed concede that servile fear is good; that is, to the extent that it denotes a good thing that is agreeable to reason or usefulness" (book 22, chapter 9), just as Augustine said on Psalm 127, "That fear is good, and is useful."

Thesis 13: Objection 1: *Man is thus an animal, in that he is not able to do good. Therefore, he is not able to be disposed, while he remains such, to regeneration.* Responses: 1. This is no consequence; if he is not able to dispose himself, then he is not able to be disposed by God. 2. Man is able to do something that is good, that is, useful to himself in order to regeneration. For example, he is able to hear the word preached. 3. He is able to do something materially good in the class of an honest[8] good; and that material good is able to be, or to leave behind, a material disposition to regeneration. 4. That which of itself is plainly evil is able by circumstance[9] to bring in a disposition to some great good. Thus the selling of Joseph disposed him to the preservation of his paternal family. The very crucifixion of Christ in some manner disposed Him to the work of redemption.

Thesis 14: Objection 2: *Unregenerate man has a taste for those things which are of the flesh. Therefore, he is not able to be disposed to regeneration.* Responses: 1. This is a consequence similar to the former. 2. Just as those who have a taste for the things which are of the Spirit are able to have such great dispositions to death that by the same dispositions they merit by condignity[10] death, so also nothing hinders that those others who have a taste

---

8. *Honestus*, morally worthy of respect.
9. *Per accidens.*
10. *Ex condigno.*

for those things which are of the flesh have such dispositions to spiritual life, although not of themselves, and not either by merit, or actually equal to those formerly mentioned. 3. Men are able to be disposed to have a taste for that for which they do not yet have a taste. 4. Those who do not taste of the good are able to be led to it, so that they might understand that they do not have a taste for the good, indeed, so that they might sip of the heavenly good, which is sufficient for a disposition.

Thesis 15: Objection 3: *In unregenerate man sin reigns. Therefore he is not able to be disposed to regeneration.* Responses: 1. Sin does not so reign in unregenerate man that that kingdom is not subject to the powerful government of God. Nothing, therefore, hinders but that, according to the will of God, even before it is removed; in this or that part, it might be diminished or impeded, which is sufficient for a material disposition. 2. Just as the kingdom of grace does not always exclude all dispositions to the sin of apostasy; so the kingdom of sin does not exclude material dispositions to the grace of regeneration.

Thesis 16: Objection 4: *Unregenerate man is dead in sins. Therefore, no disposition unto regeneration is able to be in him.* Response: The consequence is null, concerning a material disposition. For, just as in Adam's fashioned body, in itself there was a disposition to life afterwards to be instilled; and in the bones, in Ezekiel 37, gathered, conjoined, clothed with flesh and skin, before they had the spirit infused, there was a greater disposition to life, than while they remained dry and divided; so also it happens in certain men destitute of spiritual life.

Thesis 17: Objection 5: *In this manner a middle state between men regenerate and unregenerate would be granted.* Response: This does not follow because dispositions of that sort do not change the state. Those dispositions unto evil, which remain in the regenerate, do not change their state. Those dispositions of the body of Adam, and of the bones of Ezekiel, do not introduce a middle state between living and not living, man and not man. The unregenerate state, just as also the regenerate state, has a great latitude, in which dispositions varying in kind have a place. Except this be, how could it be denied that all those who have been illuminated, and made partakers of the various gifts of the Spirit, and in some measure made clean and free from sin, are to be found in the state of the regenerate.

Thesis 18: Objection 6: *If the dispositions to regeneration precede in an unregenerate man, then the unregenerate man is not merely passive in regeneration, but also active.* Responses: 1. That a man in regeneration is not merely passive ought not to appear strange to him, who taught a little before that the desire of salvation and grace, the sighing of a bleating conscience, and the initial fear, are parts of regeneration. For in those the man is not merely passive. 2. The same assertion will not appear to be a new thing to any understanding person, unless it be understood of the first act of regeneration. For in the second the man is not unregenerate. Nay more, it is not absurd to say what Perkins concedes in the name of all the orthodox: in the very first moment of conversion, there is some operation of the will, although in the order of nature it is after the operation of grace (*Reformed Catholic*, chapter 1). 3. No reason of the consequence is able to be given. For the body of Adam, in the infusion of the spirit, although it was previously disposed, was merely passive—thus also the bones of Ezekiel. 4. That consequence (from whatever sort of disposition, to cooperation in the act of regeneration) is abandoned by all reason to such an extent that, if such dispositions are granted beforehand, that would obtain regeneration by way of meritorious cause, not even thence would it follow that unregenerate man in the real act itself of regeneration is not merely passive, but active. For merit does not imply real efficient concurrence.

Thesis 19: Objection 7: *It would follow from this that those who appear better than the rest are regenerated, but those of inferior quality are not regenerated.* Response: Not at all. For, 1. Who will grant that all those who *appear* to be better than the rest are more prepared for conversion? There are many hypocrites who appear to be better than the very regenerate—much better than those who were merely led to such an extent that, with grief and a desire for redemption, they seriously acknowledge their sins. The Pharisee appeared better than the Publican (Luke 18). The pseudo-apostles, who transfigured themselves into the apostles of Christ, to many of the Corinthians appeared better than Paul (2 Cor. 11). 2. Who will grant that those material dispositions (which are treated) have a certain and definite connection with regeneration? How monstrous then is this requirement, that those of inferior quality are not able either by degrees, or even (as it sometimes happens in experience), by one sermon, to a certain extent to be disposed unto regeneration.

Two Related Questions

Question 1: *Whether the word of God, before regeneration, is heard savingly?* Response: Something is said to be done savingly, 1. When the very action presupposes the state of salvation, and in formal order, and in a certain and definite connection, cleaves to "things accompanying salvation" (Heb. 6:9). 2. When that which is done confers anything to the salvation afterwards to be communicated. In the latter sense (not the former) we respond affirmatively. Now, this often clearly appears even in the hearing of the Word, which for a significant space of time precedes regeneration. That knowledge of the sacred books which Timothy had while yet a boy (2 Tim. 3), was afterwards saving for him. Augustine, in *Confessions*, book 7, chapter 8, narrating the mercy of God, by which he was deemed fit that it should prepare him, while not yet faithful, for conversion; among other things he confesses that the perplexed and darkened battlefield of his mind, by the harsh eye-salve of *salutary* griefs, day unto day, was healed. He says he was *wholesomely* mad, and vitally dead (book 8, chapter 8). Now, concerning that hearing of the word, which immediately precedes conversion, thus it appears: that hearing of the word, which produces faith, is saving. But that hearing is before regeneration. Therefore, some hearing, which is before regeneration, is saving.

In vain is it here objected that *the word is not heard savingly, except from faith, which presupposes a regenerate man; that fruit does not come forth, except in good earth; that hearts are to be opened before application* (Acts 16). For, 1. (that we might pass over at this point, that faith, which precedes justification, is not able to presuppose regeneration according to those who by regeneration properly understand sanctification) that hearing of the word which is not formally of salvation before faith, is able through a manner of preparation effectively salvific to be before faith, to the extent that it begets faith, with which it is savingly mixed. 2. The first fruit of the word heard is, in its own manner, to make the soil good, so that, remaining in good soil, the fruit of good works is able to advance. 3. In Acts 16, these three things are conjoined, *she heard; the Lord opened her heart; she was attending*. Who is able to deny that that hearing, which was brought to completion in the opening of the heart, was salvific, although in order it preceded faith; hearing was an effect of faith, in the moral category. But the cause of the effect formally salvific is not able not to be causally salvific.

Question 2: *Whether those, who teach that the will necessarily follows the judg-ment of the intellect, so that they might decline that absurdity, which thence appears to follow (that infused gifts, therefore, are not necessary to the will), say rightly that gifts are infused into the will, illuminated by the help of the mind, as by the intervening of some means?* Response: That this is very ignorantly spoken, it is evident, 1. From the nature of the mind, or of the intellect, which does nothing to the will, except morally or objectively, an act of which sort is not able to be a proximate means of any real quality to be communicated. 2. From the nature of gifts supernaturally infused, of which this is the proper difference by which they are distinguished from acquired gifts, that they are not produced by any act of ours, and to that extent not by an act of our intellect. For on that account they are called infused, because they are immediately created by God, in such a way that they do not have means properly intervening between God and its sub-ject. Therefore, there is a contradiction in the thing added, *it is infused by the intervening of means.* 3. From the comparison of gifts which are infused into the will, with the nature of the intellect. For, charity (which is a virtue of the will) is in no way in the intellect, neither formally, nor eminently, and hence it is not able to be infused properly into the will by the help of the intellect. 4. Because, if all these things be conceded, concerning ability, yet it would be no more necessary (from that hypothesis concerning the necessary subjection of the will to the intellect), that supernatural gifts be infused into the will than into the fingers because (with that hypothesis granted) the will with equal necessity is subject to the intellect, and the fingers to the will, and even more so. No greater virtue is infusive of gifts in the intellect, with respect to the voluntary, than in the will, with respect to any inferior faculty, subjected to the government of it.

Corollary

It is crude to assert (without any distinction or limitation) that there is no other power, or disposition, in any unregenerate man, unto this, that he might be regenerate, than is in a stone. This is nothing other than stones speaking.

Bibliography

Primary Sources: Individual Authors

Ambrose, Isaac. *Works of Isaac Ambrose*. London: Thomas Tegg and Son, 1829.

Ames, William. *Conscience with the Power and Cases Thereof*. n.p., 1639.

———. *Disceptatio Scholastica de circulo pontificio… Item ejusdem Disquisitiones Theologicae, De Lumine Naturae et Gratiae, Praeparatione peccatoris ad Conversionem, Adoratione Christi Mediatoris*. Amstelodami: Joannem Janssonivm, 1644.

———. *The Marrow of Theology*, trans. and ed. John D. Eusden. 1968; repr., Grand Rapids: Baker, 1997.

———. *The Substance of Christian Religion: Or, a Plain and Easie Draught of the Christian Catechisme*. London: by T. Mabb for Thomas Davies, 1659.

———. *Theologiae Medullae, Liber Primus*, ed. James S. Candlish. London: James Nisbet, 1874.

Aquinas, Thomas. *Summa Theologica*, trans. Fathers of the English Dominican Province. London: R. & T. Washbourne, 1914.

Augustine, *Confessions*. In *A Select Library of the Nicene and Post-Nicene Fathers of the Christian Church, Volume 1*, ed. Philip Schaff. Repr., Grand Rapids: Eerdmans, 1991.

———. *The Enchiridion on Faith, Hope, and Love*. Washington, D.C.: Regnery, 1996.

———. *On Grace and Free Will*. In *A Select Library of the Nicene and Post-Nicene Fathers of the Christian Church, Volume 5*, ed. Philip Schaff. Repr., Grand Rapids: Eerdmans, 1991.

———. *On the Spirit and the Letter*. In *A Select Library of the Nicene and Post-Nicene Fathers of the Christian Church, Volume 5*, ed. Philip Schaff. Repr., Grand Rapids: Eerdmans, 1991.

Baxter, Richard. *The Practical Works of Richard Baxter.* London: James Duncan, 1830.

———. *The Practical Works of Richard Baxter.* London: George Virtue, 1837.

Bradford, John. *The Writings of John Bradford,* [Volume 1]. Cambridge: The Parker Society, 1848.

à Brakel, Wilhelmus. *The Christian's Reasonable Service,* trans. Bartel Elshout, ed. Joel R. Beeke. Grand Rapids: Reformation Heritage Books, 1999.

Bunyan, John. *A Book for Boys and Girls.* 1686; facsimile repr., London: Elliot Stock, 1889.

———. *Life and Death of Mr. Badman and Holy War,* ed. John Brown. London: Cambridge University Press, 1905.

———. *The Pilgrim's Progress.* 1678; facsimile repr., London: Elliot Stock, 1895.

———. *The Pilgrim's Progress.* London: by A. W. for J. Clarke, 1738.

———. *The Pilgrim's Progress… in Two Parts.* London: for W. Johnston, 1757.

———. *The Works of John Bunyan,* ed. George Offor. 3 vols. Glasgow: Blackie and Son, 1855.

Burroughs, Jeremiah. *The Evil of Evils, or the Exceeding Sinfulness of Sin.* London: Peter Cole, 1654.

———. *Four Books on the Eleventh of Matthew.* London: Peter Cole, 1659.

Calvin, John. *The Bondage and Liberation of the Will.* Grand Rapids: Baker, 1996.

———. *Commentaries on the Catholic Epistles,* trans. John Owen. Repr., Grand Rapids: Baker, 1996.

———. *Commentary on a Harmony of the Evangelists,* trans. William Pringle. Repr., Grand Rapids: Baker, 1996.

———. *Commentary on the Acts of the Apostles,* trans. Christopher Fetherstone, ed. Henry Beveridge. Repr., Grand Rapids: Baker, 1996.

———. *Commentary on the Gospel according to John,* trans. William Pringle. Repr., Grand Rapids: Baker, 1996.

———. *The Deity of Christ and Other Sermons,* trans. Leroy Nixon. Audubon, N.J.: Old Paths Publications, 1997.

———. *Institutes of the Christian Religion,* ed. John T. McNeill, trans. Ford Lewis Battles. 2 vols. Philadelphia: Westminster Press, 1960.

———. *Sermons on Deuteronomy.* 1583; facsimile repr., Edinburgh: Banner of Truth, 1987.

———. *Sermons on the Epistle to the Ephesians.* Edinburgh: Banner of Truth, 1987.

———. *Sermons on Timothy and Titus.* 1579; facsimile repr., Edinburgh: Banner of Truth, 1983.

Cotton, John. *A Brief Exposition with Practical Observations upon the whole Book of Canticles.* London: by T. R. and E. M. for Ralph Smith, 1655.

———. *Christ the Fountaine of Life.* 1651; facsimile repr., New York: Arno Press, 1972.

———. *The Correspondence of John Cotton,* ed. Sargent Bush, Jr. Chapel Hill: University of North Carolina Press, 2001.

———. *An Exposition of First John.* Evansville, Ind.: Sovereign Grace Publishers, 1962.

———. *Gospel Conversion… Opened by John Cotton, at a Conference in New-England… Now published for the generall good by Francis Cornwell.* London: by J. Dawson, 1646.

———. *The New Covenant, Or, A Treatise, unfolding the order and manner of the giving and receiving of the Covenant of Grace to the Elect.* London: by M. S. for Francis Eglesfield and John Allen, 1654.

———. *The Way of Life, Or, Gods VVay and Course, in Bringing the Soule into, and keeping it in, and carrying it on, in the ways of life and peace.* London: by M. F. for L. Fawne and S. Gellibrand, 1641.

———. *The Way of the Churches of Christ in New England.* London, 1645.

———. "To the Godly Reader." In *CVIII Lectures upon the Fourth of John,* by Arthur Hildersam. 3rd ed. London: by Moses Bell for Edward Brewster, 1647.

———. "To the Judicious Christian Reader." In *The Orthodox Evangelist, or A Treatise Wherein many Great Evangelical Truths… Are briefly Discussed,* by John Norton. London: by John Macock for Henry Cripps and Lodowick Lloyd, 1654.

De Sales, Francis. *An Introduction to the Deuout Life,* trans. I[ohn] Y[akesley]. Douai: by G. Patt for Iohn Heigham, 1613.

Dent, Arthur. *The Plain Man's Pathway to Heaven.* Belfast: North of Ireland Book and Tract Depository, 1859.

Dickson, David. *Therapeutica Sacra.* Edinburgh: Evan Tyler, 1664.

Edwards, Jonathan. *The Works of Jonathan Edwards, Volume 2, Religious Affections,* ed. John E. Smith. New Haven: Yale University Press, 1959.

———. *The Works of Jonathan Edwards, Volume 13, The "Miscellanies," a–500,* ed. Thomas A. Schafer. New Haven: Yale University Press, 1994.

———. *The Works of Jonathan Edwards, Volume 14, Sermons and Discourses 1723–1729*, ed. Kenneth P. Minkema. New Haven: Yale University Press, 1997.

———. *The Works of Jonathan Edwards, Volume 16, Letters and Personal Writings*, ed. George S. Claghorn. New Haven: Yale University Press, 1998.

———. *The Works of Jonathan Edwards, Volume 17, Sermons and Discourses, 1730–1733*, ed. Mark Valeri. New Haven: Yale University Press, 1999.

———. *The Works of Jonathan Edwards, Volume 18, The "Miscellanies" 501–832*, ed. Ava Chamberlain. New Haven: Yale University Press, 2000.

———. *The Works of Jonathan Edwards, Volume 19, Sermons and Discourses 1734–1738*, ed. M. X. Lesser. New Haven: Yale University Press, 2001.

———. *The Works of Jonathan Edwards, Volume 20, The "Miscellanies" 833–1152*, ed. Amy Plantinga Pauw. New Haven: Yale University Press, 2002.

———. *The Works of Jonathan Edwards, Volume 21, Writings on the Trinity, Grace, and Faith*, ed. Sang Hyun Lee. New Haven: Yale University Press, 2002.

———. *The Works of Jonathan Edwards, Volume 23, The "Miscellanies" 1153–1360*, ed. Douglas A. Sweeney. New Haven: Yale University Press, 2004.

———. *The Works of Jonathan Edwards, Volume 25, Sermons and Discourses, 1743–1758*, ed. Wilson H. Kimnach. New Haven: Yale University Press, 2006.

———. *The Works of Jonathan Edwards Online, Volume 43, Sermons, Series II, 1728–1729*. Jonathan Edwards Center at Yale University, http://edwards.yale.edu (accessed July 18, 2011).

———. *The Works of Jonathan Edwards Online, Volume 48, Sermons, Series II, 1733*, Jonathan Edwards Center at Yale University, http://edwards.yale.edu (accessed July 19, 2011).

———. *The Works of Jonathan Edwards Online, Volume 50, Sermons, Series II, 1735*, The Jonathan Edwards Center at Yale University, http://edwards.yale.edu (accessed July 20, 2011).

———. *The Works of Jonathan Edwards Online, Volume 56, Sermons, Series II, July–December 1740*, The Jonathan Edwards Center at Yale University, http://edwards.yale.edu (accessed August 5, 2011).

Erskine, Ralph. *Sermons and Other Practical Works*. Falkirk: by Patrick Mair for John Stewart, Peter Muirhead, and Hugh Mitchell, 1795.

Firmin, Giles. *The Real Christian, or A Treatise of Effectual Calling*. London: for Dorman Newman, 1670.

Flavel, John. *A Blow at the Root of Antinomianism*. Philadelphia: Presbyterian Board of Publication, [1830].

————. *The Works of John Flavel*. 1820; repr.; Edinburgh: Banner of Truth, 1997.

Gomarus, Franciscus. "Theological Disputation on Free Choice." In *Reformed Thought on Freedom: The Concept of Free Choice in Early Modern Theology*, ed. Willem J. van Asselt, J. Martin Bac, and Roelf T. te Velde. Grand Rapids: Baker Academic, 2010.

Goodwin, Thomas. *The Works of Thomas Goodwin*. 12 vols. 1861–1866; repr., Grand Rapids: Reformation Heritage Books, 2006.

Goodwin, Thomas and Philip Nye. "To the Reader." In *The Application of Redemption, By the effectual Work of the Word, and Spirit of Christ, for the bringing home of lost Sinners to God, The First Eight Books*, by Thomas Hooker. 1657; facsimile repr., New York: Arno Press, 1972.

Guthrie, William. *The Christian's Great Interest*. Glasgow: for William Collins, 1833.

Hall, Joseph. *The Works of the Right Reverend Joseph Hall*. 10 vols. Oxford: Oxford University Press, 1863.

Halyburton, Thomas. *The Works of the Rev. Thomas Halyburton*. London: Thomas Tegg & Son, 1835.

Heywood, Oliver. *The Whole Works of the Rev. Oliver Heywood*. 5 vols. Idle: by John Vint, for F. Westley et al., 1826.

Hildersam, Arthur. *CVIII Lectures upon the Fourth of John*, 3rd ed. London: by Moses Bell for Edward Brewster, 1647.

Hooker, Thomas. *The Application of Redemption, By the effectual Work of the Word, and Spirit of Christ, for the bringing home of lost Sinners to God, The First Eight Books*. 1657; facsimile repr., New York: Arno Press, 1972.

————. *The Application of Redemption By the Effectual Work of the Word, and Spirit of Christ, for the bringing home of lost Sinners to God. The Ninth and Tenth Books*. London: Peter Cole, 1657.

————. *The Soules Implantation into the Natural Olive*. London: by R. Young, 1640.

————. *The Sovles Humiliation*. London: by T. Cotes for Andrew Crooke and Philip Nevill, 1640.

————. *The Sovles Exaltation*. London: by Iohn Haviland for Andrew Crooke, 1638.

————. *The Sovles Possession of Christ*. London: by M. F. for Francis Eglesfield, 1638.

————. *The Sovles Preparation for Christ*. The Netherlands: n.p., 1638.

————. *The Sovles Vocation or Effectval Calling to Christ*. London: by John Haviland for Andrew Crooke, 1638.

———. *The Vnbeleevers Preparing for Christ*. London: by Tho. Cotes for Andrew Crooke, 1638.

———. "To the Reader." In *The Doctrine of Faith*, by John Rogers. London: for Nathanael Newbery and William Sheffard, 1627.

———. *Zielsvernedering en heylzame wanhoop* [The Soul's Humiliation, or Wholesome Desperation], trans. Jacobus Koelman. Amsterdam: J. Wasterlier, 1678.

Howe, John. *The Works of the Rev. John Howe*. 3 vols. New York: John P. Haven, 1838.

Leigh, Edward. *A Systeme or Body of Divinity: Consisting of Ten Books. Wherein the Fundamentals and main Grounds of Religion are Opened: the Contrary Errours Refuted: Most of the Controversies between Us, the Papists, Arminians, and Socinians Discussed and Handled*. London: by A. M. for William Lee, 1654.

Mather, Cotton. *Magnalia Christi Americana: Or, the Ecclesiastical History of New-England*. London: for Thomas Parkhurst, 1702.

Mather, Increase. "To the Reader." In *A Guide to Christ*, by Solomon Stoddard. Northampton: Andrew Wright, 1816.

Newton, John. *Wise Counsel: John Newton's Letters to John Ryland, Jr.*, ed. Grant Gordon. Edinburgh: Banner of Truth, 2009.

Norton, John. *The Orthodox Evangelist, or A Treatise Wherein many Great Evangelical Truths... Are briefly Discussed*. London: by John Macock for Henry Cripps and Lodowick Lloyd, 1654.

Owen, John. *The Works of John Owen*. 16 vols. 1850–1853; repr., Edinburgh: Banner of Truth, 1965.

Pemble, William. *Vindiciae Gratiae*. In *The Workes of the Late Learned Minister of God's Holy Word, Mr William Pemble*, 4th ed. Oxford: by Henry Hall for John Adams, 1659.

Perkins, William. *A Commentary on Galatians*, ed. Gerald T. Sheppard. 1617; facsimile repr., New York: Pilgrim Press, 1989.

———. *A Golden Chaine*. London: Iohn Legat, 1600.

———. *The Whole Treatise of the Cases of Conscience*. Cambridge: Iohn Legat, 1609.

———. *The Work of William Perkins*, ed. Ian Breward. Appleford: Sutton Courtenay Press, 1970.

———. *The Workes of that Famovs and VVorthy Minister of Christ in the Vniuersitie of Cambridge, Mr. William Perkins*. 3 vols. London: Iohn Legatt, 1612–1613.

Preston, John. *Remaines of that Reverend and Learned Divine, John Preston.* London: for Andrew Crooke, 1634.

———. *The Breast-plate of Faith and Love.* 1634. Facsimile repr., Edinburgh: Banner of Truth, 1979.

Reynolds, Edward. *The Works of the Right Rev. Edward Reynolds.* 1826; repr. Morgan, Pa.: Soli Deo Gloria, 1998.

Rogers, John, *The Doctrine of Faith.* London: for Nathanael Newbery and William Sheffard, 1627.

Rogers, Richard. *Seven Treatises.* London: by Felix Kyngston, for Thomas Man and Robert Dexter, 1603.

Rollock, Robert. *Select Works of Robert Rollock.* Repr., Grand Rapids: Reformation Heritage Books, 2008.

Shepard, Thomas. *The Sincere Convert, Discovering the Paucity of true Believers; and the great Difficultie of Saving Conversions.* London: by T. P. and M. S., 1643.

———. *The Sound Beleever. Or, a Treatise of Evangelicall Conversion.* London: for R. Dawlman, 1645.

Sibbes, Richard. *The Brvised Reede and Smoaking Flax,* 3rd ed. London: by M. F. for R. Dawlman, 1631.

———. *The Complete Works of Richard Sibbes,* ed. Alexander B. Grosart. Edinburgh: James Nichol, 1863.

Taylor, Edward. *The Poems of Edward Taylor,* ed. Donald Stanford. Chapel Hill: University of North Carolina Press, 1989.

Turretin, Francis. *Institutes of Elenctic Theology,* trans. George Musgrave Giger, ed. James T. Dennison, Jr. Phillipsburg, N.J.: P & R Publishing, 1994–1997.

Ursinus, Zacharius. *The Commentary of Dr. Zacharias Ursinus on the Heidelberg Catechism,* trans. G. W. Williard, 3rd ed. Cincinnati: T. P. Bucher, 1851.

Van Mastricht, Peter. *On Regeneration.* New Haven: Thomas and Samuel Green, 1769.

Vincent, Thomas. *Explicatory Catechism, or, An Explanation of the Assembly's Shorter Catechism.* New Haven: Walter, Austin, and Co., 1810.

Watson, Thomas. *A Body of Practical Divinity in a Series of Sermons on the Shorter Catechism.* London: A. Fullarton, 1845.

Wigglesworth, Michael. *The Day of Doom.* New York: American News Company, 1867.

Willard, Samuel. *A Compleat Body of Divinity.* 1726; facsimile repr., New York: Johnson Reprint Corp., 1969.

Winthrop, John. *The History of New England from 1630 to 1649,* ed. James Savage. Boston: Little, Brown, and Co., 1853.

Witsius, Herman. *Conciliatory, or Irenical Animadversions on the Controversies Agitated in Britain under the Unhappy Names of Antinomians and Neonomians,* trans. Thomas Bell. Glasgow: W. Lang, 1807.

———. *The Economy of the Covenants between God and Man,* trans. William Crookshank. 1822; repr., Grand Rapids: Reformation Heritage Books, 2010.

Primary Sources: Compilations and Confessional Standards

Adams, Charles F., ed. *Antinomianism in the Colony of Massachusetts Bay, 1636–1638.* Boston: The Prince Society, 1894.

Barker, William S. and Samuel T. Logan, eds. *Sermons that Shaped America: Reformed Preaching from 1630–2001.* Phillipsburg, N.J.: P & R Publishing, 2003.

Beeke, Joel R., ed. *Doctrinal Standards, Liturgy, and Church Order.* Grand Rapids: Reformation Heritage Books, 2003.

The Confession of Holy Christian Faith of All Three Estates (Bohemian Confession of 1575), translated from the Lissa Folios of the Unitas Fratrum. http://www.moravianarchives.org/images/pdfs/Bohemian%20Confession,%201575.pdf (accessed August 1, 2011).

Dennison, James T., Jr., ed., *Reformed Confessions of the 16th and 17th Centuries in English Translation, Volume 1, 1523–1552.* Grand Rapids: Reformation Heritage Books, 2008.

———. *Reformed Confessions of the 16th and 17th Centuries in English Translation, Volume 2, 1553–1566.* Grand Rapids: Reformation Heritage Books, 2010.

The Dutch Annotations upon the Whole Bible, trans. Theodore Haak. 1657; facsimile repr., Leerdam, The Netherlands: Gereformeerde Bijbelstichting, 2002.

Hall, David D., ed. *The Antinomian Controversy, 1636–1638: A Documentary History.* Durham: Duke University Press, 1990.

Howie, John, ed. *A Collection of Lectures and Sermons... mostly in the time of the Late Persecution.* Glasgow: J. Bryce, 1779.

Schaff, Philip, ed. *The Creeds of Christendom.* Repr., Grand Rapids: Baker, 1998.

Walker, Williston, ed., *The Creeds and Platforms of Congregationalism,* Philadelphia: Pilgrim's Press, 1969.

Westminster Confession of Faith. Glasgow: Free Presbyterian Publications, 2003.

Secondary Sources

Ball, John H., III. *Chronicling the Soul's Windings: Thomas Hooker and His Morphology of Conversion*. Lanham, Md.: University Press of America, 1992.

Battis, Emery. *Saints and Sectaries: Anne Hutchinson and the Antinomian Controversy in the Massachusetts Bay Colony*. Chapel Hill: University of North Carolina Press, 1962.

Bauckham, Richard J. "Adding to the Church—During the Early American Period." In *Adding to the Church*, 36–48. London: The Westminster Conference, 1973.

Bavinck, Herman. *Reformed Dogmatics*, ed. John Bolt, trans. John Vriend. Grand Rapids: Baker Academic, 2008.

Beck, Stephen P. "The Doctrine of *Gratia Praeparans* in the Soteriology of Richard Sibbes." PhD Dissertation, Westminster Theological Seminary, 1994.

Beeke, Joel R. *The Quest for Full Assurance: The Legacy of Calvin and His Successors*. Edinburgh: Banner of Truth, 1999.

Beeke, Joel R. and Mark Jones. *A Puritan Theology: Doctrine unto Life*. Grand Rapids: Reformation Books, 2012.

Beeke, Jonathon. "The Watchman William Ames: The Nature of Justifying Faith in Ames's Soteriology in Light of his Emphasis on the Divine and Human Wills." MA Thesis, Westminster Seminary West, 2006.

Bell, Michael D. "*Propter Potestatum, Scientiam, ac Beneplacitum Dei*: The Doctrine of the Object of Predestination in the Theology of Johannes Maccovius." ThD Dissertation, Westminster Theological Seminary, 1986.

Beougher, Timothy K. *Richard Baxter and Conversion*. Ross-shire, U.K.: Christian Focus Publications, 2007.

Blackham, Paul. "The Pneumatology of Thomas Goodwin." PhD Dissertation, University of London, 1995.

Boerkoel, Benjamin J. "Uniqueness within the Calvinist Tradition—William Ames (1576–1633): Primogenitor of the *Theologia Pietatis* in English-Dutch Puritanism." ThM Thesis, Calvin Theological Seminary, 1990.

Boone, Clifford B. "Puritan Evangelism: Preaching for Conversion in Late-Seventeenth Century English Puritanism as Seen in the Works of John Flavel." PhD Dissertation, University of Wales, 2009.

Bozeman, Theodore D. *The Precisianist Strain: Disciplinary Religion and Antinomian Backlash in Puritanism to 1638*. Chapel Hill: University of North Carolina Press, 2004.

Bulluck, F. W. B. *Evangelical Conversion in Great Britain, 1516–1695*. St. Leonards on Sea, Eng.: Budd & Gillatt, 1966.

Bush, Sargent, Jr. *The Writings of Thomas Hooker: Spiritual Adventure in Two Worlds*. Madison: University of Wisconsin Press, 1980.

Caldwell, Patricia. *The Puritan Conversion Narrative*. Cambridge: Cambridge University Press, 1983.

Caldwell, Robert W., III. "Pastoral Care for the Converting: Jonathan Edwards' Pastoral Cure of Soul in Light of the Puritan Doctrine of Preparation." MA Thesis, Trinity Evangelical Divinity School, 1997.

Chalker, William H. "Calvin and Some Seventeenth Century English Calvinists." PhD Dissertation, Duke University, 1961.

Christy, Wayne H. "John Cotton: Covenant Theologian." MA Thesis, Duke University, 1942.

Cohen, Charles L. *God's Caress: The Psychology of Puritan Religious Experience*. Oxford: Oxford University Press, 1986.

———. "Two Biblical Models of Conversion: An Example of Puritan Hermeneutics." *Church History* 58, no. 2 (June 1989): 182–96.

Come, Donald R. "John Cotton: Guide of the Chosen People." PhD Dissertation, Princeton University, 1948.

Cook, Paul E. G. "Becoming a Christian—In the Teaching of Richard Rogers and Richard Greenham." In *Becoming a Christian*, 58–67. London: The Westminster Conference, 1972.

Craig, Philip A. "The Bond of Grace and Duty in the Soteriology of John Owen: The Doctrine of Preparation for Grace and Glory as a Bulwark against Seventeenth-Century Anglo-American Antinomianism." PhD Dissertation, Trinity International University, 2005.

Dean, John W. *A Brief Memoir of Rev. Giles Firmin*. Boston: David Clapp & Son, 1866.

Dever, Mark E. *Richard Sibbes: Puritanism and Calvinism in Late Elizabethan and Early Stuart England*. Macon, Ga.: Mercer University Press, 2000.

Elliott, Bruce S. "The Wrights of Salvation: Craft and Conversion among 17th Century English Puritans." PhD Dissertation, University of California, Berkeley, 2001.

Ferguson, Sinclair B. *John Owen on the Christian Life*. Edinburgh: Banner of Truth, 1987.

Foxgrover, David L. "John Calvin's Understanding of Conscience." PhD Dissertation, Claremont Graduate School, 1978.

Fulcher, John R. "Puritan Piety in Early New England: A Study in Spiritual Regeneration from the Antinomian Controversy to the Cambridge Synod of 1648 in the Massachusetts Bay Colony." PhD Dissertation, Princeton University, 1963.

Gerstner, John. *Steps to Salvation: The Evangelistic Message of Jonathan Edwards.* Philadelphia: Westminster Press, 1960.

Gerstner, John and Jonathan Gerstner. "Edwardsean Preparation for Salvation." *Westminster Theological Journal* 42, no. 1 (Fall 1979): 5–71.

Gillies, John. *Historical Collections of Accounts of Revivals,* ed. Andrew Bonar. 1845; repr., Edinburgh: Banner of Truth, 1981.

Goode, Richard C. "'The Only and Principal End': Propagating the Gospel in Early Puritan New England." PhD Dissertation, Vanderbilt University, 1995.

Gura, Philip F. *A Glimpse of Sion's Glory: Puritan Radicalism in New England, 1620–1660.* Middletown: Wesleyan University Press, 1984.

Haas, Guenther H. "Calvin's Ethics." In *The Cambridge Companion to John Calvin,* ed. Donald K. McKim, 93–105. Cambridge: Cambridge University Press, 2004.

Hall, Basil. "The Calvin Legend," and "Calvin against the Calvinists," in *John Calvin,* ed. G. E. Duffield, 1–37. Grand Rapids: Eerdmans, 1966.

Harinck, Cor. "Preparation as Taught by the Puritans." *Puritan Reformed Journal* 2, no. 2 (July 2010): 161–73.

Harran, Marilyn J. *Luther on Conversion: The Early Years.* Ithaca, N.Y.: Cornell University Press, 1983.

Harrison, Graham. "'Becoming a Christian'—In the Teaching of John Calvin." In *Becoming a Christian,* 22–40. London: The Westminster Conference, 1972.

Helm, Paul. *Calvin and the Calvinists.* Edinburgh: Banner of Truth, 1982.

Henard, William D. "An Analysis of the Doctrine of Seeking in Jonathan Edwards's Conversion Theology as Revealed through Representative Northampton Sermons and Treatises." PhD Dissertation, Southern Baptist Theological Seminary, 2006.

Holifield, E. Brooks. *Theology in America: Christian Thought from the Age of the Puritans to the Civil War.* New Haven: Yale University, 2003.

Horn, Robert. "Thomas Hooker—The Soul's Preparation for Christ." In *The Puritan Experiment in the New World,* 19–37. London: Westminster Conference, 1976.

Horton, Michael. "Christ Set Forth: Thomas Goodwin and the Puritan Doctrine of Assurance." PhD Dissertation, Wycliffe Hall, Oxford and Coventry College, n.d.

Humphrey, Richard Alan, "The Concept of Conversion in the Theology of Thomas Shepard (1605–1649)." PhD Dissertation, Drew University, 1967.

Jones, David C. "The Law and the Spirit of Christ," in *A Theological Guide to Calvin's Institutes,* ed. David W. Hall and Peter A. Lillback, 301–319. Phillipsburg, Pa.: P & R Publishing, 2008.

Jones, James W., III, "The Beginnings of American Theology: John Cotton, Thomas Hooker, Thomas Shepard and Peter Bulkeley." PhD Dissertation, Brown University, 1970.

———. *The Shattered Synthesis: New England Puritanism before the Great Awakening.* New Haven: Yale University Press, 1973.

Kendall, R. T. *Calvin and English Calvinism to 1649.* Carlisle, U.K.: Paternoster Press, 1997.

Knight, Janice. *Orthodoxies in Massachusetts: Rereading American Puritanism.* Cambridge: Harvard University Press, 1994.

Lajeunie, E. J., O.P. *Saint Francis de Sales: The Man, The Thinker, His Influence,* trans. Rory O'Sullivan. Bangalore, India: S.F.S. Publications, 1986.

Laurence, David. "Jonathan Edwards, Solomon Stoddard, and the Preparationist Model of Conversion." *Harvard Theological Review* 72, no. 3–4 (July–October 1979): 267–83.

Lillback, Peter A. *The Binding of God: Calvin's Role in the Development of Covenant Theology.* Grand Rapids: Baker Academic, 2001.

Lloyd-Jones, D. M. *The Puritans: The Origins and Successors.* Edinburgh: Banner of Truth, 1987.

Marsden, George M. *Jonathan Edwards: A Life.* New Haven: Yale University Press, 2003.

McGiffert, Michael. ed. *God's Plot: Puritan Spirituality in Thomas Shepard's Cambridge,* rev. ed. Amherst: University of Massachusetts Press, 1994.

McNeill, John T. *The History and Character of Calvinism.* New York: Oxford University Press, 1954.

Middlekauff, Robert. *The Mathers: Three Generations of Puritan Intellectuals, 1596–1728.* Berkeley: University of California Press, 1999.

Miller, Perry. *Errand into the Wilderness.* Cambridge: Harvard University Press, 1956.

———. *Jonathan Edwards.* [New York]: William Sloane Associates, 1949.

———. *The New England Mind: From Colony to Province.* Cambridge: Harvard University Press, 1953.

———. "'Preparation for Salvation' in New England," *Journal of the History of Ideas* 4, no. 3 (June 1943): 253–86.

Morgan, Edmund S. *Visible Saints: The History of a Puritan Idea.* New York: New York University Press, 1963.

Muller, Richard A. *After Calvin: Studies in the Development of a Theological Tradition.* Oxford: Oxford University Press, 2003.

———. *Christ and the Decree: Christology and Predestination in Reformed Theology from Calvin to Perkins.* Durham, N.C.: Labyrinth Press, 1986.

———. "Covenant and Conscience in English Reformed Theology." *Westminster Theological Journal* 42, no. 2 (Spring 1980): 308–334.

———. *Dictionary of Latin and Greek Theological Terms Drawn Principally from Protestant Scholastic Theology.* Grand Rapids: Baker, 1985.

———. *Post-Reformation Reformed Dogmatics: The Rise and Development of Reformed Orthodoxy, ca. 1520 to c. 1725.* 2nd ed., 4 vols. Grand Rapids: Baker, 2003.

Murray, Iain H. *Antinomianism: New England's First Controversy.* Edinburgh: Banner of Truth, 1978.

———. "Thomas Hooker and the Doctrine of Conversion," *Banner of Truth* no. 195 (Dec. 1979): 19–29; no. 196 (Jan. 1980): 22–32; no. 197 (Feb. 1980): 12–18; no. 199 (Apr. 1980): 10–21; no. 206 (Nov. 1980): 9–21.

Najapfour, Brian G. "'The Very Heart of Prayer': Reclaiming John Bunyan's Spirituality." ThM Thesis, Puritan Reformed Theological Seminary, 2009.

Oberman, Heiko A. *The Harvest of Medieval Theology: Gabriel Biel and Late Medieval Nominalism.* Cambridge: Harvard University Press, 1963.

Ozment, Steven. *The Age of Reform, 1250–1550: An Intellectual and Religious History of Late Medieval and Reformation Europe.* New Haven: Yale University Press, 1980.

Packer, J. I. *A Quest for Godliness: The Puritan Vision of the Christian Life.* Wheaton, Ill.: Crossway Books, 1990.

———. *The Redemption and Restoration of Man in the Thought of Richard Baxter.* Vancouver, B.C.: Regent College Publishing, 2003.

Parker, David L. "Edward Taylor's Preparationism: A New Perspective on the Taylor-Stoddard Controversy," *Early American Literature* 11, no. 3 (Winter 1976/1977): 259–78.

Payne, Rodger M. "'When the Times of Refreshing Shall Come': Interpreting American Protestant Narratives of Conversion, 1630–1830." PhD Dissertation, University of Virginia, 1989.

Pettit, Norman. *The Heart Prepared: Grace and Conversion in Puritan Spiritual Life.* New Haven: Yale University Press, 1966.

Porterfield, Amanda. *Female Piety in Puritan New England: The Emergence of Religious Humanism.* Oxford: Oxford University Press, 1992.

Rooy, Sidney H. *The Theology of Missions in the Puritan Tradition: A Study of Representative Puritans: Richard Sibbes, Richard Baxter, John Eliot, Cotton Mather, and Jonathan Edwards.* Delft, Netherlands: W. D. Meinema, 1965.

Rouwendal, Pieter. "Jacob Koelman on Thomas Hooker's *The Soules Humiliation.*" *Puritan Reformed Journal* 2, no. 2 (July 2010): 174–86.

Schaefer, Paul R. Jr. *The Spiritual Brotherhood: Cambridge Puritans and the Nature of Christian Piety.* Grand Rapids: Reformation Heritage Books, 2011.

Schaff, Philip. *History of the Christian Church*, 3rd rev. New York: Charles Scribner's Sons, 1891.

Selement, George and Bruce C. Woolley, eds. *Thomas Shepard's* Confessions. Boston: The Colonial Society of Massachusetts, 1981.

Shedd, William G. T. *Dogmatic Theology.* New York: Charles Scribner's Sons, 1888.

Shepherd, Victor A. *The Nature and Function of Faith in the Theology of John Calvin.* NABPR Dissertation Series, Number 2. Macon, Ga.: Mercer University Press, 1983.

Song, Yong Jae Timothy. *Theology and Piety in the Reformed Federal Thought of William Perkins and John Preston.* Lewiston, N.Y.: Edwin Mellen Press, 1998.

Sprunger, Keith L. "The Learned Doctor Ames." PhD Dissertation, University of Illinois, 1963.

Spurgeon, Charles H. *The Metropolitan Tabernacle Pulpit, Volume 9.* 1863; repr. Pasadena, Tex.: Pilgrim Publications, 1979.

———. *Pictures from Pilgrim's Progress.* 1903; repr. Grand Rapids: Baker, 1982.

Steinmetz, David C. *Reformers in the Wings: From Geiler Von Kayserberg to Theodore Beza.* Oxford: Oxford University Press, 2001.

Stoever, William K. B. *'A Faire and Easie Way to Heaven': Covenant Theology and Antinomianism in Early Massachusetts.* Middleton, Conn.: Wesleyan University Press, 1978.

————. "Nature, Grace, and John Cotton: The Theological Dimension in the New England Antinomian Controversy." *Church History* 44, no. 1 (March 1975): 22–33.

Tipson, Baird. "Invisible Saints: The 'Judgment of Charity' in the Early New England Churches." *Church History* 44, no. 4 (Dec. 1975): 460–71.

Tipson, Lynn B. Jr., "The Development of a Puritan Understanding of Conversion." PhD Dissertation, Yale University, 1972.

Trueman, Carl R. "Calvin and Calvinism," in *The Cambridge Companion to John Calvin*, ed. Donald K. McKim, 225–44. Cambridge: Cambridge University Press, 2004.

Tuttle, Julius H. *The Libraries of the Mathers.* Worcester, Mass.: Davis Press, 1910.

Van Asselt, Willem J., et al. *Introduction to Reformed Scholasticism*, trans. Albert Gootjes. Grand Rapids: Reformation Heritage Books, 2011.

Van Dyken, Seymour. *Samuel Willard, 1640–1707: Preacher of Orthodoxy in an Era of Change.* Grand Rapids: Eerdmans, 1972.

Van Vliet, Jan. "William Ames: Marrow of the Theology and Piety of the Reformed Tradition." PhD Dissertation, Westminster Theological Seminary, 2002.

Visscher, Hugo, Karl Reuter, et al. *William Ames*, trans. Douglas Horton. Cambridge: Harvard Divinity School Library, 1965.

Watkins, Owen C. *The Puritan Experience.* London: Routledge and Kegan Paul, 1972.

Wells, Paul. "Calvin and Union with Christ: The Heart of Christian Doctrine." In *Calvin: Theologian and Reformer*, eds. Joel R. Beeke and Garry J. Williams, 65–88. Grand Rapids: Reformation Heritage Books, 2010.

White, Charles E. "Were Hooker and Shepard Closet Arminians?" *Calvin Theological Journal* 20, no. 1 (April 1985): 33–42.

Williams, Martin. "Assurance and the Preparationist *Ordo Salutis* in Puritan Thought: Calvin, English and American Puritanism from William Perkins to John Owen." ThM Thesis, Bible College of New Zealand, Auckland, 1999.

Williams, Selma R. *Divine Rebel: The Life of Anne Marbury Hutchinson.* New York: Holt, Rinehart, and Winston, 1981.

Winship, Michael P. *Making Heretics: Militant Protestantism and Free Grace in Massachusetts, 1636–1641.* Princeton: Princeton University Press, 2002.

Yuille, Stephen J. *The Inner Sanctum of Puritan Piety: John Flavel's Doctrine of Mystical Union with Christ.* Grand Rapids: Reformation Heritage Books, 2007.

Ziff, Larzer. *The Career of John Cotton: Puritanism and the American Experience.* Princeton: Princeton University Press, 1962.

Awake, Awake, O Sinner

Awake, awake, and then thou shalt perceive
Thy peril greater than thou wilt believe.
Lift up thine eyes, and see God's wrathful ire
Preparing unextinguishable fire
For all that live and die impenitent.
Awake, awake, O sinner, and repent,
And quarrel not because I thus alarm
Thy Soul, to save it from eternal harm….

Now seek the face of God with all thy heart,
Acknowledge unto him how vile thou art.
Tell him thy sins deserve eternal wrath.
And that it is a wonder that he hath
Permitted thee so long to draw thy breath,
Who might have cut thee off by sudden death,
And sent thy soul into the lowest pit,
From whence no price should ever ransom it

And that he may most justly do it still,
(Because thou hast deserv'd it) if he will.
Yet also tell him that, if he shall please,
He can forgive thy sins and thee release,
And that in Christ his Son he may be just
And justify all those that on him trust;
That though thy sins are of a crimson dye,
Yet Christ his blood can cleanse thee thoroughly.

—Michael Wigglesworth (1651–1705)[1]

1. Michael Wigglesworth, *The Day of Doom* (New York: American News Company, 1867), 99, 102.

Index

Brakel, Wihelmus à, 228, 233–37, 241,
    253, 258, 259
Bucer, Martin, 6, 60, 264
Bulkeley, Peter, 261
Bullinger, Heinrich, 6, 33, 226, 241
Bunyan, John, 34, 178, 191–200, 250, 258
    on assurance, 191, 194, 196, 198, 200
    on conviction of sin, 191–94, 198, 199
    on covenant of grace, 194
    on ordinary conversion, 191–98
    on use of law, 191, 192, 195, 196, 199
Burroughs, Jeremiah, 250
    on assurance, 138
    on burden of sin, 137–38
    on covenant of grace, 138
    life of, 135–36
    preaching of, 136, 143
    on stages of preparation, 138–40,
        149, 259
    on use of law, 136
Bush, Sargent, 76–77, 89, 90

Caldwell, Patricia, 106, 107
Caldwell, Robert, 204, 215, 217, 218
Calvin, John
    on conversion, 37, 44, 51, 68
    on conviction of sin, 78, 206
    on double knowledge, 48, 168
    misunderstandings of, 11, 251
    on predestination, 102
    on preparation, 24–35, 62, 63, 69,
        265, 267
    vs. Puritans, 6, 16–18, 81, 86, 113,
        243–48
    on use of law, 24, 29–35, 37, 51, 56,
        86, 246–48, 257
Canons of Dort. *See* Synod of Dort
Caryl, Joseph, 133
Case, Thomas, 133
Castro, Alphonsus de, 25
Chalker, William, 30
Chamier, Daniel, 63
Charles II, 161
Chauncy, Charles, 167
Christy, Wayne, 121, 121n71
Claghorn, George, 217
Cochlaeus, Johann, 25
Cohen, Charles, 2, 8, 127, 149

Come, Donald, 118
common grace, 73, 149, 153, 155, 261
congruent merit, 264, 269
    description of, 25, 112, 256, 269
    and preparation, 66, 130
    Reformed opposition to, 112, 128,
        224, 248–49, 255, 264
cooperating grace, 20, 22. *See also*
    congruent merit
Cornwell, Francis, 113
Cotton, John, 135, 250, 255, 263
    alleged opposition to prepara-
        tion by, 111–13, 127, 145, 154,
        145–47, 250
    and antinomianism, 109, 114, 117,
        121–26, 128, 249
    and Congregationalism, 161
    on covenant of grace, 108, 114–17,
        123, 127, 250
    life and ministry of, 47, 107–9, 144,
        158, 166
    on sorrow for sin, 117–19, 164
    on stages of preparation, 120–21
    on use of law, 110–11, 114–17, 121–22,
        127, 250
    and voluntarism, 74
Council of Trent, 38
covenant of grace, 123–25. *See also* Bun-
    yan; Cotton; Hooker; Preston
covenant of works, 108–10, 115, 116,
    124–27, 250
covenant theology, 11, 13, 17, 79, 114,
    233, 237–40
Culverwell, Ezekiel, 36
Cutter, Elizabeth, 175

damnation, 239, 243, 252, 258
    contentment in, 82–84, 95–97, 143,
        170–76, 252. *See also* Firmin; Fla-
        vel; Hooker; Norton; Shepard
    and fate of the lost, 29, 43, 134, 136,
        196, 206, 228
    fear of, 6, 183, 186, 188, 218–21, 230,
        235
    justice of, 37, 44, 83, 84, 239, 243, 258
    and predestination, 41
    See also judgment
Dent, Arthur, 240

Pettit, Norman (*continued*)
  on Hildersam, 40
  on Hooker, 71, 106, 121, 146, 246, 250
  on preparation in general, 12–16,
    18, 245
  on Rogers, 40
  on Shepard, 106
  on Sibbes, 45, 246, 248
  on Synod of Dort, 230
  on Westminster Standards, 130
  on Zwingli, 226
predestination
  Calvin on, 102
  and covenant, 48
  Edwards on, 204
  and free offer of gospel, 11
  Greenham on, 38
  Hooker on, 89
  and means of grace, 58
  misunderstandings of, 11, 13, 14, 250
  and morphology of conversion, 10,
    15, 41, 51
  Perkins on, 41
  See also election
Preston, John
  on covenant of grace, 48
  humiliation, 108, 152
  life and ministry of, 47–48, 92, 161,
    254
  on preparation in general, 47–51, 155
  on use of law, 49–50
prevenient grace, 20, 22, 23, 256

Remonstrants. *See* Arminianism
restraining grace, 43
Reuter, Karl, 66, 67
Reynolds, Edward, 187
Rogers, John, 240
Rogers, Richard, 39, 40, 51, 74, 80, 101,
    105
Rollock, Robert, 40, 134
Roman Catholicism, 255–56
  and Ames, 59, 60, 66, 69, 248, 263
  and Calvin, 24–46, 248
  and Church of England, 38
  and Cotton, 111–12, 117, 126–27
  and Hooker, 83, 85, 103
  and Norton, 148, 154, 157–58

and Pemble, 99, 102, 249
and Perkins, 41, 42
and Westminster Standards, 127,
    135, 142
and Wistius, 237
Rooy, Sidney, 15
Rutherford, Samuel, 140, 261

Sales, Francis de, 83, 83n75, 173
sanctification
  Ames on, 270
  Bunyan on, 198
  Cotton on, 110, 112, 113, 125–27
  divine sovereignty in, 14, 22, 80
  Goodwin on, 165
  Hooker on, 102
  and justification, 96, 110
  Norton on, 152, 154, 157
  sorrow in, 80, 81
  Winthrop on, 125
  Wistius on, 238
Schaff, Philip, 20, 23
Second Helvetic Confession, 226
Selement, George, 11
semi-Pelaginism, 41, 59, 230, 237, 241, 256
Shedd, William G. T., 256
Shepard, Thomas
  and Arminianism, 12, 93, 158
  on assurance, 106
  on contentment to be damned, 84,
    95–97, 105, 171–76, 213, 252
  on conviction of sin, 93–95, 170–71,
    206, 208
  and Cotton, 112, 116–18
  and cutting from Adam, 105,
    153–54, 158, 170
  and Edwards, 206, 208, 213–14,
    216–17
  and Firmin, 245
  on free offer of gospel, 255
  life and ministry of, 91–92, 106–7
  and Preston, 48
  on use of law, 94, 97, 98, 103
Sibbes, Richard
  on "bruising," 44–48, 51, 108, 253
  influences on, 23
  life and ministry of, 44, 108, 161
  on means of grace, 15